SOUTH KOREA'S GRAND STRATEGY

Contemporary Asia in the World

CONTEMPORARY ASIA IN THE WORLD

David C. Kang and Victor D. Cha, Editors

This series aims to address a gap in the public-policy and scholarly discussion of Asia. It seeks to promote books and studies that are on the cutting edge of their disciplines or promote multidisciplinary or interdisciplinary research but are also accessible to a wider readership. The editors seek to showcase the best scholarly and public-policy arguments on Asia from any field, including politics, history, economics, and cultural studies.

For a complete list of books in the series, see our website, https://cup.columbia.edu /books/series.

South Korea's Grand Strategy

MAKING ITS OWN DESTINY

Ramon Pacheco Pardo

Columbia University Press
New York

Columbia University Press
Publishers Since 1893
New York   Chichester, West Sussex
cup.columbia.edu

Library of Congress Cataloging-in-Publication Data
Names: Pacheco Pardo, Ramon, author.
Title: South Korea's grand strategy : making its own destiny / Ramon
Pacheco Pardo.
Description: New York : Columbia University Press, [2023] | Series:
Contemporary Asia in the world | Includes bibliographical
references and index.
Identifiers: LCCN 2023003288 (print) | LCCN 2023003289 (ebook) |
ISBN 9780231203227 (hardback) | ISBN 9780231203234 (trade paperback) |
ISBN 9780231554930 (ebook)
Subjects: LCSH: Korea (South)—Foreign relations. | Geopolitics—Korea (South)
Classification: LCC DS917.37 .P33 2023 (print) | LCC DS917.37 (ebook) |
DDC 327.5195—dc23/eng/20230405
LC record available at https://lccn.loc.gov/2023003288
LC ebook record available at https://lccn.loc.gov/2023003289

Cover credit: South Korean (Republic of Korea) National Assembly Hall,
© Alistair Ruff / Alamy Stock Photo

Contents

Acknowledgments

This work was supported by the Laboratory Program for Korean Studies of the Ministry of Education of the Republic of Korea and the Korean Studies Promotion Service at the Academy of Korean Studies (AKS-2021-LAB-223002). I would also like to thank Nagyeong Kang, Soohyoung (Sean) Kim, and Jean Song for their research assistance, as well as two anonymous reviewers for their comments and suggestions.

Abbreviations

ADB	Asian Development Bank
ADIZ	Air Defense Identification Zone
AFC	Asian financial crisis
APEC	Asia-Pacific Economic Cooperation
BCBS	Basel Committee on Banking Supervision
BIS	Bank for International Settlements
BOK	Bank of Korea
CFC	ROK/U.S. Combined Forces Command
CPTPP	Comprehensive and Progressive Agreement for Trans-Pacific Partnership
CSCAP	Council for Security Cooperation in the Asia Pacific
DEPA	Digital Economy Partnership Agreement
EDCF	Economic Development Cooperation Fund
FDI	foreign direct investment
FTA	free trade agreement
GATT	General Agreement on Tariffs and Trade
GFC	global financial crisis
IAEA	International Atomic Energy Agency
KNOC	Korea National Oil Corporation
KOCIS	Korea Overseas Culture Information Service
KOGAS	Korea Gas Corporation
KOICA	Korea International Cooperation Agency

KORUS	Korea–United States Free Trade Agreement
LNG	liquefied natural gas
MND	Ministry of National Defense
MOEF	Ministry of Economy and Finance
MOFA	Ministry of Foreign Affairs
MOFAT	Ministry of Foreign Affairs and Trade
MOTIE	Ministry of Trade, Industry and Energy
MOU	Ministry of Unification
NAPC	Northeast Asia Peace and Cooperation Platform
NAPCI	Northeast Asia Peace and Cooperation Initiative
NSP	New Southern Policy
OECD	Organization for Economic Cooperation and Development
P4G	Partnering for Green Growth and the Global Goals 2030
RCEP	Regional Comprehensive Economic Partnership
ROK	Republic of Korea
WTO	World Trade Organization

SOUTH KOREA'S GRAND STRATEGY

Introduction

Setting the Scene

The Republic of South Korea (ROK) has had a clear grand strategy since its transition to democracy and the end of the Cold War. Between 1988 and 1992, South Korea's domestic and international environment changed dramatically. South Korea became a democracy, normalized diplomatic relations with the Soviet Union and a then-rising China, was admitted to the United Nations, and witnessed the collapse of the Soviet Union. Shortly afterward, the first North Korean nuclear crisis took place in 1993–1994. These developments happened as South Korea achieved developed country status, marked by its accession to the OECD in 1996. South Korea was then hit by the Asian financial crisis of 1997, its biggest economic crisis since the Korean War.

These events helped to forge a new consensus among South Korea's political, military, diplomatic, economic, and bureaucratic elites regarding their ultimate goal: for South Korea to make its own destiny, understood as independence of action. This overriding goal underpins South Korea's long-term path to security, prosperity, and status. This path has held under both liberal and conservative governments. It is underlined and explained by shared ideas about the other goals to be achieved in order for South Korea to make its own destiny: protection from external military threats, reconciliation and reunification with North Korea, deeper integration in the world economy, and recognition as an influential middle power. In turn, South Korean elites agree on the means to prioritize to achieve these goals: growing military capabilities, the long-standing ROK–U.S. alliance, a growing and highly skilled diplomatic corps, trade, investment, and aid, public diplomacy, soft power, and, more recently, cybertools. These goals and means are, in a nutshell, South Korea's grand strategy.

Furthermore, this grand strategy is based on the consensus that the practice of the country's foreign policy can be divided into four concentric circles with South Korea at the center. They include a triangular core including North Korea, the United States, and China; East Asia including both its northeast and southeast; Greater Eurasia and the Indian Ocean including Russia, Central Asia, South Asia, the Greater Middle East, Europe, Australia, and the Indian Ocean itself; and the rest of the world and global governance. The division of South Korean grand strategy into these four concentric circles is the natural expression of the country's geographical position, foreign policy interests and goals, available resources, and, ultimately, the priorities of the country's foreign policy elites.

Certainly, South Korea's vibrant domestic politics sometimes give the impression of a permanent liberal/conservative divide, including on certain foreign policy issues. Should South Korea prioritize engagement or pressure when it comes to dealing with North Korea? To what extent should South Korea rely on the United States for its own protection? What is the right approach to relations with China? South Korean policymakers seemingly disagree on their answers to these and other foreign policy questions, which in theory would prevent the country from forging the long-term consensus that grand strategy requires. After all, debate, disagreement, and ultimately regular change are only natural in a full, strong democracy such as South Korea.

Scratch the surface and the theatrics of South Korean politics, however, and the consensus emerges. The structural factors explaining South Korea's grand strategy cut across administrations; they do not magically disappear once a new government takes office. The ultimate, grand goals that South Korean policymakers want to achieve are the result of careful thinking and discussion; administrations set up their own, lower level goals, but they do not change the grand strategic objectives. And the instruments that South Korean policymakers activate to achieve the country's goals remain unchanged over time; new administrations do not have the luxury of suddenly coming up with new tools unavailable to previous ones.

This book set outs to analyze South Korea's grand strategy by answering the following three questions:

1. What factors explain South Korea's grand strategy?
2. What are the goals of South Korea's grand strategy?
3. What are the means of South Korea's grand strategy?

These three questions build on the consensus that grand strategy is "long-term in scope, concerned with the state's most important priorities, and inclusive of all spheres of statecraft (military, diplomatic, and economic)."[1] This consensus stems from the understanding that there is an "intellectual architecture" composed of ideas from which particular goals and how to achieve them flow. In other words, states are not simply reacting to events but are instead taking a long-term view.[2] Therefore, grand strategy involves concrete initiatives a state implements in its foreign policy to pursue its most important objectives. Ultimately, these goals and their operationalization through the use of certain means aim at achieving the key, overarching objectives of security and prosperity, and, in the case of middle powers such as South Korea, status.

The time scope of the book is the Sixth Republic period from its onset until the first six months of the country's thirteenth presidency, that is, from 1988 to 2022. This period covers the full mandates of four conservative presidents (Roh Tae-woo, Kim Young-sam, Lee Myung-bak, and Park Geun-hye) and their three liberal counterparts (Kim Dae-jung, Roh Moo-hyun, and Moon Jae-in) who have held office since South Korea's most recent transition to democracy, as well as the first six months in office of the fifth conservative president since then (Yoon Suk-yeol). By examining the policies of presidents from the two different sides of the political spectrum—plus different factions within each of them—who belong to different generations, this book can demonstrate that South Korea indeed has a grand strategy that withstands the short-term political fortunes of liberals and conservatives.

Understanding South Korea's grand strategy during the Sixth Republic era matters for three reasons. To begin with, South Korea is an important foreign policy actor. Its assets include the tenth largest economy in the world, the sixth most powerful military, and the twelfth strongest soft power capabilities.[3] South Korea also boasts a seat at the G20 table, has been invited to G7 summits, and has an expanding official development assistance (ODA) budget. It is also a model of successful economic development and democratic transition and consolidation. Along with Japan and India, South Korea is one of Asia's key middle powers. Therefore, Seoul's foreign policy goals and actions matter. In the same way that developments in the global system are partially affected by the behavior of South Korea's fellow Asian middle powers or others such as Australia, France, Germany, or the United Kingdom, the way South Korea acts increasingly affects them as well.

In addition, the study of South Korean grand strategy adds a new layer to our understanding of the country itself. Korean studies covers a wide range of fields, from history to anthropology to sociology. Certainly, international relations (IR) has been and is also part of Korean studies. But the study of South Korean foreign policy is less common than the study of the country's domestic politics, particularly when focusing on it beyond a small number of issues and countries. By focusing on South Korea's grand strategy, this book takes an even deeper dive into our understanding of South Korean foreign policy. This is a topic that, simply put and as far as this author knows, has not been analyzed before through a book-length study.

And from an academic point of view, the field of international relations is ripe to analyze the grand strategy of middle powers. This includes countries beyond "the West," as the move to approach IR from non-Western perspectives gathers pace. Books such as *Comparative Grand Strategy: A Framework and Cases* are moving in this direction, analyzing the grand strategy of middle powers together with great powers.[4] This book moves beyond chapter- or article-long case studies. It also introduces a framework of analysis to study the grand strategy of middle powers that can be applied to other cases. As IR scholars seek to better understand the position and role of actors beyond the great powers, analyzing the grand strategy of middle powers draws our attention to the fact that many different types of actors have agency. Structures influence their behavior, but they are not helpless when faced with them.

Ultimately, this book serves to prove that middle powers can have a grand strategy. South Korea is the quintessential middle power, an identity that its foreign policy elites have often implicitly and sometimes explicitly embraced dating back to the Roh Tae-woo years. South Korea—and middle powers by extension—may not always be successful in achieving its ultimate objectives. But great powers also have their fair share of failures when it comes to successfully attaining their foreign policy goals. What matters is whether middle powers possess a set of long-term goals and tools to pursue them. And South Korea does. They are the objectives and instruments that are helping South Korea in its quest for its ultimate dream: to break with centuries of Korea being a "shrimp among whales," and for South Korea to be autonomous and make its own destiny.

The Study of Contemporary South Korea's Grand Strategy

The academic literature on South Korean grand strategy is scarce, as is true for most middle powers.[5] To a large extent, this is the result of grand strategy scholars having mainly focused their research on great powers hitherto—especially the United States and, more recently, China. One notable exception is David Kang's "South Korea: An Independent Grand Strategy," a chapter in his book *American Grand Strategy in the Twenty-First Century*. Adopting a strategic culture approach mixing both Korean historical experience with more recent South Korea–specific developments, Kang explains why Seoul has taken a nonconfrontational approach toward relations with China, still has frictions with Japan, and will not necessarily align with the grand strategy of the United States.[6] Kang takes a South Korea–centric approach in this chapter, with other chapters focusing on other Asian countries and thus allowing for comparison.

There is, though, a growing literature on South Korean foreign policy. Certainly, the literature on the Korean Peninsula security dilemma—and herein, South Korea's approach to relations with North Korea—is still more extensive than the literature on South Korean foreign policy *per se*. But it is also true that the scholarship on South Korean foreign policy has grown as the country has become more powerful and active in global affairs. This literature can serve as a proxy for academic debates about the country's grand strategy, for it also concerns itself with South Korean goals, determinants, and instruments even if the framework is necessarily different. And what does this literature tell us about South Korean foreign policy? What follows is a summary of some recent key works.

Uk Heo's and Terence Roehrig's *South Korea's Rise: Economic Development, Power, and Foreign Relations* is an ambitious work that focuses on how domestic factors affect South Korea's foreign policy. The authors posit that the country's economic development was the precondition for the democratic transition of the 1980s. Once the transition took place, South Korean government elites felt compelled to become more active in global affairs. This was the result of the twin forces of greater capabilities and increased national pride, which led elites to become more active and assertive. The authors then draw a comparison between the pre-1988 and post-1988 periods, examining seven different countries and regions in which this comparison applies: North Korea, the United States, Russia and China, Japan, the European Union, India, and four developing regions.[7] Heo and Roehrig convincingly show that South Korea has become a more central player to global affairs.

Jeffrey Robertson also develops an original analytical framework that he then applies to the case of South Korea's foreign policymaking. In *Diplomatic Style and Foreign Policy: A Case Study of South Korea*, Robertson draws our attention to the role played by diplomatic style in a country's foreign policy. Based on a wealth of interviews with South Korean diplomats and foreign diplomats based in Seoul, the author asserts that South Korea's style leans toward emotionalism. He also posits that status, generational change and cosmopolitanism, and concerns about estrangement from international society define South Korea's foreign policy style.[8] Robertson's book adds an interesting layer to our understanding of South Korea as an international actor, since it focuses on how psychological traits affect policy.

In *South Korea's Changing Foreign Policy: The Impact of Democratization and Globalization*, Wonjae Hwang analyzes how the twin forces of (domestic) democratization and (international) globalization have shaped South Korean foreign policy from the 1980s and, especially, 1990s onward. Hwang's develops an empirical study showing how these two forces have shaped Seoul's voting in the United Nations, trade with Japan, or ODA and trade cooperation.[9] Similarly, Patrick Flamm's *South Korean Identity and Global Foreign Policy: Dream of Autonomy* takes a case study approach. Applying an identity-based approach, Flamm analyses how South Korea's self-identification informs its policy in the areas of peacekeeping and climate diplomacy.[10] Together, the works of Hwang and Flamm serve to identify different forces shaping South Korea's foreign policy behavior. Seoul's foreign policy cannot be understood by looking at one factor only, just like any other international actor.

Other recent books on South Korean foreign policy focus on specific countries. In *South Korea's 70-Year Endeavour for Foreign Policy*, Nam Sung-Wook and colleagues focus on the country's decades-old top foreign policy goal: reunification with North Korea. Each of the seven contributors to this volume analyses a different aspect of inter-Korean relations, from the role of the two Koreas throughout history to the potential challenges that a unified Korea would face. This book prioritizes an empirical approach to the study of relations between the two Koreas.[11] Similarly, Gabriel Jonsson's *South Korea in the United Nations: Global Governance, Inter-Korean Relations and Peace Building* takes an empirical approach, with the concept of global governance guiding the analysis. Jonsson focuses on both Koreas, and dives into both the pre-UN membership years as well as the years since they both joined in 1991. The book shows both how UN membership has served foreign policy interests and the divergence between the two Koreas in terms of their position in the international system.[12]

The South Korea–U.S. alliance has also attracted the attention of several scholars recently. In *South Korea at the Crossroads: Autonomy and Alliance in an Era of Rival Powers*, Scott Snyder takes a close look at that alliance. The author analyzes the alliance dating back to its origins in 1953, but he concentrates on the post-1988 democratization period mainly. Snyder cautions that South Korea's quest for autonomy—which he thinks was reinforced following the transition to democracy—has its limits in the context of Sino-American strategic rivalry.[13] Similarly, Uk Heo and Terence Roehrig take a deep dive into South Korea–U.S. relations in their book *The Evolution of the United States-South Korea Alliance*. Heo and Roehrig anchor their analysis in Alliance Theory, and also examine the South Korea–U.S. alliance from its origins but focus more extensively on the post-democratization years. The authors take a holistic approach, delving into South Korean domestic politics, security preferences, economic growth, and the military dimensions. They explain how these forces have fundamentally transformed the alliance.[14] Meanwhile, in *Japan, South Korea, and the United States Nuclear Umbrella* Roehrig focuses on a crucial yet underdiscussed aspect of the South Korea–U.S. relationship: the role of Washington's nuclear umbrella in the security calculus of both Seoul and Tokyo. Using an extended deterrence approach, Roehrig explains how the nuclear umbrella informs the politics of how the two allies think about potential security threats and military capabilities.[15] Put together, these three works offer a very comprehensive and multifaceted analysis of a crucial South Korean foreign policy relationship. Interestingly, the three books agree that the

South Korea–U.S. alliance was transformed following the former's democratization—which happened almost simultaneously with the end of the Cold War and concomitant easing of East/West competition.

Min Ye, meanwhile, has written on South Korea–China relations. His book *China-South Korea Relations in the New Era: Challenges and Opportunities* takes a multidimensional game approach to provide a holistic analysis of the relationship between Seoul and Beijing. Ye focuses on the post-1992 diplomatic normalization period and shows how the rise of both countries— especially China—and domestic politics in each of them affect their relationship. Ye argues that the strategic interactions between both have become more complex as a result of these two forces.[16] Brad Glosserman and Scott A. Snyder have written on the relationship between South Korea and Japan. In their book *The Japan-South Korea Identity Clash: East Asian Security and the United States,* the authors posit that the national identities of South Korea and Japan impede deeper cooperation between both. A more confident South Korea and a Japan undergoing an identity crisis have resulted in this state of affairs.[17]

If there is one theme that these different authors agree on, it is that South Korean foreign policy underwent a dramatic transformation between the late 1980s and early 1990s, when South Korea became democratic and developed. In the decades since, South Korean economic, diplomatic, military, soft power, and, more recently, cyber capabilities have increased, as the literature summarized here shows. In turn, this has made South Korea more confident. This is a theme that underpins the analysis of most authors studying South Korean foreign policy. Yet none of them uses a grand strategy framework to explain the continuities in Seoul's foreign policy from 1988 onward.

This book is the first detailed analysis of South Korea's grand strategy—or South Korea's foreign policy using a grand strategy framework. The book thus systematically describes and analyses South Korea's long-term strategy and the tools to fulfil it. This way, the book counters the narrative that South Korea is a "shrimp among whales," condemned to react to the whims of great powers. In addition, this book presents an analysis of South Korea's grand strategy across the world. Most literature centers on South Korean foreign policy toward North Korea, the United States, China, East Asia, or some other narrowly defined region. While it makes sense to focus on the areas of most interest to South Korean policymakers, or on a particular area or issue, this approach does not provide a full picture of Seoul's grand strategy. This book addresses this omission in the existing literature by taking a holistic approach to South Korean grand strategy.

Methodology

This book relies on a middle power grand strategy model. This framework builds on existing theoretical debates and frameworks for the study and analysis of grand strategy. This framework is then combined with the international relations literature specific to middle powers, since their characteristics, position, and behavior is different from that of the great powers on which grand strategy studies have focused for the most part thus far. This framework is developed and presented in detail in chapter 1.

In terms of data gathering, the book is based on three main methods. First, I consulted more than 2,300 documents from the South Korean government. These include presidential national security strategies, speeches, and interviews, Ministry of Foreign Affairs (MOFA) white papers, Ministry of National Defense (MND) white papers, Ministry of Trade, Industry and Energy (MOTIE) strategies, Ministry of Economy and Finance (MOEF) strategies, and Ministry of Unification (MOU) white papers.[18] These documents were publicly available from South Korean government websites and were available in either English or Korean. They cover the period from February 1988 to November 2022; that is, they cover all the presidencies analyzed in this book. The objective of this content analysis was to capture South Korean views about its own grand strategy at the time when decisions were being made.

Second, I conducted semistructured, in-depth interviews with seventy-one South Korean high-level Office of the President and MOFA policymakers, high-ranked ROK armed forces officials, and formal advisors to the Office of the President, MOFA, MND, MOU, and the National Assembly, as well as over a hundred background conversations with South Korean diplomats, military personnel, and formal and informal advisors. Combined, interviewees worked for or advised all the South Korean presidents serving during the 1988–2022 period. In some cases, they also worked in government or the army before South Korea's transition to democracy. Interviews were conducted mainly in 2008 and 2019–2022. The objective of these interviews was to capture the reflections of South Korean foreign policymaking elites on their country's grand strategy.

Third, I conducted dozens of semi-structured interviews with policy-makers from third countries who have experience working with South Korea and interacting with the country's policy-makers. These were conducted mainly in 2007–2008 and 2019–2022. The objective of these interviews was to capture the views of the recipients of South Korean foreign policy actions, either at the time these recipients were serving or when reflecting on their interactions with South Korea.

The choice of time period for my case study is driven by a critical juncture in South Korean history. According to Giovanni Capoccia, critical junctures are "events and developments in the distant past, generally concentrated in a relatively short period, that have a crucial impact on outcomes later in time."[19] In the case of South Korea, 1988 was the year when the country democratized for good. Democratization was swiftly followed by normalization of diplomatic relations with the Soviet Union in 1990, UN membership, and the end of the Cold War in 1991, two key inter-Korean agreements in 1991–1992, and normalization with China in 1992. A few years later, South Korea joined the OECD in 1996—thus cementing its position as a developed country—and suffered the Asian Financial Crisis (AFC) in 1997. In other words, democratization and the events taking place shortly after this critical juncture fundamentally transformed South Korea, as well as its grand strategy.[20] South Korea has not undergone any similar critical juncture since.

Book Structure

This book is divided into seven chapters. In chapter 1, I discuss the meaning of the concept of grand strategy before moving on to analyze its theorization and shortcomings. I then delve into the academic literature about the foreign policy behavior of middle powers. By combining these two types of literature, I then develop a model of middle power grand strategy. This is the model that will be applied throughout the empirical chapters.

In chapter 2, I provide a historical background by analyzing South Korean foreign policy from the foundation of the country in 1948 to its last year under dictatorial rule in 1987. This historical background focuses on the key relationships of South Korea during these years: North Korea, the United States, Japan, and China, mainly. The chapter serves as a counterpoint to

South Korea's post-1988 grand strategy, showing the much narrower scope of its foreign policy and limited autonomy in 1948–1987.

In chapter 3, I build on the model presented in chapter 1 and the historical background laid out in chapter 2 to explain the key elements of South Korea's post-1988 grand strategy. In the chapter, I list, explain, and discuss the key factors explaining South Korea's grand strategy; the key ends for South Korea to fulfil its core interests of security, prosperity, and status and the means that South Korea uses to operationalize its grand strategy. This is followed by a discussion of the four concentric circles in which South Korean grand strategy has been divided since 1988.

In chapters 4–7, I provide an empirical analysis of South Korea's grand strategy in each of these four concentric circles: a triangular core involving North Korea, the United States, and China; East Asia, understood as both Northeast and Southeast Asia; Greater Eurasia and the Indian Ocean, including Russia, Central Asia, South Asia, the Greater Middle East, Europe, Australia, and the Indian Ocean *per se*; and the rest of the world and global governance. Each of these chapters delves into the core policies and conceptualizations of the eight South Korean presidents from 1988 to 2022.

Finally, I include a conclusion to the analysis developed throughout the book. I first summarize South Korea's grand strategy during the Sixth Republic era. Afterward, I explain what the analysis of South Korea's grand strategy tells us about the grand strategy of middle powers in general. To finish the book, I venture into what the future South Korean grand strategy might look like.

CHAPTER I

The Grand Strategy of Middle Powers

Grand strategy is the key concept driving the analysis presented in this book. As explained in the introductory chapter, there is no detailed analysis of South Korea's grand strategy. So far, in-depth studies of South Korea as an international actor have focused on its foreign policy. Often they have concentrated on one or a small number of issues or regions. But South Korea's grand strategy deserves attention in its own right. As this book will show, South Korea is proactive in its approach to foreign policy. This results in a grand strategy that withstands the short-term vagaries of international relations and foreign policymaking that South Korean elites have to confront. It is a long-term approach that determines South Korea's foreign policy behavior.

The concept of grand strategy is contested though. Thus, in this chapter I first delve into its meaning and how it has been operationalized by scholars of international relations, strategic studies, and cognate disciplines. I follow this with a discussion of the shortcomings of existing scholarship on grand strategy—in particular, the extent to which it has overlooked middle powers hitherto. Indeed, the study of grand strategy is overwhelmingly dominated by works on the United States and, to an extent, China. But as I explain in this chapter, middle powers can have their own grand strategy. I thus develop a model to analyze their grand strategy, which I will then apply throughout the book.

The Meaning of Grand Strategy

The origins of the concept of grand strategy can be traced back to the eighteenth and nineteenth centuries, when practitioners of foreign policy and war began to think more systematically about the military conflicts they engaged in. In his 1832 treatise *On War*, Carl von Clausewitz noted that "war is the continuation of policy by other means" and "a continuation of political intercourse, with the addition of other means," which already encapsulates the idea that war is not an end in and by itself.[1] Instead, it is part of broader strategy for a state to achieve its goals. But war remained central to the concept of strategy for decades. As Nina Silove reminds us, it was military historians who first debated this concept and who came up with the concept of grand strategy to begin with.[2]

It is generally acknowledged that the term "grand strategy" was first introduced by the military historian Basil Henry Liddell Hart in 1929. In his book *Strategy: The Indirect Approach*, he noted that "victory in the true sense implies that the state of peace, and of one's people, is better after the war than before."[3] Liddell Hart, therefore, stressed that grand strategy seeks "to co-ordinate and direct all the resources of a nation, or a band of nations, toward the attainment of the political object of the war—the goal defined by fundamental policy."[4] By referring to the "political object" of the war, Liddell Hart was drawing from Clausewitz's thought insofar there is a recognition that winning a war is not an objective *per se*. There are ulterior motivations behind a state or group of states deciding to go to war against another one. And while those motivations may lead to war as the best means to satisfy them, there may be other ways to achieve them. Liddell Hart's references to "all the resources of a nation" already suggests this. But Liddell Hart was linking these resources to the preparation or conduct of war, even if in his book he explained that grand strategy should also apply in times of peace.

As Martel explains, the thinkers of grand strategy eventually abandoned the narrower confines of war and military history. Sun Tzu, Thucydides, Machiavelli, or Clausewitz can be considered grand strategists, but their starting point and focus was war, for the most part. Following the outbreak of World War II, some scholars started to think not only about how to win the war but also about how to lay the groundwork for an enduring peace that they hoped would come afterward. And considering the importance of economic power and society's morale to the conduct of war, these two elements have to be an integral part of any grand strategy. This thinking would go on to prevail in the decades following World War II.[5] Regardless, the study of grand strategy remained heavily geared toward preparing to conduct war during the Cold War. This is what Thierry Balzacq, Peter Dombrowski, and Simon Reich label as "the classicist approach" to grand strategy, which is closely linked to the discipline of strategic studies.[6]

Toward the end of the Cold War, Paul Kennedy published *The Rise and Fall of the Great Powers*. In this monumental work, Kennedy analyzed how the combination of military and economic power had resulted in successive European powers gaining in power and then losing it in relative terms between 1500 and 1980.[7] The book renewed attention to the intersection of military and economic might in determining the fortunes of great powers. Shortly after the collapse of the Soviet Union, Kennedy edited the influential *Grand Strategies in War and Peace*. In this volume, several authors analyzed the grand strategy of European powers including Britain, France, Germany, Spain, and the Roman Empire during their heydays as a means to draw lessons for the United States. As Kennedy made clear in the introduction to the volume, grand strategy is "concerned with peace as much as (perhaps even more than) with war," and thus required "the balancing of ends and means, both in peacetime and in wartime."[8] By explicitly bringing in peacetime into his understanding of grand strategy, Kennedy helped to open the door to what Balzacq, Dombrowski, and Reich refer to as "the International Relations approach" to this concept. As the three of them explain, this perspective broadens the scope of grand strategy since it explicitly entails a long-term dimension and includes both material and social forms of power.[9]

In this book, I adopt an international relations approach to grand strategy. This approach has become more popular in the aftermath of the Cold War, as the prevalence of interstate war has declined while our definition and understanding of security has broadened. Throughout the Cold War, the realist interpretation of security as "state survival" guaranteed through military power prevailed.[10] Indeed, in a Cold War setting in which both the United States and the Soviet Union showed their willingness to topple governments and invade other countries, it made sense to focus on this interpretation. Even if after the Cold War both great powers (e.g., the United States) and middle powers (e.g., Russia) have continued to invade other countries, this interpretation has been challenged more recently. Most notably, constructivist scholars have noted that security is a social construction.[11] Starting with Wendt's axiom that "anarchy is what states make of it," scholars taking this approach have convincingly argued that different states will have different perceptions of what constitutes a security threat or how powerful their resources are.[12] Meanwhile, scholars taking other approaches such as postmodernism or feminism fundamentally reject the notion that security can be studied and understood at the level of the state. They posit that security has to be understood through the perspective of different units within the state.[13] In short, security does not only equate to survival guaranteed through military might today. Therefore, the goals and instruments of states are contingent on their circumstances.

International relations scholars analyzing grand strategy have yet to agree on a common definition of the concept, though. In his seminal work on it, Liddell Hart defined grand strategy in these terms: "While practically synonymous with the policy which guides the conduct of war, as distinct from more fundamental policy which should govern its object, the term 'grand strategy' serves to bring out the sense of 'policy in execution.'"[14] Liddell Hart then went on to explain why "grand strategy"—or "policy in execution"—is analogous to Clausewitz's concept of "strategy" but goes beyond it insofar as it coordinates all of a country's resources and is also concerned with peace.[15]

Writing decades later, Kennedy nonetheless built on Liddell Hart's definition when offering his own: "It [is] about the evolution and integration of policies that should operate for decades, or even for centuries. It [does] not cease at a war's end, nor commence at its beginning."[16] Kennedy then went on to explain that Liddell Hart was right when he argued that this was the point that Clausewitz's was trying to make when he argued "that war was 'a continuation of policy by other means.'"[17] Kennedy's definition of grand strategy, therefore, expands from Liddell Hart's and is much more explicit about the time period and the importance of grand strategy continuing outside of war.

Also writing in the final decade of the Cold War but taking a different approach, Barry Posen provided his own definition of grand strategy. In Posen's words, grand strategy is "a political-military, means-ends chain, a state's theory about how it can best 'cause' security for itself."[18] Posen's definition explicitly makes clear that grand strategy has political elements and not only military ones. And Posen is also explicit about the ultimate goal of grand strategy, which is none other than security. Since Posen was taking a realist perspective, was writing during the Cold War, and his work was examining military doctrine in the interwar period, the focus on this ultimate goal was warranted.

These three definitions laid the groundwork for those that have followed since the 1990s. But as the proliferation of definitions suggests, scholars disagree on the exact meaning of this concept. Hal Brands, who has published widely on the concept and how it applies in practice, understands grand strategy in a succinct way as "the intellectual architecture that gives form and structure to foreign policy."[19] Brands thus turns our attention to the logic that leads policymakers to use the limited number of instruments available to them to maximize the state's benefits. But he also draws attention to the process, which he considers to be as important as the principle, for Brands explains that short-term actions are linked to long-term goals.[20]

William Martel, meanwhile, has developed a more detailed definition of grand strategy. He understands it in the following way: "Grand Strategy is a coherent statement of the state's highest political ends to be pursued globally over the long term. Its proper function is to prioritize among different domestic and foreign policy choices and to coordinate, balance, and integrate all types of national means—including diplomatic, economic, technological, and military power—to achieve the articulated ends. In effect, grand strategy provides a framework of organizing principles that in a useful way help policy makers and society make coherent choices about the conduct of foreign policy."[21] Martel's all-encompassing conceptualization of grand strategy shares the focus on a long-term time horizon, as well as the focus on key goals.

Ultimately, there can be as many definitions of grand strategy as authors writing on the topic are.[22] As Silove explains, conceptualizations of this term can be divided into three categories: grand strategy as a plan, grand strategy as an organizing principle, and grand strategy as a pattern of behavior.[23] And depending on a scholar's interest, their definition of grand strategy will fall into one or another category. It is for this reason that in this book I refrain from providing a definition of grand strategy. Instead, my understanding of grand strategy stems from the consensus presented by Silove and already outlined here: grand strategy takes a long-term perspective, is focused on a state's primary ends, and makes use of all available means to achieve them.[24]

Ends and Means in Grand Strategy

The study of grand strategy has been heavily influenced by strategic studies, as explained above. Arguably, the biggest impact of this classicist approach has come from Arthur Lykke's foundational 1989 article "Defining Military Strategy = E + W + M" laying out a framework to formulate and analyze grand strategy. In his article, Lykke explains that military strategy is defined with reference to national or grand strategy and is the sum of ends, ways, and means. In this formulation "strategy equals *ends* (objectives towards which one strives) plus *ways* (courses of action) plus *means* (instruments by which some end can be achieved)" (italics in the original).[25] The sum of these three constituent components results in an end state, which would be the end of a war. Lykke explicitly builds on the work of Liddell Hart, particularly the use of the terminology of ends and means.[26] His simple formulation has become widely used by militaries across the world and has influenced grand strategy thinkers in the United States and beyond.[27]

Lykke's formulation, however, is not without its critics. Within the field of military strategy itself, Richard Berkebile posits that "the mathematics" of the ends, ways, means formulation "do not match the process."[28] According to Berkebile, the practice of strategy cannot be reduced to a mathematical formulation that fails to capture the complexities of a process involving multiple variables whose impact cannot be isolated. Besides, Berkebile believes that Lykke's formulation is too narrowly focused on conflict.[29] To this criticism we can add Lawrence Freedman's implicit rejection of Lykke's formulation when he argues that the actual fighting is only part of a broader process.[30] Strategy—whether grand or not—comprises a process involving thinking actions in advance, in consideration of both goals and capacities.[31] The implicit suggestion is that grand strategy cannot be reduced to the battlefield. Building on Freedman's work, Jeffrey Meiser adds a third criticism to Lykke's understanding of grand strategy. Meiser posits that (grand) strategy should focus on creating advantages, generating new sources of power, and exploiting an opponent's weaknesses.[32]

Having said that, the language of "ends" and "means" is common among scholars of grand strategy. This applies to those taking a classicist approach as well as those of an International Relations persuasion. As Silove points out, ends and means are the two fundamental constituent parts of grand strategy regardless of whether scholars see grand strategy as a plan, an organizing principle, or a pattern of behavior.[33] Silove specifically points out that "those associated with the US military" usually add "ways" as the third element of grand strategy. But as she explains, ways and means can be separated in the military sphere because materiel and doctrine can be separated there. However, in all other domains scholars "use the term 'means' to refer to both the resources mobilized as well as the ways in which they are mobilized."[34] Indeed, an analysis of some of the key texts informing our understanding of grand strategy shows the prevalence of this dyadic approach to its analysis. Brands, Kennedy, Liddell Hart, Martel, and Posen are among the many authors making use of these two terms.[35]

Martel even goes further by identifying the ends and means specific to the level of grand strategy as opposed to the lower levels of strategy, operations, tactics, and technology. Martel explains that grand strategy refers to the highest political ends, not the overall military victory, campaign victory, achievement of tactical objectives, and competitive advantage over enemies characteristic, respectively, of the four other levels. With regard to the means, grand strategy makes use of all types: diplomatic, informational, military, and economic. Meanwhile, strategy is linked to military, informational, and economic means; operations to military and informational; tactics to military; and technology to technical expertise.[36] The way in which Martel differentiates grand strategy from other levels of strategy is useful insofar he shows why the focus should be on ends and means, but also the wide range of means available to states. In this book, I will build on the widely accepted focus on ends and means. In addition, I will follow Martel's categorization of the different types of means that can be used as part of a state's grand strategy.

Grand Strategy Theory and the Neglect of Middle Powers

The scholarship on grand strategy has so far focused on great powers. As Balzacq, Dombrowski, and Reich explain, the study of grand strategy has so far narrowed its scope to "the well-trodden examples of a few great powers."[37] The assumption seems to be that only great powers have the necessary institutional resources to design and implement a grand strategy.[38] Plus, the policies and actions of great powers have far greater effect on the international system than their equivalent from weaker powers.[39] Murray makes the case for this focus on great powers succinctly: "Grand strategy is a matter involving great states and great states alone."[40] If one takes this view, then the study of the grand strategy of middle and weak powers is an exercise in futility.

An analysis of the existing literature on grand strategy indeed makes clear the prioritization of great powers hitherto. To begin with, there is a strand of the literature that takes a historical approach and concentrates on great powers of centuries past. Kennedy's seminal *Grand Strategies in War and Peace* is a case in point. Contributors to his volume take the historical examples of Britain, France, Germany, Spain, and the Roman Empire at different points in history and when each of them ruled—or wanted to rule—large swathes of territories well beyond their capitals. This way, Kennedy can draw a comparison among these countries and offer suggestions to the modern "empire" that is the United States.[41] For the theme of drawing lessons for the past to the present is often part of this type of literature. Athanasios Platias and Konstantinos Koliopoulos, for example, study the grand strategies employed by the warring parties in the Peloponnesian War explicitly to show how their lessons hold currency today.[42]

In other cases, scholars study the grand strategy of past great powers basically to shed light on their behavior. Edward Luttwak, for example focuses on the evolving strategy of the Roman Empire throughout its history in one of his books.[43] In another one, he turns his attention to the grand strategy of the Byzantine Empire.[44] Steven Lobell, for his part, examines the grand strategy of Britain and Spain when they were imperial powers, focusing on their reaction to rising powers.[45] Mark Brawley focuses on the grand strategy of Britain, France, the Soviet Union, and the United States at different points when they were great powers.[46] As for Richard Rosecrance and Arthur Stein, their edited volume sheds light on the grand strategy of Britain, Germany, Japan, the Soviet Union and the United States at different times when they could be labelled as great powers.[47]

Posen, meanwhile, analyzes the grand strategy of Britain, France, and Germany during the interwar period. This was a period in time when the first two still retained their colonial empires, while the latter was developing its capabilities to conquer other territories.[48] The interwar period is fertile ground for the analysis of grand strategy. Most notably, in their edited volume Jeffrey Taliaferro, Norrin Ripsman, and Steven Lobell curate chapters looking at the grand strategies of Britain, France, Germany, Japan, the Soviet Union, and the United States during these years.[49]

Given its position as the sole superpower in the aftermath of the Cold War, its present position as one of very few great powers, and the modern preponderance of American authors in the analysis of grand strategy, it is unsurprising that the United States has been the focus of a large number of studies about grand strategy over the past three decades. Some of these works take a historical approach, analyzing the evolution of its grand strategy over the decades. Brands provides a comparative analysis of the grand strategies of four American presidents: Harry Truman, Richard Nixon, Ronald Reagan, and George W. Bush.[50] In the case of Dueck, his focus is on the grand strategy of the United States at four major turning points: the aftermath of World War I, World War II, the Cold War, and the 9/11 terrorist attacks on American soil.[51] Christopher Hemmer, meanwhile, explains how U.S. grand strategy has evolved throughout the twentieth and twenty-first centuries. He starts with an analysis of grand strategy under Theodore Roosevelt, taking the reader all the way to Barack Obama.[52] As for Martel, he analyzes the evolution of theories of grand strategy over time to then apply his analysis to four distinct periods in U.S. history. These periods range from the country's foundation years under George Washington to the presidency of Barack Obama.[53]

There is also a strand of the literature on U.S. grand strategy that is prescriptive rather than analytical. A case in point is Robert Art's book in which he lays out a grand strategy for the US mixing tools such as collective security, containment, selective engagement, or offshore balancing.[54] In the case of Brands, he discusses grand strategy during the presidency of Donald Trump. Brands asks poignant questions about the dilemmas faced by Obama right before Trump took office, the death or not of American internationalism under Trump, or whether the United States possesses the military capabilities to exercise grand strategy.[55] As for Trevor Thrall and Benjamin Friedman, they have edited a volume in which the different contributors make the case for restraint in U.S. grand strategy.[56]

China is the other great power on which scholars of grand strategy have focused their attention in recent years. There is a general agreement that the Asian power is the only country that could potentially challenge the United States in the years since the collapse of the Soviet Union. As a result, books on the grand strategy of China have proliferated. Lukas Danner examines how Chinese history—particularly the Tributary System and the

"Century of Humiliation"—inform contemporary China's grand strategy.[57] Avery Goldstein, for his part, has analyzed the stimuli behind a rising China's grand strategy, the country's goals, and the extent to which China can maintain a long-term grand strategy considering the rapid changes it has undergone.[58] Sulmaan Wasif Khan takes a historical approach and offers a study of Chinese grand strategy from Mao Zedong to Xi Jinping.[59] Honghua Men, meanwhile, has presented a framework to study Chinese grand strategy. The framework brings together national resources, capabilities, orientations, objectives, content planning, and the implementation of means.[60] As for Ye Zhicheng, he focuses on the impact of domestic politics and economics on Chinese grand strategy. Ye argues that domestic weaknesses could derail China's grand ambitions.[61] Rush Doshi maintains that China has a carefully planned, decades-long grand strategy to replace the United States as a regional and global hegemon.[62]

In short, there is abundant literature on the grand strategy of great powers. Whether taking a historical perspective, examining the case of the United States as the sole superpower until recently, or looking at the emerging great power that is China, multiple authors have sought to explain how great powers tie ends to means. Even though both of them are finite, there can be little doubt that great powers tend to have a wider range of goals and a larger set of instruments to achieve their goals. Thus why some authors may have legitimate questions about whether weaker powers can also have a grand strategy.

Middle Powers and Grand Strategy

What is a middle power? There is no agreed definition of this concept. As Andrew Cooper, Richard Higgott, and Kim Nossal explain, definitions of middle powers are varied and can be divided into four categories: positional, geographic, normative, and behavioral. Positional definitions refer to the international hierarchy of states and focus on the material capabilities of different types of power. Geographic definitions refer to the geographical or ideological position of middle powers among the great powers. Normative definitions refer to the role of middle powers as "honest brokers" among major and other powers. Introduced by Cooper, Higgott, and Nossal themselves, behavioral definitions refer to the type of diplomatic behavior of states that middle powers share.[63] This categorization, however, has been disputed. Andrew Carr argues that middle power definitions can be divided into three groups: position, behavior, and identity. Position refers to quantifiable factors such as size of the economy or military power, as well as other factors such as geographical position. Behavior relates to the distinct type of behavior that middle powers display. And identity refers to states making use of the term middle power to refer to themselves.[64] Thus, we can see that both Cooper, Higgott, and Nosal on the one hand and Carr on the other agree on the categories of positional, geographic, and behavioral definitions. This suggests that they are quite common.

Eduard Jordaan arguably comes the closest to offering a definition on which there could be consensus among international relations scholars: "Middle powers are states that are neither great nor small in terms of international power, capacity and influence, and demonstrate a propensity to promote cohesion and stability in the world system."[65] In other words, middle powers can be identified on a case by case basis by discarding great powers whose actions invariably influence the international system— China and the United States being cases in point today—and weak powers with little to no influence in international relations. There is a general agreement that countries such as Australia, Canada, South Korea, or Sweden are middle powers and have been studied as such for decades. There are also former great powers that as of the twenty-first century are no more and can now be considered middle powers, including France, Germany, Japan, Russia, or the United Kingdom. And there are also emerging middle powers with increasing impact on the international system, such as Brazil, India, Indonesia, Nigeria, South Africa, and Turkey.

Balzacq, Dombrowski, and Reich on the one hand and Silove on the other are adamant that middle powers do have their own grand strategy. In the case of the former, they argue that if grand strategy is concerned with how a state thinks about its national security and uses its resources to enhance it, there is nothing *a priori* that prevents "small states"—a category that includes middle powers along with all other states that are not great powers—from having their own grand strategy.[66] In fact, their edited volume on comparative grand strategy includes their framework that they ask contributors to apply to both great and middle powers. The second group includes Brazil, India, Iran, Israel, and Saudi Arabia, plus the European Union. Balzacq, Dombrowski, and Reich therefore explicitly make the case that middle powers can have a grand strategy.

Silove explains that "small states" can produce grand plans to decide how to use their limited resources; can have their own organizing principles to take the necessary decisions to achieve long-term goals; and can establish certain patterns of behavior.[67] Thus, as long as middle powers and other "small states" have control over their means, we can argue that they can have their own grand strategy.

However, the sample of international relations scholarship on grand strategy is very limited. Richard Samuels's book-length study of Japan's grand strategy is the exception rather than the rule. In the book, Samuels analyzes the Asian country's evolving grand strategy and especially a seeming move away from pacifism.[68] More recently, Brad Williams has also analyzed the grand strategy of Japan. His focus, however, is on the evolution of Japanese foreign intelligence since the end of the Cold War and how it has affected the country's grand strategy.[69] Also recently, Michael Green has written a book-length account of Japan's grand strategy with specific focus on the Abe Shinzo era.[70] Etel Solingen takes the original approach of examining the grand strategy of different groups of middle and smaller powers: the Korean Peninsula including the two Koreas, the Middle East, and the Southern Cone including Argentina and Brazil.[71] In an article on Australia, meanwhile, Michael Wesley focuses on how the country's 2016 Defence White Paper can serve as the blueprint for a grand strategy.[72] And building on a grand strategic approach, Jeffrey Legro, Melvyn Leffler, and William Hitchcock have edited a volume analyzing the national strategies of Brazil, Germany, India, Israel, Russia, and Turkey—along with the two great powers of China and the United States.[73]

All this indicates that not only are studies about the grand strategy of middle powers limited in number, but they are also generally shorter in length than the book-long analyses of the United States, China, or historical great powers. Therefore, to develop a model to analyze the grand strategy of middle powers it is useful to make use of the literature on their foreign policy behavior. This literature has a long tradition and can illuminate the analysis of the grand strategy of middle powers.

Foreign Policy Behavior of Middle Powers

There is a rich and growing literature analyzing the foreign policy behavior of middle powers. And certainly, middle powers display a wide range of strategies, policies, and actions as part of their foreign policy. Cooper, Higgott, and Nossal, however, suggest that there is a type of foreign policy behavior that is common to most if not all middle powers. This is their support for multilateralism and multilateral solutions to international problems, their proclivity to find compromise in international disputes, and, in general, their participation in initiatives to find solutions to global problems.[74] Indeed, there is a great amount of literature analyzing middle powers' preference for multilateralism, compromise, and international cooperation.

Why do middle powers display a preference for this type of behavior which ultimately amounts to international diplomacy? Above all, middle powers have a self-interest in the stability of the international system. In general, middle powers benefit from the predictability and absolute gains that come from the absence of conflict. Their limited capabilities mean that middle powers cannot shape the international system to their benefit in the same way that great powers have the ability to do. And global instability can have unintended consequences, negatively affecting their economic or political position.[75] We should not forget that middle powers have a privileged position compared to the vast majority of countries that are weak powers. And few middle powers are able to graduate to great power status. Throughout the first two decades of the twenty-first century, China has graduated. India or perhaps even Russia might do so in future years. But for the most part, middle powers will seek to retain their status, and stability helps them in this respect.

Middle powers are also generally considered "good citizens," which is another reason why they support international diplomacy. The rationale is that middle powers believe in the utility and necessity to take cooperative approaches to deal with global issues.[76] Certainly, middle powers are not the only types of countries that may believe in cooperation. The United States, most notably, self-identifies as a liberal power with a belief in the benefits of multilateral cooperation.[77] And the European Union—one of three economic superpowers along with China and the United States—was founded on the principle of international cooperation to begin with.[78] In the case of middle powers, however, their "good citizenship" is a sine qua non characteristic, for they do not have the ability to shape the international system through other means such as war or economic carrots or sticks. In other words, being a good citizen matters more to middle powers than it does to great powers.

Furthermore, middle powers are seen as "honest brokers." This term is used both to explain why middle powers support multilateralism and cooperation, and to label a separate type of behavior that middle powers display.[79] Acting as honest brokers serves middle powers by reducing instability, but it is also a status-seeking behavior since it allows them to show their commitment to the peaceful resolution of conflict.[80] Even during the Cold War with its East-West division, middle powers tried to act as honest brokers even if this could create problems with great powers on the same bloc.[81] Great powers of course also seek to act as honest brokers, presenting themselves as neutral parties that can help to bridge the gap between warring parties—just as middle powers do.[82] But as is the case with good citizenship, middle powers do not have the same tools of economic coercion or the military power that great powers do. Thus, being an honest broker is a more important tool for middle powers compared to their more powerful counterparts.

There are other types of behavior that middle powers can engage in. Most notably, network diplomacy and coalition-building are generally regarded as trademark behaviors of middle powers. Networks and coalitions act as force multipliers for middle powers in specific issue-areas, in which otherwise the network or coalition members would not be able to effectively promote their policy preferences by themselves.[83] Networks and coalitions also serve to legitimize a particular goal or policy. One middle power's preference with regard to one or the other may be seen as an outlier. But this is not the case when it is a network or coalition of middle powers that supports a particular position. Thus, middle powers often try to act as catalysts for international cooperation through their networks and coalitions.[84] Certainly, great powers also use networks and coalitions to provide legitimacy to their position. But ultimately, great powers can use a range of tools to convince other countries to support their position, whether coercive or collaborative. In the case of middle powers, however, networks and coalitions may be the only means to promote their preferences given their limited material capabilities compared to great powers—in fact, a great power could always outmatch a middle power in military and economic terms.

Middle powers can also act as norm entrepreneurs. Given their limited resources, middle powers can enhance their leverage by specializing in one or a small number of niche issue areas. This can be labeled as "niche diplomacy."[85] Norm entrepreneurship prompts middle powers to pursue an active role in the global system, since they seek to promote not only a particular norm but also international cooperation.[86] The alternative to norm entrepreneurship would be to simply have to accept the norms promoted by great powers. The EU, in particular, self-styles as a "normative power" that promotes liberal norms,[87] which may not always be beneficial for middle powers. And the so-called Brussels Effect is helping the EU to effectively promote its standards globally.[88] For middle powers, norm entrepreneurship can prevent the need to comply with other powers' rules. But it can also foster legitimacy as an innovative and active member of the international community.

Regional integration—or at least cooperation—is another behavior of choice for middle powers.[89] Middle powers often try to lead regional integration initiatives that can foster stability in their immediate neighborhood.[90] Sometimes it is actually great powers that invite middle powers to lead regional cooperation initiatives. Even if middle powers cannot match the material influence of great powers, they can have ideational power allowing them to shape regional affairs.[91] Plus, the relative decline of the United States in recent decades has opened opportunities for middle powers to shape their regions according to their preferences. And as regional architectures have grown in importance, middle powers have greater incentives to try to promote regional integration and cooperation in their quest for stability and status.[92] Arguably, this tendency will only increase as concerns over "imperial overstretch" mean that the United States may seek to retrench from its foreign policy commitments.[93]

A word of caution is needed when it comes to analyzing the behavior of middle powers. Most literature on middle powers has been dominated by case studies referring to Western countries. In particular, countries such as Australia, Canada, the Netherlands, Norway, and Sweden have featured prominently in the analysis of great power behavior for decades. But these countries operate in a very specific environment. Generally, they have been rich and democratic for a very long period of time. They are located in fairly stable regions. They have long benefited from the U.S.-led Liberal International Order established in the aftermath of World War II, given their privileged position therein. Therefore, it could well be that the behavioral patterns observed in these Western middle powers do not hold elsewhere.

Indeed, Jordaan explicitly argues that we need to distinguish between Western middle powers—which he labels "traditional"—and "emerging" middle powers. According to Jordaan, the different histories, domestic characteristics, and geographical positions of Western and emerging middle powers explain different patterns of behavior. Jordaan holds that emerging middle powers have a stronger regional orientation compared to their Western counterparts, are more supportive of regional integration, prioritize reform of the global system, and seek to distance themselves from weak powers, whereas their Western counterparts want to distance themselves from great powers.[94] Other authors have also cautioned against applying preexisting, Western-centric understandings of middle powers and their behavior to other settings. Referring to South Korea specifically, Dongmin Shin suggests that the implicit liberal bias of existing middle power scholarship may not apply to countries located in unstable regions where a realist order prevails.[95] Also focusing on South Korea, Shin explains the importance of South Korea's geographical position and Korean history when analyzing the country's own understanding of its middlepowermanship.[96] Shin also rejects previous understandings of middle powers and their behavior. None of these authors, however, excludes the possibility that middle powers may display similar patterns of behavior regardless of their history or geographical position.

However, it is true that existing literature tends to downplay and sometimes even ignore military power as a type of behavior that middle powers may engage in. This was not the case during the Cold War, when military concerns arguably trumped economic ones for middle powers.[97] To an extent, this stems from middle power scholarship's traditional focus on a small number of countries located in stable regions such as North America, Oceania, or Western Europe. Differently, however, middle powers located in regions with a higher expectation of war develop military capacities related to national defense. For middle powers located in this type of region, survival rather than influence or status may well be the ultimate goal of their military capabilities. These middle powers are also more likely to try to pursue collective balance of power approaches.[98] Differently, middle powers that do not fear for their own survival can prioritize the use of their military capabilities to support international operations to enhance their influence and status.

The key point is that middle powers have the necessary agency and autonomy to choose their own patterns of behavior. This supports the growing evidence that middle powers are capable of effectively conceptualizing and executing their own grand strategy, as explained above.

Irrespective of the success of a middle power's grand strategy in serving to achieve a particular goal, a middle power is at least able to deploy a grand strategy. The literature on middle powers shows the means that they have at their disposal when planning and executing their grand strategy.

A Model of Middle Power Grand Strategy

Having discussed the meaning of grand strategy, its theorization including the neglect of middle powers, and the literature on middle powers, I now develop a model of middle power grand strategy. This model will serve me to analyze the grand strategy of South Korea in 1988–2022. At the same time, the model can be applied to other middle powers since it is anchored on the literature analyzing their behavior. This model builds on Martel's theorization of grand strategy, and in particular his differentiation between grand strategy, strategy, operations, tactics, and technology.[99] Martel's theorization, however, is best suited to the analysis of the grand strategy of great powers. I thus adapt Martel's theorization with a model adapted to the idiosyncrasies of middle powers, which in terms of capabilities and scope cannot match their more powerful peers.

To begin with, Martel suggests that the geographic scale of a grand strategy is global.[100] This certainly makes sense for great powers such as China or the US. After all, they have the capabilities to shape the international system by themselves as well as the interest in doing so. The most recent example is the development of the liberal international order by the United States following the end of World War II, and its reinforcement once the

TABLE 1.1

Middle power grand strategy model

Geographic scale	Temporal scope	Types of ends	Types of power (means)
Global when possible, regional always	Long-term (decades)	Autonomy, highest political ends (security, prosperity, status)	All if possible (diplomacy, military, economy; informational, soft, cyber)

Cold War was over.[101] Also during the Cold War, the Soviet Union tried to develop an alternative communist international order.[102] From the 2000s onward, China has displayed its global ambitions by trying to reshape the exiting international order.[103] And the EU has for decades been a key driving force behind the development of economic global governance structures.[104] In the case of middle powers, they do have an interested in trying to influence the international systems. This means that their interests can be global as well.

At the same time, however, middle powers understand that they cannot always shape the structures of the international system. Plus their limited resources mean that they have to be selective regarding the number of issue areas they can be involved in. Also, middle powers sometimes will have to be reactive to developments that result from decisions taken by great powers. But for a middle power to have a properly developed grand strategy, it needs to have a regional scope. A middle power that retreats upon itself and merely reacts to regional developments cannot be said to have a grand strategy. For middle powers can influence the structures of their own region to a larger extent that they can affect global structures. So while a middle power's grand strategy will be global in scope when possible, it will also always have a regional dimension.

In addition, Martel explains that the temporal scope of a country's grand strategy is long-term and spans decades. Some elements of a country's grand strategy might have a shorter term horizon measured in years, but ultimately these elements would lay the groundwork for decades-long ends.[105] This time horizon should apply to middle powers as much as it does to great powers. The logic is that grand strategy is designed to attain the "highest political ends." That is, the goals that transcend short-term considerations and that are meant to guide a country's strategy and policies well into the future. A middle power without a long-term horizon cannot be said to have a grand strategy.

Furthermore, Martel makes clear that grand strategy is concerned with the highest political ends, which he equates to "the most vital priorities of the state."[106] These are usually related to security, which would include economic security and not only military security. After all, the relationship between wealth and military power as the way to ensure survival is a key tenet of both realist and liberal thought. This applies to middle powers as much as to great powers and also to weaker powers. But in the case of middle powers, status should be added to the list of highest political ends.

As the literature on middle powers makes clear, middle powers are status-seeking. Status matters to middle powers, above all, because they want to be recognized as such and to be differentiated from weaker powers with less influence in the international system.

For middle powers, autonomy is a separate, fundamental goal and arguably takes priority. Certainly, the foreign policy behavior of great powers also suffers constraints. Even an undisputed hegemon such as the post–Cold War United States had its freedom of action affected by its own capability limitations or the actions of other powers.[107] But there is little doubt that great powers have an unparalleled freedom of action. This is not the case for middle powers, whose autonomy is compromised by the behavior of great powers, their relatively limited resources, or the structure of the international system. This is why autonomy is a key goal for middle powers, separate from their chosen higher political ends. After all, without autonomy a country can have the best laid out strategy but be unable to even start to execute it. Autonomy is thus an overarching goal that takes precedence even over higher political ends, but without which middle powers will still try to achieve their ends since it cannot be guaranteed.

Finally, Martel lists the means that countries have to pursue their grand strategies: diplomatic, informational, military, and economic. To this I add soft and cyber means, missing from Martel's list but increasingly prevalent. Martel also explains that diplomatic, military, and economic means are the key instruments for the implementation of a grand strategy.[108] Other types of power are secondary in that states do not build grand strategy around them; instead, they are used to support or supplement the three key means of grand strategy.[109] This applies to both great and middle powers. Even if the former have more capabilities, the latter can decide which one(s) to invest in and prioritize to pursue their different goals. Middle powers can also decide how to mix the use of different instruments. Since grand strategy is about the fundamental goals that a country wants to achieve, it is unlikely that the use of a single instrument will be sufficient. At the end of the day, grand strategy requires a level of planning and an attention to detail in its execution that demands the mobilization of all layers of power a state is in possession of.

In short, the grand strategy of middle powers can be as complex as the grand strategy of great powers even if more limited in scope owing to their power differentials. And indeed, as I will show in this book, South Korea's grand strategy since the onset of the Sixth Republic has become increasingly complex. It is global; long-term; concerned with security, prosperity, and status, as well as autonomy as the overarching goal; and inclusive of all available means (military, economic, diplomatic, informational, soft, and, more recently, cyber). But before analyzing South Korea's grand strategy, I will discuss the country's foreign policy in the years 1948–1987. These were decades when South Korea was still a weak power, but understanding its foreign policy behavior during them helps to shed light on the country's contemporary grand strategy.

CHAPTER II

Historical Background, 1948–1987

S outh Korea was founded on August 15, 1948, exactly three years after Korea became independent again following the surrender of Japan that put an end to World War II. North Korea was founded less than a month later, on September 9, 1948. Thus, Korea's de facto division following its independence, as the Soviet Union occupied the northern half and the United States controlled the southern half, was confirmed de jure within three years. The division between the two Koreas along the thirty-eighth parallel had been the result of a decision made by two junior officers in Washington, whose only goal was to keep Seoul inside the territory occupied by the United States. The division did not have any significant historical precedent, since Korea had been a unified country for more than a thousand years by the time of its partition. In other words, Korea's division and therefore South Korea were mainly a by-product of the power politics of the early Cold War years.

The division of Korea into two halves certainly has had a profound impact on the foreign policy and the grand strategy of the two Koreas. To begin with, the ultimate goal of both South Korea and North Korea is reunification under their own terms. In addition, division has been a key determinant in the country that is closest to each Korea when it comes to their foreign policy: the United States in the case of South Korea and China, along with the Soviet Union during the Cold War, in the case of

North Korea. Furthermore, Korea's division has been one of the reasons why historical wounds are yet to heal. From the perspective of the two Koreas, the effects of colonization by Japan were a key reason why the country was divided. Furthermore, division helps to explain why South Korea maintains a lingering mistrust toward China and why North Korea and the United States have yet to establish diplomatic relations. Division also serves to understand why the two Koreas have been in competition over international recognition from the moment they were founded.

From a South Korean foreign policy perspective, the period between its division in 1948 and the final democratization of 1987–1988 was broadly marked by the goal of reunification, strong links with the United States, a tense relationship with Japan even after bilateral diplomatic normalization, antagonistic relations with China and the Soviet Union, and diplomatic competition with North Korea to be recognized as Korea's legitimate representative. I will distill and discuss the nuances of this policy throughout this chapter.

Yet, South Korean foreign policy throughout its first four decades was less complex than it would become from 1988 onward because the country was a weak power throughout the period. South Korea was a weak military power, dependent on the ROK–U.S. alliance for its security and unable to compete with China, the Soviet Union, or even North Korea. Indeed, Washington's participation in the Korean War was crucial in preventing South Korea from being completely overrun by North Korea. South Korea was also a weak economic power. By the end of the Korean War, it was one of the poorest countries in the world: an agrarian country with almost no industry to speak of, devastated by the military conflict with its northern neighbor. South Korea was also a weak power with reference to the structure of the international system, dominated by the United States, while the North was effectively a satellite of the Soviet Union.

In other words, South Korea did not have the geographic scale, temporal scope, or means that a middle power grand strategy requires (see table 1.1). South Korea did have the types of ends that middle powers pursue: security, prosperity, status, and, to an extent, autonomy. But ends do not make middle powers. South Korea remained a weak power throughout 1948–1987, and its foreign policy reflected this reality.

The Founding of South Korea and
the Korean War, 1948–1953

South Korea's foreign policy originated even before the country was founded. Neither of the two soon-to-be separate Koreas recognized the other. Thus, South Korea's goal was to reunify as an independent country— as was North Korea's. To this end, the UN General Assembly passed Resolution 112 (II) in November 1947 on "the problem of the independence of Korea," calling for elections to be held and for foreign troops to be withdrawn. The resolution also called for the establishment of a United Nations Temporary Commission on Korea to facilitate the election and, therefore, independence as a unified country.[1] In theory, the election would have settled the question of the type of country a unified Korea would have been through the free vote of Korean voters.

In practice, North Korea boycotted the election. Urged by the Soviet Union, Kim Il-sung declared that there would be no vote north of the thirty-eighth parallel. Nonetheless, a Constitutional Assembly election was held in May 1948 in South Korea. A few weeks later, North Korea convened a conference in Pyongyang. Several political parties and organizations from South Korea attended the Pyongyang conference with counterparts from North Korea. Some of the South Korean attendees returned alarmed, thinking that northern forces could easily take over the south if they wished.[2] But this did not deter the newly formed Constitutional Assembly. In July, assembly members held a presidential election. Rhee Syngman, Provisional Government of the ROK president in 1919–1925 and 1947–1948, was elected as the new president.[3] He was South Korea's first president when the country was founded in August. Rhee was known for his staunch anticommunism and pro-American views. Thus, he adopted a hardline approach toward North Korea from the moment he became president until he left office in 1960.

Meanwhile, South Korea also formed the National Defense Force in January 1946. A constabulary force, it was established with the support and training of the U.S. armed forces. The force was the predecessor of the ROK Armed Forces. In May, South Korea established the Southern Chosun National Defense Security Military Academy to train its own officers.[4] This was an early step in the quest for eventual independence from the United States in terms of security policy. On the same day that South Korea was founded, the command of the National Defense Force was renamed the Ministry of National Defense (MND).[5] This is the name that the ministry retains to this day. Less than a month later, the ROK Armed Forces was officially established. In December, its different branches were launched.[6] The ROK Armed Forces had two main tasks in its early stages: preventing a possible strike from North Korea and domestic policing to prevent a communist takeover from within South Korea. In other words, the ROK Armed Forces were a pillar of the Rhee government's anticommunism.

However, South Korea did not have operational control over its own military. The U.S. Army Military Government in Korea (USAMGIK) set up in September 1945 officially ruled over the southern half of the Korean Peninsula until South Korea was official established in 1948. Shortly after, Rhee signed an executive order together with the head of USAMGIK whereby Washington would retain control of the South Korean armed forces until U.S. troops withdrew from the Korean Peninsula. Full withdrawal took place by June 1949, with the United States leaving a small contingent of military advisers behind.[7] South Korea now had operational control of its own armed forces.

Despite growing tensions between the two Koreas and several skirmishes around the thirty-eighth parallel, the South Korean government and the ROK Armed Forces were caught unprepared when North Korea launched an invasion in June 1950. This was the start of the Korean War. The (North) Korean People's Army (KPA) had received training and equipment from the Soviet Union and had combat experience, having supported China in the final stages of the Chinese civil war. In sharp contrast, the ROK Armed Forces had been denied heavy weaponry and sufficient combat training.[8] On top of that, the Truman administration had explicitly excluded South Korea from Washington's "defensive perimeter" in January 1950. The perimeter defined a line in East Asia running through Japan, the Ryukyus, and the Philippines that the United States was ready to protect from communism.[9] South Korea was conspicuously absent from the perimeter. A week after its exclusion, the U.S. Congress voted against a $60 million aid package for South Korea.[10] In addition, the U.S. Army was withdrawing from South Korea since elections had already been held and there was a functioning independent government in Seoul. These developments probably emboldened Kim Il-sung to try to take over South Korea, given that the United States seemed not to be ready to protect the country.

However, the United States did intervene. In April, the Truman administration had approved the United States Objectives and Programs for National Security. Better known as NSC-68, the statement argued for the militarization of U.S. policy in its confrontation against the Soviet Union and communism in general. North Korea's invasion of South Korea was the first test of the new policy. The United States immediately called for the United Nations Security Council to convene. With the Soviet Union boycotting the council, the United States was able to steer Resolution 82 demanding that North Korea immediately withdraw from the South.[11] Two days later, the council passed Resolution 83, authorizing UN members the use of any assistance to repel the North Korean invasion and restore peace and security in the Korean Peninsula.[12] Within days, the U.S. Army was back in South Korea leading a UN contingent fighting along the ROK Armed Forces and against North Korean troops. The UN forces fought under the United Nations Command (UNC), established in July as the first collective security arrangement set up under the United Nations Charter.[13] A few days later, Rhee made the decision to grant U.S. General Douglas MacArthur operational control of the ROK military in his capacity as commander of the UNC.[14] This was a return to the situation before June 1949. The United States would retain operational control until 1994 in peacetime, and it continues to retain control in case of war until today.

The intervention of the U.S.-led UN forces pushed North Korean troops almost all the way back to the Amnok River (Yalu River) separating the Korean Peninsula from China by October 1950. As a result and fearing an invasion by the United States, China then sent "volunteer" troops to fight against the UN and South Korean forces. By early 1951, the two warring factions had reached a stalemate around the thirty-eighth parallel. From then on, the battle lines barely moved.[15] In July, the United States on behalf of the United Nations and North Korea supported by China launched peace talks.[16] Rhee opposed the talks, though. He feared the threat that the existence of a communist North Korea posed to the South, and he believed that his country would be able to defeat the North—and China—with U.S. support. And even if that support was not forthcoming, Rhee thought that South Korea should build up its military capabilities to take over the North.[17] In any case, the United States, North Korea, and China signed an armistice putting an end to the Korean War in July 1953.[18] This put an end to hostilities, even if no formal peace agreement was signed. Thus, the three parties agreed to create a demilitarized zone (DMZ) around the thirty-eighth parallel to have a buffer that would prevent new hostilities. But South Korea was not a signatory to the armistice. And Rhee predicted that the armistice would fail because the communist side would undoubtedly breach it.[19]

Throughout these early stages in South Korean foreign policy history, Rhee also sought to advance the country's recognition and autonomy. Most notably, South Korea gained observer status at the United Nations. Under resolution 195, South Korea was recognized by the UN General Assembly as a lawful government and became an observer in December 1948.[20] Since Taiwan represented China in the UN Security Council, however, North Korea was not able to be accepted as an observer. And both Koreas were rejected as members after they applied in early 1949, in the case of Seoul due to Soviet opposition.[21] In any case, South Korea was able to use its observer status to advance relations with the United States and other capitalist countries. Most notably, South Korea established diplomatic relations with permanent UN Security Council members France and the United Kingdom, as well as with Spain.[22] Furthermore, the Rhee government sought to use its seat at the UN General Assembly to promote its preferred solution to the division of the Korean Peninsula. Seoul, however, was unsuccessful. The "Korean question" became a regular feature in UN discussions, but the Soviet Union's veto power in the UN Security Council once it had ceased its boycott plus the presence of a large number of communist countries sympathetic to North Korea prevented the South from obtaining any greater benefits from its observer status.[23]

The nationalistic Rhee government also moved to assert (South) Korean territorial claims after the decades of Japanese occupation. In January 1952, Rhee issued the Presidential Declaration of Sovereignty Over Adjacent Seas, claiming sixty nautical lines of territorial waters from the Korean coast. The Dokdo Islands that Japan also claimed under the name of Takeshima fell within these territorial waters.[24] Since the islands were not explicitly included in the San Francisco Treaty signed in 1951 that had reestablished peaceful relations between Japan and the Allied Powers after World War II, Rhee was able to reassert (South) Korean claims to them. Pointedly, Rhee also refused to normalize diplomatic relations with Japan even as South Korea established relations with the Philippines and Taiwan—two other U.S. allies.[25]

The Post–Korean War Syngman Rhee Years, 1954–1960

Following the end of the Korean War, the ROK–U.S. alliance and strong relations with Washington more generally became the key pillar of South Korea's foreign policy. In October 1953, Seoul and Washington signed the Mutual Defense Treaty Between the United States and the Republic of Korea.[26] The treaty sealed the ROK–U.S. alliance that continues to be a crucial element of South Korean foreign policy well into the twenty-first century. Essentially, the treaty committed the United States to defend South Korea from the North. As a result, the United States stationed troops in South Korea permanently. This included the UNC, which was maintained following the Korean War to fulfill its duty to protect South Korea and which was mainly staffed by U.S. troops. A few months after they signed their Mutual Defense Treaty, Seoul and Washington launched Focus Lens. Led by the UNC, these were their first joint military exercises. And in November 1954, Seoul agreed to an "Agreed Minute" appended to the treaty whereby South Korean troops would remain under the command of the United States—technically, the UNC—as long as it retained its function to guarantee South Korea's security.[27] By the time that Rhee left office in 1960, South Korea was host to fifty thousand U.S. troops. Furthermore, in 1954–1960 Washington provided $3.6 billion in aid to Seoul. The United States placed tactical nuclear weapons in South Korea in January 1958.[28] The United States wanted South Korea and other noncommunist countries such as Japan, the Philippines, and Taiwan to become economically successful as a way to show the superiority of capitalism and to prevent the expansion of communism throughout Asia. At the same time, the United States saw the treaty signed with South Korea as well as a similar agreements signed with Japan and Taiwan around the same time as a means to restraint their leaders from potentially launching an attack on their communist foes.[29]

The ROK–U.S. alliance was signed and entered into force in the context of the Truman Doctrine and NSC-68. The Truman doctrine dated back to 1947 and established that the United States would provide political, military, and economic assistance to all democratic countries—or at least noncommunist countries—under the threat of communism. The Truman Doctrine informed Washington's decision to support Western European countries through the 1948 Marshall Plan and the creation of the

North Atlantic Treaty Organization (NATO) in 1949.[30] With NSC-68, the Truman administration further militarized its response to communism. In the case of East Asia, this led the United States to sign its alliance treaty with South Korea together with similar alliances with Japan (1950), the Philippines (1951), and Taiwan (1954). The United States also signed the Southeast Asia Treaty Organization (SEATO) in 1954. This organization included, among others, the Philippines, Thailand, and the United Kingdom—which still maintained its colony of Hong Kong.[31] With China having won the Chinese Civil War in 1949 and threatening to expand, the United States feared that East Asian countries would not be able to repel an attack from Beijing's People's Liberation Army (PLA).

In the particular case of South Korea, the U.S. commitment to its security included the deployment of nuclear weapons. In January 1958—four years after Washington began forward deployment of nuclear weapons in Europe—the first nuclear weapons systems arrived in South Korea. Within weeks, the United States had deployed 150 warheads. Both the Rhee government and the United States agreed that nuclear weapons were a necessary deterrent to prevent a potential new invasion from North Korea. They also saw nuclear weapons as a deterrent against potential Chinese and Soviet support for a North Korean invasion.[32] The United States had become the only country to use nuclear weapons to achieve its military goals when it dropped two bombs over Japan in August 1945, as a way to force the country's surrender. And besides Europe, the United States was also deploying nuclear weapons in other locations across Asia and the Pacific. From a South Korean perspective, the deployment of U.S. nuclear weapons was indeed a commitment to their use if necessary.

For Rhee, the treaty with the United States not only brought the promise of security and economic development. It could also serve as a springboard to potential reunification by force. Indeed, in May 1954 Foreign Minister Byeon Yeong-tae gave a speech at the Geneva Political Conference to settle outstanding issues from the Korean and First Indochina wars. In the speech, Byeon reiterated that the South Korean government was the only legal representative of Korea, so elections should be held also in the North, China should withdraw its troops, and UN forces should remain in the Korean Peninsula.[33] In other words, the Rhee government refused to move away from its maximalist position, which predated the Korean War. Rhee maintained this position during his presidency. In fact, both the Truman administration and the Dwight D. Eisenhower administration that took office in 1953 considered the South Korean president to be stubborn.[34] Certainly, Rhee was single-minded in his ultimate goal when it came to relations with North Korea.

The ROK–U.S. alliance assuaged one of South Korea's greatest concerns. Led by Rhee, South Korean policymakers feared that the United States would one day abandon South Korea. After all, South Korea had originally been excluded from the defensive perimeter when announced in 1950. And some South Koreans suspected that the United States had only come to the rescue of their country to prevent a unified, communist Korea from posing a threat to Japan and Formosa (the future Taiwan) along with China and the Soviet Union.[35] The Rhee government thus became a staunch supporter of U.S. foreign policy, which in any case came naturally to the president given his anticommunism. But this fear of abandonment also resulted in a push to develop domestic military capabilities in case the United States withdrew its troops and support to South Korea.

Relations with the United States aside, the Rhee government sought to have South Korea recognized as part of the anticommunist camp by establishing diplomatic relations with countries across the world. The Rhee government thus established diplomatic relations with countries such as Brazil, Denmark, Germany, Italy, Malaysia, Norway, Sweden, Thailand, and Turkey during the 1954–1960 period.[36] Engaged in competition with a North Korea that had been recognized by most of the communist bloc, it was important for the Rhee government to demonstrate that South Korea was not isolated and that its diplomatic relations extended beyond the United States. Even though these relations did not yield the same security and economic advantages that Seoul obtained from its alliance with Washington, they had a clear political benefit. The main exception continued to be Japan. The Rhee government continued to be opposed to the establishment of relations with Korea's former colonial power.

In the meantime, South Korea continued to play an active role in the United Nations. Every year, the UN General Assembly discussed the "Korean Question" with a position that remained unchanged since the first discussion back in 1947: Korea should be unified as an independent and democratic country. Thanks to its alliance with the United States and the fact that Western countries predominated in the United Nations, South Korea was able to present Korea's position nominally on behalf of both Koreas.[37] However, the Soviet Union continued to exercise its veto power over South Korea's potential membership in the organization. Therefore, Korea continued to be restricted in its activities. It could participate in meetings and debates, but it could not vote. Similar to Germany or Vietnam, a divided Korea was the victim of geopolitics when it came to UN membership.

The Park Chung-hee Era, 1961–1979

In May 1961, Park Chung-hee led a military coup against the democratically elected government that had replaced Rhee in 1960. Park would go on to lead South Korea until his death in 1979. During his almost two decades of authoritarian rule, South Korea underwent a period of industrialization and economic growth that put it in the path toward development. An archetypical Developmental State, South Korea's economic growth was the result of a state-led capitalist model in which the government, bureaucratic elites, and selected *chaebol* (big conglomerates) worked together for the benefit of the country as well as their own. For Park, the goal was clear: to become an advanced nation (*seonjinguk*). He wanted South Korea to join the ranks of modern countries.[38] His goal was to transform South Korea into a developed economy to reduce reliance on foreign powers—including the United States—and to present the South as the most successful of the two Koreas.

Indeed, Park's foreign policy doctrine included self-reliant national defense (*chaju kukbang*). A general himself, Park wanted to improve the military preparedness of the ROK Armed Forces to defend South Korea from a possible second North Korean invasion with as little external support as possible. At the same time and arguably even more importantly, Park wanted to develop a strong domestic weapons production program to reduce reliance on foreign weapons. In particular, Park was wary of South Korea's overreliance on U.S. weapon systems. He was particularly afraid that withdrawal of U.S. support could make South Korea vulnerable if it did not have its own domestically produced military capabilities.[39] As a result, Seoul's defense budget increased from $820 million when Park took office in 1961 to $8.9 billion in 1979, when he was assassinated.[40] From Park's perspective, economic modernization should help sustain bigger and stronger armed forces.

But South Korea remained a weak power. And North Korean provocations across the DMZ intensified during the mid-1960s.[41] Therefore,

Park recognized the value of strengthening links with the United States. As a result, anywhere from 47,000 to 66,000 troops were stationed in South Korea in 1961–1970 in any given year.[42] And the number of U.S. nuclear weapons hosted by South Korea continued to increase, reaching a peak of 950 in 1967.[43] Furthermore, one year earlier Seoul and Washington signed the U.S.-ROK Status of Forces Agreement (SOFA). The agreement provided a legal framework for the treatment of U.S. forces stationed in South Korea for the first time.[44] Bringing predictability to the treatment of South Korea–based-U.S. troops was proof that Seoul and Washington acknowledged that the ROK–U.S. alliance would endure in time. Also in 1966, the first ninety-eight U.S. Peace Corps volunteers arrived in South Korea.[45] From the perspective of the Park government, this was further proof that the United States was committed to strong relations with South Korea, since the Peace Corps would foster people-to-people exchanges and better mutual understanding. This was reinforced by the United States granting South Korean exporters preferential access to its market, thus giving them a comparative advantage. Plus, South Korea and the United States launched Ulchi in 1968, a second joint military exercise. And in 1976 they launched Team Spirit, an exercise bringing together smaller ones, while merging Focus Lens and Ulchi into Ulchi-Focus Lens.

Even more important in terms of strengthening the ROK–U.S. alliance was South Korea's decision to send troops to the Vietnam War to support Washington's war against communism. Among the several reasons why Park decided to contribute his country's troops, four stood out: South Korea would be supporting its ally and security guarantor, thus showing that it also brought value to the ROK–U.S. alliance; South Korea would accrue economic benefits from its participation in the war that should help economic development, just as Japan had benefited from providing material support to the United States during the Korean War; the ROK Armed Forces would gain much-needed combat experience that would come handy in case of a new war with North Korea; and the Park government would gain international legitimacy or at least political acceptance. South Korea made its first deployment in 1965, only withdrawing in 1973.[46] It also helped that Park was staunchly anticommunist by the time he took power, much like Rhee before him. At their peak, 48,000 South Korean troops were deployed to Vietnam.[47]

With regards to inter-Korean relations, throughout the 1960s the Park government continued the policy pursued by the Rhee government—which the short-lived democratic government of 1960–1961 had also pursued. In other words, Park refused to recognize North Korea, still formally pursued reunification by all means necessary, and called for a free general election across the two Koreas under the auspices of the United Nations. The Park government, however, introduced a tweak to this last demand. The general election should be based on population ratio.[48] Since South Korea's population was 25.7 million in 1961—the year of Park's coup—compared to an estimated 11.4 million in North Korea, this would favor South Korean parties.[49] In November 1964, the South Korean National Assembly voted in favor of this approach.

However, as the decade went by the Park government took a more realistic view about potential reunification. In 1961, North Korea had signed a Treaty of Friendship, Co-operation and Mutual Assistance with the Soviet Union, followed by a treaty with exactly the same title with China only five days later.[50] Pyongyang therefore had official military alliances with Moscow and Beijing. If there was a second Korean War, both the Soviet Union and China would be legally required to assist North Korea. At the same time, however, North Korea had not attempted to invade South Korea since the end of the Korean War. Likewise, China had not sought to invade Taiwan. And the United States was opposed to South Korea attempting an invasion of the North. In other words, it was highly unlikely that Seoul would be able to take over North Korea by force. In January 1968, North Korean commandos had attempted an unsuccessful raid on the Blue House (Cheong Wa Dae), the official residence and executive office of the president from 1948 through 2022, in order to kill Park. Three days later, the North Korean military seized the USS *Pueblo* near its territorial waters. The crew would only be freed after months of negotiations. And in April 1969, North Korea shot down a U.S. reconnaissance jet flying over the East Sea (Sea of Japan).[51] But the number of cross-DMZ troop clashes dramatically declined in 1969 compared to the previous year, suggesting that North Korea was decreasing its hostility toward the South.[52] Thus, in August 1970 Park introduced the Peaceful Unification Initiative. The document called for economic and people-to-people exchanges, as well as the removal of barriers between the two Koreas.[53] It was an implicit recognition that reunification could only take place peacefully, not by force.

Throughout the 1960s, the most dramatic change in South Korean foreign policy was normalization of diplomatic relations with Japan in June 1965. The Treaty on Basic Relations Between Japan and the Republic of Korea established diplomatic relations between them, and also included the following economic reparations from Tokyo to Seoul for its past colonization: $200 million in aid loans, $300 million in aid grants, and $300 million in loans for public trust.[54] The democratic government of 1960–1961 had also contemplated normalization with Japan, so this was not an original idea from the Park government. But the Park government encountered huge domestic opposition nonetheless, spurred by liberals who thought that South Korea was "selling" itself to its former colonial master.[55] The Park government pressed ahead with normalization. However, bilateral relations did not immediately improve after the establishment of diplomatic relations. There was a period of better relations in the early 1970s, followed by tensions in the mid-1970s before a new thaw in relations allowed the Park government and Japan to exchange visits by high-ranked military officials and to hold their first security conference in 1979.[56] Despite the fluctuation in relations, Park saw the advantages of normalization with Japan: economic aid, private investment, and further recognition.

In terms of South Korea–U.S. relations and inter-Korean links, the 1970s started very differently compared to the 1960s. Richard Nixon was inaugurated as U.S. president in 1969. In July of that year, the new president announced the Nixon doctrine (also known as Guam doctrine)—which he spelled out in more detail in November. Nixon stated that the United States would keep all of its treaty commitments and that its nuclear umbrella would continue to protect allies. But he also announced that allies should assume primary responsibility for their own defense.[57] In practice and from a South Korean perspective, this led to the United States reducing its military footprint in the country by twenty thousand troops in March 1971.[58] Aid went down to below $700 million in 1975 compared to $4.5 billion in 1969.[59] The fear of abandonment was palpable in the Park government, which doubled down on the development of South Korea's domestically produced capabilities.

Most notably, Seoul considered launching a nuclear weapons program. Following the announcement of the Nixon doctrine and subsequent removal of thousands of U.S. troops from South Korea, Park started to mull over the development of a domestically produced nuclear weapons program in case the United States withdrew its own nuclear weapons. In the early 1970s, Park authorized a program to develop nuclear weapons. South Korea turned to Canada, France, and overseas scientists—especially of Korean origin—to obtain the necessary technology. In 1975, Park officially announced that South Korea aspired to have nuclear weapons. Seoul, however, came under heavy criticism from Washington. The Park government was forced to ratify the Treaty on Non-Proliferation of Nuclear Weapons (NPT) in April 1975, which it had signed eight years earlier. This should have put an end to South Korea's nuclear ambitions, but the end of the Vietnam War reignited fears that Washington could abandon Seoul. Thus, the Park government encouraged South Korean scientists to conduct research on the development of nuclear technology.[60] Park would thus never fully abandon his nuclear ambitions.

On top of the Nixon doctrine, the U.S. president also stunned the world including South Korea when he visited China in 1972 and met with Chairman Mao Zedong.[61] Potential normalization between Washington and Beijing signaled a thaw in relations between the United States and its greatest communist foe in Asia. South Korea reacted positively to the visit. And the Park government actually pursued accommodation and some links with China and other communist countries, such as quietly promoting economic links or lifting a ban on mail exchanges.[62] With China replacing Taiwan in the UN Security Council in 1971, it made sense for the Park government to try to improve relations with its neighbor because they would be in contact in the United Nations. But above all, Park saw Sino-American links as an opportunity to double down on his policy for South Korea to pursue better relations with the North.

In August 1971, Red Cross delegations from the two Koreas held talks in Panmunjom—the village in the DMZ were the 1953 armistice had been signed—and then set up a hotline the following month.[63] Proposed by Seoul, these were the first talks between representatives from the two Koreas since 1948, when a group of South Korean delegates had attended the Pyongyang conference. The two Koreas also established a hotline to communicate across the DMZ shortly after. A few months later, the two Koreans set up a secret phone line to communicate at the highest level.[64] Several rounds of meetings over the following months were followed by official government-level talks from May 1972. These government talks yielded the historic July 4 North–South Joint Communiqué. This document established the three principles of reunification: independence without depending on foreign powers and without foreign interference; use of peaceful means without resorting to the use of force; and national unity that transcended differences in ideas, ideologies, and systems.[65] This meant that Seoul recognized Pyongyang as a subject of peaceful coexistence.

Indeed, the Park government's June 23 Declaration of 1973 enshrined the new approach.[66]

Inter-Korean rapprochement was unsuccessful, and that same year North Korea's Supreme People's Assembly sent a letter to U.S. Congress urging the removal of U.S. troops from South Korea.[67] The following year, another letter from the Assembly asked the United States to engage in a direct bilateral dialogue with North Korea.[68] Both demands proved fruitless. Relations deteriorated, and the Panmunjom ax incident of 1976 in which North Korea troops killed two U.S. Army officers who were cutting down a tree in the DMZ was a low point in inter-Korean relations.[69] Following the incident, Pyongyang cut off the direct lines with Seoul for the first time. It would be reopened only in 1980, starting a pattern of cutting off and reopening them over the following decades.[70] By the mid-1970s, it was becoming clear that South Korea had the bigger economy.[71] Kim Il-sung, therefore, would have been unwilling to improve inter-Korean relations only to confirm the growing gap between the two Koreas. However, Park's approach to North Korea from the 1970s laid the initial basis for the *Nordpolitik* approach that South Korea would pursue after its democratization.[72] This policy would consist of the South and its partners' establishing diplomatic relations and economic ties with the North in a bid to open it up to improve inter-Korean relations, and it would go on to be implemented from the late 1980s onward (see chapter 4).

The deterioration in inter-Korean relations after the failed implementation of the joint communiqué did serve to improve South Korea-U.S. ties. In 1978, the two countries signed an agreement to form the ROK/U.S. Combined Forces Command (CFC).[73] By the mid-1970s, only U.S. troops remained in the UNC. And in 1976, UN General Assembly Resolution 3390 had called for the UNC to be dissolved by the following year.[74] North Korea had gained observer status in the United Nations after China had replaced Taiwan in the organization, and large numbers of newly independent countries from Africa and Asia were becoming members. Thus, there was a threat that the United Nations could exercise enough pressure for the UNC to be dissolved. Even though this did not happen, the CFC guaranteed the military presence of the United States in South Korea. In keeping with tradition, a U.S. general had operation control of the command. And even though Jimmy Carter openly criticized Park's human rights record upon becoming president in 1977, a bribery scandal involving the South Korean intelligence services and U.S. congressmen weakened the standing of the Park government, SEATO was dissolved that same year, and the U.S.–Taiwan mutual defense treaty expired in 1979, U.S.–South Korea security relations continued to be strong.[75] Park also felt forced to propose trilateral talks with the United States and North Korea at the end of 1979, at the suggestion of Carter.[76] But Pyongyang rejected the offer, so the proposal actually reinforced links between Seoul and Washington.

In fact, Seoul and Washington signed an agreement on Ballistic Missile Guidelines in 1979. South Korea had become one of the few countries in the world to successfully test-fire a domestically manufactured surface-to-surface missile the year before.[77] The deal with the United States restricted South Korea's autonomous missile development and possession, capping its ballistic missiles to a range of 180 kilometers and a payload of five hundred kilograms. This was a blow to South Korea's development of domestically produced capabilities. But the Carter administration agreed to transfer military technology to South Korea in return.[78] And to further reinforce its commitment to South Korea's defense, the United States send submarines capable of launching ballistic missiles with nuclear warheads to South Korean waters annually in 1976–1981.[79]

One last area in which the Park government built on the policy pursued during the Rhee years but significantly expanded in ambition and scope was relations with third parties and also within the United Nations. South Korea normalized relations with dozens of countries across the world in 1961–1979. Park took a pragmatic approach, and South Korea also established relations with countries that also recognized North Korea.[80] Rhee had refused to do this. Park also sought to join or create a collective security mechanism that Seoul could be part of, similar to SEATO. In 1966, South Korea hosted an Asian and Pacific Council (ASPAC) meeting.[81] Seoul hosted eight other noncommunist countries from Asia and the Pacific including Australia, Japan, the Philippines, and Taiwan. Three years later, South Korea tried to promote ASPAC as a potential source of collective security, after its bid to join SEATO was rebuffed.[82] One year later, Seoul once again try to promote ASPAC as an institution to promote security.[83] Even though ASPAC failed, it was proof of Park's ambitions. Once South Korea became a democracy, other South Korean leaders would also try to promote regional security organizations.

With regard to the United Nations, North Korea's presence as an observer meant that South Korea had to change its tactics within the organization. Thus, Park announced in the June 23 Declaration that he would not be opposed to both Koreas joining international organizations if North Korea so wished.[84] In the following years, the UN General Assembly urged both Koreas to continue their dialogue.[85] But in 1977, the "Korean Question" was not discussed—and the following year it was only discussed once. Since Seoul had ceased to be the only representative of Korea in the United Nations and other organizations, the Park government had more incentives to formally become a member of the UN system and less incentives to discuss the question of a divided Korea.

One final notable aspect of South Korean foreign policy during the Park years was the launch of overseas development programs and incipient attempts to develop soft power, with a view at dominating the narrative in its competition with North Korea. In 1963, South Korea accepted its first batch of trainees from developing countries. In 1967, the country dispatched its experts overseas for the first time ever. In 1969, the Ministry of Science and Technology initiated South Korea's first development project. And in 1977, MOFA provided South Korea's first development grant.[86] Having said that, South Korea would only establish a proper centralized aid system also supporting the country's grand strategy in the early 1990s. Also in 1977, Seoul established the Korea Overseas Culture Information Service (KOCIS). Two years later the agency would open the first two Korean cultural centers in New York and Tokyo.[87] These centers would start to become ubiquitous only in the mid-2000s.

The Chun Doo-hwan Years, 1980–1988

Chun Doo-hwan replaced Park Chung-hee as South Korean president following Park's assassination and a coup led by Chun himself. Officially confirmed as the new South Korean president in September 1980, Chun was another general whose rule would be marked by authoritarianism and anticommunism. Chun would go on to rule until South Korea inaugurated a new democracy in February 1988. Similar to that of Park, Chun's rule would focus on economic growth and making South Korea an advanced nation.[88] Chun shared Park's goal of making South Korea a developed country that would be less reliant on the United States, and therefore more able to pursue an autonomous foreign policy. Chun also wanted to continue to grow the economic gap between the two Koreas, which by the early 1980s was obvious.

Throughout Chun's time in office, however, South Korea remained a weak power. Its economy had grown exponentially since the end of the Korean War, but South Korea was not a developed economy yet. The ROK Armed Forces were arguably stronger than the KPA, but North Korea still had two allies in China and the Soviet Union. Plus, the development of South Korea's domestically produced capabilities was now constrained by the Ballistic Missile Guidelines, while operational control of the South Korean forces remained in the hands of the United States as a result of the CFC. Also, South Korea remained an observer rather than a member of the United Nations. This constrained its diplomatic power.

The Chun government, therefore, sought to strengthen the alliance with the United States. Serendipitously for Chun, Ronald Reagan was inaugurated as the new U.S. president in January 1981, a mere four months after Chun was confirmed as head of government in South Korea. Reagan reassured Chun that he would put an end to the troop reductions of the Carter years, while also emphasizing that South Korea would continue to be covered by Washington's nuclear umbrella.[89] In return, Chun put a definitive end to South Korea's nuclear weapons ambitions shortly after Reagan took office.[90] Reagan kept his word. The number of U.S. troops in South Korea remained stable at around forty thousand throughout the 1980s.[91] And even though Washington's nuclear arsenal in South Korea went down from three hundred warheads in the early 1980s to around one hundred by the end of the decade, South Korea did continue to be under the U.S. nuclear umbrella.[92]

The strength of the ROK–U.S. alliance allowed it to withstand two important headwinds. The first of them was about of anti-Americanism in the early 1980s among large numbers of South Koreans. The direct cause was the Gwangju Uprising, a popular prodemocracy revolt taking place in May 1980 violently repressed by the military under Chun orders. The United States acquiesced to Chun's use of force to repress the uprising. When South Koreans found out, many viewed Washington as complicit and turned against the United States—especially since many liberals resented the presence of U.S. troops in their country to begin with.[93] The second issue putting pressure on the ROK–U.S. alliance was the Reagan administration's open criticism of the Chun government's human rights record and, as the decade went by, calls for the democratization of South Korea.[94] Common interests prevailed though, and South Korea-U.S. relations ran relatively smoothly throughout Chun's time in office nonetheless.

With regard to North Korea, the Chun government sought to build on Park's official policy. The new government continued to recognize North Korea as a subject of peaceful coexistence and suggested a general election as the way to decide the government of a reunified Korea. In January 1981, Chun invited Kim Il-sung to visit Seoul without any preconditions.[95] Chun laid out his approach toward Pyongyang in January 1982, when he presented his Formula for National Reconciliation, Democratic Peace and Unification. Chun wanted reunification based on the principle of equality and reciprocity, peaceful resolution of problems, the recognition of each other's institutions, maintaining the armistice, an increase in all types of exchanges, the honoring of existing bilateral and multilateral treaties, and the establishment of liaison offices.[96] By then it was clear that South Korea was richer than North Korea and had a more active international policy. Chun's proposal therefore came from a position of strength. And even though South Korea's proposals ultimately proved unsuccessful, it informed the *Nordpolitik* that Roh Tae-woo would implement after becoming South Korea's president in 1988.

Inter-Korean relations suffered a major blow in October 1983. Chun was visiting Rangoon (today Yangon) at the invitation of the government of Burma (today Myanmar). North Korean agents planted a bomb to try to kill him. Luck saved the president, but twenty-one people died in the attack and forty-six were injured. Only a visit from Reagan to South Korea stopped the Chun government from retaliating against North Korea.[97] Then inter-Korean relations took an unexpected turn for the better. South Korea suffered from damaging floods a few months later, and Pyongyang offered relief aid. Seoul agreed, and the South Korean Red Cross suggested launching talks. Pyongyang agreed, and for the first time in over a decade the two Koreas engaged in negotiations. The result was that the two Koreas agreed to allow South–North family reunions. In September 1985 and for the first time since the Korean War, citizens from the two Koreas legally crossed the DMZ to meet Koreans on the other side of the border.[98]

The family exchange did not result in improved inter-Korean political links. On the contrary, North Korea resorted to violence toward the end of Chun's time as president. In 1986, North Korean agents planted a bomb in Gimpo Airport—Seoul's main airport then—shortly before South Korea was due to host the Asian Games.[99] In 1987, another group of North Korean agents planted a bomb on a Korean Air flight.[100] The explosion killed everyone on board, only a few months before Seoul was scheduled to host the Olympic Games. North Korea's actions were a desperate attempt to undermine South Korea, which was clearly winning the competition for international recognition between the two sides.

Indeed, the Chun government significantly expanded South Korea's relations with its neighbors. In 1983, Prime Minister Nakasone Yasuhiro made history as he became the first post–World War II Japanese leader to visit Korea. The visit proved very controversial, but it went ahead all the same, and South Korea and Japan held their first-ever summit. Furthermore, one year later Chun visited Japan to become the first South Korean president to set foot in the homeland of its former colonial master.[101] Political and economic relations received a boost from these reciprocal visits, which also pleased the Reagan administration as its two allies were looking for ways to boost cooperation with each other.

More surprisingly, South Korea–China relations improved markedly over the decade after Deng Xiaoping implemented his "Opening Up" policy first launched in late 1978. In 1983, a group of Chinese would-be defectors hijacked an airplane, redirected it to Chuncheon Airport, and requested political asylum upon arriving in South Korea. Deng dispatched an official delegation to South Korea to discuss the matter. This was the first time that Chinese officials had set foot in their neighbor, which implied mutual recognition by Seoul and Beijing. The defectors were allowed to leave for Taiwan, and South Korea returned the plane to China.[102] Two years later, two Chinese navy officers killed six of their colleagues and fled to South Korea in their ship. Beijing officially requested the return of the two officers and the ship, to which the Chun government agreed.[103] In return, China decided to participate in the 1986 Asian Games and 1988 Olympic Games to be hosted by South Korea. (China was due to host the 1990 Asian Games, which also informed its decision to participate in the two events held in South Korea.) Besides political relations, trade links between China and South Korea also improved. In 1984, South Korea surpassed North Korea as the biggest Chinese trade partner between the two Koreas.[104] From then on, the difference between the two Koreas only grew as South Korean firms and individuals saw the economic opportunities offered by Deng's opening-up policy.

In the case of the Soviet Union, bilateral relations suffered an important setback in 1983. A Korean Air flight accidentally flew into Soviet airspace, where it was shot down, killing everyone on board. Chun reacted furiously, but there was little that South Korea could do, and political contacts resumed the following year.[105] With Mikhail Gorbachev becoming the Soviet Union's leader in 1985 and the subsequent improvement in relations with the United States, South Korea saw an opportunity to improve political relations as well as trade. Thus, the Chun government increased the number of political contacts with the Soviet Union, and trade between South Korea and its neighbor increased.[106]

In fact, the Chun government skillfully made use of its economic growth and hosting of the Olympic Games to reach out to the communist bloc. There were initial contacts with countries in the bloc keen on attracting South Korean investment, especially from Central and Eastern Europe. In addition, South Korea maneuvered to ensure that the 1988 Olympic Games would not suffer the boycotts that had afflicted the 1980 Games in Moscow and the 1984 Games in Los Angeles.[107] Indeed, there were some incipient economic exchanges toward the end of Chun's years in office, and almost all communist countries confirmed their participation in the Seoul Olympic Games, despite calls from North Korea to boycott them. Furthermore, the Chun government launched the Economic Development Cooperation Fund (EDCF) in 1987 to provide loans for economic development.[108] This initiative, however, only came toward the end of the government's tenure.

For the 1980s were a period in which South Korea started to escape its weak power status and be recognized as a more relevant global actor. Above all, in 1981 South Korea was awarded the right to host the 1986 Asian Games and the 1988 Olympic Games. Seoul beat Pyongyang for the right to host the former, with North Korea withdrawing its bid after it became clear that South Korea would win.[109] Seoul defeated Nagoya in neighboring Japan in the vote to decide the host of the Olympic Games, a victory that for South Korea carried great symbolism, given the troubled history between both countries.[110] The two games were to become coming-out parties for South Korea, much as the 1964 Olympic Games in Tokyo had helped to rehabilitate Japan in the eyes of the international community. Less noticed at the time, South Korean *chaebol* growing involvement in infrastructure development overseas—particularly in the Middle East—started to show the role that the country's firms and investment could play in its foreign policy. This involvement had started in the 1970s but became more central to South Korean foreign economic relations only in the 1980s.[111]

There was one area in which South Korea failed to make any breakthrough: membership in the United Nations. Allowing South Korea to become a member was a step too far for China and the Soviet Union. Even though both Koreas were UN observers and the membership of the organization had grown dramatically, it seemed that the "Korean Question" could not be solved. It was still discussed during the 1980s, though.[112] By the end of the Chun government, South Korea had the largest economy since its foundation, the largest number of diplomatic partners ever, a stronger military, and an undisputed "victory" over North Korea. But South Korea's foreign policy remained crippled by its lack of UN recognition.

CHAPTER III

South Korea's Grand Strategy

Factors, Ends, and Means

Postdemocratization South Korea has a long-standing grand strategy. In this chapter, I lay out the factors serving as stimuli for Seoul's grand strategy, the ends that South Korea wants to achieve, and the means to pursue them. After all, we cannot argue that South Korea has a grand strategy unless we can show that it indeed has goals and tools that transcend the country's five-year-long, nonrenewable presidencies and that have held consistently over the decades. As I will explain, some of South Korea's grand strategy factors, ends, and means predate democratization in 1988. But as the discussion of South Korean foreign policy in 1948–1987 shows, during those decades South Korea was a weak power with a mainly reactive foreign policy. It was only in the years after democratization that a new set of factors, ends, and means made of South Korea a middle power with a clear grand strategy.

The geographic and temporal scale of South Korean foreign policy has become—respectively—global and long-term. This is a precondition for a middle power to be able to claim that it has a grand strategy. This was not the case during the pre-1988 years, when South Korea foreign policy essentially had a regional remit. Plus, arguably reunification with North Korea and perhaps autonomy were South Korea's long-term objectives, but there was no clear path to attain them. It was only from the late 1980s and early 1990s onward that South Korean elites both articulated clear long-term

TABLE 3.1
South Korea's grand strategy

Factors (independent variable)	Ends (intervening variable)	Means (dependent variable)
Division of Korea	Autonomy (overarching end)	Growing military capabilities (military)
ROK–U.S. alliance	Protection from external military threats (security)	Cybertools (military)
Rise of China	Inter-Korean reconciliation and reunification (security, status)	U.S. alliance (military)
Economic development	Deeper integration in the world economy (prosperity)	Diplomatic corps (diplomatic)
Democracy	Recognition as an influential middle power (status)	Trade, investment, and aid (economic)
Middle power identity		Public diplomacy (informational)
Regional integration and globalization		Soft power
Asian financial crisis		

goals and—crucially—had a growing number of instruments at their disposal. The critical juncture that South Korea underwent during this period was matched by new strategic thinking from the country's elites. Also, both high-aiming ends and a wide range of means are essential to have a grand strategy, as per my model based on Martel's theorization of grand strategy. After 1988, South Korea's geographically widened and temporarily ambitious ends have been matched by the necessary means. Table 3.1 introduces the factors, ends, and means of South Korean grand strategy between 1988 and 2022, which we will discuss in more detail.

Numerous factors underpin and explain South Korea's grand strategy. These are the independent variables that explain South Korea's grand strategy. The ends of South Korea's grand strategy are to fulfill the core interests of security, prosperity, and status. These would be the intervening variables. I follow with an analysis of the means available for South Korean foreign policymakers to operationalize their grand strategy goals. These are the dependent variables. South Korea divides its grand strategy in four concentric circles. The discussion of these four sections builds on primary data from official South Korean documents and speeches together with interviews.

South Korea's Grand Strategy: Key Factors

Grand strategy, ultimately, is the result of adjustments that states make in response to the threats and opportunities that the regional and global security environment offer. These adjustments depend on the institutional arrangements, resources, and geopolitical circumstances of each state.[1] In other words, a number of factors affect a state's grand strategy. These factors can be structural, the environment that a state confronts. But they also relate to the agent, the domestic circumstances, and capabilities that a state has. This explains why the grand strategy of similar types of states located in close proximity to each other may be different. Regardless of whether the environment they face is exactly the same or not, their circumstances and capabilities mean that they will develop a different grand strategy. In the case of South Korea, for example, its grand strategy is different from Japan—the other undisputed middle power in northeastern Asia.

In the case of South Korea, eight factors explain its grand strategy. Two of these factors are long-standing and date back to the early stages of South Korea as an independent state: the division of Korea and the ROK–U.S. alliance. Three other factors can be traced back to the years before South Korea became a democracy but became more relevant after democratization: China's rise, economic development, and regional integration and globalization. The last three factors are specific to South Korea's postdemocratization years: democracy itself, middle power identity, and the AFC.

Division of Korea

The division of Korea into two separate countries is and remains a key factor influencing South Korean domestic politics, foreign policy, and grand strategy. Arguably it was the key influence in South Korea's foreign policy before 1988. It continues to be an essential element affecting Seoul's grand strategy after 1988. Indeed, all South Korean presidents during the democratic era have had a strategy to pursue inter-Korean reconciliation and reunification. To an extent, all these different strategies have built on the foundations of Roh Tae-woo's *Nordpolitik*.[2] This shows the centrality that the division of Korea plays as part of Seoul's grand strategy. No South Korean president can have a credible grand strategy that does not incorporate the division of Korea and how to address it.

There are three main reasons why the division of Korea is a key factor influencing South Korean grand strategy. To begin with, originally the division was an external imposition agreed upon by the two great powers of the era—the United States and the Soviet Union—shortly after Korea gained independence from Japan. Both Koreas have sought to redress what they consider to be an artificial state of affairs, returning Korea to the single entity that it was for centuries. In the case of South Korea, article 3 of its constitution states, "The territory of the Republic of Korea shall consist of the Korean peninsula and its adjacent islands," while article 4 states that "The Republic of Korea shall seek unification and shall formulate and carry out a policy of peaceful unification based on the principles of freedom and democracy."[3] In other words, it is a constitutional obligation for all South Korean governments to pursue reunification. It is the ultimate task for the South Korean state.

In addition and in sharp contrast, the division of Korea is a factor in South Korean grand strategy because of the military threat that North Korea poses. This was most clearly laid bare when North Korea sought to invade South Korea, a move that resulted in the Korean War. Ever since, Seoul has had to prepare against a possible North Korean strike. The preamble of the North Korean constitution states, "The great Comrades Kim Il Sung and Kim Jong Il are the sun of the nation and the lodestar of national reunification. Regarding the reunification of the country as the supreme national task, they devoted all their efforts and care for its realization," with article 1 stating, "The Democratic People's Republic of Korea is an independent socialist state representing the interests of all the Korean people."[4] Coupled with North Korea's decades-long military buildup, these words in Pyongyang's constitution explain why South Korea has no option but to consider a strategy against a possible North Korean strike. South Korea's defense white papers do exactly this.[5]

Last, Korea's division into two separate states is a factor influencing South Korean grand strategy because there is a belief among policymakers that reunification would make Korea stronger.[6] Despite any short-term challenges that reunification might bring, in the long run a unified Korea would have a bigger territory, a larger population, a bigger economy, and the opportunity not to have to devote a large share of its military capabilities to preempt an inter-Korean conflict. Certainly, therefore, a stronger Korea is a key reason why South Korean policymakers want a unified Korea. And it is one of the reasons why the division of Korea is a factor influencing South Korean grand strategy.

The ROK–U.S. Alliance

The history of the alliance between South Korea and the United States is almost as long as the history of South Korea itself, for it dates back to the immediate aftermath of the Korean War armistice. Together with the division of Korea, the ROK–U.S. alliance was the other main factor informing South Korean foreign policy until 1988. Since democratization, the alliance has continued to be a key element influencing the grand strategy of South Korea. Every single president from Roh Tae-woo to Yoon Suk-yeol has made clear that they consider the alliance to be a pillar behind the country's grand strategy.

There are three main reasons why the ROK–U.S. alliance has been and remains a key factor explaining South Korean grand strategy. To start with, the alliance is part of South Korea's deterrence policy toolkit.[7] Due to restrictions including operational control over its military forces and the 1979 Ballistic Missile Guidelines—scrapped only in 2021—South Korea lacks the autonomy and full range of capabilities that it could possess. Furthermore, Seoul continues to be under Washington's nuclear umbrella.[8] The ROK–U.S. alliance, therefore, acts as a deterrent against a possible North Korean strike.

Furthermore and to an extent related, South Korean policymakers see the ROK–U.S. alliance as a useful and necessary addition to their country's military capabilities. The United States has the most advanced and powerful military forces in the world. It also remains the biggest military spender worldwide by a wide margin.[9] As a treaty ally and in spite of recurrent fears of abandonment, South Korea can count on U.S. military support as a way to enhance its deterrent capabilities against other potential threats such as China or Russia.[10] In fact, the alliance has evolved since its original purpose of deterring North Korea. Successive South Korean presidents have said as much.[11] In common with other U.S. treaty allies such as Japan or NATO members, South Korea sees the value of a strong alliance with one of the two great powers of the twenty-first century.

Finally, South Korean policymaking elites see the ROK–U.S. alliance as an enabler of Seoul's grand strategy. This is another reason why the alliance is a factor behind South Korea's grand strategy: it enhances the country's reach and policy options.[12] From a South Korean perspective, the alliance provides Seoul with an instrument that can support its grand strategy at the regional and global levels. Thanks to the ROK–U.S. alliance, South Korea's position and actions have an added layer of legitimacy.[13] As well, South Korea and the United States can bring together their economic capabilities. This is another enabler of South Korean grand strategy that would not necessarily be available without the alliance. In return, South Korea supports U.S. policy in issue areas such as the Afghanistan and Iraq wars, boosting the credibility of the G20, or Washington's Indo-Pacific strategy.[14]

The Rise of China

China's rise affects the international system as a whole. But its impact on China's immediate neighborhood is even greater, given that China considers its near abroad its sphere of influence. This includes the Korean Peninsula. Therefore, the rise of China is a major factor affecting South Korea's grand strategy. Even before China started to open up its economy, China's power and behavior certainly were a key consideration in South Korean foreign policy. This dates back to the Korean War itself, due to China's role in preventing South Korean and UN forces from taking over North Korea. And it was also the case in the interim decades before Deng

Xiaoping introduced his first economic reforms in 1978, for the China–North Korea alliance plus Sino-North Korean economic exchanges were a lifeline for Pyongyang. But it has been since the 1980s and especially the 1990s–2000s that China has become a major economic, military, and diplomatic power. Every South Korean president since the country's transition to democracy has had to grapple with China's rise as part of its grand strategy.[15]

There are three main reasons explaining the centrality of the rise of China to South Korea's grand strategy. The first one is that China continues to have a treaty alliance with North Korea and is also a signatory of the 1953 armistice that ended the Korean War. Therefore, Beijing is a crucial player in dealing with one of South Korea's key foreign policy concerns. In fact, North Korea is often considered a buffer state for China that prevents U.S. troops from being stationed even closer to its territory. Furthermore, the potential collapse of North Korea is often considered a threat for the Chinese government, which could see a flood of refugees crossing the Amnok River.[16] In case of a new inter-Korean conflict, China would be legally required to assist North Korea, given their treaty commitment. As per article 2 of the treaty: "The Contracting Parties undertake jointly to adopt all measures to prevent aggression against either of the Contracting Parties by any state. In the event of one of the Contracting Parties being subjected to the armed attack by any state or several states jointly and thus being involved in a state of war, the other Contracting Party shall immediately render military and other assistance by all means at its disposal."[17] In short, Beijing has a role to play in South Korea's inter-Korean and North Korea strategies.

Besides, China has become South Korea's largest trading partner. And Beijing does not refrain from exercising its economic leverage, as Seoul itself found out when the Xi Jinping government imposed sanctions on South Korea after its neighbor agreed to the deployment of Washington's THAAD antimissile defense system on its territory. For South Korea, the economic rise of China is a crucial factor in the economic component of its grand strategy. On the one hand, China's uninterrupted economic growth dating back to the 1980s to become the second biggest economy in the world already in 2011 offers an opportunity for South Korea, given their complementarity. On the other hand, not only can China exercise its coercion, but it is also trying to move up the value-added chain to compete with South Korea and other developed economies.[18] China is therefore a threat to the South Korean economy.

Finally, China's military rise and Sino-American rivalry poses a strategic dilemma for South Korea affecting its grand strategy. As of the 2020s, China is the second biggest military spender in the world.[19] And Beijing has shown its willingness to use its military to assert its territorial and other claims.[20] South Korea has to consider this reality as part of its grand strategy. In addition, the United States considers China its greatest competitor and a potential threat to the liberal international order it has led since the end of World War II.[21] South Korea, therefore, is "sandwiched" between its decades-old military ally and its biggest trading partner, and Seoul has to consider this as part of its grand strategy.

Economic Development

South Korea's own economic development is another crucial factor with a strong influence on the country's grand strategy. By the 1980s, South Korea had become a middle-income economy.[22] This started to be incorporated into the country's foreign policy, for communist countries were among the many that sought to improve relations with South Korea as a means to boost inward investment and trade.[23] South Korea's economy continued to grow in the years following democratization, and in 1996 the country became only the second in Asia to join the Organization for Economic Cooperation and Development (OECD).[24] One year later, the Bank of Korea (BOK) formally joined the Bank for International Settlements (BIS).[25] Later on, South Korea went on to join the G20, joined the OECD's Development Assistance Committee (DAC), was invited to participate at G7 meetings, and became one of the ten largest economies in the world.[26] South Koreans take pride in their country's transition from one of the poorest in the world in the 1950s to a rich country by the 1990s, an attitude that has remained constant over the decades.[27] South Korean presidents since democratization have been able to use South Korea's economic development as a tool of economic statecraft.

There are two reasons why economic development is a factor explaining South Korea's grand strategy. The first reason is that it gives South Korea a new means. Third parties are attracted to trade, investment, and aid opportunities plus the South Korean market itself. As an economic power, South Korea is not at the same level as the "big three" of China, the European Union, and the United States. But it is part of a second tier of middle economic powers including Australia, Canada, Japan, or the United Kingdom that can leverage their economic capabilities. South Korean governments have made strategic use of these capabilities and understand that they are part of their policy toolkit.

At the same time, economic development influences South Korean grand strategy because it imposes new obligations and responsibilities on Seoul. Demands for market openness, aid provision, or participation in economic governance institutions tend to be greater on bigger and/or more developed economies. Certainly South Korea has come under greater pressure to increase its aid, provide funds for international economic organizations such as the World Bank or the Asian Development Bank (ADB), and contribute other public goods such as equipment and vaccines to address the COVID-19 pandemic.[28] These demands are a factor influencing South Korea's grand strategy, for they cannot simply be brushed aside as a less economically powerful country would be able to.

Democracy

South Korea's transition to democracy and subsequent consolidation as a democratic country is a factor that has had an influence on South Korea's grand strategy since—logically—its transition to democracy itself. South Korea was part of the "third wave" of countries in Central and Eastern Europe, East Asia, Latin America, and Southern Europe that democratized between the 1970s and the 1990s.[29] It was also one of these third wave countries that rapidly consolidated its democracy along with others such as Portugal, Spain, or Taiwan, becoming one of the strongest democracies in the world by the 2010s already. Indeed, South Korea ranks as one of Asia's three only full democracies along with Japan and Taiwan.[30] South Koreans are proud of their democratic transition and consolidation.[31] This has thus become a factor influencing the grand strategy pursued by policymakers.

There are two main reasons why democratization has become an issue affecting South Korea's grand strategy. The first reason is that South Korea is under domestic and international pressure to live up to and incorporate its democratic credentials as part of its grand strategy. The South Korean population attaches great importance to democracy as a value, an attitude that has not changed over the decades.[32] And as a democratic country, South Korean policymakers should at least consider the population's preferences. And indeed, South Korean policymakers do consider values such as democracy as part of the country's grand strategy.[33] On top of that, South Korea is also called upon by fellow democracies to side with them when calling out nondemocratic practices.[34]

The other reason why democratization affects South Korea's grand strategy is that being a democracy provides South Korea with the opportunity to be part of groups and organizations that otherwise it would be shunned from. For example, all OECD members are democracies. And when South Korea has been invited to attend the G7 as a guest, a key reason has been its status as a democracy located in Asia.[35] Similarly, democratization allowed South Korea to be invited to the 2021 Summit of Democracies.[36] Therefore, democratization has brought new responsibilities for Seoul but also new opportunities that it has taken advantage of.

Middle Power Identity

A country's self-identity matters in grand strategy. Identity might not be a self-fulfilling prophecy, but it is well established that ideational factors affect a state's behavior along with material factors. This is because self-identity informs the roles that a state assigns to itself as well as the expectations from others.[37] South Korea saw itself as a weak—or small—power in the decades before its democratization. This changed shortly after democratization, which coincided with the end of the Cold War and gave South Korean policymakers a new perspective of their country's position in the international system. In 1991, Roh Tae-woo labeled South Korea a middle power. Ever since, South Korean policymakers and officials have considered their country as such.[38]

Two main reasons explain why South Korea's self-identification as a middle power matters. They key one is that Seoul itself has greater expectations about its own role in the international system. As explained in chapter 1, middle powers tend to support multilateralism and diplomacy, are usually considered "good citizens" and "honest brokers," tend to employ network diplomacy and coalition-building, like to act as norm entrepreneurs, and usually support regional integration. International relations theory does not always match a state's behavior in the international system. But it is true that South Korea has displayed this type of behavior since its democratization. Among South Korean policymakers, there is an expectation that their country will behave in a way that has long been associated with middle powers.[39]

Additionally, middle powerness implies being in possession of a certain amount of capabilities that are not available to weak powers and that give the middle power more agency. This means that middle powers have at their disposal more means to implement a grand strategy that suits their interests. Indeed, South Korea is a case of a country with greater agency thanks to greater capabilities. Thus, the country's policymakers are aware that the middle power status of South Korea in recent decades allows it to display greater autonomy than was the case before democratization This informs their grand strategy choices in a way that was not possible in the past.

Regional Integration and Globalization

The democratization of South Korea coincided with the onset of regional integration and globalization, which rapidly became another factor influencing the country's grand strategy. Certainly, globalization had already started before 1988. But the collapse of the Soviet Union and subsequent end of the Cold War opened the door to a globalization process touching all corners of the world. And South Korea embraced this process, with Kim Young-sam's *segyehwa* (globalization) policy becoming a pillar of South Korean grand strategy from the moment it was formulated.[40] Relatedly, regional integration involving both Northeast Asia and Southeast Asia became possible thanks to the end of Cold War hostilities. In 1989, the Asia-Pacific Economic Cooperation (APEC) group was launched, with South Korea among its founding members.[41] From then on, different regional institutions, groups, and agreement including the Council for Security Cooperation in the Asia Pacific (CSCAP), ASEAN Regional Forum (ARF), ASEAN+3, the East Asia Summit, the Comprehensive and Progressive Agreement for Trans-Pacific Partnership (CPTPP), and the Regional Comprehensive Economic Partnership (RCEP) have fostered cooperation and integration. Economic integration was prioritized, but security and political cooperation also moved ahead. And South Korea has been a founding member and active participant in most of these initiatives. There has been a tension between Asia-Pacific integration (involving the United States) and East Asian integration (excluding the United States), and in recent years Indo-Pacific cooperation (involving India but excluding China) has become yet another geographical area to consider. From a South Korean perspective, in any case, what has mattered most is that integration has involved most of East Asia.

South Korea's backing of regional integration and globalization is explained by two dynamics. The first one is that South Korea has benefited from globalization more than most other countries. South Korea is a trade-dependent economy, with its trade-to-GDP ratio standing at 69 percent as of 2020. This is one of the highest ratios among large developed economies, trailing only Germany.[42] In addition, South Korea benefited from the openness of other markets during its developmental decades. South Korean policymakers are very aware of this fact.[43] South Korea's own history therefore helps to explain why Seoul is a strong supporter of regional integration and globalization in the area of economics.

In addition, South Korean policymakers perceive regional and global institutions as extra venues to promote diplomatic exchanges.[44] In line with its identity as a middle power, Seoul prefers diplomacy and cooperation over the use of coercion or even conflict. Also, South Korea has sufficient diplomatic capabilities to actively participate in a large number of institutions and groups. This further reinforces South Korean policymakers' support for regional and global integration processes.[45] Before democratization, the South Korean diplomatic corps was not sufficiently large for the country to be an active voice in this type of process.

One risk associated with regional integration and globalization is that it can curtail independence of action. Thus, the positive connotations of this factor influencing South Korea's grand strategy has to be balanced with this risk. Most notably, economic grand strategy can be influenced by the power that globally integrated, open markets hold over even the biggest economies in the world.[46] The AFC is an example of this. Regional and global integration also means that security and political developments in one part of the world can have ripple effects in other parts. The 9/11 terrorist attacks on the United States are a case in point, for they led to the Global War on Terror that sucked in many other countries, including South Korea.

Seoul's independence of action was constrained even though South Korea was not directly threatened.

The Asian Financial Crisis

The Asian financial crisis (AFC) of 1997–1998 is the last key factor influencing the grand strategy of South Korea. Also known to South Koreans as the IMF crisis because of the role of this institution in exacerbating its effects, the crisis was the biggest hit that the South Korean economy had taken since the Korean War.[47] The crisis came as a major shock for South Korea, which had joined the OECD only one year before. One of its main causes was the sudden withdrawal of foreign capital from South Korea, which had left the country's firms and government unable to fully serve their U.S. dollar–denominated debt. South Korea had to ask for a $57 billion bailout package to avoid defaulting on its debt.[48] This was the IMF's biggest-ever package hitherto. The international dimension of the crisis—both in its origins and its resolution—explains why the AFC became a factor in South Korean grand strategy.

A crucial reason why the AFC affects South Korean grand strategy is that it acts as a constrain on the country's independence of action. Every single South Korean government since the Kim Dae-jung administration in power from shortly after the AFC has sought to avoid a repeat of the crisis.[49] South Korean policymakers have been well aware of the terrible effects of the economic shock that South Korea suffered, both for South Koreans themselves and for the standing of the country at the international level. This explains why Seoul seeks to avoid a repeat of the AFC.

On the other hand, the AFC opened up new venues for cooperation for South Korea. ASEAN members, China, Japan, and South Korea launched ASEAN+3 in 1997 as a result of the crisis.[50] The G20 finance ministers' meeting was created in 1999 in response to the AFC and other financial crises. South Korea was one of the founding members.[51] It would eventually evolve into the G20 after the global financial crisis (GFC) of 2007–2008. The BOK also joined the Basel Committee on Banking Supervision (BCBS) in 2009.[52] This was following the GFC, but the origins of the BOK potentially joining the organization can be traced back to the AFC. In other words, the AFC made South Korea one of the voices to be consulted on global economic governance. This has affected Seoul's grand strategy.

South Korea's Grand Strategy: Key Ends

What are the ends that South Korea is trying to achieve with its grand strategy? As the title of this book explains, Seoul has a very clear overarching goal: to make its own destiny. In other words, autonomy. This is logical for a country that was colonized by Japan for thirty-five years when Korea remained unified, was created as a result of the division of Korea as decided by the United States and the Soviet Union, needed the intervention of the U.S.-led UN forces to survive the Korean War, and was unable to pursue an independent foreign policy as a weak power throughout the Cold War. In short, the analogy of a "shrimp among whales" that illustrated the influence of great powers on Korean actions over the centuries still applied to South Korea until a little over three decades ago.

Certainly, South Korea is not the only middle power whose ultimate end is autonomy. As explained in chapter 1, middle powers strive for independence of action because they cannot take it for granted. Undoubtedly, all powers strive for autonomy. Not even great powers have full agency, unconstrained by the structures of the international system. But great powers have the muscle and authority to create and constantly shape the international system: the U.S.'s liberal international order and the Soviet Union's Eastern bloc are cases in point.[53] In the case of East Asia, China created and for centuries led a Sinocentric international system with itself at the top and other countries positioned under or in opposition to it.[54]

In contrast, middle powers can sometimes shape the existing international system but cannot create a new one. And even when shaping the international system, structural constraints affect them more than is the case for great powers. The liberal international order again serves as a case in point. It was a U.S. creation after World War II, with middle powers such as France, Germany, Japan, and the United Kingdom helping to shape it. But ultimately, these middle powers operated within the boundaries set by the United States. Likewise, since South Korea's transition to democracy the international system has been defined by the last few years of Cold War bipolarity, U.S. unipolarity in a liberal international order, and more recently the reemergence of incipient bipolarity due to China's rise. South Korea can perhaps shape this order, but it cannot redefine it. Thus, its quest for autonomy to pursue the grand strategy of its choice. I will show in later chapters not only how South Korea has strived for strategic autonomy, but also how it has continued to do so when facing constraints coming from great powers.

But what does autonomy mean for post-1988 South Korea? It means achieving four grand strategic ends: protection from external military threats (i.e., security); inter-Korean reconciliation and reunification (i.e., security as well as status); deeper integration in the world economy (i.e., prosperity); and recognition as an influential middle power (i.e., status as well). These are the global, long-term goals that South Korean policymakers are trying to achieve. The ends that would help South Korea to make its own destiny.

Protection from External Military Threats

Protection from external military threats is a fundamental end of South Korean grand strategy. Certainly, security from military intervention arguably remains the basic goal for all states. After all, survival as a unitary state continues to be a challenge for many countries even as inter-state conflict has decreased dramatically since the end of the Cold War. The cases of Afghanistan, Iraq, Libya, Ukraine, Yemen, and Yugoslavia show that more powerful states do not hesitate to intervene in weaker counterparts to invade them, change their government, support the independence of a particular group, or even seize part of their territory.

Arguably, South Korea is more powerful and safer from external military intervention than the states that have suffered one since the end of the Cold War. But this does not mean that South Korea does not need to protect itself against a potential military strike. This has been the case almost since the foundation of the country, considering that the North Korean invasion that precipitated the Korean War took place only two years after South Korea was established. Throughout the Cold War, there were inter-Korean military clashes and North Korean attempts to infiltrate South Korea. And even since the end of the Cold War, there have been several military clashes. Most notably, in 2010 a North Korean torpedo sank ROKS *Cheonan*, killing forty-six crew members, and the North Korean military shelled Yeonpyeong Island, which resulted in four casualties.[55] It is unsurprising that South Korean defense white papers show the country's security strategy seeks to contain North Korea and protect South Korea against a possible strike by its neighbor.[56] Furthermore, North Korea's development of its nuclear weapons adds a new threat to South Korea.

In addition, South Korea also feels threatened by a possible military attack from China or Russia. Certainly, the threat from these two other South Korean neighbors has decreased since the end of the Cold War. But both countries have challenged South Korea's territorial integrity. The air forces of both countries routinely fly over South Korea's air defense identification zone (ADIZ), occasionally also flying into South Korean air space.[57] Chinese vessels, meanwhile, has also sailed through South Korea's territorial waters in the West Sea (Yellow Sea).[58] And China remains a treaty ally with North Korea, which puts a legal obligation on Beijing to assist Pyongyang in case of a new inter-Korean conflict.[59] As a result, Seoul sees Beijing and Moscow as potential military threats, even if not to the same extent that Pyongyang is.[60]

Also, security threats extend beyond traditional military strikes in the era of hybrid warfare. Cyberattacks, disinformation campaigns, and economic pressure are among the most common means to destabilize an opponent. In the case of South Korea, it has to confront cyber warfare from China, North Korea, and Russia—especially from Pyongyang.[61] Thus, the military threat to South Korea not only comes from a traditional military strike but also from cyberattacks targeting both military and civilian objectives. As a grand strategy end, therefore, protection from external military threats refers to both traditional and hybrid warfare threats.

Inter-Korean Reconciliation and Reunification

South Korea lays claim to the whole of the Korean Peninsula in its constitution. And during the Cold War, some South Korean policymakers thought that it would be possible to attempt forceful reunification. But over the years, it became clear that this was not possible considering both the constraints that South Korea faced because of its alliance with the United States, as well as the alliances between North Korea on the one hand and China and the Soviet Union on the other. Thus, Seoul moved away from a maximalist position of reunification by force and toward a position of inter-Korean reconciliation as a step toward eventual reunification. Therefore, reconciliation and reunification are not contradictory insofar the latter is the ultimate goal that may or may not entail the former as an interim stage. The end of South Korean grand strategy therefore is reconciliation and reunification today.

Both security and status underpin this end. When it comes to security, North Korea remains the main external military threat for South Korea as just explained. Pyongyang's foremost goal continues to be reunification under its own terms. North Korea has formidable conventional military capabilities, as well as weapons of mass destruction, including nuclear bombs. North Korea's armed forces have struck South Korea in the not too distant past. For Seoul, reconciliation between the two Koreas would reduce tensions and reinforce its own security.[62] This is, therefore, a very practical reason for South Korean policymakers to seek reconciliation and reunification.

Enhancing the country's status also explains the goal of reconciliation and reunification. To begin with, Korea was divided not out of its own volition but due to external intervention. For South Korean leaders, reunification has a strong and understandable emotional component.[63] In addition, reunification under South Korean terms would obviously make clear that South Korea is "superior" to North Korea.[64] In other words, Seoul would have "won" the battle for legitimacy between the two Koreas. Reconciliation and eventual reunification would also result in a country with more than double the size and one-third more population than today's South Korea. As small as the North Korean economy is, a reunified Korea would have a bigger economy than South Korea's. A bigger, more populous country with a bigger economy and with the political and economic system of South Korea would have a greater status in East Asia and globally.

This explains why all South Korean leaders from Roh Tae-woo to Yoon Suk-yeol have implemented policies to promote inter-Korean reconciliation and eventual reunification. Regardless of the name of their policies and the role that pressure placed in them, all South Korean leaders in power since democratization have sought dialogue and engagement including the possibility of inter-Korean summits at the highest level. South Korean leaders have also pursued policies involving (the possibility of) economic and people-to-people exchanges. These policies have also included the end of reunification, whether de jure or de facto through different formulas. And all South Korean presidents since 1988 have stressed the need for peaceful reunification under terms acceptable to both Koreas. Arguably, this has been South Korean policy dating all the way back to the 1972 Three Basic Principles for Peaceful Unification. It is thus a grand strategy goal with deep roots.

Deeper Integration in the World Economy

South Korea's grand strategy also has deeper integration in the world economy as one of its ultimate grand strategy ends. Prosperity or wealth is of course a goal for most if not all leaders across time and place. Whether trying to realize liberal-style absolute gains or realist-informed relative gains, countries seek wealth maximization as a means to achieve more power and enhance the security of the state and the population. South Korea is no exception. Dating back to the aftermath of the Korean War, South Korean leaders have been no different. With the advent of democracy in 1988, the country's leaders have had even more incentives to pursue prosperity as a way to maintain their political parties in power.

South Korea is often characterized as a developmental state. This suggests an economic model in which the state plays a central role. And even though there have been discussions regarding the extent to which South Korea continues to adhere to this model considering the growing importance of the market from the 1980s onward, it remains true that the country continues to display the characteristics of a developmental state.[65] Certainly, South Korea is far away from the neoliberal model pursued by countries such as the United States or the United Kingdom. In terms of grand strategy, this implies that the state plays an important role in South Korean foreign economic policymaking and actively plots ways to help maximize the country's overall prosperity.

Integration in the world economy is the main way in which the South Korean state has sought to maximize prosperity. Certainly, the roots of this policy can be traced back to the pre-1988 era. Back then, the government promoted trade and inward foreign direct investment (FDI) to ensure this integration. After 1988 and coinciding with the end of the Cold War, successive South Korean administrations have sought to reinforce economic integration through trade and FDI flows. In this respect, Seoul has supported the General Agreement on Tariffs and Trade (GATT) and its successor the World Trade Organization (WTO), the OECD, and bilateral and regional free trade agreements (FTAs).[66] This means that South Korean integration in the world economy has rested on two pillars: market-led private commercial and investment flows, and state-driven initiatives and organizations to remove barriers to said private flows.

Ultimately, deeper integration in the world economy is the obvious choice for Seoul. Its market is one of the ten biggest in the world, but much smaller than the market of the "big three." Led by *chaebol* such as Hyundai, LG, or Samsung, export-oriented, globally competitive firms able to withstand foreign competition dominate the South Korean economy. And South Korea's own history was predicated on the openness of the U.S.-led liberal international (economic) order. Therefore, both structural factors and South Korean elites thinking and ideas about the reasons behind their country's advanced economy status underpin support for the goal of deeper integration in the world economy. Not even the AFC or the GFC have dented this enthusiasm. For South Korean policymakers, their grand strategic goal is the only way to bring economic prosperity.

Recognition as an Influential Middle Power

A final key end of South Korean grand strategy is recognition as an influential middle power. Dating back to the Roh Tae-woo government, South Korean presidents have put middle powerness at the center of their country's grand strategy. In contrast, self-identification as a middle power was not part of South Korea's foreign policy pre-1988. Before democratization, South Korea wanted to be recognized as the "true" representative of Korea. But democratization in 1988 coincided with the Seoul Olympic Games in the same year and came in the midst of countries in the Eastern bloc seeking to establish diplomatic relations with South Korea. Shortly after, South Korea joined the UN and started the process to become part of the OECD—which Seoul finally achieved in 1996. Therefore, South Korea's perception of its own status changed and added this new layer of becoming an influential middle power.

For South Korean leaders, middle power relates to the country's power, role, and position. The capabilities of South Korea in the military, diplomatic, or economic sphere make the country a middle power according to South Korean policymakers.[67] In addition, South Korea is a middle power because it behaves as such. The behavior of middle powers is characterized by certain features such as the prioritization of diplomacy and cooperation over conflict. In general, South Korean leaders adhere to and follow this type of behavior.[68] Finally, the geographical position of South Korea as well as its position in the global system also informs Seoul's self-identification as a middle power.[69] Geographically, South Korea is in the middle of the two great powers of the twenty-first century: China and the United States. In terms of its position in the global system, South Korea sees itself in the middle of different types of countries: developing and developed, since South Korea used to be the former and is now the latter; East and West, since South Korea is located in the latter and still shares some of its values, while other values now resemble those of the former; and authoritarian and democratic, as South Korea has transitioned from the former to the latter.

But self-identity does not mean recognition by third parties. South Korea's grand strategy aims at obtaining this recognition because South Korean policymakers understand that they have to gain this status. Australia, France, Germany, Japan, and the United Kingdom have been widely recognized as middle powers for many decades. In some cases, they even used to be great powers pre–World War II. But South Korea's historical trajectory is very different. Thus, why South Korea is in constant search for recognition as a middle power. There is an anxiety among South Korean policymakers that third parties may not consider the country as developed, fully democratic, or indeed a middle power in terms of its diplomatic and other capabilities.[70]

Recognition as a middle power is an end in and by itself, since it confers status on South Korea. But there are also benefits to this recognition, including invitation to and membership of forums such as the G20 or the G7. Middle powerness also allows South Korea to be able to lead groups such as MIKTA or initiatives like Partnering for Green Growth and the Global Goals 2030 (P4G), to be invited to joint military exercises in the Indo-Pacific region, to contribute to antipiracy missions such as in the Gulf of Aden, or to be seen as an honest broker in organizations such as ASEAN+3. Therefore, this grand strategy end has a clear status dimension but can also contribute to South Korean security and prosperity.

South Korea's Grand Strategy: Key Means

What are the preferred means that South Korea uses when trying to implement its grand strategy successfully? In common with other great and middle powers and following from Martel's division of means by category, South Korea prioritizes three types of tools: military, diplomatic, and economic. In the case of Seoul, military means include both its own, ever-growing armed forces and military equipment plus also the ROK–U.S. alliance, which celebrated its seventieth anniversary in 2023. Diplomatic means refers to South Korea's sprawling diplomatic corps. As for economic means, South Korea prioritizes the use of trade, investment, and aid to third countries.

In addition and still following from Martel's categories, South Korea also makes use of other types of ends as part of its grand strategy: informational, soft power, and cyber. With regards to informational tools, South Korea makes use of public diplomacy. Seoul is a keen user of soft power. In the case of South Korea cyber means are more recent and are so far included as part of its military capabilities. These means supplement the main triad, which has been and remains the core of Seoul's grand strategy. These means have also served South Korea when facing constraints to pursue the ends described earlier.

Growing Military Capabilities

South Korea has sought to develop a strong autonomous military since the days of its foundation. The Korean War demonstrated the inadequacy of these capabilities, for the North Korean army was able to advance through South Korean territory relatively easily until U.S.-led UN forces intervened. In the decades after the armistice that halted Cold War hostilities, South Korea sought to use a significant share of its still-limited resources to improve its own military capabilities. Throughout the 1960s, for example, South Korea's military budget amounted to 4.1–6.9 percent of its GDP annually.[71] This was a significant amount for a developing country, especially considering the ROK–U.S. alliance. And in the 1970s, the Park Chung-hee regime sought to develop nuclear weapons as explained in the previous chapter.

Following its transition to democracy in 1988 and the launch of a grand strategy, South Korea has continued to emphasize boosting its military capabilities as a mean to fulfill its goals. As of 2021, South Korea's army is ranked as the sixth most powerful in the world, similar in strength to the militaries of fellow middle powers such as France, Japan, and the United Kingdom.[72] In terms of military spending, Seoul ranked tenth in the world with a budget of $45.7 billion in 2020.[73] As a percentage of its GDP, however, South Korea was above any other Asian power bar India. Seoul spent 2.8 percent of its GDP on its military.[74] Furthermore, South Korea had the eighth largest armed forces in the world as of 2022. With 555,000 active military personnel and a further 3,100,000 in reserve, South Korea's armed forces were similar in size to those of fellow East Asian countries including China or North Korea.[75]

In addition, South Korea has one of the most technologically advanced militaries worldwide. This includes its own air jet fighters, ballistic missile submarines, and short-range, medium-range, and submarine-launched missiles, along with plans to build a domestically produced aircraft carrier, an attack helicopter, and intermediate-range missiles. In 2021 Seoul and Washington also reached an agreement to remove any limits to the range and payload of South Korean missiles as mandated by their 1979 agreement.[76] This suggests that Seoul will continue to develop its missile program substantially. In fact, both liberal and conservative administrations have invested heavily in the modernization of the South Korean military. This includes cyberwarfare capabilities, which were fairly underdeveloped in South Korea until the Moon Jae-in government decided to prioritize them.[77]

Ultimately, South Korea sees the development of strong domestically produced military capabilities as a way to become more autonomous from the United States. This fits with Seoul's overarching grand strategy goal. As we will see throughout this book, growing military capabilities are a way for South Korea to pursue other goals such as its own security or greater international recognition as an influential middle power. In terms of grand strategy, it could be argued that South Korean policymakers consider an independent strong military the most important means to achieve their goals.

Alliance with the United States

The ROK–U.S. alliance is both a factor explaining South Korea's grand strategy and a means for Seoul to implement this same grand strategy. With regard to the former, the alliance informs South Korea's policy choices as explained earlier. As to the latter, the ROK–U.S. alliance augments South Korea's military capabilities insofar in case of conflict with North Korea the two allies would act as one. This is because the United States retains operational control of the South Korean armed forces in case of war. (Up until 1994, Washington also retained peacetime operational control of the

South Korean army.) In case of conflict, the South Korean armed forces would be under the command of the U.S. commander of the CFC. Evidently, this is a strong deterrent against a strike by North Korea—or any other country—on South Korea.

The alliance also facilities the acquisition of U.S. military technology by Seoul. South Korea spends more on arms transfer than almost any other country in the world. Between 1988 and 2020, South Korea spent $39.4 billion in military imports. This ranked the country fourth in the world by spending during the period.[78] U.S. firms accounted for $29.1 billion of the total, or 74 percent. For the United States, South Korea has become one of the most important arms clients, ranking third overall in the period 2017–2021.[79] Most of these arms transfers involve high-tech equipment, including jet fighters, helicopters, surveillance systems, and missiles.[80] Most of Washington's arms clients are close allies. It is therefore unlikely that South Korea would have been able to purchase so much world-leading military technology without their bilateral alliance.

Over time and especially as South Korean democracy has consolidated and the country has become more active in global affairs, Seoul's diplomatic muscle has also benefited from the ROK–U.S. alliance. The partnership between both countries has long gone beyond the deterrence of North Korea, and successive U.S. presidents have sought to strengthen the alliance in other areas of regional and global cooperation. Some of these relate to traditional security, but many others fall within the remit of global politics including trade, climate change, the functioning of international institutions, or participation in or membership of exclusive clubs such as the G7 or the G20.

It should be noted, however, that while the ROK–U.S. alliance amplifies Seoul's means, successive South Korean presidents have sought to build capabilities to strengthen their country's autonomous capabilities. This is clearest with reference to the transfer of operational control of the South Korean armed forces or the development of domestically produced military capabilities. But it can also be seen in other areas, such as South Korea's seeking to develop its independent economic and diplomatic capabilities. There is a debate in South Korea about the extent to which the ROK–U.S. alliance curtails the country's autonomy. But there is an agreement that, on balance, the alliance is beneficial for South Korea in the implementation of its grand strategy.

The Diplomatic Corps

As a self-identified middle power, South Korea prioritizes the use of diplomacy and negotiations in its grand strategy. Throughout most of the Cold War, Seoul's diplomacy was mainly focused on its battle with North Korea for recognition as the "true" representative of Korea. The situation started to change following the 1987–1988 democratization process, and especially after communist and postcommunist countries normalized diplomatic relations with Seoul, South Korea joined the United Nations in 1991, and afterward joined the OECD in 1996. South Korean diplomacy started to become more active and diversified, both as part of Seoul's bilateral relations and in relationship to its membership of the UN system and other international organizations.

As of 2019, South Korea ranked thirteenth worldwide and fourth in Asia in terms of its diplomatic network.[81] At the end 2021, the Ministry of Foreign Affairs (MOFA) had 167 diplomatic posts overseas and was staffed by 2,512 diplomats.[82] And even though Asia, Europe, and the United States were the main hosts of South Korean diplomatic missions, the country's diplomatic reach touched every corner of the world. This included previously fairly neglected regions such as Latin America or sub-Saharan Africa. This is a means that South Korean governments have consistently considered central to their country's grand strategy.

The use of diplomatic corps as a means of grand strategy also involves the placement of South Korean diplomatic corps in international institutions. This enhances the profile of South Korea as a diplomatic actor and underscores its commitment to diplomacy as a tool to advance its interests. Undoubtedly, Ban Ki-moon's tenure as UN secretary general in 2007–2016 is the best-known example of this.[83] Ban was only the second Asian secretary general and the only one from a developed Asian country. But South Korean diplomats are also active in wide range of international institutions and climate-related organizations.[84] In fact, South Korea actively seeks leadership positions in international institutions by putting forward candidates to key posts and lobbying for its diplomats and other professionals to be elected or selected to them.

For South Korea, its identity as a middle power matters. But the realities of being one also do. The country's diplomatic corps are a useful tool to reinforce this identity, but also serve to pursue its goals in a way that is realistic. Bilateral diplomatic partnerships or alliances with fellow middle powers within or outside international institutions have thus become a staple of South Korean grand strategy. This is particularly the case in issue areas that are farther away from the Korean Peninsula but nonetheless are of great interest for postdemocratization South Korea.

Trade, Investment, and Aid

As the South Korean economy has become bigger, so has Seoul's use of economic means to implement its foreign policy. Before the 1988 democratization and up until the 1990s, South Korea remained a developing economy. It actually received aid from the World Bank and other aid agencies in the amount of $12.7 billion.[85] In 1997, South Korea received the biggest bailout package from the IMF hitherto. But as South Korea joined the ranks of developed countries, it started to deploy trade, investment, and aid as strategic means to pursue its goals. Actually, South Korea's ODA program was already launched in 1987. That year, the Economic Development Cooperation Fund (EDCF), South Korea's aid agency, gave $23.5 million.[86] In the second half of the 1980s the Chun Doo-hwan government used the carrot of trade and investment to improve relations with communist countries, as explained in the previous chapter. In other words, South Korean policymakers believed in the potential to use economic tools to support South Korean foreign policy goals even before the country was developed and democratized.

It was from the late 1980s and early 1990s onward, however, that South Korean elites designed a grand strategy with trade, investment, and aid at the center. With regard to trade and investment, in the late 1990s South Korea joined the race initiated by the United States and other developed countries to sign bilateral and regional trade agreements that would facilitate exports, imports, and investment flows. In the over two decades during which South Korea has been pursuing bilateral and regional trade deals, successive presidents have had a clear strategy. Most notably, the Roh Moo-hyun government launched an FTA Roadmap in August 2003. This roadmap established that South Korea ought to sign FTAs following economic reasons, political and diplomatic considerations, the willingness of third parties to sign a deal with Seoul, and the potential of third parties to serve as stepping stones for larger deals. Furthermore, the roadmap established that South Korea should pursue FTAs with big trading countries.[87] This roadmap built on previous policy and has survived subsequent changes in government.

South Korean FTAs come with the promise of investment by South Korean *chaebol* and other firms. This is an incentive for third parties to sign agreements with Seoul. In this respect, firms such as SK, Samsung, LG, or Hyundai implicitly and informally support South Korea's grand strategy because the factories or research centers they might open appeal to countries seeking better trade relations with South Korea. And indeed, big conglomerates are an important force in shaping South Korea's FTA strategy.[88]

South Korea opened the EDCF in 1987, months before its democratization. The fund was set to provide loans to developing countries.[89] MOFA then launched the Korea International Cooperation Agency (KOICA) in 1991.[90] This was the country's first centralized agency directly embedding aid in South Korean foreign policy and grand strategy, with a focus on grants. From 1991 onward, South Korean aid started to steadily increase.[91] Plus, South Korea became the first former aid recipient to become part of the OECD's DAC in 2010. From the mid-2010s onward, South Korea has been disbursing around $2 billion annually in aid. Even though South Korea lags behind other donors, it is one of the three biggest in Asia along with China and Japan. And the country has made strategic use of its ODA. To begin with, around 50 percent of South Korean aid goes to infrastructure.[92] While this lags behind China and Japan, whose aid is mainly linked to infrastructure rather than social development,[93] it nonetheless gives Seoul leverage. The geographical distribution of South Korean aid also suggests that Seoul prioritizes countries and regions it wants to strengthen links with.

Public Diplomacy

Modern public diplomacy traces back its origins to the Cold War, when the United States and the Soviet Union competed to win the "hearts and minds" of people worldwide. The United States used media, universities, foundations, firms, and even private individuals to spread the idea that its system was superior.[94] Arguably, public diplomacy was also part of South Korea's policy toolkit during this period as it sought to dominate the narrative in its competition with North Korea. Thus, the Park Chung-hee government launched the Academy of Korean Studies in 1978 to educate about Korean culture.[95] In 1980, Seoul founded Yonhap News Agency, which was tasked with providing a South Korean perspective on domestic and international news.[96]

It was only after democratization and from the 1990s onward that South Korea started to put public diplomacy at the center of its means to pursue its grand strategy. In 1991, the Korea Foundation was founded to promote knowledge about South Korean culture, domestic affairs, and international relations.[97] In 1997, Arirang TV began airing. The TV channel covers news stories from a South Korean perspective, including covering stories that otherwise might not gain international attention.[98] In other words, South Korean elites started to develop a sophisticated understanding of public diplomacy, moving it away from Cold War era–style propaganda and into the realm of direct communication and knowledge dissemination with international audiences. Thus its categorization as informational power.

Public diplomacy explicitly became a central component of South Korean grand strategy in 2010. That year, the Lee Myung-bak government made public diplomacy one of the three pillars of South Korea as a foreign policy actor, alongside diplomacy and economic diplomacy. MOFA was put in charge of coordination of public diplomacy work. And in 2017, South Korea passed the Public Diplomacy Act. MOFA is explicit that public diplomacy aims at deepening understanding of South Korea, its history, and its policies, as well as gaining support for the latter.[99]

For middle powers whose military and economic capabilities cannot compete with those of the great powers, public diplomacy serves to level the playing field. And in the case of countries like South Korea, public diplomacy also serves to promote its own vision of domestic and international affairs. Considering that the global media and educational landscape continues to be dominated by the United States, Western Europe, and a small number of English-speaking countries,[100] public diplomacy serves South Korea and other middle powers from nondominant regions as a means to pursue their grand strategies.

Soft Power

Soft power can be understood as "the ability to obtain preferred outcomes by attraction rather than coercion or payment."[101] It was initially linked to the post–Cold War United States, when its relative power was bound to diminish but talk about its decline was qualified thanks to its unrivaled soft power. The United States, however, is certainly not the only country consciously or unconsciously employing soft power. In the case of South Korea, governments in office have been promoting the use of soft power as part of Seoul's grand strategy dating back to the mid-1990s.

Above all, South Korea has promoted *Hallyu* (Korean wave) as a way to boost its prestige and change minds internationally. The movies, pop music, and dramas often included in *Hallyu* emerged and continue to be the creation of individual South Koreans. But the state has made use of *Hallyu* as a means to pursue its goals. Initially, the Kim Young-sam government saw *Hallyu* as a means to boost the South Korean economy. Likewise, the Kim Dae-jung government taking office right in the middle of the AFC was keen in using *Hallyu* for postcrisis economic recovery.[102] In 1999, it adopted the Framework Act on the Promotion of Cultural Industries pledging state support for South Korean contemporary culture.[103] But already in the late 1990s and early 2000s, *Hallyu* was seen as a soft power tool that the government could use to pursue its broader grand strategy. Therefore, government agencies supported and sometimes organized film screenings, K-pop concerts, exhibitions, and other activities to promote (South) Korean culture and boost the image of the country. In 2020, the Ministry of Culture, Sports and Tourism launched the Hallyu Support and Cooperation Division.[104] This further solidified the role of *Hallyu* in South Korean foreign policy.

In 2007, the King Sejong Institute Foundation was established to promote *Hangeul* (Korean language). By the middle of 2021, there were 234 King Sejong institutes across the world teaching the Korean language.[105] And from the mid-2000s, the South Korean government started to dramatically increase the number of Korean Cultural centers across the world. In 1977, the Korea Overseas Culture Information Service (KOCIS) was established. Shortly after, the agency launched the first Korean cultural centers. The first four were set up in New York and Tokyo in 1979 and in Los Angeles and Paris in 1980. With centers later established in other regions such as Africa, Latin America, South Asia, and Southeast Asia, there were forty-two of them by 2022.[106] The centers were closely linked to South Korean grand strategy, strengthening links with MOFA throughout the 2010s and moving beyond their more limited initial remit of promoting Korean culture.

For South Korea, soft power has become an important grand strategy means thanks to the global popularity of the country's modern culture. As of 2021, the country was ranked twelfth in the world in terms of soft power. In Asia, only Japan can compete with South Korea in terms of the popularity of its modern culture. Therefore, soft power is an asset that South Korean governments have had at their disposal to try to move ahead with their goals, including in regions that traditionally had limited interest in South Korea.

The Four Concentric Circles of South Korea's Grand Strategy

For middle powers, grand strategy always has a regional component and can also be global in scope when possible. In the case of South Korea, its grand strategy indeed includes a strong and clear global component on top of its regional elements. While the regional aspect of South Korean international relations dates back to the years of dictatorial rule during the Cold War, the more global elements are more recent. They started to emerge once South Korea democratized in 1988, the Cold War finished, the country joined the United Nations, and Seoul developed a clearly defined grand strategy focusing on both its immediate neighborhood and the rest of the world. Nonetheless, the regional element arguably continues to be the most relevant in South Korean grand strategy as is common for most states.

Based on my interviews and South Korea's official policy documents, there seems to be an implicit agreement among South Korean policymakers that the grand strategy of the country can be divided into four concentric circles. The inner circle is a triangular core including North Korea, the United States, and China. There is a second circle around it: East Asia, including both Northeast and Southeast Asia. A third circle comes next, involving Greater Eurasia and the Indian Ocean which includes Russia, Central Asia, South Asia, the Greater Middle East, Europe, Australia, and the ocean itself. Finally, there is an outer circle with the rest of the world and global governance in it. There are similarities but also differences in the grand strategy of South Korea toward each of these circles, cutting across the factors, goals, and ends of the country's grand strategy.

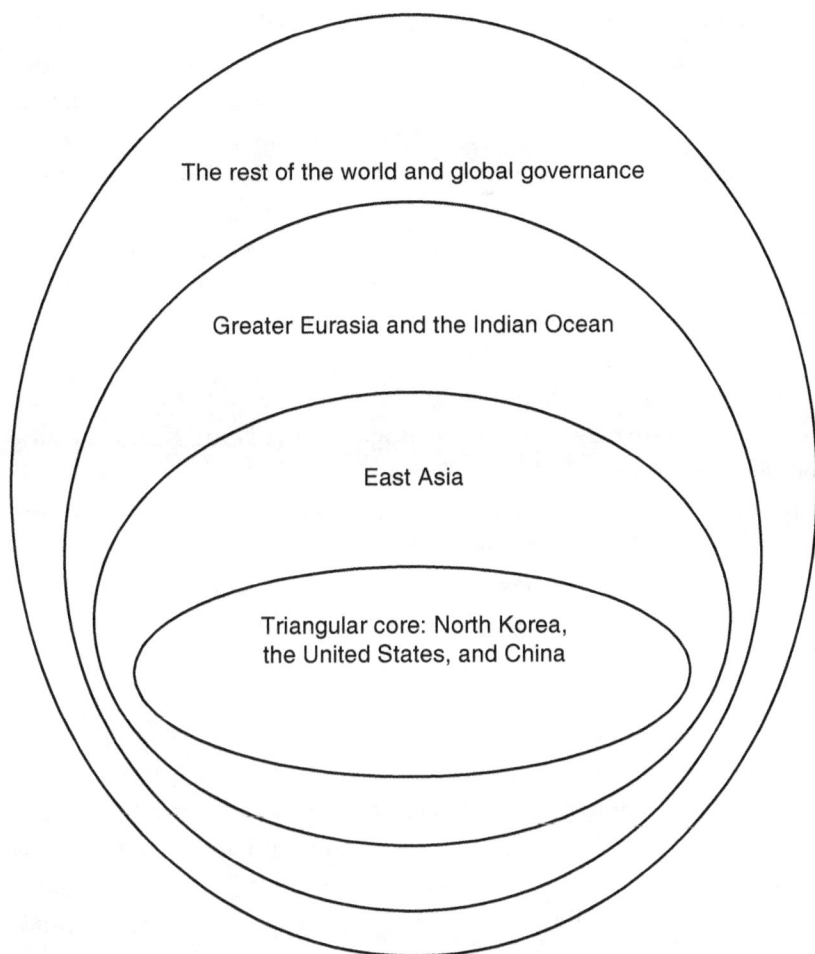

Figure 3.1 The four concentric circles of South Korea's grand strategy.

Triangular Core: North Korea, the United States, and China

Relations between South Korea and North Korea, the United States, and China, respectively, are very different. But in terms of South Korean grand strategy, the three of them are intimately linked to each other. This has been the case since shortly after the division of Korea and subsequent foundation of South Korea, for the United States and China were the main reasons why the Korean War ended in a stalemate and the two Koreas remained divided. And throughout the rest of the Cold War, it was South

Korea's alliance with the United States and North Korea's alliance of its own with China that helped prevent a second inter-Korean war and maintained the status quo. Since the end of the Cold War and the collapse of most communist regimes, China has been a key reason behind North Korea avoiding the same fate. Meanwhile, the ROK–U.S. alliance has consolidated and expanded. In the minds of South Korean policymakers, North Korea, the United States, and China are the triangle at the core of their country's grand strategy.[107] Crucially, this is the region in which South Korea has to strive the hardest to achieve strategic autonomy—including where it faces the biggest constraints.

A key reason why the three countries are the cornerstone of South Korean grand strategy is, undoubtedly, geography. North Korea of course occupies the northern half of the Korean Peninsula. China is South Korea's largest neighbor, and the country sharing the largest border with the Korean Peninsula. And the United States is de facto present in South Korea thanks to its troops stationed in the country, where Washington has maintained a military presence almost uninterruptedly since Korea was divided following the end of Japanese colonization in 1945. Geography certainly is a central component of any country's grand strategy, and South Korea is no different in this respect.

This inner circle of South Korea's grand strategy is closely related to two key goals: protection from external military threats and inter-Korean reconciliation and reunification. For South Korea, the biggest military threat it strategizes against is a possible North Korean strike.[108] Increasingly, however, South Korea also strategizes against a possible conflict against China. Indeed, China's rise is seen in Seoul as both an opportunity and a potential threat—and in the area of security, mainly as the latter.[109] Therefore, for South Korea its biggest security threats are regional in nature. Differently from other parts of the world such as North America or Western Europe where states in the region do not feel threatened by their neighbors as much as by outside actors, in the case of South Korea it is the closest neighbors that make policymakers fear for the security of their country.

The matter of reconciliation and reunification between the two Koreas is fairly simple from a South Korean perspective. North Korea is the main actor because, after all, reconciliation and reunification involves the two Koreas. But the United States and China are also crucial.[110] There are two reasons for this. De jure, they signed the armistice agreement that ended the Korean War so they would be part of any discussions to put an end to the conflict. De facto, the United States and China are the two greatest powers in the international system today and the closest allies, respectively, of South Korea and North Korea. Therefore, North Korea, the United States, and China are intertwined when it comes to inter-Korean relations along with South Korea itself.

But the triangular core is also related to South Korea's two other main grand strategy goals. China and the United States are South Korea's two largest trading partners. The United States was its largest trading partner until 2004, when it was replaced by China at the top.[111] As of 2021, China accounted for 23.9 percent of South Korean trade and the United States for 13.5 percent.[112] They are also important investment partners. Thus, Seoul's deeper integration in global economic flows starts with both of them. And when it comes to recognition as an influential middle power, several South Korean administrations have understood middle powerness as taking a middle or balanced position between the United States and China, even if this does not mean equidistance because the former is a treaty ally with the same values so Seoul will gravitate toward it. There is a line of thought in Seoul that understands South Korea's identity as a middle power in terms of its position vis-à-vis the two superpowers.

East Asia

East Asia has become an increasingly important region for the grand strategy of South Korea after democratization, especially post-AFC. Certainly, Japan was important for South Korea even during the Cold War. Colonial era–related animosity, normalization of diplomatic relations, or the potential for strong economic ties informed a complex relationship. But it was from the 1990s onward that Japan became more central to South Korean grand strategy. Southeast Asia joined toward the end of the decade. Despite some interest in the region during the years of dictatorship due to the possibility of alignment with anticommunist states, Seoul did not become strategic in its relations with Southeast Asia until the Cold War ended.

Once again, geography informs the importance of East Asia in South Korean grand strategy. If the triangular core were South Korea's immediate back alley, East Asia would be the immediate neighborhood. Japan is of course South Korea's closest neighbor in the region, separated by a few miles across the East Sea and the Korea Strait. Southeast Asia, meanwhile, is certainly further away but it is still closer to the Korean Peninsula than most other regions. And inasmuch as South Korea has a maritime grand strategy, Southeast Asia including its waters is a key region in it. This would include ASEAN primarily, since it encompasses most Southeast Asian countries. This further underscores the importance of geography in Seoul's prioritization of East Asia.

East Asia matters for South Korea's goal of deeper integration in the world economy too. East Asia is the second most integrated region in the world in terms of trade links, only trailing the EU.[113] This integration involves both market-led regionalization and state-led regionalism or institution-building. And South Korea has been a strong supporter of both processes, whether through its firms being part of regional manufacturing chains, the government signing FTAs including RCEP, or the country joining regional economic governance initiatives—most notably, ASEAN+3. What is more, South Korean policymakers see economic links with Japan and Southeast Asia as an opportunity to reduce economic dependence on China and the United States.[114]

For South Korea, East Asia also matters due to its objective of being recognized as an influential middle power. This includes participation in regional institutions, in which South Korea seeks to play a balancer role especially between the competing interests of China and Japan. In this respect, Seoul benefits from the perception that it is not interested in becoming a regional hegemon as China and Japan may be.[115] For South Korean policymakers, if there is one region in which South Korea may be able to exercise leverage thanks to its economic influence, geographical proximity, participation in regional fora, and diplomatic presence, it is East Asia.

South Korea's two other goals have an East Asian component as well. When it comes to protection from external military threats, potential military clashes in the East China Sea and South China Sea as well as other armed clashes such as piracy or terrorism are considerations for South Korea.[116] They may not be latent threats such as North Korea and China, but they do pose a threat to South Korea. Meanwhile, when it comes to inter-Korean reconciliation and reunification none of the countries in East Asia is a central player. But Japan has become more involved in dealing with North Korea from the late 1990s, after Pyongyang conducted a missile test across it. Most notably, Tokyo was involved in the Six-Party Talks throughout the 2000s.[117] As for Southeast Asia, it is tangentially linked to inter-Korean relations from a South Korean grand strategy perspective mainly because Seoul believes that the postcommunist countries in the region could serve as an example for Pyongyang to reform and open up.[118]

Greater Eurasia and the Indian Ocean

From a South Korean perspective, Greater Eurasia and the Indian Ocean include Russia, Central Asia, Australia, South Asia, the Greater Middle East, Europe, Australia, and the ocean itself. This is the landmass to which the Korean Peninsula belongs, as well as the closest ocean to its eastern half where South Korea is based. In the case of the Indian Ocean, even though it is not part of the Eurasian landmass it is inextricably linked to it for economic and security reasons. In other words, the western half of the Indo-Pacific region is a core part of Greater Eurasia from a South Korean perspective. Greater Eurasia and the Indian Ocean is a region to which South Korea did not pay much attention before democratization. The only exceptions were incipient economic relations with Australia, (Western) Europe, the Greater Middle East, and the Soviet Union, as well as through the Indian Ocean. But there was no overarching foreign policy toward the region before 1988.

The situation started to change after 1988. To begin with, the end of communism in the Soviet Union and Central and Eastern Europe facilitated the establishment and strengthening of diplomatic relations with South Korea. Furthermore, the expansion of South Korea's diplomatic and military scope created new links with the Greater Middle East and throughout the Indian Ocean.[119] As a result, Greater Eurasia started to become a region of more importance to South Korean policymakers. Eventually, Central Asia and South Asia also become more relevant to South Korea grand strategy throughout the 1990s and 2000s—especially India in the case of the latter.

Certainly, the diversity of Greater Eurasia and the Indian Ocean means that not the whole region is important to Seoul for the same reasons. Arguably, however, deeper integration in the world economy is a South Korean goal that indeed spans its strategy throughout the whole region. Some parts of the region such as Russia, Central Asia, and the Greater Middle East matter to South Korean policymakers because South Korea imports 99 percent of the oil and gas that it consumes and the three of them are rich in the energy resources that the country needs to fuel its economy.[120] India, meanwhile, is increasingly becoming part of East Asian-centric manufacturing chains, a potentially vast market, a destination for South Korean aid, and home to ports that facilitate trade between South Korea and Europe. Europe is one of the biggest economies in the world, the largest investor in South Korea, a manufacturing base for South Korean *chaebol*, and a crucial trade partner. This applies, especially, to the European Union. Australia is a major provider of the natural resources that the South Korean economy needs. The Indian Ocean, meanwhile, is the main route for South Korean trade with Europe and the Greater Middle East.[121]

Russia, the Indian Ocean, and Australia are also important to South Korean grand strategy goals due to their connection to protection from external military threats. Similarly to Japan, Russia is not a crucial player in inter-Korean affairs. However, Moscow is one of North Korea's closest partners, a permanent member of the UN Security Council, and has become increasingly involved in trying to address the North Korean nuclear conundrum from the 2000s onward.[122] Most noticeably, it was part of the Six-Party Talks during that decade. Plus, potential inter-Korean economic cooperation would link the Korean Peninsula with Central Asia and Europe through Russia.[123] As for the Indian Ocean, piracy and territorial claims threaten the stability of its waters. This could pose a threat to South Korean economic security. Australia has become an increasingly more active security actor in the Indo-Pacific region.[124] Inevitably, this has boosted military and diplomatic ties with South Korea.

South Korea's objective of being recognized as an influential middle power also applies to parts of Greater Eurasia and the Indian Ocean. In Central Asia there is a sizable population of Korean origin that can trace its roots back to immigrants who moved to Russia in the nineteenth century and early twentieth century. In particular, Uzbekistan and Kazakhstan are each home to more than 100,000 ethnic Koreans.[125] For Seoul, these links provide a window of opportunity to have some influence in the region. Meanwhile, in the case of Europe South Korea sees opportunities to cooperate with like-minded partners such as the European Union or fellow middle powers France, Germany, Italy, Poland, Spain, and the United Kingdom. Seoul shares similar views about economic governance, trade openness, the importance of diplomacy, or values with them.[126] Thus, Europe can serve as a multiplier of South Korean middle power. The same applies to Australia, with which South Korea also shares values and a middle power identity.

The Rest of the World and Global Governance

South Korea's grand strategy includes one final circle that spans the rest of the world and global governance. When it comes to regions outside of the three first concentric circles, Seoul paid limited attention to them before democratization. South Korean dictatorial regimes did establish diplomatic relations with most Latin American countries or the newly independent states of sub-Saharan Africa. But political contacts were minimal, economic links were modest, and in terms of security there was no real common threat despite rhetorical agreement with pro–United States countries about the dangers of communism. As for global governance, South Korea played a negligible role throughout the Cold War. Since Seoul was not part of the United Nations, its presence in the other international institutions that were part of the UN system was either symbolic or nonexistent.

The situation changed from the 1990s. Middle powers aspire to have a grand strategy of global scale. And South Korean policymakers dating back to Kim Young-sam and his policy of *segyehwa* have had global ambitions. Thus, membership in the United Nations, WTO, OECD, and other international institutions that South Korea accomplished throughout the 1990s gave the country a platform to expand the geographical reach of its grand strategy. Meanwhile, the South Korean economy provided its policymakers and elites with a means to strengthen links with other parts of the world hitherto neglected. As a poignant example, Seoul signed its first-ever FTA with Chile in 2003.[127] Economic links with the Americas have also made South Korean policymakers to pay greater consideration to the Pacific, which of course is also the western part of the Indo-Pacific region.

The rest of the world and global governance matter for South Korea's goal of deeper economic integration. When it comes to regions such as Latin America or sub-Saharan Africa, South Korean businesspeople consider them potential markets and manufacturing bases. This is especially the case for Latin America.[128] In the sphere of global governance, international institutions including the WTO, BIS, BCBS, and G20 provide Seoul with the opportunity to try to influence the rules of international trade, investment, or taxation. Over time, Seoul has become more active in these institutions and sought to forge alliances with countries that have similar views about the balance between economic openness and a state's economic sovereignty.[129]

South Korea also sees the rest of the world and global governance as a platform to be recognized as an important middle power, especially the latter. Indeed, South Korea is an active player in the UN system. Similarly to other middle powers, Seoul seeks to be recognized in certain areas rather than trying to become a central player in every single one of them.[130] A case in point is climate change and green growth, an issue on which South Korea has sought to forge its own voice and narrative dating back to the Lee Myung-bak years. When it comes to the rest of the world, Seoul has followed a strategy to enhance its voice by strengthening links and cooperation with countries such as Canada and Mexico or institutions such as the Pacific Alliance.[131] To sum up, South Korea acknowledges that recognition as a middle power requires deeper engagement with regions and institutions even when its core interests are not at stake.

South Korea's Grand Strategy

Dating back to its most recent democratization in 1988, South Korea has developed a stable and long-lasting grand strategy. As befits a middle power, this grand strategy is global in geographic scale and long-term in temporal scope. Before 1988, South Korea lacked a grand strategy. But from the late 1980s onwards, the country's foreign policy, political, and business elites have reached a common understanding about the ends that South Korea should prioritize above everything else, as well as the means that the country has at its disposal to achieve them. This common understanding allows goals and ends to stand and survive across administrations, regardless of the political leaning of the president in power.

A key reason why there is elite agreement about the ends and means that South Korea should pursue is the set of factors that that explain the country's grand strategy. They include factors already dating back to the early years of the existence of the country itself, including the division of Korea and the ROK–U.S. alliance. They also include other factors that can be traced back to the years when South Korea was an authoritarian weak power, such as the rise of China and the country's own economic development. Other factors are unique to South Korea's post-1988 years, including democracy, a middle power identity, regional integration and globalization, and the AFC. The combination of these factors imposes a set of structural constrains that do not neglect South Korean agency per se, but that set some limits to the country's realistic ends and available means.

South Korea is similar to other middle powers in that its overarching goal is autonomy. South Korea strives to gain strategic autonomy and has to overcome the constraints imposed by great powers to attain it. Leaving aside this end, four others stand out as the ultimate objectives of South Korean grand strategy: protection from external military threats, inter-Korean reconciliation and reunification, deeper integration in the world economy, and recognition as an influential middle power. Certainly, some administrations may put more emphasis on one or another, as we will see in subsequent chapters. Yet, all South Korean presidents have pursued these four ends and implemented policies to achieve them. This is the result of the just-mentioned elite consensus. Beyond the expected partisanship of South Korea's vibrant democracy, there is an underlying agreement that these are the key ends that the South Korean state should pursue.

Regarding the means at South Korea's disposal to achieve its preferred ultimate ends, seven stand out: the country's growing military capabilities, cybertools integrated in these military capabilities, the ROK–U.S. alliance, diplomatic corps, trade, investment, and aid, public diplomacy, and soft power. Certainly, these means are common to many middle and great powers. And some of them were available to South Korea in the years before its democratization of 1988, when it was a weak power and a developing country under authoritarian rule. It is since democratization, however, that South Korea has developed and used well-defined tools to achieve its goals. Different administrations may have showed an inclination toward certain means over others. But ultimately, elite consensus has resulted in successive administrations using a combination of all of them, as we will see over the next chapters. Consensus in terms of both ends and means owes to the structural factors affecting South Korean grand strategy as well as to the agency that the country has as a middle power.

CHAPTER IV

Triangular Core

Inter-Korean Relations, the U.S. Alliance, and China's Rise

Geography is destiny, as the saying goes. For South Korea, geography means that North Korea since the division of Korea into two halves, the United States since its troops were stationed in the country, and China since the founding of the People's Republic have been the country's "destiny." This was the case before the 1988 democratic transition, and it has not changed since then. The three of them form an inextricable triangular core for South Korea's grand strategy planning and implementation, for the actions of any of them have consequences on the other two. In fact, if anything the importance of this triangular core has only grown over time as North Korea has become more powerful and China's rise has resulted in strategic competition with the United States.

Inter-Korean reconciliation and unification is an inescapable end for any South Korean president. No matter their personal background or political ideology, every single South Korean president has sought to achieve reconciliation as a way to lay the groundwork for eventual reunification. Reunification is a constitutional imperative insofar as the South Korean constitution lays claim to the whole of the Korean Peninsula and mandates that South Korea should seek reunification under its own terms. To this end, successive South Korean administrations have sought engagement with North Korea. At the same time, North Korea remains a key security concern for Seoul, with several military clashes over the years reminding South Korean administrations that North Korea continues to threaten the lives of South Korean citizens. Therefore, South Korea has sought to strengthen its military capabilities and to bolster the alliance with the United States to address this threat. This military buildup also supports the goal of reconciliation and reunification by making clear to Pyongyang that the use of force against South Korea is not an option and that diplomacy is preferable to manage inter-Korean differences.

In the case of the United States, successive South Korean presidents have seen the bilateral alliance between Seoul and Washington as an indispensable component of their security calculus. The alliance acts as a deterrent against a possible North Korean strike. Over the years, however, the ROK–U.S. alliance has grown in terms of its scope. The United States supports South Korea's security against other potential military threats, most notably China. But it also acts as an enabler of other grand strategic ends, including deeper integration in the world economy and recognition as a middle power. Thus, South Korean administrations generally see the United States as an enabler of their country's autonomy. The United States also influences inter-Korean relations insofar its relationship with North Korea is a big determinant of Pyongyang's actions and, consequently, policy toward Seoul. When it comes to dealing with the United States, South Korea has used a wide range of means to ensure that bilateral relations continue to be strong and that Washington remains committed. For there is a lingering "fear of abandonment" on the South Korean side, exacerbated by the way in which sometimes U.S. presidents have dealt with—and sometimes even dispatched—allies. Yet sometimes there is a "fear of entrapment" that Seoul will have to support U.S. policy against its wishes.

South Korea's biggest neighbor has become more central to its grand strategy in recent decades. China was always a presence that South Korea had to acknowledge and contend with, but its economic rise, growing politico-diplomatic clout, and military buildup have made it ever more central to South Korean grand strategy. Thus, China plays a paradoxical role in Seoul's grand strategy. On the one hand, Seoul sees Beijing as a growing security threat due to its alleged assertiveness. On the other hand, economic relations with China are key to South Korean prosperity. And meanwhile, China influences inter-Korean relations as North Korea's closest partner, or at least the closest relationship that Pyongyang has to a partnership. To deal with China, South Korea employs a variety of means. They include deterrents such as stronger military capabilities or the ROK–U.S. alliance, as well as carrots such as diplomacy, trade agreements, or soft power.

TABLE 4.1
South Korea's grand strategy toward the triangular core

Key factors	Key ends	Key means
Division of Korea, ROK–U.S. alliance, rise of China, economic development, democracy, middle power identity, regional integration and globalization	Autonomy, protection from external military threats, inter-Korean reconciliation and reunification, deeper integration in the world economy, recognition as an influential middle power	Growing military capabilities; cybertools; U.S. alliance; diplomatic corps; trade, investment, and aid; public diplomacy; soft power

A combination of carrots and sticks manages inter-Korean relations, while the endurance of the alliance with the United States and the economic and military rise of China underpin the operationalization of South Korea's grand strategy toward the triangle, even as South Korea seeks to ensure its autonomy of action.

Roh Tae-woo (1988–1993)

North Korea

Roh Tae-woo launched the *Nordpolitik* strategy to approach relations with North Korea in July 1988.[1] Roh came to office having served as a minister under Chun Doo-hwan. As a result, his approach toward North Korea was informed by Chun's. However, *Nordpolitik* was a bold strategy that reset relations between the two Koreas—particularly following the end of the Cold War and the collapse of the communist bloc. Indeed, *Nordpolitik* has influenced South Korea's grand strategy toward North Korea since it was formulated. This was one of Roh's main legacies in the foreign policy and grand strategy of the country.

The importance and success of *Nordpolitik* related to the way in which it clearly placed inter-Korean relations in the broader context of relations with the United States, China, and other countries. This was a recognition that the United States and China, as the two greatest powers in East Asia, constrained South Korea's grand strategy. Roh decided that South Korea could achieve its aims of autonomy and reconciliation and reunification with North Korea only by involving both the United States and China in his inter-Korean policy. Inspired by Western Germany's *Ostpolitik*, Roh based his North Korea strategy on cross-recognition between the two Koreas, rapprochement, and a holistic approach to improve relations between South Korea and its partners on the one hand and North Korea and its own partners on the other.[2] *Nordpolitik* also came as communist countries were starting to reach out to Seoul in a bid to launch trade and investment relations, and only a few weeks before the Seoul Olympic Games were due to open. In other words, South Korea was in a position of strength vis-à-vis North Korea. Roh formulated six principles in the speech that gave birth to *Nordpolitik*, including the promotion of trade with North Korea; visitor exchanges at all levels and humanitarian contacts; dropping Seoul's opposition to its allies' establishing nonmilitary trade with North Korea; and support for Pyongyang in its efforts to normalize diplomatic relations with the United States and Japan.[3]

North Korea proved receptive to Roh's overtures, and the two Koreas launched several rounds of dialogues covering politics, security, economics, sports, culture, and Red Cross exchanges.[4] For the Roh government, these would serve as initial steps toward eventual reunification, which remained the ultimate goal. As per Roh's Korean National Community Unification Formula, cross-recognition between the two Koreas would set the stage for a Korean commonwealth, after which there would be a general election based on the constitution of a unified Korea.[5] A concrete outcome of Roh's policy and these subsequent exchanges was the admission of the two Koreas to the United Nations in September 1991.[6]

Furthermore, the two Koreas signed the Agreement on Reconciliation, Non-aggression and Exchanges and Cooperation Between the South and the North in December 1991. The agreement established the principles of cross-recognition, peace, dialogue, and exchanges as the basis for inter-Korean relations.[7] In short, the ideas espoused by Roh with his *Nordpolitik* were now enshrined in a document signed by the two Koreas. This document has been a crucial component of Seoul's North Korea policy ever since. It included the key end of reconciliation and reunification, as well as the prioritization of tools including diplomacy and economic power.

Concurrently, however, the Roh government continued to see North Korea as a potential threat. This is a dichotomy that has influenced South Korea's grand strategy ever since: how to achieve reconciliation and reunification while protecting the country from a potential North Korean strike. In fact, the potential threat coming out of North Korea became even clearer during the first North Korean nuclear crisis of 1993–1994. In September 1991, U.S. President George H. W. Bush announced that his country would withdraw all tactical nuclear weapons from overseas. In the case of South Korea, the last of them were removed in December.[8] This reduced South Korea's relative power vis-à-vis the North and could constrain its autonomy and push for reconciliation and reunification, since Pyongyang would be aware of this shift in relative power. Barely one month later, in January 1992, the two Koreas signed the Joint Declaration on the Denuclearization of the Korean Peninsula. In the declaration, the two Koreas committed not to develop nuclear weapons.[9] And indeed, North Korea signed and ratified its safeguards agreement with the International Atomic Energy Agency (IAEA) shortly after.[10] However, IAEA inspectors found inconsistencies in North Korea's initial report on its nuclear program.[11]

This precipitated the first North Korean nuclear crisis of 1993–1994. Coupled with the withdrawal of U.S. tactical nuclear weapons, the crisis reinforced the sense among South Korean policymakers that they needed to bolster their independent capabilities. Seoul thus continued development of the Haeseong and Hyunmoo missile short-range missile programs as a deterrent against North Korea.[12] In the meantime, the Korea Aerospace Institute (KARI) began development of a rocket program in 1990. KARI successfully launched two KSR-1 in June and September 1993.[13] Concurrently, Seoul signed an agreement with Moscow in November 1992 to acquire military technology and gain access to Russian expertise.[14] As South Korea's first-ever publicly available Defense White Paper had made clear, the military situation in the Korean Peninsula continued to be unstable, and the country continued to be under threat from North Korea.[15]

The United States

In terms of relations between South Korea and the United States, the Roh government pursued a strategy labeled "Korea-U.S. Partnership" (한미동반관계).[16] The key emphasis was on the "partnership" component, in other words, South Korea being an equal to the United States rather than its subordinate. On the one hand the Roh government was seeking greater autonomy for South Korea to develop and implement its own grand strategy. But the ongoing threat from North Korea—particularly during the first nuclear crisis—led the South Korean government to seek to reinforce the alliance with the United States as well. To an extent, this policy was also out of fear of abandonment caused by Washington's changing military posture following the collapse of the Soviet Union and most of the communist bloc more broadly. In other words, Roh reacted to the twin fears of potential dependence on and abandonment by South Korea's great power ally by seeking to reinforce the alliance while stressing that—from Seoul's perspective—it was a partnership. This became a constant as successive governments continued to pursue strategic autonomy, as well as other ends, over the years.

The Bush administration's decision to completely remove Washington's nuclear weapons from South Korean territory, in particular, was perceived as a sign of weaker U.S. commitment and greater need to develop autonomous capabilities. Between October–December 1991, the United States first removed sixty artillery shells, followed by forty B61 bombs. By mid-December, Roh announced that no nuclear weapons remained in South Korea. The decision to remove the nuclear weapons from South Korean territory was partly informed by a push to make North Korea consent to IAEA inspections of its nuclear facilities, which Pyongyang actually agreed to a few months later.[17] South Korea was also seeking to reduce tensions with North Korea and forge a different relationship. But on the other hand, the removal of U.S. tactical nuclear weapons weakened the deterrent against a possible North Korean strike. This reinforced the idea that Seoul had to reinforce its own autonomy, without questioning the alliance *per se*.

It was in this context that the Roh government announced the 818 Plan in August 1988. The plan called for South Korea to restructure the military to strengthened the air force and navy independently from the United States, to procure new weapons to boost the independent capabilities of the South Korean armed forces, and to develop a stronger domestic arms industry.[18] Roh wanted South Korean firms including Daewoo, Hyundai, LG, and Samsung to become more involved in the development of domestically produced capabilities such as helicopters, naval vessels, and tanks.[19] For South Korea, this was a key mean to achieve its goals. Yet the 818 Plan did not imply security decoupling from the United States. In fact, South

Korea's development of its own capabilities involved partnerships and joint ventures with the United States, most notably with McDonnell Douglas.[20] South Korean military technology remained dependent on sales from and partnerships with the United States.

In its quest for greater autonomy, the Roh government thought about pressing for transfer of peacetime operational control (OPCON) of the South Korean armed forces, which remained in the hands of the United States. In November 1991, Seoul and Washington agreed that peacetime OPCON transfer would take place at some point between 1993 and 1995.[21] This was crucial for South Korea to achieve its end of autonomy, for it meant that South Korean armed forces were under the actual control of a South Korean general rather than the ROK/U.S. CFC.

The Ministry of National Defense (MND) made South Korea's Defense White Paper available for the first time in late 1988. The paper made clear the importance that Seoul afforded to its alliance with Washington. Above all, the white paper had a whole section on CFC collaboration as part of the chapter on South Korea's defense posture.[22] This showed the centrality that the Roh government afforded to close cooperation with the United States. And indeed, South Korea would go on to deploy its military during the Gulf War of 1990–1991, in support of the U.S.-led coalition to free Kuwait after its invasion by Iraq. South Korean troops provided transport and medical support.[23] Plus, the ROK Navy participated in the Rim of the Pacific Exercise (RIMPAC) in 1990 for the first time. Launched in 1971 and led by the United States, this was a joint maritime drill for the U.S. Navy to improve interoperability with allies. South Korea would go on to participate in RIMPAC ever since.[24] Similarly to the situation during the Park Chung-hee years, the Roh government was supporting U.S. policy and activities elsewhere, among other things, as a way to reinforce the alliance.

At the same time, South Korea's transition to democracy and middle power identity, the changing international environment with the end of the Cold War, and the evolving ROK–U.S. alliance itself made the Roh government rethink its grand strategy in terms of other means that could be used to both strengthen relations with Washington and influence it. The Roh government thus started to take a strategic approach to the use of trade and investment. Accordingly, South Korea was actively involved in the Uruguay Round of trade negotiations whereby the GATT was to be replaced by the WTO.[25] Certainly Seoul was taking part in these negotiations out of self-interest. But it was also a way to support another U.S.-led initiative by adding to its legitimacy and push to expand the liberal international order. That is, South Korea believed that strategic autonomy could be achieved by supporting U.S.-led initiatives of interest to Seoul itself. This would reinforce the ROK–U.S. alliance and reduce the possibility of abandonment, but it would also strengthen South Korea as these initiatives strengthened Seoul's position and capabilities at the global level.

China

Roh's *Nordpolitik* had a very important China element, on top of its North Korea component. For one of the policy's six key principles was the improvement in relations between South Korea and China and other communist countries.[26] With China's opening up from the late 1970s, its rise seemed inexorable for South Korean policymakers.[27] Relations between Seoul and Beijing had already started to improve during the Chun government, including through economic, cultural, and sports exchanges. And the latter became central to South Korea's strategy toward China, in an early use of soft power after the democratic transition. For an opportunity to improve relations with China came shortly after South Korea's transition to democracy, when Seoul hosted the Olympic Games in September 1988. Having already participated in the Asian Games also hosted by the South Korean capital in 1986, China joined most other communist countries to commit to the 1988 Olympic Games.[28] The Games, therefore, served as a launching pad for Roh's grand strategy toward South Korea's neighbor. South Korea reciprocated by sending a delegation of its own including sportspeople, politicians, businesspeople, and tourists to the Asian Games hosted in Beijing in 1990.[29]

Improvement in relations with China could serve South Korea to achieve several ends. Certainly, it could strengthen autonomy as it would broaden the scope of South Korean foreign relations and therefore reduce dependence on the United States and its allies and partners. Among other ends, recognition as an influential middle power needed better relations with China. South Korea wanted to join the United Nations, and China was a permanent member of its Security Council and therefore had veto power.[30] Furthermore, South Korea wanted to become more integrated in the global economy to diversify trade and investment partners. China's rapid growth after opening up was an opportunity in this area. Plus, the Roh government wanted better relations with North Korea, and as an ally of Pyongyang, Beijing might be able to help improve inter-Korean links.

With China looking for trade partners and investors, South Korea used its economic leverage to improve bilateral relations. Between 1990—two years after Roh took office—and 1992 when his successor was elected, trade between South Korea and China increased from $669 million to $5.06 billion.[31] South Korea was exporting higher-tech goods to its neighbor, with China shipping lower-cost goods the other way. By 1992, China was South Korea's fourth largest trading partner.[32] South Korea, for its part, was China's fourth largest partner (excluding Hong Kong).[33] Also important in terms of South Korea's grand strategy, investment by the country's firms started to pour into China.[34] On the South Korean side, trade and investment was of course mainly the prerogative of the *chaebol* and other private firms. But the government was encouraging it because of the economic and diplomatic benefits that it could accrue. Most notably, the Bank of Korea (BOK) and the People's Bank of China negotiated the opening of branches in each other's country, which would materialize shortly after Roh left office.[35]

But the Roh government's biggest strategic gamble was the normalization of diplomatic relations with China. Following diplomatic normalization between Seoul and the Soviet Union in 1990, this was the biggest prize for South Korea, as well as one of the greatest changes in diplomatic strategic thinking, since it would involve abandoning formal recognition of Taiwan. China, meanwhile, was looking for new partners following from the isolation to which it was subject as a result of the Tiananmen Square crackdown of June 1989.[36] Dating back to 1985, Deng Xiaoping had signaled China's intent to improve relations with South Korea. This could have economic benefits and also facilitate Chinese reunification.[37] By the early 1990s, therefore, both Seoul and Beijing were bent on their own reunification goals.

In October 1991, South Korea's Foreign Minister Lee Sang-ock met with his Chinese counterpart, Qian Qichen. What followed was a flurry of diplomatic activity, with South Korea and China launching working-level talks in May 1992.[38] Finally, the two sides established diplomatic relations in August 1992, with South Korea agreeing to China's request that it was "the only legitimate government of China" and Beijing vowing to "support the peaceful reunification of the Korean Peninsula."[39] Roh would then become the first South Korean president to visit China in September of the same year.[40] For South Korea, normalization was proof of the power of two of its grand strategy means: its diplomatic corps and its economic tools. With the decision to normalize relations, the Roh government established that Seoul would seek to benefit from China's economic rise but also to have good diplomatic relations. This, in turn, would help underpin autonomy by diversifying South Korea's foreign relations.

Kim Young-sam (1993–1998)

North Korea

Kim Young-sam's policy toward North Korea followed from his predecessor's, in a sign that Seoul's grand strategy toward Pyongyang was becoming formalized and transcended changes in leadership. Kim's policy was based on the idea of "cooperative coexistence" (협력적 공존관계).[41] But crucially, the ultimate goal remained reunification—albeit only when conditions allowed.[42] This approach sought to assuage North Korean concerns about a possible takeover by South Korea at a time when West Germany's absorption of East Germany was a recent memory and communist regimes were folding across different parts of the world. Indeed, there was an open discussion about whether North Korea would collapse.[43] Differently, the Kim government portrayed Pyongyang as a partner for reconciliation and cooperation, which could lead to a commonwealth as an interim step toward peaceful reunification.[44]

Kim continued to place inter-Korean relations in the broader context surrounding the Korean Peninsula, even more explicitly than his predecessor. This context was marked by the first nuclear crisis of 1993–1994 and Washington's response. The crisis had started after North Korea was confronted with evidence of its plutonium program, in contravention of its safeguards agreement with the IAEA.[45] As a result, Pyongyang had announced its intention to withdraw from the NPT in March 1993.[46] Foreign Minister Han Sung-Joo suggested the launch of a Northeast Asia Security Dialogue (NEASED) in May 1994.[47] This was a way to make South Korea central to security discussions in the Korean Peninsula, but also a means to place North Korea's nuclear program in the context of broader security issues. It was a case study of Seoul using its diplomatic corps as the means to address the security conundrums of the region. But the idea did not take off.

Instead, Seoul believed that the Clinton administration had made plans to launch a strike on North Korea to destroy its main nuclear reactor in Yongbyon without prior consultation with South Korea. It seems that Washington had indeed considered a strike before backing down following private consultation with countries in the region and internal dissent in the Clinton administration.[48] Yet Washington's initial thinking that a strike may have been possible rattled the Kim government, which vehemently opposed such a move once it found out considering the havoc it could had brought to the Korean Peninsula had Pyongyang retaliated.[49] Furthermore, once Washington and Pyongyang launched the negotiations that led to the Agreed Framework of October 1994 that put an end to the first North Korean nuclear crisis, Seoul was excluded from the negotiating table.[50] Throughout the negotiations, Washington consulted with Seoul but ultimately reached an agreement that fitted its interests best. For the Kim government, Clinton's actions showed that the United States could make foreign policy decisions even if they put South Korea at risk or if they did not necessarily suit it. Yet, once the Agreed Framework was signed, South Korea, the United States, and Japan established the Korean Peninsula Energy Development Organization (KEDO) to provide light-water reactors to North Korea in exchange for the dismantlement of its nuclear facilities.[51] And in August 1997, the two Koreas, China, and the United States launched talks to address the North Korean nuclear problem following a proposal from Seoul and Washington.[52] Even though KEDO and the four-way talks were no NEASED, they showed that South Korea's idea of a Northeast Asian security framework could be applied to specific cases. Furthermore, the Kim government was following the template of involving the United States and China in the resolution of the inter-Korean standoff as a way to support its own, autonomous policy. Without their support, South Korea could see its approach toward North Korea derailed and therefore its autonomy curtailed.

The Kim government's grand strategy indeed also wanted to put South Korea in the driving seat of developments in the Korean Peninsula, a decision exacerbated by the Clinton administration's pursuit of the Agreed Framework without South Korea being in the negotiations. Seoul emphasized that South and North Korea should take the leading role in solving the issues affecting the Korean Peninsula (남북한 주도).[53] In other words, Seoul wanted autonomy to pursue its preferred approach to inter-Korean relations. The Kim government secretly exchanged messages with Pyongyang to set up what would have been the first-ever inter-Korean summit between the leaders of the two countries. The summit, however, did not take place, since Kim Il-sung passed away unexpectedly in July 1994.[54] But Kim's plans would become a staple of South Korea's approach toward the North for subsequent governments. Without neglecting the role of the United States and China in solving inter-Korean tensions, South Korea—or, sometimes, the Koreas—taking the driver's seat would show Seoul's autonomy in being able to shape developments in the Korean Peninsula.

At the same time, the Kim government worked to boost its deterrent against a possible North Korean strike. In March 1994, when U.S.–North Korea and inter-Korean negotiations seemed to be going nowhere, a North Korean official threatened to make Seoul a "sea of fire."[55] This drove home the risk that North Korea still posed to the South. The risk was reinforced in 1996, when Pyongyang announced that it would cut off inter-Korean communication lines.[56] The Kim government confronted ongoing tensions in the Korean Peninsula by seeking to develop Seoul's independent military capabilities. In November 1995, the Kim government launched negotiations with the Clinton administration to review the 1979 Ballistic Missile Guidelines and develop missiles with a range of up to three hundred kilometers (185 mi).[57] U.S.–South Korea negotiations could not be finalized during Kim's time in office, but they set a template for future governments, which also saw the development of domestically produced military capabilities as a way to boost autonomy in deterring North Korea and to address potential abandonment by the United States.

South Korea thus looked beyond Washington to develop its deterrent against Pyongyang. In 1994, as a result of the first North Korean nuclear crisis, Kim ordered the Korea Atomic Energy Research Institute to explore the design of nuclear-powered submarine reactors.[58] That same year, Seoul launched the "Brown Bear Project" (불곰사업) to acquire military technologies and expertise from Russia. This included long-range missile technology.[59] In April 1996, the National Science and Technology Council announced a Medium- and Long-Term National Space Development Plan. This was South Korea's first proper space program, which would be followed by several more, building on each other over the years.[60] In July 1997, meanwhile, KARI launched the KSR-II rocket.[61] In other words, Seoul was looking into the development of its autonomous capabilities to supplement the protection afforded by the ROK–U.S. alliance.

The United States

For Seoul, South Korea–U.S. relations during the Kim years in office were underpinned by the idea of a "Future-oriented Alliance" (미래지향적 동맹 관계).[62] Its key aspect was that the alliance between Seoul and Washington had to move beyond a narrow focus on the North Korean threat to consider other security issues beyond the Korean Peninsula.[63] In addition, the alliance should not be based on a subordinate relationship, and the Kim government emphasized the idea of a mutually beneficial relationship.[64] Certainly the United States remained the senior partner. The Kim government understood this.[65] But South Korea remained an important ally to the United States and could offer it material and ideational support. That is, a strong alliance was not in opposition to autonomy and could actually help to boost it by showing the value of South Korea as a partner, as well as helping Seoul to achieve other goals and increase its capabilities.

The alliance, however, suffered from the aforementioned lack of consultation between Washington and Seoul during the Agreed Framework negotiations. In addition, the Kim government was displeased with Washington's unwillingness to reduce barriers to Seoul's missile development in any meaningful way.[66] Furthermore, the U.S. Nuclear Posture Review of 1993–1994 raised doubts that Washington's nuclear weapons could act as a deterrent against would-be nuclear powers. The review also called for the denuclearization of all U.S. aircraft carriers patrolling the oceans across the world.[67] Thus, not only was the United States not consulting with the Kim government, but now Seoul also had doubts about Washington's commitment to using its nuclear deterrent against North Korea. It is in this context that South Korea continued to develop its own military capabilities to deter the North, as explained above. Using the means of its own capabilities made sense for a Kim government doubtful about the commitment of the Clinton administration to provide for South Korean security.

This quest for greater autonomy was further reinforced when peacetime OPCON transfer was realized in 1994. This meant that South Korea was fully responsible for the training, equipment, and maintenance of its own armed forces during peacetime. Even though Seoul did not question the

ROK–U.S. alliance, this was a significant step toward greater control of its own grand strategy insofar many South Koreans believed that not having operational control of the country's armed forces meant that South Korea was not fully sovereign.[68] Thanks to OPCON transfer, the South Korea–U.S. relationship could indeed be more interdependent.

Having said that, the alliance with the United States continued to be an indispensable means for South Korea to achieve its end of protection from external military threats. The MND issued annual defense white papers throughout the Kim government's term in office. Invariably, the ROK–U.S. alliance was presented in its own section and as a core component of South Korean security and defense—as was customary beforehand and continues to be to this date.[69] Simply put, the ROK armed forces did not conceive of any deterrent against North Korea that did not involve South Korea's closest ally. Plus, U.S. firms continued to sell arms systems to South Korea and to partner with South Korean firms to develop joint programs.[70] South Korea's growing military capabilities would build on U.S. technology and expertise.

The Kim government engaged more closely with the United States in addressing the North Korean nuclear issue through diplomatic means as the years went by. In August 1997, the Four-Party Talks were launched. The Kim government saw them as an opportunity to deal with U.S. concerns about nuclear weapons and its own goal of inter-Korean reconciliation in a single forum.[71] Seoul was seeking coordination between its approach and Washington's, which was recognition that its own relationship with Pyongyang could improve only in parallel with better U.S.-North Korea relations.

Leaving security and defense aside, South Korea's self-identification as a middle power meant greater use of diplomacy. This included relations with the United States. Under Kim, South Korea continued to actively participate in the Uruguay Round of trade negotiations that resulted in the launch of the WTO in 1995.[72] The Kim government also supported UN Framework Convention on Climate Change (UNFCC) negotiations launched in 1995 that led to the Kyoto Protocol of December 1997, which South Korea signed a few months later.[73] Seoul understood that it was important for the Clinton administration to conclude these two deals, which would showcase its post–Cold War leadership role. South Korea embraced the two negotiation processes, among others, to provide diplomatic support to these U.S.-led initiatives. In addition, Seoul started to make use of its military capabilities to support the United States beyond the Korean Peninsula. In 1993, South Korea dispatched peacekeepers to the UN Assistance Mission in Somalia, where the United States also deployed its troops.[74] South Korea saw this as a sign of autonomy, which at the same time also boosted the ROK–U.S. alliance by showing to Washington that it had value well beyond the Korean Peninsula. The Kim government also sought to increase its soft power vis-à-vis the United States. In 1993, Seoul opened a Korean Cultural Center in Washington, DC.[75]

China

The Kim government continued the Roh Tae-woo's government policy of embracing China as a partner for economic and political cooperation. Seoul labeled its approach toward Beijing a "Real Partnership" (실질협력 관계). In the economic front, this essentially meant manufacturing outsourcing to China by South Korean *chaebol* and other firms, the import of cheap goods such as textiles or toys no longer produced in South Korea, and the export of higher-end goods. As a result, bilateral trade grew from $8.22 billion in 1993 to $24.02 billion by the end of 1997.[76] Investment into China, meanwhile, continued to flow.[77] Furthermore, in April 1993 the BOK and the People's Bank of China decided to open branches in each other's countries. This was a clear sign that the governments of both countries wanted to boost bilateral economic relations. For Seoul, it was another step toward its end of deeper integration in the world economy by taking advantage of the phenomenal economic growth of its neighbor. It also boosted autonomy and reduced dependence on the United States, by securing a stronger partnership with the other East Asian great power.

South Korea also wanted to improve political relations with China though, for this would support its quest to be seen as an influential middle power. And its skillful use of its diplomatic corps yielded a big reward. Kim had visited China in March 1994, as his predecessor had done.[78] But in November 1995, Jiang Zemin became the first Chinese head of state to visit South Korea. During his five-day visit, Jiang held talks with Kim, Foreign Minister Gong Ro-myung, and business leaders, among others. Jiang expressed China's support for South Korea's North Korea policy, and he sided with Seoul in chastising Japan for refusing to acknowledge its role in starting World War II in the Pacific.[79] And Jiang's support for Seoul's

North Korea policy, as well as criticism of Japan for not acknowledging its past wrongdoings also showed that South Korean diplomacy could support the country's grand strategy. To this, Seoul added soft power as part of its toolkit to smooth relations with China. In 1993, Seoul opened a Korean Cultural Center in Beijing.[80]

In fact, the Kim government saw a broader role for China in addressing the North Korean nuclear conundrum. Certainly, Kim wanted South Korea and the Koreas to be in the driving seat. And cooperation with the United States was crucial to its North Korea policy. But Beijing was Pyongyang's closest ally and main economic benefactor, and China was one of the parties to the armistice agreement that put an end to the Korean War. Therefore, de jure it had a role to play in any peace agreement in the Korean Peninsula that could facilitate inter-Korean reconciliation. Seoul thus welcomed Beijing's participation in the Four-Party Talks launched in 1997.[81] The talks would ultimately fail, but for South Korea they marked the beginning of open efforts across administrations to engage China in dealing with North Korea. After all, Seoul's autonomy when it came to pursuing the goal of inter-Korean reconciliation and reunification would be curtailed if China was not part of its outreach to the North.

China's rise, however, had a more negative undertone from a South Korean perspective. For Beijing's economic rise came hand in hand with its military rise. This became apparent during the Taiwan Strait Crisis of 1995–1996, when Beijing conducted a series of missile tests and naval exercises after Taiwanese President Lee Teng-hui was allowed to visit the United States and later on in the runup to Taiwan's first-ever democratic presidential election. The United States responded by sending its navy to international waters near Taiwan, which further inflamed tensions in the region.[82] For South Korea, this was an indication that China might intervene in the case of conflict in the Korean Peninsula.[83] But it was also proof that Beijing could be willing to mobilize its military in case of tensions in Northeast Asia.

As a result, Seoul's grand strategy in relation to China incorporated a new element. South Korea would seek to engage Beijing and help "socialize" it in international norms such as multilateralism and the peaceful resolution of conflicts.[84] Seoul would also seek to get Chinese support for its North Korea policy. This way, Seoul wanted to use its diplomatic skills and economic tools as a means to influence Chinese behavior and benefit from the country's opening up. On the other hand, South Korea had to be wary of the potential threat coming from China's rise. Thus, Seoul started to see the ROK–U.S. alliance as a possible deterrent against China and pursued its military buildup as a way to deter possible Chinese aggressiveness.[85] Without these means, South Korea could see its autonomy curtailed as a result of its military weakness vis-à-vis China—and vis-à-vis a potential Sino–North Korean military strike.

Kim Dae-jung (1998–2003)

North Korea

In December 1997, Kim Dae-jung was elected as South Korea's fist liberal president since the 1960s. After decades of conservative rule, this was a seismic change for the Asian country. Furthermore, Kim took office in February 1998, when South Korea was engulfed in the AFC. The crisis dominated the country's domestic and foreign policy, for it threatened to wipe out decades of economic progress. And yet, Kim did not move South Korea away from its previous foreign policy trajectory in any significant way. This signaled that post-1988 South Korean grand strategy had indeed taken hold, for the factors behind it were relatively unaffected, the ends also remained unchanged, and the means were relatively stable as well.

Kim's signature foreign policy was his "Sunshine Policy" toward North Korea. Formally known as "North Korea Reconciliation and Cooperation Policy" (대북화해협력정책), the policy sought to reduce tensions in the Korean Peninsula by giving the Kim Jong-il regime incentives to cooperate with Seoul. To this end, the Sunshine Policy was based on three principles: no toleration for armed provocations from North Korea, no attempt to absorb the North by South Korea, and active promotion of inter-Korean cooperation and reconciliation.[86] Kim later added two major policies or quasi-principles: separation of politics from economics and a demand for the North to reciprocate.[87] Furthermore, Kim emphasized that the Koreas should be in the driving seat of inter-Korean relations rather than being subject to the policies and interests of the great powers around the Korean Peninsula. The Sunshine Policy built from Kim's decades-old Three-stage Unification Formula dating back to the early 1970s. The three stages were peaceful coexistence, with the two Koreas de facto recognizing each other,

China and the Soviet Union recognizing the South, and the United States and Japan recognizing the North; peaceful exchange, with the two Koreas promoting people-to-people, economic, and political exchanges; and peaceful unification.[88] Kim had updated his formula in 1987 and then in 1991 to peaceful coexistence, exchange, and unification. But the stages were essentially the same as in the 1970s formula, as were the tools to move through them.[89] Crucially, the United States and China were assigned an important role in solving inter-Korean tensions. Similarly to his conservative predecessors, the liberal Kim understood that Seoul's autonomy to drive inter-Korean relations necessitated buy-in and involvement from Washington and Beijing.

Indeed, the Sunshine Policy was building on Kim Young-sam's cooperative coexistence that recognized North Korea as a potential partner, prioritized people-to-people and economic exchanges, saw unification as the last stage in a prolonged process, and included a deterrent component. Arguably, the Sunshine Policy could trace its roots back to the July 4 North-South Joint Communiqué that de facto established peaceful coexistence as a principle and also called for the Koreas to lead inter-Korean engagement. The South Korean ends of autonomy and inter-Korean reconciliation and reunification remained unchanged.

Possibly, the key difference between Kim and his predecessors was that he was actually able to implement his North Korea policy. In other words, he was able to carry out Seoul's grand strategy toward Pyongyang. Thus, in June 2000 Kim and his North Korean counterpart Kim Jong-il held the historic first-ever inter-Korean summit in Pyongyang.[90] Where Kim Young-sam had failed following the death of Kim Il-sung, Kim Dae-jung succeeded. Furthermore, Kim launched inter-Korean economic projects, a feat that his predecessors were also unable to accomplish. In November 1998, the Kim regime opened Mount Kumgang to tourists from the South following an inter-Korean agreement signed earlier in the year.[91] Plus, there were regular inter-Korean family reunions following the 2000 summit between the two Kims.[92] Cultural exchanges became relatively frequent.[93] With Kim Jong-il having consolidated his power and North Korea suffering the effects of the great famine of the mid-1990s, it felt the need to reciprocate in a way that would have been unnecessary earlier.[94] Yet, the Four-Party Talks involving the two Koreas, China, and the United States would be last convened in 1998. And Kim's suggestion to launch a multilateral forum—similar to Kim Young-sam's NEASED—did not take off. Still, the fact that Kim had similar views about the benefits of a mul-tilateral forum showed the extent to which his North Korea policy built on similar ideas from previous South Korean administrations.

In this respect, it is telling that Kim continued to seek to develop a power-ful deterrent against Pyongyang. Indeed, the first principle of the Sunshine Policy was not to tolerate North Korean provocations. Seoul condemned Pyongyang's August 1998 ballistic missile test, when the North Korean regime launched a missile toward the East Sea and over Japan.[95] The ROK Navy then repelled its Northern counterpart during the June 1999 Battle of Yeonpyeong, when North Korean ships crossed the Northern Limit Line (NLL) separating the two Koreas on several occasions over a period of one week. The (North) Korean People's Navy suffered heavy losses as well as at least seventeen casualties during the battle.[96] In June 2002, the second Battle of Yeonpyeong took place. A North Korea ship crossed the NLL and opened fire on a South Korean patrol boat, killing six sailors. The ROK Navy retaliated, sinking a North Korean vessel and killing at least thirteen North Koreans. The Kim government requested and received an apology from North Korea. Seoul also successfully requested from the United States the right to change the rules of engagement so that its troops could shoot first if threatened by the North.[97] Furthermore, the Kim gov-ernment successfully concluded Ballistic Missile Guidelines negotiations in March 2001. South Korea was allowed to develop missiles with a three-hundred-kilometer (185 mi) range.[98] This was significant in that South Korean missiles could now target anywhere in North Korea up to its bor-der with China. And South Korea was indeed improving its domestically produced missile technology during the Kim government. In short, the Sunshine Policy did not prevent the Kim government from continuing to develop a powerful deterrent against North Korea nor to criticize Pyong-yang's military developments or respond to its provocations. And Kim also believed that South Korea needed autonomous military capabilities to supplement the ROK–U.S. alliance, in case Washington abandoned its ally.

The United States

The advent of South Korea's first liberal government in decades brought questions as to whether Seoul might reexamine the ROK–U.S. alliance.

As it turns out, the approach of the Kim government built on his predecessors, reinforcing South Korean grand strategy. Kim even dubbed his approach toward the alliance as "A Higher-Level Partnership for the 21ˢᵗ Century" (21세기를 향한 한차원 높은 동반자 관계).[99] Continuity was a key element. The Kim government believed that the ROK–U.S. alliance remained a key pillar of South Korea's grand strategy, helping Seoul to be a stronger international actor and therefore reinforcing its foreign policy reach.[100] For the Kim government, the alliance would remain a crucial element of its grand strategy regardless of whether Clinton, a Democrat, or his successor, the Republican George W. Bush, was U.S. president, in spite of their different views of the Sunshine Policy.[101] In common with his conservative predecessors, Kim also believed that Seoul could enhance its autonomy by broadening the scope of South Korea–U.S. relations and showing and benefiting from the value that the alliance could bring beyond the Korean Peninsula.

Clinton and Bush had fundamentally different approaches toward North Korea, and therefore toward relations with South Korea in this area. Kim held his first summit with Clinton in June 1998, and the U.S. president conceded that the new South Korean president should "lead the Korean Peninsula matter," that is, relations with North Korea.[102] In fact, Washington's National Security Strategy published later that year described Seoul as the "lead interlocutor with the North Koreans."[103] From the perspective of the Clinton administration, the United States had a wide range of foreign policy issues to deal with. North Korea was "only" one more of them. But for Seoul, it was the main issue. It thus made sense to assign South Korea this role.[104] Kim seized the opportunity, since it promised to allow him to fulfill Seoul's ends of autonomy as well as inter-Korean reconciliation.

The situation changed dramatically after Bush took office in 2001. The new U.S. president dismantled the Agreed Framework signed by the Clinton administration by cancelling oil shipments to North Korea.[105] This effectively terminated KEDO. Bush also made clear his dislike for North Korea, including Pyongyang in an "axis of evil" that sponsored terrorism and harbored weapons of mass destruction together with Iran and Iraq.[106] But Kim actually sought to work with Bush as part of his North Korea policy and tried to steer the new administration toward dialogue and engagement, even if it did not succeed.[107] Seoul did not deviate from its grand strategy in terms of the ends and means to deal with North Korea together with the United States.

Furthermore, relations with the United States were not only about engagement with North Korea. Deterrence was also part of the equation. The Kim government continued to work toward a revision of the Ballistic Missile Guidelines. The revision was finally agreed after the Bush administration took office, as mentioned above. In other words, the ROK–U.S. alliance continued to serve its purpose of facilitating South Korea's goal of protection from military threats, in this case by removing impediments to South Korea's development of its own military capabilities. The Kim government had problems with the Bush administration, but even in the area of security relations were not as negative as sometimes portrayed.[108]

Commensurate with its position as a middle power, South Korea also used other means to reinforce relations with the United States as a way to support its overall grand strategic ends. The Korea Foundation continued to provide funding to encourage projects and events to strengthen knowledge about South Korea. But the foundation now shifted its focus toward foreign policy, security, and politics and away from culture.[109] The Korean cultural centers in Los Angeles and New York, meanwhile, continued with their programs of activities to boost the image of South Korea.

Equally relevant, South Korean investment toward the United States continued to grow. Certainly, investment was the remit of the private sector. But the South Korean government made sure to publicize the benefits of this investment for job creation.[110] In other words, Seoul was working to create favorable views of South Korea among U.S. politicians and the general public. This could indirectly support South Korean foreign policy by showing Washington the benefits that good relations with Seoul brought to its own country.

On the other hand, the Kim government added a new means to South Korea's grand strategy toward the United States: WTO disputes. As a result of its economic development and globalization, South Korea was competing head-to-head with other developed economies, including the United States. This brought trade frictions. But whereas in the past a weak South Korea would have had no choice but to accept restrictions on its exports, middle power South Korea felt that it could stand up to bigger economies. Taking advantage of the WTO's dispute-settlement mechanism that brought de jure equality to all its members, the Kim government brought six cases against the United States related to TV receivers, dynamic random access memory semiconductors, stainless steel, line pipes, dumping and subsidies, and steel products. In the first two cases brought by Seoul, it settled the dispute with Washington. But in the other four, the dispute went all the way to the WTO's dispute-settlement body.[111] This showed that South Korea was willing to use its trade prowess as a tool to support its economic prosperity, even if it meant directly confronting its closest ally.

China

Following from the burgeoning economic relationship between Seoul and Beijing, Kim sought to expand ties into other areas. In particular, the Kim Dae-jung government was interested in strengthening bilateral ties with China. Thus, the government pursued a policy of expanding South Korea–China political and economic cooperation.[112] Political relations were broadly understood, in that they included both bilateral diplomatic relations between South Korea and China but also security matters, including the North Korean nuclear issue.[113] Kim's interest in improving political relations with Beijing made sense considering that China's rise was becoming a factor that Seoul had to grapple with to achieve a range of ends, from reconciliation with North Korea to deeper integration in the world economy. Stronger South Korea–China relations would also help boost Seoul's autonomy by reducing dependence on the United States.

Building on this approach, Kim visited China in November 1998 and established a "cooperative partnership."[114] Seoul hoped to develop diplomatic and security cooperation with Beijing as a way to build a productive bilateral relationship, garner support for its Sunshine Policy, create a stable environment in Northeast Asia in the aftermath of the AFC, and diversify its foreign policy links.[115] South Korea was using its diplomatic corps as a way to foster its autonomy by strengthening links with one of its closest geographical neighbors, one that technically remained an ally of North Korea but that was pursuing an strategy of economic, societal, and diplomatic opening up that made it look more like South Korea with every passing day.

As part of its grand strategy, the Kim government also continued to encourage trade and investment links with China. Bilateral trade grew from $21.28 billion in 1998—following a slump due to the AFC—to $44.08 billion in 2002 when Kim's successor was elected.[116] China's accession to the WTO gave a significant boost to bilateral trade, as Beijing started to

lower tariffs and other barriers to imports while other countries including South Korea also reciprocated. By 2002, China (excluding Hong
Kong) had become South Korea's third largest trading partner and South
Korea had become China's third largest (excluding Hong Kong and with
ASEAN and the EU disaggregated by country).[117] South Korean invest-
ment continued to pour into China as well.[118] China's entry into the WTO
led a growing number of South Korean firms to outsource production to
China. From a South Korean perspective, by not pursuing the devaluation
of its currency during the AFC, China's behavior had been positive.[119] Had
China done so, South Korea would have probably suffered a deeper reces-
sion and taken longer to recover. China was also attracting a larger share of
South Korean exports, which also helped its economy rebound more
quickly from the AFC. Therefore, the Kim government sought to support
stronger economic relations with China by promoting consultation between
the two countries' central banks and ministries of Finance.[120] This was done
at the bilateral level, but also multilaterally via the newly created ASEAN+3
framework.

The Kim government added two new means to its arsenal to deal with
China: soft power and public diplomacy. South Korean cultural industry
had been growing since the early 1990s, with creative musicians, cinema-
tographers, and other artists developing cutting-edge pop, films, or dramas.
The Kim government launched a plan to take advantage of this creativity,
with a view at promoting economic growth in a post-AFC environment
but also at boosting South Korean soft power. The Ministry of Culture
and Tourism worked together with the private sector to find new markets
for South Korean cultural products, and also raised the cultural industry's
budget.[121] China was at the top of the list, in consideration of its geographical and cultural proximity.[122] In 1999, public TV broadcaster KBS
partnered with CCTV to launch the Korea-China Music Festival. The
festival featured pop singers and bands from both South Korea and China.[123]
It would become an annual feature. And South Korean pop and dramas
started to arrive in China, leading Chinese journalists to coin the term
Hallyu or Korean wave.[124]

But China's economic opening up had negative consequences for South
Korea as well. Cheap Chinese garlic started to inundate the South Korean
market. As a result, the Kim government hiked tariffs on Chinese garlic
from 30 percent to 315 percent in June 2000. China retaliated by banning

imports of South Korean mobile phones and polyethylene. The two countries solved their feud over garlic one month later.[125] But this feud led South Korea to use a new means in its grand strategy toward China: trade restrictions. Even though Seoul would not make use of this often in subsequent years, the Kim government opened the door to South Korea's using its economic leverage to try to achieve its goals.

Roh Moo-hyun (2003–2008)

North Korea

Roh Moo-hyun was inaugurated as South Korea's second liberal president in 2003. Labeled "Peace and Prosperity," his approach toward North Korea was essentially a continuation of Kim Dae-jung's Sunshine Policy. If anything, the Roh government took a more dovish approach toward North Korea. Most notably, the first Defense White Paper published by the MND after Roh took office omitted a reference to North Korea as the South's "main enemy."[126] For the first time, Pyongyang was not addressed in this way. This characterization of North Korea had survived during the early years of the Kim Dae-jung government. Seoul had then refrained from publishing its scheduled 2002 Defense White Paper to a large extent due to the changing relationship with Pyongyang following the 2000 inter-Korean summit.[127] With the Roh government in office, Seoul stopped labeling North Korea as the South's "main enemy," as reflected in the 2004 white paper but also in the 2006 version.[128]

From Roh's perspective, the Sunshine Policy had allowed Seoul to reduce tensions in the Korean Peninsula and also to play a leading role in addressing U.S.–North Korea differences over the latter's nuclear program.[129] In other words, engagement with Pyongyang enabled South Korean autonomy, protection against external threats, and, certainly, inter-Korean reconciliation. Therefore, his preferred means to deal with the Kim Jong-il regime was through talks and diplomacy. Taking office shortly after the second nuclear crisis broke out in October 2002, following North Korea's admission of possession of highly enriched uranium in breach of the Agreed Framework, the effective termination of KEDO by Bush, and North Korea's withdrawal from the NPT, Roh called for a diplomatic resolution to Korean Peninsula tensions starting from his inauguration address.[130]

Furthermore, Roh doubled down on economic engagement with North Korea. In 2004, the Kaesong Industrial Complex was inaugurated.[131] Combining South Korean capital with North Korean labor, the complex became a symbol of inter-Korean economic cooperation and hope that one day there would be a single Korean economy. Furthermore, aid to North Korea increased from $262.85 million in the final full year of the Kim Dae-jung government to $358.09 million in Roh's final full year.[132] Tours for South Korean civilians to Kaesong and Pyongyang were also launched in 2005, even if only for a brief period of time.[133] That is, South Korea was using trade, investment, and aid as a preferred means to improve inter-Korean relations. Roh's prioritization of diplomacy and economic engagement was rewarded when North Korea reopened inter-Korean communication lines in 2005.[134]

Roh believed in the possibility of Northeast Asian cooperation and integration as well, and he launched a Northeast Asian Cooperation Initiative for Peace and Prosperity proposal shortly after taking office in 2003. Among others, this initiative was a way to integrate North Korea in regional structures to support inter-Korean reconciliation, using multilateral diplomacy to support other means to deal with Pyongyang.[135] There were clear parallels between Roh's proposal and Kim Young-sam's NEASED. Yet the situation in Northeast Asia had changed, and Roh was able to partially realize his vision when the Six-Party Talks were launched in August 2003. Involving the two Koreas, the United States, China, Japan, and Russia, the talks would last throughout the full Roh administration, with their last round held in September 2007. From a South Korean perspective, the Six-Party Talks confirmed that its autonomy in terms of grand strategy toward North Korea could be realized only if China and the United States were involved. Indeed, in a 2005 joint statement the six parties "agreed to explore ways and means for promoting security cooperation in Northeast Asia."[136] In February 2007, the six parties issued a new joint statement that, among others, announced the creation of a working group to implement this agreement.[137] This way, the Northeast Asia Peace and Security Mechanism involving the six parties was born. Chaired by Russia, the working group met twice.[138] However, it did not survive the dissolution of the Six-Party Talks.

Roh's prioritization of diplomacy as the way to deal with Pyongyang arguably was most clearly demonstrated toward the end of this tenure. In

October 2006, North Korea had conducted its first-ever nuclear test. This had upended the geopolitics of the Korean Peninsula and was a major blow to efforts to solve the North Korean nuclear issue peacefully. The UN Security Council had imposed sanctions on Pyongyang as a result of the test.[139] Yet, in October 2007 Roh traveled from Seoul to Pyongyang by land for the second-ever inter-Korean summit. The three-day summit resulted in a joint declaration that reaffirmed the validity of the June 2000 inter-Korean declaration, the centrality of the Koreas to peace in the Korean Peninsula, and, more generally, their wish to promote exchanges and cooperation in areas ranging from military security to economic links.[140]

But despite Roh's dovish approach toward North Korea, he maintained South Korean grand strategy of also promoting hawkish policies to deal with Pyongyang. Barely a few weeks after his inauguration, Roh reactivated South Korea's plans to build nuclear-powered submarines. The plans were halted within a year, but the new president's wishes to deter North Korea autonomously were clear.[141] In 2005, Roh introduced the Defense Reform Plan 2020 for South Korea to develop a long-term blueprint to strengthen its autonomous capabilities.[142] Indeed, Seoul continued to develop its missile, rocket, jet fighter, submarine, and other programs to strengthen its armed forces. Most notably, South Korea established its Guided Missile Command in 2006. The command was in charge of a Hyunmoo missile battalion.[143] In the mind of Roh government officials, the "Peace and Prosperity" policy and the removal of the designation of North Korea as the South's "main enemy" did not imply military de-escalation. To the contrary, Seoul needed to build up its military to show Pyongyang that it was capable to protect itself thanks to the combination of its own capabilities and the ROK–U.S. alliance.[144] Roh emphasized "cooperative self-reliant defense" in multiple speeches, indicating that Seoul should be able to protect itself but the alliance with Washington continued to be part of South Korea's strategy to deal with Pyongyang.[145] That is, autonomous capabilities were central to deter North Korea along with the alliance with the United States.

The United States

Roh came to office with the intention to establish a more equal relationship between South Korea and the United States, but not with the goal of disentangling Seoul from Washington as some of his critics argued. He dubbed his approach "Comprehensive and Dynamic Alliance" (포괄적, 역동적 동맹), with "comprehensive" being the key word.[146] For the Roh government, the ROK–U.S. alliance was not circumscribed to North Korea or Korean Peninsula security issues. Instead, the alliance had to serve the interests of South Korea at the regional and global levels. And the alliance should broaden the range of issues that it covered and focus on politics and economics and not only security.[147]

It is in this context that the Roh government tried to move ahead South Korea's grand strategic autonomy from the United States—but with the caveat that the alliance with Washington actually served to underpin this autonomy. To begin with, the government's Defense Reform Plan 2020 was designed to provide South Korea with the necessary capabilities to protect itself against North Korea without or with minimal U.S. assistance. However, South Korea relied on U.S. arms and military technology sales and transfers to develop its capabilities. In fact, South Korea was the largest arms importer from the United States under Roh.[148] This made sense both because of the degree of integration between the South Korean and U.S. armed forces and because the United States had the most advanced weapons systems. Furthermore, the Roh government accelerated plans to develop a blue water navy, and in 2007 launched its first-ever destroyer with an advanced weapons system to shoot down missiles and aircraft.[149] On top of that, the United States committed over $11 billion to modernizing its forces in the Korean Peninsula to make up for a one-third reduction in the number of its troops from 2004 to 2005.[150]

Furthermore, the Roh government picked up the discussions about wartime OPCON transfer from its predecessor. Discussions dragged on until 2007 but resulted in an agreement between Seoul and Washington. The agreement was that OPCON transfer would be completed by 2012, and the two sides would establish a new command with a South Korean commander at the helm supported by a U.S. counterpart.[151] The plan was not implemented until after Roh was replaced by a conservative president in 2008. But the agreement between the two sides signaled that the Roh government did not want to end the role of the United States in the security of the Korean Peninsula. Autonomy meant Seoul leading its own defense even in time of war, not abandonment of the ROK–U.S. alliance. In fact, the "cooperative self-reliant defense" policy pursued by the Roh government established that Seoul wanted to combine autonomy with the alliance to protect the country.

The United States and the ROK–U.S. alliance continued to play a necessary role for the deterrence of North Korea under the Roh government. But Roh was also continuing Kim Dae-jung's engagement policy, which the Bush administration had initially showed doubts about. The situation changed shortly after Roh was inaugurated. In August 2003, South Korea and the United States were among the countries that launched the Six-Party Talks. Within this framework, Seoul and Washington cooperated closely to try to put an end to the second North Korean nuclear crisis. Negotiators from both countries worked hand in hand to come up with the agreements and incentives that could support North Korean denuclearization and better relations between the two Koreas and between Washington and Pyongyang.[152] The Six-Party Talks and the constructive role that the Bush administration played in trying to come up with incentives to offer North Korea provided support to Roh's pro-engagement policy.[153] South Korean diplomats were crucial in renewing the ROK–U.S. alliance.

Another signature policy of the Roh government was "strategic ambiguity" toward the U.S.–China relationship. This meant that South Korea would not take sides in any potential competition between the two and that Seoul would try to act as a balancer between Washington and Beijing if competition indeed took place.[154] Roh pursued this policy enabled by the ROK–U.S. alliance. In other words, the Roh government believed that it was the alliance with the United States that actually allowed South Korea to actually contemplate playing this role. Any balancing role did not mean "choosing China" over the United States. It meant avoiding falling prey to the problems derived from Sino-American competition and supporting Washington in incorporating Beijing into the international community.[155] Thus, Roh was implicitly supporting long-standing U.S. policy dating back to at least the 1980s.

As part of South Korea's grand strategy, the Roh government was seeking to have a more active role beyond the Korean Peninsula and Northeast Asia to be recognized as an influential middle power. In 2003, South Korea sent peacekeepers to the UN mission in Liberia along with the United States and other countries.[156] But it was the Global War on Terror launched by the Bush administration that laid the groundwork for Seoul to play this role, in strong support of U.S. policy. In February 2004, the National

Assembly voted overwhelmingly in favor of authorizing the dispatch of South Korean combat troops to Iraq. The Roh government led efforts for the National Assembly to provide authorization, with Roh himself arguing for the need to support Washington and laying out the benefits of doing so for South Korea.[157] Seoul went on to dispatch the third largest contingent among all U.S.-led Coalition of the Willing contributors to the war in Iraq, until all troops were withdrawn in December 2008.[158] This was the first time that South Korean troops had been dispatched to fight overseas since the Vietnam War. The Roh government was signaling that South Korea's alliance with the United States was indeed "comprehensive."

Roh sought to significantly emphasize that comprehensive component of South Korea–U.S. relations with the launch of free trade agreement (FTA) negotiations. The FTA Roadmap announced by the Roh government in 2003 laid the groundwork for South Korea–U.S. FTA negotiations, with initial talks launched in November 2004.[159] From a South Korean perspective, its status as a developed economy and the rise of China were crucial factors in explaining its push to sign an FTA with the United States. An FTA would strengthen Seoul's integration in the world economy. It would also enhance its autonomy by reducing the risk of economic diversification from South Korea to China, since South Korean firms would enjoy better conditions to access the U.S. market. South Korea thus was making use of its economic means. In fact, China had approached South Korea to launch FTA negotiations. This had helped convince the Bush administration of the need to do the same.[160] Seoul and Washington finally launched FTA negotiations in February 2006, and they reached an agreement in April 2007.[161] However, the U.S. Congress slowed down ratification of the Korea-U.S. Free Trade Agreement (KORUS), which would only come into effect under the Lee Myung-bak government after some aspects were renegotiated. By then, South Korea had already put in place an FTA with the European Union.

As a middle power, South Korea also continued to use other tools in its relationship with the United States. Investment from South Korean firms into the United States continued its upward trajectory, particularly from the mid-2000s onward.[162] This included Korea National Oil Corporation (KNOC) investment in an offshore oil production project toward the end of Roh's tenure in 2008.[163] On the other hand, the Roh government also continued to take the United States to the WTO dispute-settlement mechanism, albeit only once compared to six times under the Kim Dae-jung government.[164] Along with economic means, the Roh government continued to use soft power in its approach toward the United States. The Korean cultural centers in Los Angeles and New York continued to operate; the Korea Foundation opened an office in Washington, DC, in 2005, while continuing to provide grants with a growing focus on foreign affairs; and in 2007 the South Korean government launched the King Sejong Institute to promote Korean language and culture learning.[165] The United States would eventually become the host of the third largest number of these institutes. Also, the South Korean government provided sponsorship to the Korean Music Festival launched in 2003 in California.[166] The festival brought K-pop acts to the United States, thus helping spread South Korean soft power.

China

China's (economic) rise and its accession to the WTO in December 2001 reinforced South Korea's grand strategy toward its neighbor. For the Roh government, China's rise was inevitable and would be having repercussions beyond trade and investment. Thus, Seoul had to use different means to deal with its neighbor and achieve its ends, including protection from China's (potential) military threat, better inter-Korean relations, and deeper economic integration. Roh visited China in July 2003 and announced his policy toward Beijing: "Comprehensive Cooperative Partnership" (전면적 협력 동반자관계).[167] The name of Roh's policy inevitably drew parallels with Kim Dae-jung's own, labeled "Cooperative Partnership." By using the term "comprehensive"—also applied to Roh's U.S. policy—the new government was indicating that it wanted to deepen ties beyond trade and investment. Furthermore, Roh's "strategic ambiguity" approach to Sino-American competition indicated that he did not want to have an antagonistic approach toward Beijing and perhaps even facilitate its integration into existing regional and global governance structures. From this perspective, better South Korea–China relations would enhance South Korean autonomy through the diversification of Seoul's foreign relations.

The economic relationship inevitably dominated Seoul's grand strategy toward Beijing. In December 2003, China became South Korea's largest export destination.[168] And in December 2004, it became the largest trading partner. Meanwhile, bilateral investment between the two countries shot up from $2.72 billion in annual flows in 2002—China's first full year of WTO membership—to $3.67 billion in annual flows in 2007.[169] South Korean firms were outsourcing to China at record rates. Building on stronger economic ties, Roh's FTA Roadmap, and a request by China, Seoul and Beijing launched consultations to study the feasibility of an FTA in 2006.[170] However, actual negotiations would only be launched under the Lee Myung-bak government. The Roh government decided to prioritize FTA negotiations with the United States, which suggested that Seoul's decades-old ally still took precedence in South Korean grand strategy. Furthermore, an FTA with the United States would enhance the competitiveness of South Korean firms at a time when they were trying to withstand the competition of their cheaper Chinese counterparts.

South Korea's relations with China were also strengthened thanks to South Korea's diplomatic corps. In particular, South Korea and China were part of the Six-Party Talks to address North Korea's nuclear program. Participants in the talks were complimentary of China's role as host of the talks.[171] For the Roh government, Beijing's involvement in dealing with North Korea was necessary to ensure that South Korea could indeed have the autonomy to pursue better inter-Korean relations. And South Korean diplomats felt that their regular interactions with their Chinese counterparts created stronger bonds between the two countries.[172] Symbolizing the stronger political relations between South Korea and China as a result of the latter's role in dealing with North Korea as well as stronger economic links, Chinese president Hu Jintao visited South Korea in November 2005.[173] The visit proceeded without any problems.

Soft power was also part of Roh's toolkit to implement South Korea's preferred strategy toward China. The Roh government, in fact, pushed forward the idea of "Creative Korea" to take advantage of *Hallyu* to support South Korea's grand strategy. In the particular case of China, Seoul opened a second Korean Cultural Center in Shanghai.[174] Furthermore, the South Korean government prioritized the opening of King Sejong institutes in China when they were first launched in 2007 as well. China would eventually become the country hosting the largest number of these centers.[175] These government efforts were aided by the growing number of K-pop acts touring China and K-dramas being shown in the country's TV networks. On top of that, the Korea–China Music Festival sponsored by KBS and CCTV continued to be aired.[176] Soft power was supplemented with public diplomacy when the Korea Foundation opened an office in Beijing in 2005.[177]

Not everything was positive in the relationship between South Korea and China, though. In 2004, Beijing's Northeast Asia Project argued that the ancient kingdom of Goguryeo had been part of China. This revisionist interpretation of Chinese history and Sino-Korean links created a diplomatic spat with South Korea.[178] It was a reminder that the rise of China could create diplomatic frictions that South Korea needed to address through its diplomatic corps and public diplomacy. In addition, the Defense Reform Plan 2020 targeted China, not just North Korea.[179] The Roh government was aware that the rise of China could create security frictions, so that South Korea's military capabilities ought to be part of the mix of means that Seoul would use to deal with Beijing.

Lee Myung-bak (2008–2013)

North Korea

Lee Myung-bak's election in late 2007 and inauguration in early 2008 returned a conservative president to office after a decade of liberal rule. Lee was critical of the pro-engagement policy of his two liberal predecessors, which he thought had failed to produce any meaningful result for South Korea and had also failed to prevent North Korea's development of a nuclear weapons arsenal. Yet Lee did not turn against engagement. His approach toward North Korea was labeled "Policy of Mutual Benefits and Common Prosperity" and promised a "grand bargain" whereby South Korea would help the North achieve a GDP per capita of $3,000 within a decade in exchange for denuclearization. Furthermore, the Lee government wanted reciprocity from the Kim Jong-il regime so that South Korea would also benefit from stronger inter-Korean links. Lee's plan also called for the continuation of the Six-Party Talks to promote cooperation among countries in the region including North Korea.[180] The latter also implied that Lee believed that South Korean autonomy to pursue its policy toward the North could not neglect the role of the United States and China.

Significantly, Lee's policy toward North Korea included diplomatic and economic engagement among its means to implement its strategy. The Lee government held secret talks with Pyongyang government officials to hold a summit with Kim Jong-il,[181] as his two liberal predecessors had done. And the Kaesong Industrial Complex and Mount Kumgang tourism tours continued to operate. Also, Lee envoys discreetly approached North Korean officials to ascertain whether it would be possible to hold official inter-Korean talks.[182] Furthermore, the 2008 Defense White Paper again refrained from labeling North Korea as an "enemy."[183] This was the first white paper issued under Lee's presidency, and it followed from the line established during the Roh Moo-hyun government that North Korea would not be considered as such.

However, the approach of the Lee government also included pressure and deterrence. And North Korea's behavior over the first three years of the Lee government led the latter to prioritize diplomatic, economic, and military pressure to address inter-Korean relations. In 2008, a North Korean soldier shot a South Korean tourist dead in Mount Kumgang. The Lee government requested an apology and a joint investigation of the killing. When North Korea refused, the Lee government decided to suspend tours to the mountain.[184] Later in the year, Seoul joined a UN resolution condemning North Korea's human rights record. Indeed, the Lee government's policy toward Pyongyang emphasized the role of values. The Kim Jong-il regime retaliated by closing communication lines between the two Koreas. They would reopen a few months later.[185] This suggested that the Lee government was not ruling out engagement, but pressure was part of its strategy.

Inter-Korean tensions escalated dramatically throughout 2009–2010. In May 2009, Pyongyang conducted its second nuclear test shortly after Barack Obama had become the new U.S. president.[186] North Korea also conducted a record number of missile tests throughout the year.[187] This ratcheted up tensions between the two Koreas. In July, Pyongyang conducted large-scale DDoS attacks against South Korea and the United States. It was one of North Korea's first publicly known, large scale cyberattacks against Seoul.[188] From then on, this became a new variable for South Korea to consider in its relations with the North. In November of the same year, a North Korean vessel crossed the NLL separating the territorial waters of the two Koreas in the West Sea. The ensuing battle between the two Koreas left at least one North Korean sailor dead.[189] In March 2010, North Korea sank the ROK Navy corvette *Cheonan*, killing forty-six South Korean personnel.[190]

This was the gravest confrontation between the two Koreas since the Korean War, and it considerably strained inter-Korean relations.

The Lee government responded to the *Cheonan* sinking with the "May 24 Measures," which included "proactive deterrence" allowing a preemptive attack by the South Korean armed forces, suspension of all official economic exchanges with the exception of the Kaesong Industrial Complex, and a halt to all transfers to North Korea including humanitarian aid.[191] As a result of the measures, Pyongyang once again cut off the communication lines between the two Koreas.[192] Furthermore, Pyongyang engaged in a new provocation in November. North Korea fired around 170 artillery shells in the direction of Yeonpyeong Island, a South Korean territory located just south of the NLL. Two South Korean soldiers and two civilians were killed.[193] The Lee government responded by temporarily suspending visits to the Kaesong Industrial Complex and by prohibiting inter-Korean Red Cross exchanges.[194] Furthermore, the 2010 South Korean Defense White Paper had a noticeably harsh approach toward North Korea for the first time since the Kim Dae-jung years.[195] And Seoul developed its first cybersecurity strategies: the Comprehensive Countermeasures for National Cyber Security Crisis of 2009 and the Masterplan for National Cybersecurity of 2011.[196] However, they were relatively limited in their scope.

Yet the Lee government continued to pursue engagement with North Korea as well. The two Koreas held secret talks in April–June 2011 to hold a bilateral summit. Lee thought that the talks could reset inter-Korean relations after the tensions of 2010.[197] Meanwhile, the Kaesong Industrial Complex continued to operate. And South Korea resumed aid to the North, albeit in more modest amounts compared to the Roh Moo-hyun years.[198] In addition, the two Koreas restored communication lines in 2011 as well.[199] The Lee government also stood ready to resume the Six-Party Talks.[200] In short, the Lee government continued to believe that diplomacy should be part of its toolkit to approach relations with Pyongyang.

The Lee government clearly emphasized deterrence as its preferred approach toward North Korea following the *Cheonan* sinking and Yeonpyeong shelling. In 2011, the South Korean government published Defense Reform Plan 307. The plan refocused South Korean defense strategy on the immediate threat posed by North Korea. Significantly, deterrence was seen as a way to move Pyongyang toward nonbelligerent positions by making it clear that forceful reunification was not an option.[201] In 2012, Seoul unveiled the Kill Chain strategy and the Korea Air and Missile Defense (KAMD) system. The Kill Chain strategy involves the early detection of an imminent North Korean missile attack through surveillance and intelligence assets and the preemptive destruction of Pyongyang's missile launch capabilities through precision-guided munitions.[202] The KAMD, meanwhile, is a domestically produced early warning radar system to track down North Korean missile launches together with a domestically produced missile system to destroy the North Korean missiles.[203] In order to develop these programs, the Lee government successfully negotiated a review of the Ballistic Missile Guidelines with the Obama administration. After the review, the range limit for South Korean missiles went up from three hundred kilometers (185 mi) to eight hundred kilometers (~500 mi).[204] For the Lee government, these deterrence systems also served the end of increasing South Korean autonomy, particularly in the hypothetical case of abandonment by the United States.

In fact, the Lee government sought to develop a wide array of military capabilities to deter North Korea beyond missile systems. In 2008, Seoul became only the fifth operator of the Aegis Combat System worldwide. The system allows the ROK Navy to track and guide weapons against enemy targets.[205] The contract to acquire the system had been signed by the Kim Dae-jung government and survived the Roh Moo-hyun government, demonstrating continuity in South Korean defense policy and, more broadly, grand strategy. Lee also discussed with the United Kingdom the possibility of acquiring nuclear-powered submarines.[206] The talks proved unsuccessful but were proof of Seoul's willingness to acquire a capability that would give it a significant advantage over Pyongyang. South Korea also started development of a homegrown space rocket in 2010, conducting its first test in 2013.[207] Even though the space rocket program had civilian purposes, it also had military ramifications. And as a result of the Defense Reform Plan 307, South Korea established a cyber command to counter Pyongyang's cyberattacks.[208] South Korean grand strategy toward North Korea now included the development of holistic military capabilities.

The United States

Lee thought that the two previous liberal administrations had weakened the alliance between Seoul and Washington due to their pursuit of autonomy and an (alleged) narrow focus on North Korea. Once inaugurated as president he argued that he would "restore" the alliance. He referred to his approach as the "Future-oriented Alliance" (미래지향적 동맹관계).[209] This was an obvious nod to the policy pursued by the Kim Young-sam government, with Lee using the same term. Both Kim Dae-jung and Roh Moo-hyun had expanded the scope of the ROK–U.S. alliance beyond the North Korean security threat. Thus, Lee built on the grand strategy already under implementation by his two predecessors, who in turn were building on their own (conservative) predecessors' approaches. Plus, Lee continued to take steps toward enhancing South Korean autonomy within the framework of the alliance.

In June 2009, Lee and Obama issued the Joint Vision for the Alliance of the United States of America and the Republic of Korea.[210] The joint declaration indeed focused on cooperation in the areas of trade, Asia-Pacific politics and security, and global governance. But before focusing on those matters, the declaration stated: "The United States-Republic of Korea Mutual Defense Treaty remains the cornerstone of the U.S.-ROK security relationship, which has guaranteed peace and stability on the Korean Peninsula and in Northeast Asia for over fifty years."[211] That is, the primary focus continued to be the deterrence of North Korea. And indeed, in 2010 Seoul and Washington agreed to the Strategic Planning Guidance to address the new threats coming from Pyongyang, including its expanding nuclear and missile program. The guidance, thus, called for "extended deterrence" and closer cooperation between the two allies.[212] The alliance continued to be a cornerstone of Seoul's strategy to protect itself against Pyongyang.

The Lee government also saw the *Cheonan* sinking and Yeonpyeong shelling as catalysts to stronger cooperation with Washington. The ROK Navy conducted joint naval exercises with its U.S. counterpart in the East and West Seas.[213] South Korea and the United States also held their first-ever "2-plus-2" talks, involving the foreign and defense ministers of both countries.[214] They also launched a trilateral dialogue with Japan, first suggested by the Obama administration, to discuss North Korean issues and display trilateral unity.[215] The Lee government thereby mixed the ROK–U.S. alliance with diplomatic means to deter North Korea.

At the same time, the Lee government continued to move ahead with increasing South Korea's independent military capabilities to protect itself against North Korea autonomously. Certainly, Lee renegotiated the

OPCON transfer agreement agreed under Roh Moo-hyun. In June 2010 the South Korean president and Obama announced that transfer would happen in 2015 rather than in 2012, as previously agreed.[216] But Lee was indeed committed to the transfer, even though he thought that Seoul needed more time to be ready, especially following North Korea's second nuclear test.[217]

The Lee government also prioritized renegotiation of KORUS after approval by the U.S. Congress had stalled. From its perspective, KORUS would allow South Korea to make use of trade as a means to solidify the ROK–U.S. alliance and to deepen Seoul's integration in the world economy. A businessman before entering politics, Lee believed in the benefits of free markets and economic flows.[218] Seoul and Washington renegotiated the deal to give U.S. carmakers easier access to the South Korean market, after which the U.S. Congress approved the deal in October 2011. KORUS entered into force in March 2012.[219] This was one of several economic means that the Lee government used to deepen ties with the United States and boost economic integration. In October 2008 and as the global financial crisis (GFC) was spreading from the United States to the rest of the world, the BOK and the Federal Reserve signed a $30 billion swap deal.[220] As recovery from the crisis took hold, South Korean trade and investment levels went up. They reached a record $104.09 in exports and imports and a stock of $31.79 billion, respectively, by 2013, the year when Lee left office.[221] They included KNOC's participation in a shale gas production project.[222] On the other hand, there were two disputes between South Korea and the United States in the WTO during Lee's presidency.[223] And in 2008, Lee had to backtrack on his decision to completely lift a ban on beef exports from the United States following massive street protests in South Korea.[224]

South Korea's end to be recognized as an influential middle power also benefited from strong relations with the United States. To begin with, Seoul made use of its diplomatic corps to host the fifth G20 summit in 2010 and the second Nuclear Security Summit (NSS) in 2012. Both were initiatives from the Obama administration, the first one a response to the GFC and the second one with the goal of preventing nuclear terrorism. South Korea was the first Asian country to host the G20 summit, which resulted in a declaration focusing on economic matters.[225] It was also the first country other than the United States to host the NSS, with the Seoul summit resulting in a joint communiqué.[226] South Korea was therefore using its diplomatic power to strengthen the alliance with the United States, along with the benefits that the hosting brought to its middle power status.

In addition, the Lee government also harnessed its military capabilities to strengthen relations with the United States and promote South Korea's role as a middle power. In March 2009, the Lee government dispatched the Cheonghae Unit to the Gulf of Aden. Formally known as the ROK Navy Somali Sea Escort Task Group, the unit joined a multilateral coalition fighting against piracy in the waters off the coast of Somalia. The Cheonghae Unit joined Combined Maritime Forces 151 (CMF 151), a multilateral maritime partnership put together by the United States.[227] In April 2010, the Cheonghae Unit led CMF 151 for the first time.[228] Also, in 2009 South Korea dispatched peacekeepers in support of the UN stabilization mission in Haiti, where the United States was also a contributor.[229] In 2010, Seoul dispatched its army to Afghanistan after Obama launched a military surge to bring stability to the country.[230] This was a signature policy of the Obama administration. Support from the Lee government would thus show that the alliance mattered beyond the Korean Peninsula. On top of that, Seoul contributed its troops to the UN mission in South Sudan, established in 2011 and also involving Washington's army.[231]

In 2010, Lee posited that public diplomacy was one of the three pillars of South Korean foreign policy. Along with soft power, it continued to be part of Seoul's toolkit to influence relations with Washington. Most notably, the South Korean Embassy opened a Korean Cultural Center in the U.S. capital in October 2010.[232] That same year, the Korea Foundation opened its second U.S. office in Los Angeles.[233] It also continued to provide funding to U.S. organizations. Concurrently, new King Sejong institutes opened across the country. Meanwhile, the South Korean government continued to provide sponsorship to the Korean Music Festival in California. (The name changed to Korea Times Music Festival in 2013.) And in October 2012, the South Korean government sponsored KCON's first-ever edition. Held in Los Angeles, this private initiative led by one of the biggest South Korean entertainment companies would go on to become the biggest K-pop festival in the world.[234] The Lee government was supporting the private sector, which in turn was promoting South Korean soft power in the United States. In March 2013, the South Korean government took a step further as the Korea Creative Content Agency (KOCCA) affiliated with the Ministry of Culture, Sports and Tourism launched a K-pop and South Korean contemporary music festival in Texas called K-Pop Night

Out.[235] Even though it took place a few days after Lee left office, the festival was planned during his tenure. This was a case of the Lee government's directly promoting South Korean culture, as a way, among others, to support the country's grand strategy.

China

Under the aegis of its "Strategic Cooperative Partnership," Lee built on the rapprochement between South Korea and China brought about by his predecessors to strengthen links with Beijing.[236] But Lee went a step further, making use of trade as a means to deepen economic relations with Seoul's neighbor. Thus, South Korea and China launched negotiations for a bilateral FTA in May 2012.[237] Lee thought that stronger trade relations with China were crucial for South Korea's economic prosperity. In particular, he wanted South Korean firms to have a competitive advantage to target China's growing middle classes.[238] The South Korean president also thought that the country's firms could maintain a technological advantage over their Chinese competitors and therefore would not be disadvantaged by a bilateral FTA.[239] By the time negotiations with China were launched, too, South Korea already had its trade deals with the United States and the European Union in place. South Korea could become the first country in the world to have bilateral trade agreements with the "big three" global economies in place. Negotiations to sign a bilateral agreement, in any case, would finish only under the Park Geun-hye government.

The BOK, meanwhile, signed a bilateral swap arrangement with the People's Bank of China in 2009. The $27 billion deal was almost as big as the deal signed between the BOK and the Federal Reserve.[240] In addition to this government-led deal, South Korean firms continued to invest heavily in China. By 2013, when Lee left the presidency, South Korean investment stock had grown to $61.26 billion—up from $32.22 billion in 2009, a year after Lee was inaugurated.[241] The bilateral FTA that Lee supported would also help to boost investment. South Korea was thus using its economic means to balance its economic relationship with China vis-à-vis the United States. Lee was not openly suggesting that South Korea could play a balancing role as Roh Moo-hyun had done, but he indeed believed that Seoul could benefit from its economic relationship with both in spite of any tensions between Washington and Beijing.[242] In common with his predecessors, Lee believed that economic diversification via stronger trade and investment links with China would enhance Seoul's autonomy.

With the Six-Party Talks effectively over, it became more difficult for South Korea to use its diplomatic corps to address relations with its neighbor. Yet Lee was among dozens of world leaders who traveled to China for the opening of the 2008 Beijing Olympic Games. Shortly after, Chinese leader Hu Jintao reciprocated by visiting South Korea for a summit.[243] South Korean diplomats increasingly engaged with their Chinese counterparts in international organizations and other fora. This helped to foster understanding and better relations with China.[244] Noticeably, South Korea, China, and Japan held their first-ever separate trilateral summit in December 2008.[245] An idea first proposed by Roh Moo-hyun that did not materialize during his time in office, the summit became an annual feature during Lee's tenure, and three parties decided to establish a Trilateral Cooperation Secretariat in 2011 in Seoul.[246] In addition, the South Korean and Chinese ministries of Defense agreed to establish a direct hotline to prevent accidental clashes between their militaries during their first-ever strategic defense dialogue.[247] The Lee government also engaged with the Hu administration to address the North Korean nuclear issue including potential resumption of the Six-Party Talks.[248] Diplomacy was one of the tools used by Lee to pursue its end.

Public diplomacy and soft power were two other means that Seoul continued to use in its relationship with Beijing, following Lee's call to make the first a pillar of South Korean foreign policy. By the time Lee had taken office, these means were firmly included in the country's grand strategy. Thus, the government continued to open King Sejong institutes across China. KBS also continued to run its Korea-China Music Festival with CCTV.[249] And the Korea Foundation increased the number of projects and level of funding to Chinese institutions.

Yet South Korea also used its military capabilities and diplomatic corps to protect itself against the potential military threat coming from China. The new Ballistic Missile Guidelines agreed between Lee and Obama theoretically put Chinese territory within South Korea's range for the first time. Furthermore, trilateral cooperation between South Korea, the United States, and Japan targeted China and not only North Korea.[250] In 2009, Lee proposed five-party talks excluding North Korea to discuss Pyongyang's nuclear issue. This had the potential to downgrade China's role as host of the Six-Party Talks. In 2010, China refused to condemn North

Korea for the *Cheonan* sinking, implicitly casting doubt on whether North Korea was the culprit. Lee hit back at China's inaction, arguing that no country could deny that North Korea was behind the attack.[251] Meanwhile, China argued that the Lee government's approach toward Pyongyang was counterproductive and was exacerbating nuclear tensions in the Korean Peninsula.[252] This led to a new diplomatic rift between Seoul and Beijing. The rise of China was a factor influencing South Korean grand strategy, and the Lee administration was willing to use the means at its disposal to limit the harm that this could create for South Korea.

Park Geun-hye (2013–2017)

North Korea

Park Geun-hye took office in 2013 as the second conservative president in a row. Even though she was from the same party, Park had been critical of several of Lee Myung-back's policies, including his North Korea policy. According to Park, Lee's approach to relations with Pyongyang had been counterproductive.[253] The new president sought to prioritize engagement without abandoning deterrence and pressure. Park's approach to North Korea was labeled the "Trust-building Process," and it focused on boosting trust between the governments, militaries, and peoples of the two Koreas, economic support for North Korea, as well as the internationalization of a potential inter-Korean peace process through the Northeast Asia Peace and Cooperation Initiative (NAPCI). (This would include China and the United States, which showed that Park agreed that the two East Asian great powers had to be part of any attempt to deal with North Korea or otherwise Seoul would not be able to autonomously move ahead with an improvement in inter-Korean relations.) At the same time, the Park government committed to continuing to strengthen South Korea's defense capabilities.[254] The MND would continue to take a harsh approach toward North Korea in its white papers during Park's tenure.[255] In short, Park's North Korea policy carried on from South Korea's well-established grand strategy means. This was logical, since the end of inter-Korean reconciliation and reunification was a core component of Park's trust-building process.

The Park government continued to implement engagement policies pursued by previous administrations, which made use of South Korean economic means. Starting with trade, Seoul continued to operate the Kaesong Industrial Complex together with Pyongyang. The complex was briefly shut down in April 2013 after North Korea made it more difficult for South Korean employees to access it, but it reopened in September.[256] Seoul also continued to provide aid to North Korea.[257] And Park herself was willing to hold a summit with Kim Jong-un, who had replaced his father as North Korean leader upon his death.[258] The Park government also indicated that South Korea supported the resumption of the Six-Party Talks.[259]

Moreover, Park launched NAPCI as a flagship initiative to support inter-Korean trust-building. According to the Park government, NAPCI should focus on nontraditional security issues as a way to build trust and promote cooperation between participating countries—helping to create a multilateral framework in support of inter-Korean cooperation. Furthermore, Seoul would use NAPCI to promote economic cooperation between the two Koreas, China, and Russia in areas such as energy and logistics.[260] This way, the Park government was reinvigorating the centrality of Northeast Asian initiatives that previous presidents had also suggested—especially Kim Young-sam's NEASED—and which the Lee government had not been able to pursue because the Six-Party Talks had not reconvened.

North Korea's actions eventually made the Park administration prioritize deterrence and abandon most engagement initiatives. Two weeks before Park's inauguration, North Korea had conducted its third nuclear test.[261] Also in 2013, Pyongyang had cut off communication lines with Seoul before reopening them. North Korea continued to strike the South with cyberattacks, including on the military and government units.[262] Throughout 2014–2016, North Korea set new annual records in its number of missile tests. Furthermore, the range of the missiles tested increased, and in 2015 Pyongyang conducted its first submarine-launched ballistic missile (SLBM) tests.[263] Finally, North Korea conducted two new nuclear tests in January and September 2016, respectively.[264]

In this context, the Park government decisively pursued the deterrence and pressure component of its North Korea approach. Seoul issued the National Cybersecurity Measure in 2013.[265] Directly related to North Korea and as a starting point, Seoul continued to develop the Kill Chain strategy and the KAMD system unveiled by the Lee government. In December 2014 and leveraging the ROK–U.S. alliance, South Korea signed the Trilateral Intelligence Sharing Arrangement (TISA) with the United States and Japan. TISA allowed Seoul and Tokyo to access Washington's military intelligence on North Korea.[266] Following North Korea's fourth nuclear test in January 2016, the Park government took the decision to shut down the Kaesong Industrial Complex in an exercise of its trade power.[267] North Korea reacted by again closing the direct communication lines with Seoul.[268] But this did not stop the latter from continuing to strengthen its deterrence and pressure measures. The Park government also encouraged the National Assembly to pass the North Korea Human Rights Act. First introduced by conservative lawmakers in 2005, the act was finally adopted in March 2016.[269] In addition, Seoul also started to pursue development of a domestically produced jet fighter in earnest following Pyongyang's fourth nuclear test, as its own military capabilities became even more central to the Park government's North Korea policy.[270] In July 2016, Seoul and Washington agreed that the latter would deploy its Terminal High Altitude Area Defense (THAAD) missile defense system in South Korea. The South Korean military had requested information about the system in 2013, but the Park government had hesitated about whether to formally request its deployment. Following North Korea's fourth nuclear test and missile test campaign, Seoul decided to go ahead with the request.[271]

After Pyongyang conducted its fifth nuclear test in September, the Park government further upped the ante. Shortly after the test, the MND announced the Korean Massive Punishment and Retaliation (KMPR) strategy. This strategy leverages a range of kinetic and nonkinetic South Korean capabilities to strike military and government facilities in North Korea in retaliation to any attack from Pyongyang.[272] Together with the Kill Chain and KAMD, KMPR came to be part of a "three axis" defense system. Seoul also continued to develop its own missile programs, as well as other military capabilities to deter and retaliate against Pyongyang. In November 2016, the Park government signed the General Security of Military Information Agreement (GSOMIA) with Japan. The agreement allowed Seoul and Tokyo to share military intelligence related to North Korea and other matters directly.[273] It was the first military agreement between both countries since Korea had become independent in 1945. This showed the extent to which Seoul had decided to focus on deterrence. In any case, Park continued to be open to hold a dialogue with Kim Jong-un if Pyongyang shifted its behavior and considered the possibility of denuclearization.[274]

The United States

In May 2013, Park traveled to the United States. Upon her arrival, Seoul and Washington issued the Joint Declaration in Commemoration of the Sixtieth Anniversary of the Alliance between the Republic of Korea and the United States. The joint declaration elevated the alliance to a "Comprehensive Strategic Alliance" involving security, politics, economics, culture, and people-to-people, and spanning beyond the Korean Peninsula into regional and global affairs. The joint declaration also brought values to the forefront of the alliance, stating that the "shared values of liberty, democracy, and a market economy" underpinned relations between the two countries.[275] Following from and reinforcing South Korean grand strategy, the Park government saw the ROK–U.S. alliance as a cornerstone of Seoul's foreign policy and international relations. It was not an impediment to South Korean autonomy, but an enabler instead.

The joint declaration, certainly, reinforced Washington's commitment to supporting South Korea's security in the face of the threat posed by Pyongyang. The two allies stated, "The United States remains firmly committed to the defense of the Republic of Korea, including through extended deterrence and the full range of U.S. military capabilities, both conventional and nuclear." Indeed, South Korea and the United States reinforced cooperation to address the North Korea threat. The TISA agreement signed in 2014 allowed Seoul—as well as Tokyo—to access U.S. intelligence on North Korea's nuclear and missile programs. This way, South Korea could request access to intelligence that it otherwise would not be able to get hold of, given Washington's superior intelligence gathering capabilities, including via satellites and international networks. TISA reinforced trilateral South Korea–U.S.–Japan dialogue on North Korea, which the Park government continued.[276] In addition, the Strategic Planning Guidelines signed by the Lee Myung-bak government and the Obama administration continued to be in place. Seoul continued the development of its missile program with support of U.S. firms during the Park years as well. Above all, Washington agreed to Seoul's request to deploy the THAAD missile defense system. This made South Korea only the fourth country and the first one in Asia to acquire this system.

Furthermore, South Korea joined the U.S.-led campaign to increase pressure on North Korea. Making use of its economic means, the Park government duly implemented the UN Security Council resolutions passed in January and March 2013 after North Korea conducted a satellite launch and its third nuclear test, respectively. The Park government was then involved in discussions about new UN Security Council sanctions following Pyongyang's fourth nuclear test. A new round of sanctions was passed in March 2016, with yet another round approved the following November.[277] In addition, South Korea's North Korea Human Rights Act supplemented a similar act passed by the U.S. Congress in 2004.[278]

The Park government continued OPCON transfer discussions but shifted from a fixed date to a conditions-based approach. In 2013, Seoul and Washington agreed that transfer would happen when South Korea met certain conditions. These conditions were agreed by the ministries of Defense of the two countries during their 2014 Security Consultative Meeting: acquisition by the South Korean military of the necessary capabilities, development of the ability to counter North Korea's missile and nuclear weapons programs, and a stable security environment in the Korean Peninsula.[279] Once South Korea met these three conditions, its autonomy would be enhanced. However, meeting these conditions did not mean weakening the ROK–U.S. alliance. Seoul's 2014 Defense White Paper indicated that Seoul should focus on autonomous and future-oriented defense capabilities, but it also made clear that the ROK–U.S. alliance would continue to be a cornerstone of its security and would be called upon as necessary.[280]

In fact, South Korea continued to use its ever-expanding military capabilities and aid as means to support U.S. security goals elsewhere. The Cheonghae Unit continued to be deployed in the waters of the Gulf of Aden. The army continued to be deployed in Afghanistan until 2014, when the Obama administration announced a plan to withdraw from the country.[281] Seoul continued its contribution to UN missions also involving the United States such as those in Liberia and South Sudan. The South Korean military was also dispatched to the Philippines after it was hit by Typhoon Haiyan in November 2013, with the United States leading assistance and rehabilitation efforts.[282] South Korea, meanwhile, continued to provide economic support and capacity-building expertise to the U.S. reconstruction missions in Afghanistan and Iraq. Certainly, these actions also allowed Seoul to be more widely recognized as a middle power addressing issues beyond East Asia.

With KORUS having entered into force, trade and investment between South Korea and the United States continued to grow. This continued to allow Seoul to use trade and investment as a means to strengthen the alliance with the United States to protect against external threats, as well as to become better integrated in the world economy. Most notably, in 2013 South Korean investment to the United States exceeded investment in the other direction for the first time. By 2017, the year Park left office, South Korean investment stock in the United States had reached $55.56 billion. This was more than 2.5 times the amount in 2011, the year when KORUS had been approved.[283] Meanwhile, trade grew from $104.09 billion in 2013 to $118.53 in 2017.[284] On the other hand, the Park government decided against South Korea's joining the Trans-Pacific Partnership (TPP). This was a signature policy of the Obama administration, but Seoul did not see the economic benefit of joining considering its network of FTAs including KORUS itself.[285] This demonstrated that Seoul was willing to exercise its autonomy in its relations with Washington. Furthermore, South Korea launched two WTO disputes against the United States during the Park government.[286]

Similarly to previous South Korean presidents, Park also emphasized soft power and public diplomacy as part of Seoul's policy toolkit to implement its grand strategy. The Korea Foundation continued to collaborate with U.S. institutions, Korean cultural centers continued their program of activities, and the King Sejong Institute opened new centers across the United States. KOCCA continued to run K-Pop Night Out in Texas as well. KCON added New Jersey to its California festival. The expansion was supported by South Korean government agencies covering culture, tourism, and food. The government also continued to support the Korea Times Music Festival in California. This was a sign that the Park government saw K-pop as a means to enhance South Korea's middle power status and reinforce its grand strategy.

China

Park continued the grand strategy pursued by previous South Korean presidents when it came to relations with China, mixing engagement using different means while seeking to strengthen its security against a possible military threat. Park, however, took engagement to new heights in the history of South Korea–China relations. Shortly after taking office, the Park government released its strategy toward China. Labeled "New Korea-China Relations," the strategy called for multifaceted relations between Seoul and Beijing, including politics, economics, security, and culture.[287] The strategy made clear that the Park government favored engagement and good relations with Beijing. In a symbolic gesture, Park sent an envoy to China before sending one to the United States while president-elect.[288] This showed the importance that she ascribed to good relations with the Chinese government, which could help to enable South Korean autonomy via the diversification of its foreign relations.

Park used diplomacy as an entry point to foster good relations with China. In June 2013, Park traveled to China.[289] During the visit, Park reaffirmed Seoul's commitment to reinforcing the strategic cooperative partnership between the two countries.[290] Thirteen months later, Chinese President Xi Jinping reciprocated and traveled to South Korea.[291] South Korean and Chinese diplomats, meanwhile, engaged in discussions about potential resumption of the Six-Party Talks as well as, more broadly, diplomatic cooperation to address security issues in East Asia.[292] In 2014, Seoul and Beijing finally signed a memorandum of understanding to establish a bilateral hotline between their ministries of Defense, as agreed years before.[293] One year later, the armed forces of the two countries established another hotline to prevent accidental clashes at sea and in the air. The People Liberation Army's (PLA) Northern Theater Command, with responsibility for the Korean Peninsula, Russia's Siberia, Mongolia, and the West Sea signed the deal on behalf of the Chinese side.[294] Diplomatic links between Seoul and Beijing arguably reached their peak since their diplomatic normalization when Park visited Beijing in September 2015 to attend a military parade to commemorate the seventieth anniversary of the end of World War II. Park was the only president of a major democratic country to attend the parade.[295] Shortly after, Park met her Chinese and Japanese counterparts to resume the trilateral dialogue between the three countries.[296] The dialogue had been paused while China underwent a change in president. Diplomacy with China was helping South Korea to bolster its autonomy by diversifying its foreign policy links and strengthening relations with one of East Asia's two great powers.

The Park government, in any case, prioritized trade and investment as the means to improve relations with China, exercise its autonomy, and achieve deeper integration in the world economy. Furthermore, trade and investment could help to reduce potential tensions between the two countries and thus enhance South Korea's security. Above all, the Park government moved swiftly with bilateral FTA negotiations after they had proceeded relatively slowly under Lee Myung-bak. In fact, Park had decided that trade negotiations would move from MOFA to the new Ministry of Trade, Industry and Energy (MOTIE). But trade continued to be as geostrategically important to South Korea as it had been until then. Seoul and Beijing announced that they had reached a deal in November 2014, signed the FTA in June 2015, and quickly approved it so that it entered into force in December of the same year.[297] In addition, South Korea launched trilateral FTA negotiations with China and Japan upon Park's taking office.[298]

Seoul also made use of its economic means to strengthen links with China in other ways. In 2015, South Korea became a founding member of the Asian Infrastructure Investment Bank (AIIB). This was China's response to the World Bank, where it felt underrepresented. Even though the Obama administration was opposed to the AIIB and urged its allies and partners not to join, South Korea was among several that did become members of the bank.[299] In addition, the investment stock by South Korean firms in China stood at an all-time record $95.06 in 2016.[300]

South Korea also continued to use its soft power and public diplomacy to deepen links with China. The Korean Cultural centers in Beijing and Shanghai continued their programs of activities. The King Sejong Institute opened new sites across the country. The Korea-China Music Festival continued to be held annually.[301] And the Korea Foundation continued to fund activities that enhanced knowledge about South Korea and its foreign policy in China.

Still, South Korea also was one of the first countries to become cautious about the rise of China. In December 2013, South Korea extended its Air Defense Identification Zone (ADIZ) in response to China's decision to do the same. The ADIZs of both countries now overlapped in the West Sea and even over Ieodo, an islet that is part of South Korea.[302] Furthermore, the GSOMIA agreement signed by South Korea and Japan could potentially include intelligence sharing related to Chinese activities as well given the close relationship between Beijing and Pyongyang. South Korea's missile and other programs such as a domestically produced jet fighter could potentially target China. Also, Beijing labeled the Park government's North Korea policy "counterproductive" once Seoul decided to prioritize pressure.[303] This showed frictions in their approach toward

Pyongyang. This was also the time when China started to ramp up cyber-attacks on South Korea, introducing a new threat for Seoul to contend with.[304]

Most notably, however, China reacted negatively to South Korea's announcement that it would host the U.S. THAAD system. Even before the deployment, Chinese Foreign Minister Wang Yi warned that the deployment could affect China's "legitimate national security interests."[305] THAAD was targeted at North Korea, but it could indeed be seen as a tool to deter China and potentially protect South Korea against missile launches by its neighbor. China implemented a series of economic sanctions on South Korea, including inspections on Lotte eventually forcing the South Korean conglomerate to leave China. This was the *chaebol* on whose land THAAD would be deployed. In addition, Beijing banned tourist group visits to South Korea and effectively stopped K-pop acts from performing in China.[306] The Xi administration also suspended the bilateral strategic defense dialogues between its Ministry of Defense and South Korea's in 2015.[307] Beijing also increased its number of cyberattacks on South Korean targets.[308] The Park government, nonetheless, did not relent. The THAAD dispute showed that the ROK–U.S. alliance, the division of Korea, and the rise of China were important factors driving South Korean grand strategy toward putting the U.S. alliance about other means to achieve its goals.

Moon Jae-in (2017–2022)

North Korea

Moon Jae-in came to power in 2017, restoring liberal rule after two consecutive conservative presidents. The new South Korean leader set about to introduce a new North Korea strategy that would address what in his view were the failures of the policies implemented by his two conservative predecessors. The Moon government issued its policy, "A Korean Peninsula of Peace and Prosperity," to pursue the "peaceful coexistence and coprosperity of the two Koreas," a necessary interim step leading to eventual reunification.[309] Moon explicitly referred to the inter-Korean agreements signed following the bilateral summits of 2000 and 2007.[310] Having served under Roh Moo-hyun including leading preparations for the 2007 inter-Korean summit, Moon was committed to prioritizing an improvement in relations with North Korea. To this end, he sought ways to restart inter-Korean summits, restore economic cooperation between the two Koreas, and reduce tensions in the Korean Peninsula. At the same time, however, Moon emphasized "peace through strength."[311] This was a code word for an acceleration in military spending that significantly boosted the autonomous deterrence capabilities of the South Korean military. The thinking behind it was that North Korea would opt for nonbelligerent options after realizing that a military takeover of the South was not possible.

In fact, North Korea's behavior and the ROK–U.S. alliance were the main factors driving the Moon government's policy toward Pyongyang throughout 2017. The Kim Jong-un regime conducted another nuclear test, its first-ever ICBM tests, and a record number of missile tests that year.[312] It also continued its cyberattacks on South Korea.[313] At the same time, Donald Trump had been inaugurated as U.S. president shortly before Moon had taken office. The new U.S. president engaged in a campaign to criticize partners and cast doubt on the value of U.S. alliances.[314] As a result, the Moon government launched several projects to boost its autonomous deterrence capabilities against North Korea while also seeking to work together with the United States as much as possible. In July 2017, the new president announced Defense Reform 2.0, which, among others, called for South Korea to develop asymmetric capabilities to counter the nuclear threat from North Korea.[315] The Moon government also agreed to continue implementation of the THAAD antimissile system.[316] Furthermore, the new U.S. president and Trump agreed to new Ballistic Missile Guidelines that removed payload limits on South Korean missiles.[317] South Korea continued to implement existing sanctions on North Korea. The Moon government also issued the National Cyber Security Strategy in 2019. More generally, the Moon government was the first to develop a comprehensive cybersecurity strategy also including the MND.[318] Meanwhile, the MND continued to label Pyongyang an "enemy" in its white papers,[319] which showed that the Moon government was willing to take a tough stance against North Korea if necessary.

At the same time, the Moon government pressed for the resumption of diplomacy with North Korea to a larger extent than Lee Myung-bak and Park Geun-hye had done. The new South Korean president stressed that he saw diplomacy, trade, and economic aid—means that Seoul possessed—as the way to improve inter-Korean relations.[320] South Korea prioritized this approach toward North Korea throughout 2018, when the PyeongChang Winter Olympic Games provided a diplomatic opening with the North. Throughout the year, the two Koreas held three summits, as well as several bilateral meetings including between their militaries.[321] The two Koreas also restored severed communication lines that year.[322] South Korea also sought to implement an economic plan initially centered around the reopening of the Kaesong Industrial Complex, the resumption of tourism tours in Mount Kumgang, and the rebuilding and upgrading of railroad tracks connecting South Korea with Russia and therefore Eurasia through North Korean territory.[323] Seoul also supported the historic summits that Trump and Kim Jong-un held in Singapore in June 2018 and in Hanoi in February 2019. And in 2020, the MND removed the designation of Pyongyang as an "enemy" from its white paper.[324] Furthermore the MND also rebranded the "three axis" defense system to a "system to respond to nuclear and other weapons of mass destruction" and focused it on omnidirectional threats rather than North Korea only.[325] The hope was that this would make it seem less threatening to Pyongyang. Meanwhile, the Moon government increased aid to North Korea compared to the final years of the Park government.[326] Political and cultural exchanges resumed after they had stopped toward the end of Park's years in office.[327]

Concurrently, the Moon government launched the Northeast Asia Peace and Cooperation Platform (NAPC) including the Northeast Asia Plus Community of Responsibility (NAPCR). Building on Kim Young-sam's NEASED and Park's NAPCI, NAPC and NAPCR called for multilateral cooperation in Northeast Asia as a way to strengthen regional links and integrate North Korea in cross-country networks.[328] Seoul believed that the economic integration of North Korea in Northeast Asia would provide incentives for the Kim regime to become less provocative and prioritize economic development over nuclear weapons and missiles.[329] With the Six-Party Talks effectively over, NAPC highlighted the possibility of including actors from outside the region such as ASEAN or the EU contributing to the initiative.[330] Crucially, NAPC also indicated that Moon understood that China and the United States would have to be part of any resolution to inter-Korean enmity, so South Korean autonomy in this respect could be served only by involving Beijing and Washington in diplomacy with Pyongyang. U.S.-North Korea diplomacy faltered, and the program was never implemented.

Following the failure of the Hanoi summit, North Korea again shifted its behavior and resumed missile tests. As a result, the Moon government accelerated development of "peace through strength." In particular, Seoul focused on the development of its autonomous deterrent. The deployment of the "three axis" system was accelerated, with North Korea remaining the main target.[331] Deployment of THAAD continued unchanged. Likewise, Seoul continued to pursue its plans to acquire a nuclear-powered submarine.[332] In late 2019, South Korea joined the "Five Eyes" countries plus France and Japan to launch a group to share intelligence about North Korea.[333] In 2020, South Korea announced that it would develop a domestically produced aircraft carrier.[334] This could support any confrontation with the North. The Moon government continued to press for a diplomatic solution to the inter-Korean conundrum throughout 2020–2022, including a proposal for an end-of-war declaration that would help create the conditions for sustainable diplomacy to resume.[335] Pyongyang also restored bilateral communication lines again in 2021 after cutting them off in 2020.[336] Even so, following its grand strategy, Seoul continued to strengthen its military capabilities.

Indeed, 2021–2022 was a key period in the development of these capabilities. In March 2021, South Korea's Defense Acquisition Program Administration (DAPA) unveiled a new 2021–35 Core Technology Plan to develop high-tech defense capabilities.[337] In May of the same year, Seoul and Washington agreed that the Ballistic Missile Guidelines would be abolished and South Korea would be able to develop its missile program with no range or payload limitations. Moon hailed this as Seoul having "missile sovereignty."[338] That same year, Seoul rolled out its first domestically produced air fighter, announced acquisition of a domestically produced attack helicopter, decided to develop its first domestically produced frigate, became only the eighth country in the world to test an SLBM deployed from its first domestically produced submarine with SLBM capabilities, and tested its first domestically produced supersonic missile.[339] South Korea also unveiled its first homegrown space rocket, the NURI, which could have military as well as civilian uses.[340] Following a new North Korean ICBM test in March 2022, the Moon government reacted with an exceptional volley of missile tests launched from the ground, jets, and navy ships.[341]

Arguably, Moon took military capabilities and autonomous deterrence of North Korea to unprecedented levels.

The United States

Moon became South Korean president at a time when the ROK–U.S. alliance already clearly transcended the Korean Peninsula and even Northeast Asia. Thus, Moon labeled his U.S. policy "Comprehensive Alliance in All Fields" (모든 분야에서의 포괄적 동맹), going well beyond addressing the North Korean conundrum.[342] The Moon government believed that its alliance with the United States acted as a multiplier of South Korean grand strategy, not only in terms of relations with North Korea but also with regard to its global projection and ability to pursue autonomous goals and interests.[343] At the same time, the Moon government sought to become more autonomous from the United States and Seoul's alliance with Washington to develop a more independent grand strategy.[344] This built on the approach from previous governments pursuing both autonomy and joint work with the United States to amplify South Korean power.

When it came to North Korea policy, the Moon government understood that it needed to work together with the United States. Thus, Seoul sought to act as a balancer between Washington and Pyongyang as they embarked on a diplomatic path in 2018–2019. It was South Korea that shortly after the PyeongChang Winter Olympic Games transmitted Kim Jong-un's message to Trump that he would like to hold a bilateral summit.[345] At the same time, South Korea continued the rollout of THAAD and the implementation of sanctions on North Korea. These were policies pursued by both the Trump and Biden administrations. Seoul even acquiesced to a bilateral North Korea coordination policy working group that the Trump administration asked for in late 2018. The group halted the potential implementation of inter-Korean economic projects, a goal that the Moon government put on hold even if it was a core component of its North Korea policy.[346] This created tensions between Seoul and Washington, as did the Trump administration's refusal to provide sanctions exemptions to Seoul to pursue economic engagement with North Korea.[347] Once Biden took office, the Moon government coordinated policy to influence Washington's but was unable to obtain sanctions exemptions.[348] But in 2021, Seoul and Washington announced that they would conduct a full review of the Strategic Planning Guidance agreed in 2011 to better address the threats coming from a better-armed North Korea.[349]

The Moon government resumed negotiations to achieve wartime OPCON transfer as well. This goal was included in the Defense Reform 2.0, and Moon initially pushed for transfer to happen before the end of his nonrenewable five-year term.[350] Progress was slow during the Trump administration's term in office. However, in 2019 there was an initial operation capability assessment to proceed with OPCON transfer. This was a necessary step to fulfill the conditions set during the Park government. It involved an assessment of the South Korean military capabilities, and the Moon government accelerated acquisition of military assets and technologies from the United States. With the Biden administration in office, Seoul was able to reach agreement in 2021 to conduct a full operational capability assessment in 2022.[351] This would be a second phase to ascertain whether South Korea could fulfill the conditions for OPCON transfer. (The third phase would be full mission capability assessment.) Together with the termination of the Ballistic Missile Guidelines, these steps toward OPCON transfer fitted within Seoul's push for greater autonomy.

South Korea also sought to use its military capabilities to support Washington's policy. The Cheonghae Unit continued its deployment, as did South Korean peacekeepers in Liberia. Furthermore, in August 2021 the South Korean armed forces joined the United States and other allies in airlifting Afghan citizens out of Kabul as the city fell to the Taliban following the Biden administration's announcement that it would terminate the U.S. mission in Afghanistan.[352] Most notably, Seoul quietly joined Washington's strategy to contain China. Trump launched the Free and Open Indo-Pacific (FOIP) policy to counter what Washington saw as China's assertiveness in Asia and the Indian Ocean.[353] Following his first summit with the U.S. president, Moon posited that his New Southern Policy (NSP) was complementary to FOIP. Once Biden took office, Moon issued a joint statement with the new U.S. president pledging his support for freedom of navigation in the Taiwan Strait and the South China Sea, among others.[354] This was a clear reference to Beijing's alleged threat to international law in these waters. The ROK Navy also joined the United States and other countries such as Australia or Japan in conducting joint exercises designed to improve interoperability.[355] And in 2021, the South Korean Air Force signed an agreement with its U.S. counterpart to form a consultative body on space policy.[356]

South Korea also continued to make use of its economic means to manage relations with the United States. The Trump administration came to office threatening to tear apart FTAs that it thought were detrimental to the United States. Trump drafted a letter to terminate KORUS.[357] The Moon government was the first to reach an agreement, though, to revise its bilateral FTA with the United States. KORUS was revised in September 2017, with South Korea making a small number of concessions to avoid a protracted trade war with the United States.[358] Even so, the Moon government brought three cases against the United States in the WTO during the Trump years in office.[359] On a more positive sign, in March 2020 the BOK and the Federal Reserve signed a new bilateral swap arrangement as the onset of the COVID-19 pandemic brought financial stability.[360] Even though trade and investment were affected by this pandemic, they had achieved an annual volume of $132.29 billion and a record total stock of $63.66 billion, respectively, by the end of 2020.[361] Equally relevant, as competition between the United States and China heated up, South Korea became a key supporter of Washington's push to develop "resilient supply chains" not dependent on China.[362] South Korean world-leading *chaebol* in areas such as semiconductors or electric batteries announced the opening of factories in the United States, indirectly supporting South Korea's end to continue to be integrated in the world economy.[363]

Arguably, the Moon government sought to better integrate South Korean soft power into the country's grand strategy as well. In 2020, the Ministry of Culture, Sports and Tourism established Hallyu Support and Cooperation Division.[364] This could create a symbiotic relationship between South Korea's soft power and the country's grand strategic goals. KOCCA continued to run its music festival in Texas, rebranded as Korea Spotlight in 2018.[365] The Moon government had continued to support KCON in the United States. This was the case also in 2021, after the Hallyu Support and Cooperation Division was launched. The government also supported the Korea Times Music Festival. Meanwhile, the Moon government continued to make use of public diplomacy, with the Korean cultural centers, the King Sejong institutes, and the Korea Foundation continuing their activities across the United States.

China

Moon's grand strategy toward China mixed engagement and the strengthening of Seoul's defense capabilities against Beijing, as had been the case with his predecessors. Moon branded his policy "Substantive and Mature Strategic Cooperative Partnership," emphasizing similar themes to previous South Korean presidents. However, the Moon government had inherited poor relations with China as a result of the THAAD deployment. Throughout his presidency, China became more assertive toward its neighbors. As a result, the Moon government's policy leaned more toward containment of China as the years went by—especially compared to the Lee and Park governments. Yet there was no push to "decouple" from China, which indicated that Seoul understood that having cordial relations with Beijing enhanced its autonomy.

Emblematic of South Korea's policy toward China under Moon was the decision on THAAD. Seoul agreed to allow to continue the deployment of this antimissile system, despite criticisms from Beijing. But the Moon government also announced a "three no's" policy: no additional THAAD deployment, no participation in Washington's missile defense system network, and no trilateral military alliance with the United States and Japan.[366] This served to improve relations with China, and Moon visited South Korea's neighbor in December 2017.[367] Throughout 2018–2019, Seoul restarted its trilateral dialogue with Beijing and Tokyo, which had been interrupted partly due to the fallout from the THAAD issue.[368]

The Moon government implemented a policy of "strategic ambiguity" to approach the Sino-American competition.[369] In theory, this meant not choosing sides in the bilateral competition between Washington and Beijing. In practice, however, this was not the case. Most notably, Seoul's military buildup targeted Beijing and not only Pyongyang. The rebranding of the "three-axis" defense system was partly a way to manage relations with North Korea. But it was also related to Moon's policy to contain China.[370] Likewise, the 2021–35 Core Technology Plan had Beijing in mind, and not only Pyongyang.[371] The termination of the Ballistic Missile Guidelines allowed South Korea to develop missiles that could target anywhere in China; the announcement of the building of an aircraft carrier made sense in the context of defending freedom of navigation in the South China Sea and elsewhere; the unveiling of a domestically produced jet fighter was at least partly related to the PLA's violations of South Korea's ADIZ and, in joint exercises with Russia, even airspace; and the SLBM test had China in mind and not only North Korea. Increasingly, South Korea was seeking an autonomous deterrent against China to supplement the ROK–U.S. alliance.

Furthermore, the 2019 intelligence sharing agreement with the Five Eyes, France, and Japan in theory focused only on North Korea, but its close relations with Beijing meant that there was also a China component. Meanwhile, the GSOMIA agreement with Japan continued to be in place. And South Korea's cooperation with the Quad—an Indo-Pacific group including the United States, Australia, India, and Japan—the G7, and other U.S.-led groups was an attempt to counter China's assertiveness.[372] "Strategic ambiguity" eventually became a slogan that did not reflect South Korean policy, and the Moon government stopped using it.

Notwithstanding all this, the Moon government did try to work together with China to address the North Korea conundrum and prevent accidental military clashes. Moon called on Beijing to cooperate in bringing a diplomatic solution to tensions in the Korean Peninsula.[373] This was also China's preferred approach. Most notably, Xi Jinping met with Kim Jong-un after the two Koreas announced that they would hold a summit following the PyeongChang Winter Olympic Games. Xi went on to meet with Kim a total of five times in 2018–2019.[374] China also called for the resumption of multilateral talks including North Korea, as well as for sanctions relief on the Kim regime.[375] Thus, Beijing's North Korea policy preferences were similar to Seoul's. To an extent, this was the result of South Korea's skillful use of its diplomatic corps to sway Chinese policy. This made sense in the context of the Moon government believing that Beijing would need to be involved in the resolution of inter-Korean tensions. Similarly, the Moon government used diplomacy to improve relations between the South Korean military and China's. In March 2021, the two ministries of Defense revised their bilateral memorandum of understanding to allow their militaries to establish an air and navy hotline. On the Chinese side, this was signed by the Eastern Theater Command with responsibility for China's Eastern provinces and East China Sea.[376]

The Moon government also used economic means to manage relations with China. Seoul and Beijing agreed to explore the launch of negotiations to upgrade their FTA in 2018. In March 2021, the two partners started consultations to launch the actual negotiations.[377] In the meantime, both of them were founding members of the Regional Comprehensive Economic Partnership (RCEP). The agreement was signed in November 2020 and entered into force in January 2022.[378] In December 2021, too, Seoul announced that it would seek membership in the Comprehensive and Progressive Agreement for Trans-Pacific Partnership (CPTPP), the agreement replacing TPP after Donald Trump had withdrawn the United States from this agreement upon becoming president. This came two months after China officially applied to join the CPTPP.[379] In other words, Seoul saw regional FTAs as a way to improve economic relations with China. Furthermore, by the end of 2020 and in spite of the COVID-19 pandemic, South Korean firms' investment stock in China stood at $82.69 billion, having started to recover from the THAAD controversy.[380] South Korean firms had started to shift production away from China following the THAAD-related sanctions, a move further accelerated by the disruptions brought by the pandemic. But they were not ready to fully abandon or decouple from China, which remained important for their growth strategy.[381]

Seoul also sought to use its soft power-public diplomacy combo to smooth relations with Beijing. In 2018, a new Korean Cultural Center opened in Hong Kong.[382] The two in Beijing and Shanghai continued to operate, as did the King Sejong institutes across China. The Korea-China Music Festival continued to be held, and the Korea Foundation also continued its activities throughout the country.[383] Eventually, the Xi government had to start removing its sanctions on K-pop acts to perform in China. K-pop was too popular among the Chinese population. South Korean soft power actually had led Beijing to change its policy.

Yoon Suk-yeol (2022)

North Korea

Yoon Suk-yeol took office in 2022, restoring conservative rule after a five-year hiatus. From his perspective, the previous government had spent too much time and political capital in dealing with North Korea and had been too deferential. Furthermore, Yoon wanted to deemphasize North Korea as part of South Korea's grand strategy and increase attention on other regions and areas. Having said that, Yoon's approach toward North Korea built on the tried-and-tested South Korean grand strategy dating back to the Roh Tae-woo years. Yoon's "Audacious Initiative," as the president labeled his North Korea strategy, offered Pyongyang economic incentives, military confidence-building measures, and the prospect of peace in the Korean Peninsula in parallel to North Korea pausing and reversing development of its nuclear program.[384] In this respect, Yoon's approach followed closely from the policy of his two conservative predecessors, Park Geun-hye and Lee Myung-bak.

Yoon's North Korea strategy married incentives and deterrents. Yoon indicated that he was open to holding a summit with Kim Jong-un, as long as it could produce material results.[385] The government sought to take a holistic approach toward North Korea, and this included providing incentives for North Korea to engage in negotiations about a range of issues including its nuclear program, but also economic cooperation, human rights, and Korean Peninsula peace.[386] This way, Yoon settled for a more realistic short-term goal of launching a peace process—for which negotiations were necessary.[387] Reunification could wait.

At the same time, the Yoon government continued to bolster South Korea's capabilities to protect itself against North Korea. Seoul reinvigorated its extended deterrence dialogue with Washington, which had been weakened during the Moon years.[388] In addition, the ROK Navy and its U.S. counterpart conducted joint naval drills to deter North Korea for the first time in five years.[389] These actions demonstrated the enduring importance of the ROK–U.S. alliance as part of South Korea's North Korea strategy. Furthermore, Seoul responded to North Korea's missile tests with tests of its own.[390] This was a way to show its resolve to use its own military capabilities to protect itself. In fact, South Korea launched its first home-grown rocket in June 2022.[391] Developed by KARI, the rocket gave South Korea a new capability that it could weaponize to protect itself against Pyongyang. Yoon also indicated that South Korea was open to launching a preemptive strike against the North.[392] In addition, the Yoon government appointed a North Korea human rights ambassador after the position had remained vacant for five years, and also went back to cosponsoring a North

Korea human rights resolution at the United Nations.[393] The Yoon government was thus raising diplomatic pressure on North Korea as well.

The United States

Yoon made clear that the ROK–U.S. alliance was a key cornerstone of his grand strategy. He held his first summit with Biden less than two weeks after taking office, when the U.S. president traveled to South Korea. This underscored the importance that Yoon attributed to good relations with the United States. In the joint statement coming out of the summit, Seoul and Washington vowed to "evolve and expand" the alliance, focusing on North Korea but also on a host of other matters such as economic and technological cooperation, "peace and stability in the Taiwan Strait"—a clear reference to China—the pandemic, or cooperation in the Indo-Pacific.[394]

In fact, the Yoon government vowed to publish its own Indo-Pacific strategy. Coordinated by MOFA's North American Affairs Bureau, the strategy would emphasize strong coordination with the U.S.'s FOIP.[395] In addition, the Yoon government indicated that it wanted to formally join the Quad, joined the Biden administration's Indo-Pacific Economic Framework (IPEF) from its inception in May 2022, and participated in the inaugural meeting of Washington's "Chip 4" alliance designed to create a resilient, China-free semiconductor supply chain alliance and also involving Japan and Taiwan.[396] Similarly, South Korean *chaebol* announced the opening of factories for high-end tech products in the United States.[397] As emphasized previously, the *chaebol* were separate from the state but their investments supported South Korea's grand strategy. South Korea also sent its largest-ever naval force to the U.S.-led RIMPAC joint exercise.[398] The Yoon government was therefore making use of South Korea's military capabilities, economic tools, and diplomatic corps to strengthen relations with the United States.

On the other hand, the Yoon government also continued to pursue autonomy. This was informed by South Korea's long-term strategic goals as well as the memories of instances when Seoul's and Washington's interests had not been aligned—most recently, during Trump's presidency.[399] As a clear case in point, Yoon maintained the goal of OPCON transfer. During the combined military drills of August–September 2022, South

Korea and the United States held a full operational capability assessment of a future CFC to be led by the former.[400] This was the second of three-phase approach toward moving ahead with the transfer. Furthermore, the Yoon government also continued the policy of diversifying diplomatic, military, and economic ties pursued by his predecessors, as a means to strengthen South Korean autonomy.

China

Yoon came to office emphasizing the importance of values for his grand strategy, which raised questions about relations between South Korea and China given their different value systems. Yet, Yoon continued South Korea's grand strategy toward China, involving both robust military capabilities and diplomatic stances along with engagement. This approach built on that pursued by South Korea ever since the normalization of diplomatic relations with China in 1992. Containment was thus an important component, but there was no intention to decouple or break ties with Beijing.[401]

South Korea engaged in two diplomatic quarrels with China in the first few months of Yoon's time in office, symbolizing this robust approach. First of all, South Korea rebuked China for seeking to change "the status quo by force" in the Taiwan Strait.[402] Coupled with the joint statement issued by Yoon and Biden, this made clear Seoul's opposition to a potential military action by China to take over Taiwan. In addition, South Korea's MOFA rejected Chinese assertions that South Korea had agreed not to deploy more antimissile batteries to boost THAAD. This came only one day after the foreign ministers of the two countries had met in Beijing.[403] In fact, South Korea continued the development of its own military programs under Yoon. On top of that, in October 2022 South Korea voted at the UN Human Rights Council in favor of an investigation into China's alleged human rights abuses in the Xinjiang Uyghur Autonomous Region, one of only two Asian countries to do so.[404] This was an extremely sensitive issue for Beijing, which denied the abuses. Seoul was making use of its military capabilities and diplomatic corps to deal with China.

At the same time, however, South Korea continued to pursue engagement with China. Yoon issued an invitation to Xi to visit Seoul shortly after taking office.[405] Seoul and Beijing signed a supply chain cooperation memorandum of understanding, indicating that the Yoon government did not want to break its economic and technological ties with China even as it sought to ensure supply chain resilience, and South Korean firms were shifting production away from their neighbor.[406] And the defense ministers of the two countries held a meeting only a month after Yoon took office, pledging to reinvigorate military exchanges across the different branches of the armed forces.[407] From the perspective of the Yoon government, it was necessary to maintain ties with China as part of the country's grand strategy.[408]

Relations with North Korea, the United States, and China are South Korea's top foreign policy priorities. As such, they are marked by a degree of domestic bickering. This is particularly the case when it comes to approaches to inter-Korean relations and the ROK–U.S. alliance. Yet, South Korea has a clear grand strategy to manage relations with the triangular core of its foreign relations. This grand strategy traces its roots back to at least South Korea's transition to democracy. It has held all the way until at least the early stages of the Yoon Suk-yeol presidency.

Starting with North Korea, Seoul has a clear end: inter-Korean reconciliation and reunification. Every single South Korean president has launched a policy to improve relations between the two Koreas and create the conditions for eventual reunification. In order to achieve this end, South Korean presidents have sought to use diplomacy, economic tools, and a growing military deterrent. Some presidents, such as Kim Dae-jung, Roh Moo-hyun, and Moon Jae-in, have prioritized diplomatic means and economic engagement. Others, including Lee Myung-bak and Park Geun-hye, have prioritized economic coercion and deterrence. But all presidents have sought a combination of these means. Another end, at the same time, is protection from external military threats. To this end, all South Korean presidents have focused on boosting defense autonomy, including cybertools from the Lee Myung-bak administration onward, while also strengthening the ROK–U.S. alliance. Conservative and liberal presidents alike have employed these means.

Focusing on the United States, South Korea has sought to pursue several key ends concurrently: autonomy, protection from external military threats, deeper integration in the world economy, and recognition as an influential middle power. South Korea sees the United States as a potential constrain on its autonomy but also as an enabler of other ends. Therefore,

South Korean grand strategy across different presidencies has been complex when it comes to dealing with the United States. In any case, successive South Korean presidents have used a combination of means to influence the United States and, crucially, to make the ROK–U.S. alliance global in nature. This has been particularly clear from the Lee Myung-bak presidency onward. Thus, the ROK–U.S. alliance has been a means for South Korea to achieve other ends in and of itself. Meanwhile, Seoul has used its growing military capabilities, diplomatic corps, trade and investment, public diplomacy, or soft power to seek to influence the United States and its bilateral alliance.

In the case of China, Seoul has two key ends in mind: protection from its military threat and deeper economic integration. Thus, South Korea has used growing military capabilities and the ROK–U.S. alliance to deter potential Chinese aggressiveness. This has become clearer as the rise of China has moved ahead, reaching its zenith during the Moon Jae-in and Yoon Suk-yeol presidencies. Regarding deeper economic integration, successive South Korean presidents dating back to Roh Tae-woo have sought to use the country's diplomatic corps and trade and investment to influence relations with its neighbor and strengthen ties. This was particularly the case during the Lee Myung-bak and, especially, Park Geun-hye governments, and continued under the Moon Jae-in and Yoon Suk-yeol governments even as relations with China deteriorated. Meanwhile, South Korea has also seen diplomacy with China as a means to help pursue another end: inter-Korean reconciliation. This was particularly the case during the Roh Moo-hyun administration. But as China's influence over North Korea has dwindled, so has the possibility of Seoul's using its means to make Beijing more integral to its policy toward Pyongyang.

CHAPTER V

East Asia

Regionalism and Regionalization

South Korea is located in East Asia. This is a truism that nonetheless needs to be repeatedly underscored, for it informs South Korea's grand strategy beyond the triangular core that has long dominated South Korean thinking. From the perspective of policymakers and other elites in Seoul, East Asia includes Northeast Asia, Southeast Asia, and the burgeoning economic, political, and security links between the two sub-regions, resulting in regionalism and regionalization across them. This means that South Korean grand strategy is not only based on South Korea's geographical location in East Asia, but also on the idea and, increasingly, reality of the region as a single economic and security community. East Asia already featured in the thinking of South Korean leaders, including Park Chung-hee, before the 1987-1988 democratization. However, it was only the end of the Cold War that allowed East Asian policymakers to truly develop regional links and institutions—including with South Korean participation.

In terms of South Korean grand strategy in and toward East Asia, Japan certainly features most prominently. Geographically and North Korea aside, it is South Korea's closest neighbor. The history of (South) Korea–Japan relations is obviously very complex, informing South Korean grand strategy since 1988. Every single South Korean president since the restoration of democracy has had to grapple with how to approach the relationship with the country's neighbor across the East Sea, and every South Korean president has sought to improve relations with its fellow Northeast Asian middle power. Japan matters for South Korean grand strategy since bilateral relations matter for a host of Seoul's ends, including its deeper integration in global trade and financial flows, protection from external military threats especially China and North Korea, and recognition as an influential middle power. Japan has also become increasingly involved in dealing with North Korea, sometimes becoming a consideration in South Korea's goal of achieving inter-Korean reconciliation and reunification. When pursuing its grand strategy toward Japan, South Korea has been using its full spectrum of means.

Southeast Asia—and especially ASEAN and its ten members—certainly is another relevant region for South Korean grand strategy. As ASEAN and some of its members have become more active and central to East Asian and, to an extent, global politics, so has South Korean interest in the region grown. Dating back to the 1990s, successive South Korean governments have focused on the goals of deeper integration in the world economy and recognition as an influential middle power. Furthermore, the rise of China and the potential security threat that it poses to its neighborhood from the perspective of many policymakers in the region means that South Korean grand strategy also addresses Southeast Asia from the prism of the goal of protection from external military threats. In terms of the means employed by South Korea in its grand strategy toward the region, they include military capabilities, diplomatic corps, trade, investment, and aid, public diplomacy, and soft power. That is, a very comprehensive set of tools.

Another crucial aspect that is part of South Korea's grand strategy toward East Asia relates to its links with its approach toward the United States and China, and to an extent North Korea. East Asia is a region with a strong U.S. presence, both through its military imprint including alliances as well as through its on-and-off role in shaping regional trade and security agreements. In the case of China, obviously it is part of East Asia. Thus, the region is shaped by but also shapes Beijing's behavior. This is particularly the case when it comes to regional economic, political, and security integration and institutionalization. As for North Korea, its participation in a small number of regional initiatives and the example that some countries in Southeast Asia could be for North Korea has led South Korean grand strategists to include the region in their approach toward Pyongyang.

TABLE 5.1
South Korea's grand strategy toward East Asia

Key factors	Key ends	Key means
ROK–U.S. alliance, rise of China, economic development, democracy, middle power identity, regional integration and globalization, Asian financial crisis	Autonomy, protection from external military threats, inter-Korean reconciliation and reunification, deeper integration in the world economy, recognition as an influential middle power	Growing military capabilities; U.S. alliance; diplomatic corps; trade, investment, and aid; public diplomacy; soft power

Roh Tae-woo (1988–1993)

Roh Tae-woo came to office with a plan to improve relations with Japan. Under the label "Historical Reconciliation" (미야자와), Roh introduced a policy whereby South Korea would seek to separate contemporary relations between Seoul and Tokyo from the thorny historical issue of Japanese occupation and subsequent colonization of Korea.[1] This approach became a blueprint for subsequent presidents. After all, stronger relations with Japan could boost South Korean autonomy. Under Roh, this goal was facilitated by apologies from Japanese Emperor Akihito and Japanese Prime Minister Kaifu Toshiki, who in May 1990 held separate meetings with the South Korean president and apologized for the "suffering" that Japan inflicted upon the Korean people.[2] Japanese apologies, their sincerity, and potential compensation to South Koreans who directly suffered under Japanese colonial rule—or their descendants—became a feature of South Korea–Japan relations. (This included both sex slaves, euphemistically called "comfort women," and slave labor.) They inevitably affected relations between the two countries, but the blueprint established by Roh became part of South Korean grand strategy.

In order to strengthen its economic ties with the outside world, Roh sought to address the trade imbalances between South Korea and Japan.

South Korea suffered a chronic trade deficit, due to Japanese products still being more high-tech than South Korean ones. To this end, Seoul sought to push for technology transfer from Japanese firms. However, the Japanese government was wary of the growing competitiveness of South Korean firms that it increasingly perceived as direct rivals, and there were unresolved economic tensions between the two neighbors.[3] South Korea sought to use diplomacy to address them, but to no avail.

The Roh government also focused on the potential role of Japan in smoothing inter-Korean relations, the potential military threat from Tokyo, and the use of soft power to improve bilateral relations. With regard to inter-Korean relations, Roh's *Nordpolitik* called for better relations between Japan and North Korea. However, the Roh government became wary of potential full diplomatic normalization between the two.[4] Therefore, it used its diplomatic corps to seek to slow down potential rapprochement between Tokyo and Pyongyang. As for the potential military threat that Japan could pose, the MND 1988 white paper emphasized the need for cooperation with its neighbor.[5] Despite these reassuring words, South Korea's military buildup and particularly missile development was also seen as a deterrent against Japan.[6] The possibility of a Japanese strike against South Korea was remote. But South Korean officials nonetheless thought that they had to be ready for this eventuality. Plus, Japanese claims over Dokdo—under South Korean administration since 1952—could result in military clashes.[7] The ROK Armed Forces had started annual defense drills to protect Dokdo in 1986, and these continued during the Roh years.[8] Finally, Seoul had opened one of its first Korean Cultural centers in Tokyo in 1979.[9] And the Korea Foundation prioritized projects in Japan upon its launch.[10] With South Korea having transitioned into a democracy, the center could promote (South) Korean culture with the added value of the country having left behind its dictatorial past. This was a boost to the country's soft power.

With regard to Southeast Asia, South Korea focused on strengthening relations making use of its diplomatic and economic means. Diversifying relations could boost South Korean autonomy, and Southeast Asia was the logical place to start outside of Northeast Asia due to its geographical proximity and degree of cultural affinity.[11] Starting with ASEAN, the Roh government established official bilateral relations through a sectoral dialogue partnership in 1989, a Special Cooperation Fund in 1990, and a full dialogue partnership in 1991.[12] ASEAN members including Indonesia, Malaysia, the Philippines, and Thailand had been trying to replicate the development model of South Korea and fellow developmental states. This allowed South Korea to present itself as a development model for these countries and use this as means to advance its foreign policy interests.

In fact, the establishment of the Korea International Cooperation Agency (KOICA) in 1991 provided the MOFA, and by extension the South Korean government, with a powerful tool to implement its grand strategy toward the region. From the beginning, Southeast Asia became a key recipient of South Korean aid provided by KOICA, the Economic Development Cooperation Fund (EDCF), and other bodies.[13] Interestingly, Seoul focused on both infrastructure and social development as the pillars of its aid policy toward Southeast Asia. This way, Seoul hoped to influence not only Southeast Asian governments but also the region's people. Aid was supplemented with investment as Seoul signed several bilateral investment treaties across Southeast Asia.[14] In addition, Southeast Asia played a key role in South Korea's resource diplomacy. Indonesia and later on Malaysia provided South Korea with almost all the liquefied natural gas (LNG) that it consumed.[15] And in 1992, the Korea National Oil Corporation (KNOC) signed a production sharing contract with the Vietnamese government to procure gas from a new project in the country.[16] These developments supported South Korea's goal of economic integration at the global level.

The end of the Cold War, meanwhile, brought a new, less hostile paradigm to the region. The Roh government took advantage of the situation to normalize diplomatic relations with Vietnam in 1992.[17] The two of them were already trade and investment partners.[18] But in the context of *Nordpolitik* and Seoul's establishment of diplomatic relations with Moscow and Beijing, normalization of relations with Hanoi boosted South Korea's economic goals and also credentials as a middle power.

Also in the context of decreasing tensions in post–Cold War East Asia, South Korea became part of Asia–Pacific initiatives including East Asian countries, the United States, and other partners. The Asia-Pacific Economic Cooperation (APEC) initiative launched in November 1989, with South Korea as one of the founding members. APEC promised to strengthen trade and investment links between East Asia and the United States. Seoul hosted the third APEC summit in 1991.[19] And in November 1992 Seoul hosted discussions about the establishment of a regional track-2 security dialogue. Institutes from South Korea, other East Asian countries, the United States, and some other countries from the Asia–Pacific region agreed to launch the Council for Security Cooperation in the Asia Pacific (CSCAP).[20] This would become one of the two central track-1.5/track-2 security dialogues in East Asia, along with the ASEAN Regional Forum (ARF) launched in 1994. It was a case of South Korea using its diplomatic corps to strengthen its security but also to boost its middle power credentials.

Kim Young-sam (1993–1998)

Kim Young-sam introduced a policy of friendship and cooperation toward Japan on taking office. Similarly to Roh, Kim's policy sought to draw a line between history-related frictions and contemporary relations. In particular, Kim wanted to deepen relations with Japan as a way to boost the South Korean economy through trade and investment, as well as to receive support in dealing with North Korea.[21] In his first meeting with a Japanese prime minister, Hosokawa Morihiro, Kim was able to focus on cooperation as Hosokawa apologized for Japan's mistreatment of the Korean population and especially its sex slaves during the years of colonialism and World War II.[22] Hosokawa was the first president outside of the conservative Liberal Democratic Party (LDP) in power since the 1950s, which facilitated South Korea–Japan relations.

In order to support South Korean integration in the world economy and general economic growth, Kim sought to boost trade with and investment from Japan. Most notably, South Korea joined the OECD. This way, it became only the second Asian country to join this organization of developed economies along with Japan. The Kim government saw this as an opportunity for Seoul and Tokyo to promote a different type of economic policy.[23] This policy would be less anchored in the (neo)liberal model and more related to the developmental state. This way, South Korea could try to use its diplomatic corps to present a common position with Japan, and this could have a positive impact on economic relations between South Korean and Japanese firms. However, this did not work out. On a more positive note, in December 1997 the BOK and the Bank of Japan agreed to a bridging loan facility that the former could activate to address the effects of the AFC.[24] This was a case of South Korea adeptly using its diplomacy to protect its economy.

With regard to inter-Korean relations, Japan became North Korea's largest trading partner by the mid-1990s, a position that it maintained until 2002 when relations between Tokyo and Pyongyang nosedived.[25] Once China and Russia had taken a market-led approach to economic relations with North Korea, their trade had collapsed. This made Japan one of North Korea's main economic lifelines at a time when inter-Korean cooperation was very limited. The Kim government sought to work with Japan to steer North Korea toward a more cooperative stance toward South Korea.[26] This, however, did not work mainly due to North Korea's domestic problems. Concurrently, the Kim government made use of the U.S. alliance to improve coordination with Japan in relation to its inter-Korean policy but also to boost its protection against the North Korean security threat. In 1994 and spearheaded by Washington, the United States, South Korea, and Japan launched Defense Trilateral Talks (DTT).[27] Trilateral cooperation to deal with North Korea—and later, with other security matters—would become a feature of Seoul's grand strategy for years to come.

Seoul's grand strategy toward Tokyo continued to pursue the ends of protection against external military threats and recognition as an influential middle power. With regard to the former, annual military drills to defend Dokdo continued during the Kim years. On the other hand, in 1994 Lee Byung-tae became the first South Korean minister of defense to visit Japan, while an ROK Navy ship called at a Japanese port for the first time.[28] This inaugurated an era of regular bilateral exchanges going all the way until at least 2023. Also, recognition as a middle power seemed to be a more important end for the Kim government. Most notably, in May 1996 Seoul and Tokyo won the rights to cohost the 2002 World Cup.[29] For South Korea, this would imply use of its soft power to strengthen ties with Japan but also to present itself in a new light to the outside world. The Korea Foundation supplemented this by continuing to prioritize projects in Japan.

In the case of Southeast Asia, trade, investment, and aid consolidated as the preferred means for South Korea to strengthen links with the region and deepen its integration in the world economy as well as to be recognized as middle power. Trade between South Korea and ASEAN grew from $16.74 billion in 1993 to $29.24 billion in 1997 as more South Korean firms set their sights on Southeast Asia's growing middle class.[30] Trade also increased because of South Korea's resource diplomacy. Most notably, Indonesia and Malaysia along with, after 1994, Brunei continued to provide South Korea with almost all its LNG imports during this time.[31] In 1995, Seoul signed an agreement with Kuala Lumpur to gain preferential access to its energy and mineral resources.[32] In addition, South Korea made strategic use of aid. KOICA, EDCF, and other bodies disbursed $7.5 million in Asia in 1993 and up to $18.6 million in 1997, with Southeast Asia as a whole being the preferred destination of South Korean aid.[33] At the same time, Seoul continued to sign bilateral investment treaties with other countries in the region.[34]

In addition, Seoul also made use of diplomacy to boost its presence in the region. In 1995, South Korea normalized relations with Lao.[35] One year later, Kim became the first South Korean president to visit Vietnam.[36] In 1997, South Korea and Cambodia normalized diplomatic relations.[37] With South Korea having established relations with communist countries across Europe and ASEAN expanding by incorporating its former communist foes, it made sense for the Kim government to boost ties with these countries for economic and middle power credential reasons. This was supplemented through public diplomacy as the Korea Foundation started to implement projects in Southeast Asia.[38]

At the same time, the Kim government also prioritized regional cooperation (지역협력), albeit with a focus on the Asia–Pacific (아시아-태평양 지역 협력 심화) region as much as East Asia alone. In 1993, CSCAP Korea was one of the founding members of CSCAP.[39] That same year, ASEAN and its dialogue partners agreed to establish the ARF. The forum was launched the following year, with South Korea as one of its founding members.[40] It became an important track-1.5 and track-2 forum. In 1994, North Korea also joined CSCAP, and the following year, the group launched a working group on "Frameworks for Stability on the Korean Peninsula." North Korea did not attend the first meeting of the group, though.[41] Meanwhile, South Korea continued to be an active participant in APEC. Then, in the midst of the AFC, ASEAN officially invited China, Japan, and South Korea to a meeting in December 1997.[42] An ASEAN+3 Head of Government summit thus became an annual feature. Regional cooperation allowed Seoul to use diplomacy to pursue goals including protection from external threats, inter-Korean reconciliation, and deeper economic integration.

Kim Dae-jung (1998–2003)

Kim Dae-jung had a long history of positive views and experiences with Japan. The new South Korean president had been in exile in Japan in the early 1970s, and the Japanese Maritime Self-Defense Force had saved Kim's life in August 1973 after he was kidnapped and was about to be thrown to the East Sea.[43] In terms of grand strategy, once he became president of South Korea, Kim followed the approach of his predecessors of separating history from contemporary relations. However, he pressed ahead with improvement in relations to a larger extent than the two previous South Korean presidents. In October 1998, Kim visited Japan and signed the Republic of Korea-Japan Joint Declaration: A New Republic of Korea-Japan Partnership toward the 21st Century. This was the first agreement between the two countries since the 1965 Treaty on Basic Relations, and it included provisions for cooperation on the economy and North Korea, among other matters.[44] The declaration was made possible, among others, by Prime Minister Obuchi Keizo's issuing the first-ever written apology for Japan's colonial past and behavior during World War II delivered to any specific country. Emperor Akihito also reiterated his apology for the suffering that Japan had brought upon the Korean people.[45]

With Kim taking office shortly after the onset of the AFC, the new president used diplomacy and trade and investment to seek the support of Japan and improve South Korea's economic situation. In the 1998 joint declaration, Seoul and Tokyo agreed to cooperate in multilateral fora such as the OECD, WTO, and APEC. Japan also agreed to have the Export-Import Bank of Japan provide South Korea with loans.[46] Also, the Kim government removed all remaining restrictions on Japanese imports in 1999.[47] These restrictions had been in place for decades to protect South Korean firms against some high-tech Japanese imports. From Kim's perspective, South Korean firms had to compete head-to-head with their Japanese counterparts. This decision did not have a significant impact on South Korea's trade deficit with Japan. But it reduced economic frictions between both, even if some frictions continued as South Korean firms were moving up the value-added chain.

Arguably, Kim was most successful in obtaining the support of Tokyo for his inter-Korean strategy. The South Korea-Japan joint declaration stated: "Prime Minister Obuchi expressed support for the policies of President Kim Dae Jung regarding North Korea under which the Republic of Korea is actively promoting reconciliation and cooperation while maintaining a solid security system."[48] Kim also supported Japanese Prime Minister Koizumi Junichiro's visit to Pyongyang and summit with Kim Jongil in September 2002.[49] Japan indeed provided diplomatic support to Kim's reconciliation efforts. Furthermore, Japan continued to be North Korea's largest trading partner until 2002. This provided support to Kim's North Korea strategy. In addition, South Korea also made use of the U.S. alliance to get Japan more involved in its inter-Korean policy and protection against the North Korean military threat. In 1999 and at the behest of the Clinton administration, Washington, Seoul, and Tokyo launched the Trilateral Coordination and Oversight Group (TCOG). With its focus on foreign policy, TCOG would supplement the defense-focused DTT.[50]

The Kim government also made use of soft power and public diplomacy to boost its links with Japan. In 1999, the Ministry of Culture and Tourism opened a new Korean Cultural Center in Japan, this time in Osaka.[51] The Korea–Japan World Cup of 2002, meanwhile, served to strengthen relations between Seoul and Tokyo. The Korea Foundation continued its activities in Japan. More important, arguably, the Kim government launched a plan to support the export of *Hallyu*, the Korean pop-culture wave.[52] The plan aimed at supporting South Korean cultural industry to boost the country's economy and create better perceptions of South Korea as a middle power overseas. Japan was one of the first countries targeted with the plan.

The Kim government also continued its military buildup and made use of its diplomatic corps to pursue its ends. With regard to the former, tensions over Dokdo persisted. The ROK armed forces continued their annual military drills to protect the islands. As for the latter, in 2001 Japan's Ministry of Education approved a new history textbook that South Korea protested over claims that it contained several inaccuracies.[53] Furthermore, newly elected Japanese Prime Minister Koizumi Junichiro started annual visits to the Yasukuni Shrine that same year.[54] Fourteen Class A war criminals and more than a thousand war criminals in total are honored in the shrine. Koizumi's visits created a diplomatic spat with South Korea. Yet, Seoul also used its growing military capabilities to boost relations with Japan to protect against external threats. Starting from 1999, the ROK Navy and Japan's Maritime Self-Defense Force launched combined search and rescue exercises that would go on to be held every two years.[55] Japan also participated in a South Korean fleet review in 1998 for the first time ever. Seoul then reciprocated by partaking in a Japanese fleet review in 2002.[56]

With regard to Southeast Asia, the Kim government came to office shortly after the onset of the AFC. The crisis had originated in Thailand before spreading throughout Southeast Asia and then reaching South Korea and other parts of Northeast Asia. It was clear that the economies of the two East Asian subregions were closely linked. Kim doubled down on the goal of his predecessors to use trade, investment, and aid to deepen economic integration in a way that would be beneficial to South Korea. Trade went up from $21.8 billion in 1998—following an AFC-induced slump—to a record $36.55 billion in 2003. Annual investment flows, meanwhile, reached $611 million in 2003.[57] In terms of resource diplomacy, Indonesia, Malaysia, and Brunei continued to be key suppliers of LNG to South Korea.[58] In 1998 KNOC signed a second deal with the Vietnamese government to procure oil and gas.[59] Meanwhile, South Korean aid continued to increase in spite of the knock-on effects of the AFC. By 2002, KOICA and EDCF along with other government bodies were delivering $28.8 million to Asia, which remained one of the largest recipients of South Korean direct aid.[60] Last, South Korea also dispatched peacekeepers to East Timor in 1999–2003.[61] Seoul was using its military capabilities to boost its middle power credentials.

The Kim government also employed diplomacy to strengthen links with Southeast Asia and create pan–East Asian economic links in a way that would deepen integration across the region. Kim enthusiastically embraced the concept of ASEAN+3. In his view, the AFC had proved that "it [was] now meaningless to distinguish Northeast Asia and Southeast Asia."[62] In addition, an annual ASEAN+3 Finance Ministers' Meeting was also launched in 2000.[63] Kim also proposed the launch of an East Asian Vision Group (EAVG) during a December 1998 heads of government meeting.[64] Chaired by Seoul, the EAVG was introduced in 1999 with a mandate to revitalize trade, investment, supply chain, and resource cooperation between Northeast and Southeast Asian countries. In 2001, the EAVG issued a report also focusing on politics and security, environment and energy, and society, culture, and education.[65] In the meantime, Seoul also supported the Chiang Mai Initiative (CMI) launched in 2000, a series of bilateral currency swap arrangements among ASEAN+3 central banks to activate in case of currency crisis and thus reduce dependence on IMF loans.[66] Similarly, the Kim government supported the launch of the ASEAN+3 Bond

Markets Initiative, designed to develop local-currency bond markets and therefore avoid the need to issue bonds in U.S. dollars.[67] These events spear-headed truly pan–East Asian cooperation and integration. From a South Korean perspective, they complemented the annual South Korea–ASEAN summit that continued to be in place. All these initiatives were not only supporting South Korea's deeper integration in the world economy, but they were also reinforcing Seoul's goal of recognition as an influential mid-dle power. After all, the EAVG had been Kim's idea. They also under-pinned South Korea's push for autonomy by creating stronger bonds with the region where the country was located.

The Kim government also institutionalized soft power as a means to boost links with Southeast Asia and support its grand strategic goals. Kim's plan to support *Hallyu* identified Southeast Asia as a key region to target. Even though actions in the region were slow to take off during the Kim years, his government had created a blueprint for South Korea to use soft power. With regards to his North Korea policy, at the 2001 South Korea–ASEAN summit which came less than a year after the first-ever inter-Korean summit, Kim asked for ASEAN's support for this North Korea policy.[68] Furthermore, Kim asked for North Korea to be allowed to join APEC at the organization's 2000 summit. The Kim government also sup-ported North Korea's entry in the ARF that same year.[69]

Roh Moo-hyun (2003–2008)

Roh Moo-hyun's Japan policy followed the grand strategy of his prede-cessors by seeking to separate history from contemporary cooperation. Roh based his approach toward Japan on mutual respect. Essentially, Roh wanted to build on the joint declaration signed by Kim Dae-jung to promote coop-eration in areas of mutual interest—above all, trade and investment links. Cooperation would take place regardless of the state of disputes about history. And since Roh wanted South Korea to play a "balancer" role in North-east Asia, in 2004 he proposed a trilateral summit also including China and Japan focusing on political and economic matters.[70] The summit would have supported South Korean autonomy.

The prioritization of trade as a means to support South Korean goals became clear shortly after Roh took office. In December 2003, Seoul and Tokyo launched FTA negotiations.[71] This was a bold move by the Roh government, considering that many South Korean officials and business-people still baulked at the trade deficit that South Korea had with Japan. But Roh believed that an FTA with Japan would make the South Korean economy more competitive, and therefore accelerate its integration at the global level.[72] On another positive note, in May 2005 the BOK and the Bank of Japan signed a bilateral currency swap arrangement to be activated in case of currency crisis in any of the two countries.[73] At the same time, however, South Korea was becoming more self-confident in the use of other means to address economic relations with Japan. In 2004, South Korea would raise a WTO dispute against Japan related to import quotas on dried laver and seasoned laver. In 2006, Seoul raised a second dispute over countervailing duties on dynamic random access memories for computers.[74]

The Roh government also saw Japan playing a role in its North Korea policy. The Six-Party Talks were launched in 2003. South Korean diplomats often found themselves in agreement with their Japanese counterparts, even if their ultimate goals were different. Seoul supported the inclusion of Japanese goals—most notably, addressing the abduction of Japanese nationals by North Korea—as well as the Six Party Talks' Joint Statement call for Japan and North Korea to normalize diplomatic relations.[75] Tokyo, in return, provided support to Roh's inter-Korean normalization efforts.[76] At the same time, trilateral cooperation with the United States continued.[77]

The Roh government also made use of soft power and public diplomacy to improve relations with Japan and attain its ends, under the general label of Creative Korea. The South Korean government provided support for K-pop concerts in Japan. It also encouraged the export of K-dramas, with *Winter Sonata* becoming especially popular in Japan and changing perceptions about South Korea in its neighbor.[78] The Korea Foundation continued to provide support for projects carried out by Japanese think tanks and universities, and in 2007 it opened an office in Tokyo.[79] That same year, the Ministry of Culture and Tourism opened its first King Sejong Institute in Japan. Eventually, South Korea's eastern neighbor would become the host of the second largest number of King Sejong institutes worldwide.[80]

On the other hand, South Korea's military buildup continued to target Japan. In 2003, South Korea conducted biannual military drills to protect Dokdo for the first time. The move from annual to biannual exercises remained ever since.[81] In 2005, Japan's Defense White Paper claimed Dokdo as a Japanese territory.[82] This claim would remain in the white paper until at least 2021.[83] That same year, the Shimane Prefectural Government in Japan announced the celebration of "Takeshima Day," to commemorate the hundredth anniversary of the Japanese government unilaterally granting the prefecture jurisdiction over Dokdo.[84] These were points of friction during Roh's time in office, for they drew a direct link between the convoluted history of Korea–Japan relations to the present. Even though the Roh government did not consider Japan a military threat and the MND white papers emphasized bilateral cooperation, Seoul was compelled to protect its territory.[85] This was part of Roh's plan to develop regional force projection capabilities in Northeast Asia.[86]

In the case of Southeast Asia, Roh continued down the path traced by Kim Dae-jung but took relations to a new level. In 2004, South Korea and ASEAN elevated their relationship to a Comprehensive Cooperation Partnership.[87] Under this label and also building on Roh's general FTA strategy, South Korea and ASEAN launched negotiations for a Comprehensive Economic Cooperation Agreement (labeled AKFTA) in 2004. They would go on to sign the agreement in June 2007.[88] South Korea and Singapore also launched negotiations in parallel for a more ambitious and comprehensive agreement in 2004. They reached a deal barely a year and a half later, in 2005.[89] Trade, investment, and aid continued to thrive. Bilateral commercial flows almost doubled, increasing from $36.55 billion in 2003 to $69.68 billion by 2007. Annual investment flows topped $1.13 billion in 2007.[90] Meanwhile, aid flows to Asia reached $107 million in 2008.[91] Roh wanted South Korea to become the trade and investment hub of East Asia.[92] This necessitated stronger links with Southeast Asia.

The Roh government also accelerated the use of soft power and public diplomacy in Southeast Asia to support Seoul's grand strategy. In 2005, the Korea Foundation opened an office in Ho Chi Minh City.[93] The institution also increased its disbursement in Southeast Asia. In 2006, Seoul opened its first Korean Cultural Center in Southeast Asia. The location was Vietnam as well.[94] And the South Korean government provided support to South Korean artists participating in festivals and giving concerts across Southeast Asia.

In addition, the Roh government also supported pan-East Asian activities. In 2005, South Korea hosted its second APEC summit. Even though this institution focused on the Asia-Pacific, the summit took place in Busan.[95] South Korea's second largest city and host of its biggest port was becoming a hub for trade relations with Southeast Asia. Thus, hosting the

APEC summit there was hugely symbolic. Furthermore, the Roh government supported the launch of the East Asia Summit in 2005.[96] Originally including ASEAN+3 countries along with Australia, India, and New Zealand, the East Asia Summit was launched as a forum to discuss security, economics, and politics. And the Roh government continued to be an active participant in the ASEAN+3 process.

Lee Myung-bak (2008–2013)

Following ten years of liberal rule, Lee Myung-bak became South Korean president in 2008. His approach toward Japan continued to implement the grand strategy that South Korea had been pursuing since its transition to democracy. Lee labeled his policy "Future-oriented Relationship" (새로운 협력의 시대), seeking to draw a line between contemporary (and future) South Korea–Japan relations and their past history.[97] The two key pillars of Lee's policy were economics and security. From the president's perspective, Japan could be not only a strong trade and investment source and destination but also a defense and military partner. The Lee government pursued this policy not only bilaterally but also through the U.S. alliance. To a much larger extent than previous U.S. administrations, the Obama administration was pursuing trilateral U.S.–South Korea–Japan cooperation. The Lee government keenly supported this approach.

The prioritization of a combination of bilateralism and trilateralism—or the U.S. alliance—to boost protection from the North Korean military threat but also to support Lee's inter-Korean policy started as soon as the new president took office. Only a month after becoming president, Lee visited Japan and pledged to restore trilateral meetings that had been interrupted in 2007.[98] In 2008 Seoul launched the Defense Trilateral Talks with Washington and Tokyo.[99] The talks became a permanent feature all the way up to and including the Yoon Suk-yeol government. That same year, the ROK Navy joined Japan's fleet review for the first time since the Kim Dae-jung government.[100] One year later, the three countries launched an annual minister of defense–level dialogue that also became permanent.[101] South Korea, the United States, and Japan also held regular trilateral foreign minister–level meetings. And from 2010 onwards and following the ROKS *Cheonan* sinking and the Yeonpyeong Island shelling, South Korea also made use of its growing military capabilities to protect itself against the North Korean military threats in cooperation with Japan and the United States. The ROK Navy and the Japanese Maritime Self-Defense Force increased the frequency of their combined naval drills, along with trilateral exercises with the U.S. Navy.[102] South Korea and Japan even launched negotiations for a bilateral intelligence-sharing agreement between their militaries, which would be signed a few years later.

The presence of Democratic Party of Japan (DPJ) prime ministers in the period 2009–2012 greatly facilitated Seoul–Tokyo cooperation. For only the second time since the 1950s the LDP was not in power, and Japan was ruled by left-leaning prime ministers who seemed more genuinely remorseful of their country's imperialist past.[103] This was welcome by the Lee government. Even so, in August 2012 South Korea–Japan relations sank to their arguably lowest point since the restoration of diplomatic relations as Lee became the first South Korean president—and as of early 2023, also the last one—to visit Dokdo in response to renewed Japanese claims over the island.[104] This created considerable frictions during the reminder of the Lee presidency. He maintained regular military drills to protect Dokdo in any case.

Outside of security matters, the Lee government also continued to employ trade and investment to deepen economic links, diplomacy to protect against external military threats, and soft power and public diplomacy to support recognition as a middle power. In 2012, South Korea and Japan were among the ASEAN+6 countries—ASEAN+3 plus Australia, India, and New Zealand—that launched negotiations to establish RCEP.[105] Significantly, Seoul, Beijing, and Tokyo launched a trilateral head of government summit in 2008 that met annually during Lee's time in office. As for soft power and public diplomacy, public broadcaster KBS held its first Music Bank World Tour show in Tokyo in 2011, the South Korean government continued to sponsor other K-pop concerts, and the Korea Foundation, Korean Cultural centers, and King Sejong institutes continued their activities in Japan.[106] After all, Lee had labeled public diplomacy one of the tree pillars of his foreign policy.

In the case of Southeast Asia, Lee took an even more holistic approach to the grand strategy of South Korea toward the region compared to his predecessors. This was a bid to increase autonomy and deepen integration in the world economy to diversify relations away from other partners, as well as an attempt to continue to boost Seoul's middle power credentials.

To begin with, Lee expanded the diplomatic footprint of South Korea in the region. In 2010, South Korea and ASEAN elevated their relationship to a strategic partnership. Two years later, Seoul opened a diplomatic mission to ASEAN in Jakarta.[107] The Lee government also made use of South Korea's growing military capabilities by targeting arms sales toward the region. Indonesia became one of the two largest markets for South Korean arms exporters.[108]

Certainly, in any case, trade, investment, and aid continued to be central to Seoul's grand strategy toward Southeast Asia. In 2012, the Lee government launched FTA negotiations with Indonesia and Vietnam.[109] Trade, meanwhile, increased to $131.61 billion annually in 2012, the investment stock reached $19.32 billion that same year, and aid to Asia was boosted to $206.4 million also in 2012.[110] In 2009 the Korea Gas Corporation (KOGAS) signed an agreement with Jakarta to participate in an LNG exploration project.[111] Furthermore, soft power and public diplomacy received a boost. In 2011, the Ministry of Culture, Sports and Tourism opened Korean Cultural centers in Indonesia and the Philippines.[112] KBS's Music Bank held a concert in Indonesia during Lee's tenure, in 2013.[113] The South Korean government continued to provide support for K-pop festivals and concerts across the region. The Ministry of Culture, Sports and Tourism started to open King Sejong institutes across Southeast Asian countries, and the Korea Foundation continued its projects with universities and think tanks in the region.[114]

The Lee government had launched a New Asia Initiative to connect Southeast Asia, Northeast Asia, Southwest Asia, Central Asia, and the South Pacific.[115] Certainly it had a very ambitious geographical scope. But it served to guide Lee's policy toward East Asia. Seoul was part of the Chiang Mai Initiative Multilateralization (CMIM), a multilateral swap arrangement that replaced the CMI by pooling together the resources of ASEAN+3 and Hong Kong's central banks.[116] CMIM was a response to the inadequacy of CMI, which no country activated during the GFC. South Korea also was a founding member of the ASEAN Defense Ministers Meeting-Plus (ADMM-Plus), a platform launched in October 2010 for ASEAN+6 countries along with Russia and the United States to use diplomacy to address security conundrums in the region.[117] The Lee government used this platform as well as the ARF to ask for support for its North Korea policy. One year later, Russia and the United States also joined the East Asia Summit. Also in 2011, South Korea was one of the founding members of the ASEAN+3 Macroeconomic Research Office (AMRO), a regional macroeconomic surveillance office that was the region's first inter-governmental organization.[118] In 2012, Seoul agreed to RCEP negotiations that included the ten ASEAN members. That same year, South Korea was part of the ASEAN+3 Finance Ministers and Central Bank Governors' Meeting.[119] The inclusion of central bank governors acknowledged the close links between financial and monetary policies. Seoul's participation in these two initiatives would help to boost its integration in the world economy through trade and diplomatic means, respectively.

Park Geun-hye (2013–2017)

Park Geun-hye labeled her policy toward Japan "Future-oriented Friendly Partnership" (미래지향적인 우호 협력관계) upon becoming the new South Korean president. The parallels with her predecessor's approach were clear, even in terms of the policy's label. This in turn indicated that Park would continue the grand strategy set by previous presidents. Indeed, Park's approach called for a focus on positive forward-looking relations separated from historical disputes.[120] To this end, Seoul used its full set of means to achieve its full range of ends.

Starting with its growing military capabilities and U.S. alliance, the Park government sought to boost bilateralism with Japan and trilateralism also including the United States to protect against external military threats, obtain support for its inter-Korean policy, and increase recognition as a relevant middle power. The Defense Trilateral Talks, the also trilateral Minister of Defense annual meetings, and bilateral and trilateral combined naval exercises continued. Japan also joined South Korea's fleet review for the first time since the Kim Dae-jung years.[121] Trilateral Minister of Foreign Affairs meetings also carried on. All of this was supplemented with three significant developments. In 2014, Seoul, Washington, and Tokyo signed the Trilateral Information Security Agreement (TISA) to share intelligence.[122] TISA was meant to only focus on North Korea initially. But eventually it would also involve intelligence-sharing on China, which was inevitable considering the close links between Beijing and Pyongyang.[123] This indicated that South Korea–Japan cooperation now also involved protection against what both of them perceived to be China's growing aggressiveness. The two of them would then finally sign General Security of Military Information Agreement (GSOMIA) in 2016, which again nominally focused on North Korea but also had a China component. In 2016–2017, South Korea, the United States, and Japan conducted trilateral missile exercises for the first time.[124] Again focusing on the North Korea threat, they also had a component of deterrence against China.

At the same time, however, South Korea also used its military capabilities to protect against the potential threat coming from Japan. Similarly to her predecessors, Park thought of a military clash with Japan unlikely unless related to Dokdo.[125] Thus, the ROK Navy continued with its biannual drills.[126] However, growing tensions in Northeast Asia had a knock-on effect on Seoul's policy toward Tokyo. In December 2013, South Korea extended its Air Defense Identification Zone (ADIZ) in response to China's decision to extend its own. With the extension, there was an overlap between South Korea's and Japan's respective ADIZs.[127] At the same time, the Park government accelerated development of South Korea's indigenous jet fighter program.[128] Even though the program was related to the threat that South Korea perceived from China, North Korea, and, to an extent, Russia, the extension of the country's ADIZ along with the program also served as a deterrent against potential incursions by Japan's Air Self-Defense Force.

With regard to trade and investment, South Korea launched trilateral FTA negotiations with China and Japan barely a month after Park came to office.[129] The talks, however, proceeded slowly. A key reason was that ASEAN+6 launched RCEP negotiations in early 2013 as well. In November of the same year the Park government expressed its interest in joining Trans-Pacific Partnership (TPP) negotiations.[130] South Korea, China, and Japan could be part of RCEP, and Seoul and Tokyo could also be part of TPP. (As explained earlier, the Park government eventually withdrew its interest in joining TPP.) There continued to be frictions between South Korea and Japan, particularly since South Korean firms were already competing head to head with Japanese counterparts. These tensions were an important reason why the BOK and the Bank of Japan did not extend their bilateral swap arrangement once it expired in 2015.[131]

In addition, the Park government also deployed South Korea's diplomatic corps, public diplomacy, and soft power to improve relations with Japan and boost its autonomy and recognition as an influential middle power. In 2013, Japanese Prime Minister Abe Shinzo visited Yasukuni

Shrine. His government also announced that it was reviewing a 1993 government apology for Japan's World War II atrocities that included Korean and other sex slaves.[132] This raised tensions with South Korea. However, in December 2015 the Abe administration agreed to a deal whereby Japan admitted responsibility for World War II sexual slavery and agreed to pay around $8.3 million in reparations to a foundation of surviving victims.[133] In addition, Seoul held a round of its trilateral summit with Beijing and Tokyo in 2015. Tensions among the three of them and especially between China and Japan prevented more rounds during Park's tenure though. As for public diplomacy and soft power, the Korea Foundation, the Korean cultural centers, and the King Sejong institutes continued their activities. Meanwhile, the South Korean government continued to provide support to concerts in Japan. In fact, KCON held its first two concerts in Japan in 2015 and 2016 with the support of official government bodies such as the Korea Creative Content Agency, the Korea Tourism Agency, and the Korea Trade-Investment Promotion Agency.[134]

In the case of Southeast Asia, the Park government continued with the grand strategy of previous governments. Trade, investment, and aid continued to be central to Seoul's policy in order to boost autonomy from the United States, deepen integration in the world economy, and obtain recognition as an influential middle power. In 2015, South Korea and Vietnam signed their bilateral FTA that entered into force only a few months later.[135] This was only South Korea's second FTA with a Southeast Asian country, and it marked a significant milestone for it allowed South Korean firms to shift production away more easily from an increasingly expensive China. Meanwhile, ASEAN became Seoul's fourth largest trading partner by 2017 (if the European Union were considered as a single entity).[136] Between 2013 and that year, bilateral commerce went up from $135.54 billion to $152 billion. The investment stock grew to $45.4 billion by 2017, making Southeast Asia the third biggest destination for South Korean firms.[137] Aid reached $190.8 million that same year, which meant that Southeast Asia continued to be among the largest recipients of South Korean grants and loans.[138]

South Korea also pursued other ends with its grand strategy toward Southeast Asia while Park was in power. With regard to the end of inter-Korean reconciliation and reunification, Park invited ASEAN as an observer to her Northeast Asia Peace and Cooperation Initiative (NAPCI).[139] This was a significant move, since it gave the organization a seat at a multilateral diplomatic initiative that the Park government hoped would help to improve inter-Korean relations. Similarly, Park used diplomacy to boost South Korea's role as a middle power with the launch of MIKTA. The "I" stood for Indonesia, one of the five members of the initiative along with Mexico, Turkey, South Korea itself, and Australia. MIKTA held several meetings during Park's presidency.[140] Moving away from diplomacy, Park also used South Korea's growing military capabilities to boost its middle power role. Arms sales continued to increase during her time in office, with Indonesia, the Philippines, and Vietnam among the largest clients for South Korean defense firms.[141] In addition, South Korea continued to use its public diplomacy and soft power in the region. The Korea Foundation, Korean cultural centers, and a growing network of King Sejong institutions maintained their activities. For example, a new Korean Cultural Center opened in Thailand in 2013.[142] Meanwhile, KBS took its Music Bank World Tour to Vietnam in 2015.[143] Sponsorship of concerts by government agencies also carried on.

As for East Asia as a whole, Park continued to support ASEAN+3 initiatives as well as ASEAN-led institutions such as ADMM-Plus or the ARF.[144] Interestingly, her government consciously prioritized East Asia regionalism over Asia-Pacific cooperation when it decided to remain part of RCEP negotiations while withdrawing from TPP. To an extent, this was recognition that South Korea's deeper integration in the world economy and economic autonomy from China and the United States could be best attained through RCEP, since the deal would boost South Korean economic links with Japan and Southeast Asia.

Moon Jae-in (2017–2022)

Moon Jae-in took office in 2017 as the first liberal president following two terms of conservative rule. Yet his approach toward Japan did not differ from his two predecessors or indeed from that pursued by South Korean presidents since the restoration of democracy in the late 1980s. Moon implemented a two-track approach to address historical issues and develop a future-oriented partnership separately.[145] The Moon government also continued to approach relations with Japan via bilateral and multilateral channels, as previous South Korean presidents dating back to Kim Young-sam had been doing. Indeed, trilateralism continued even during the Trump years, despite the U.S. president's disdain for allies and multilateral cooperation.

In the area of security, the Moon government continued to use South Korea's burgeoning military capabilities and the U.S. alliance to boost links with Japan. The Defense Trilateral Talks, annual minister of defense–level meetings, and bilateral and trilateral combined naval exercises continued in place. They were supplemented with U.S.-led multilateral exercises as Washington took an increasingly confrontational approach toward China. Australia joined the three countries for joint drills in the Western Pacific in 2019.[146] Another quadrilateral exercise involving the four countries was held in 2021.[147] And in 2022, the four of them conducted a six-way exercise together with Canada and India.[148] In 2020 South Korea and Japan joined EUNAVFOR for joint exercises in the Gulf of Aden without the United States.[149] These were among the many joint drills that strengthened interoperability between the ROK Navy and Japan's Maritime Self-Defense Force together with the navies of other like-minded partners.

When it came to protection from the North Korean threat and inter-Korean reconciliation and reunification, there was a period during the Trump administration years in which Seoul and Tokyo did not cooperate much with each other due to diverging approaches toward Pyongyang.[150] TISA and GSOMIA continued to serve Seoul and Tokyo to exchange intelligence. Once Joe Biden took office in 2021, trilateral coordination on North Korean issues was restored.[151] Once again the U.S. alliance served to bring Seoul and Tokyo closer to each other.

In the area of trade and investment, there was a landmark occasion when South Korea and Japan signed the RCEP deal in November 2020. (India had withdrawn from RCEP by then.) The agreement entered into force in January 2022, marking the first time that South Korea and Japan had been part of the same FTA. Also, the Moon government announced in December 2021 that it would seek membership of the Comprehensive and Progressive Agreement for Trans-Pacific Partnership (CPTPP), a decision that it officially announced the following April.[152] If South Korea joined the deal, this would mark even stronger economic relations with Japan since CPTPP covered a wider range of issues. On the negative side, historical disputes related to Japan's use of slave labor during World War II created economic frictions between Seoul and Tokyo. In June 2019, Japan announced that it would remove South Korea from its "whitelist" of fast-tracked trade partners after the South Korean Supreme Court ordered two

Japanese firms to pay compensation to slave workers they had employed. Japan proceeded with the removal in August, and South Korea's Ministry of Economy and Finance then reciprocated.[153] As a result, bilateral trade decreased in 2019 for the first time since the AFC. In addition, the Moon government brought a dispute against Japan in the WTO one month later. The dispute focused on measures related to the exportation of products and technology from Japan to South Korea.[154]

The impact of history on bilateral relations led the MND to downgrade Japan to "neighboring country" in its 2020 white paper.[155] In this respect, Japan's reaction to the Supreme Court's decision on the past use of slave labor by Japanese firms had an impact on relations between Seoul and Tokyo, as the two of them reduced the number of military exchanges and joint exercises. South Korea also continued its biannual military exercises in Dokdo. Yet South Korean diplomatic corps, public diplomacy, and soft power were deployed to support ends such as autonomy or recognition as an influential middle power. Most notably, Moon held trilateral summits with his Japanese and Chinese counterparts in 2018 and 2019, before the COVID-19 pandemic struck. Furthermore, the Korea Foundation, Korean cultural centers, and King Sejong institutes continued to carry out their activities normally. And the South Korean government continued to actively support K-pop concerts too. KCON returned to Japan in 2017, 2018, and 2019. The same South Korean government bodies as well as new ones such as the Small and Medium Business Administration and some regional governments lent their support.

Arguably, Southeast Asia was the region outside of South Korea's triangular core that Moon prioritized most clearly. Shortly after his inauguration, Moon sent a special envoy to Southeast Asia and then launched his flagship New Southern Policy (NSP) in Indonesia—later relabeled NSP+.[156] NSP built on the grand strategy that previous South Korean presidents had been pursuing, but it took that strategy to a new level in terms of the extent to which Seoul's means were activated to pursue its ends. In 2019, South Korea and ASEAN held a special commemorative summit in Busan to celebrate the thirtieth anniversary of the establishment of bilateral relations. The leaders of all ASEAN countries attended. Meanwhile, Moon was the first South Korean president to visit every single of the ten ASEAN members during his presidential tenure.[157] This type of diplomacy set the tone for the NSP.

South Korea prioritized trade, investment, and aid to boost its integration in the world economy. Seoul signed an FTA with Indonesia in 2020, a very significant development given that it was the biggest economy in Southeast Asia and had historically been reluctant to sign FTAs.[158] The Moon government also launched FTA negotiations with Cambodia and Malaysia.[159] Trade between South Korea and ASEAN continued to thrive in spite of the pandemic, making ASEAN South Korea's third largest trading partner by 2021. Vietnam became the fourth largest partner by itself.[160] The bilateral investment stock, meanwhile, reached a record $75.49 billion in 2020. This made ASEAN the second biggest destination of South Korean investment.[161] Aid to Asia reached $202.5 million that same year.[162]

The Moon government also made extensive use of public diplomacy and soft power to strengthen its position as a middle power. In September 2017, the Korea Foundation opened an ASEAN Culture House in Busan.[163] (This had been planned under the Park government.) KBS's Music Bank World Tour traveled to Singapore and Indonesia in 2017.[164] KCON, meanwhile, was also held in Thailand in 2018 and 2019.[165] Also in 2019, the Korea Foundation opened its second Southeast Asian office in Jakarta.[166] When the Ministry of Culture, Sports and Tourism opened its Hallyu Support and Cooperation Division in 2020, Southeast Asia was one of its key target regions. Similarly, the Moon government also made greater use of South Korea's military capabilities to boost links with Southeast Asia, mainly to deepen economic integration. Most notably, South Korea and Indonesia signed an agreement to jointly develop a jet fighter. In addition, South Korean arms sales to Southeast Asia reached a new high in 2021.

Moon also sought to use diplomacy to get Southeast Asian countries' support for his inter-Korean reconciliation and unification policy. The NSP included peace as one of its pillars, a reference to inter-Korean peace.[167] In his summit with ASEAN leaders, Moon called for their support with North Korea.[168] Furthermore, Moon included ASEAN as a member of his Northeast Asia Peace and Cooperation Platform (NAPC).[169] Like Park's NAPCI, NAPC sought to bring about better inter-Korean relations within a Northeast Asian framework.

Focusing on East Asia as a whole, Seoul continued to be part of and support ASEAN+3 and ASEAN-centered initiatives. But it was in the area of trade and investment that South Korean concentrated most efforts. Along with its involvement in RCEP negotiations and its interest in CPTPP, Seoul applied to join the Digital Economy Partnership Agreement (DEPA) in 2021.[170] Led by Singapore while also involving Chile and New Zealand, the agreement was potentially poised to become a standard-setter for digital commerce in East Asia and the Asia–Pacific region.

Yoon Suk-yeol (2022)

Yoon Suk-yeol took office with a strong focus on improving relations with Japan, which in his view had deteriorated under the previous government. Seoul's approach toward Tokyo under Yoon, in any case, built on the pillars of South Korea's grand strategy. In short, the Yoon government advocated a two-track approach delinking historical issues from contemporary relations. Yoon vowed to build a "Future-oriented Cooperative Relationship,"[171] a well-known phrase to indicate that the two countries should focus on what unites them as opposed to what separates them. In particular, Yoon emphasized cooperation with like-minded partners, a list including Japan.[172]

Therefore, the Yoon government engaged in different policies to reinvigorate ties with Japan. This included South Korea's diplomatic corps, with several meetings taking place including bilateral talks between Yoon and Japanese Prime Minister Kishida Fumio in September 2022, the first between the leaders of the two countries since 2019.[173] This was supplemented by multiple trilateral meetings also including the United States at the head of government, minister of foreign affairs, and minister of national defense levels.[174] South Korea also engaged in joint trilateral military exercises with the United States and Japan designed to contain North Korea. These included both regular drills, such as antimissile exercises, and others that had been dormant, including antisubmarine manuevers.[175] In addition, the Yoon government set on improving intelligence exchanges via GSOMIA, which had suffered from the 2019 trade dispute.[176] The ROK Navy once more joined Japan's fleet review for the first time since the Park Geun-hye years.[177]

In the case of Southeast Asia, the Yoon government continued the strategy pursued by previous governments. Yoon launched an "ABCD Strategy" focusing on advancing human capital, building health security, connecting cultures, and digitizing Asian infrastructure.[178] The strategy built on Moon's NSP/NSP+ and relied on South Korea's economic means to advance relations with Southeast Asian countries. In addition, the Yoon government continued to emphasize military cooperation with countries in the region, including arms sales and transfers.[179] Plus, the ROK army participated in the U.S.–Philippines Kamandag military drills in October for the first time ever, upping Seoul's military commitment to the region.[180] This showed that the more holistic approach already launched under previous governments continued under Yoon.

Furthermore, the Ministry of Trade, Industry and Energy (MOTIE) also reiterated the Yoon government's commitment to joining CPTPP and DEPA.[181] Along with membership of ASEAN+3 bodies plus the RCEP trade agreement, this symbolized Seoul's ongoing diplomatic and economic support to East Asian regionalism. In this respect, the Yoon government's aim to further diversify economic links away from China, especially, and the United States meant that Seoul's focus on stronger East Asian regionalism was seen as a way to facilitate trade and investment links with the region.[182]

South Korea's geographical location obviously and understandably informs its grand strategy. In recent decades, South Korean policymakers have clearly positioned their country within East Asia, understood as both Northeast Asia and Southeast Asia, along with regional initiatives led by or including the countries in the region, also in the Asia–Pacific. Considering that East Asia is the region where South Korea sits, there could be some differences as a result of domestic politics, particularly when it comes to relations with Japan, given its troubled history with (South) Korea. However, Seoul actually has a clear grand strategy toward East Asia.

Starting with Japan, South Korea has clear ends: above all protection from external military threats with the support of Japan (and the United States) but also the lingering threat of Tokyo itself with regard to Dokdo, deeper integration in the world economy, inter-Korean reconciliation and reunification, and recognition as an influential middle power. South Korea has used a number of different means to achieve these ends. Seoul has used its growing military capabilities to cooperate with Japan in the area of security but also to deter Tokyo in Dokdo, as well as its alliance with United States also for the purpose of trilateral security cooperation. The latter was particularly prominent during the Lee Myung-bak and Park Geun-hye presidencies, as well as toward the end of Moon Jae-in's and the start of Yoon Seok-yul's. Meanwhile, Seoul has used its diplomatic corps and trade and investment to pursue deeper economic ties with Tokyo, and it has deployed its diplomatic corps, public diplomacy, and soft power to be seen as a middle power.

In the case of Southeast Asia, successive South Korean presidents have prioritized autonomy, deeper integration in the world economy, and recognition as an influential middle power. In terms of tools, South Korea has employed a mixture of trade, investment, and aid, diplomacy, public diplomacy, soft power, and its growing military capabilities. Arguably, the use of economic tools and diplomacy dates back to the Roh Tae-woo and Kim Young-sam governments, respectively. As for public diplomacy and soft power, their use increased significantly from the Roh Moo-hyun and Lee Myung-bak years onward. South Korea's use of military capabilities to pursue its goals vis-a-vis Southeast Asia is a more recent phenomenon that really blossomed only after Moon Jae-in took office.

Finally, South Korea has seen state-led regionalism as an opportunity to boost its autonomy, integration in the world economy, and middle power recognition. In this case, South Korea has mainly focused on the use of its trade, investment, and aid, together with its diplomatic corps. Indeed, there has been great emphasis in regional East Asian or Asia-Pacific initiatives. It was in the aftermath of the AFC and once Kim Dae-jung took office that South Korea focused on having a potentially leading role in regional initiatives, which eventually also covered Northeast Asian security once Park Geun-hye took office.

CHAPTER VI

Greater Eurasia and the Indian Ocean

reater Eurasia and the Indian Ocean make a vast region. From
the perspective of South Korean policymakers, it is the region
that matters the most beyond its immediate vicinity. Greater Eurasia is the landmass of which South Korea is part. Meanwhile, the Indian
Ocean is the waterway that connects the different parts of the landmass.
Historically, South Korea did not pay much attention to this region beyond
limited links with some parts of it for economic, energy, and resource-
related reasons. But the importance of Greater Eurasia and the Indian
Ocean for South Korea has increased as the country has become more powerful and has developed a more proactive grand strategy. Whereas initially
South Korea's interest in this vast region focused on its own economic interests, over time the country's policymakers have also developed a grand
strategy related to political and security developments.

South Korean strategy toward Greater Eurasia and the Indian Ocean pays
particular attention to Russia, which has a land border with the Korean Peninsula, has had a historical interest in it, and is the only truly Eurasian country connecting the European and Asian parts. In fact, Russia has strived to
become more central to Asian geopolitics in recent decades, and especially
since President Vladimir Putin first took office in 2000. Even so, Russia
continues to be secondary in Asia, and particularly in East Asia. It is
excluded from East Asian and more recent Asia–Pacific economic activities. Its role in East Asian security discussions and institutions is secondary.

And it is excluded from the main political forums in the region. But Russia matters when it comes to Eurasia and in South Korean grand strategy, both in its own right and separate to the rest of the Eurasian landmass. It affects South Korean ends in issues including autonomy, protection from external military threats, deeper integration in the world economy, or recognition as an influential middle power. South Korea uses all available means to tackle relations with Russia.

Europe is the second most important part of this region from a South Korean perspective. This includes the main trade route between South Korea and the European continent: the Indian Ocean. Europe matters to South Korea primarily for economic reasons, particularly the European Union as one of the "big three" economies together with China and the United States. Increasingly, however, the European Union, North Atlantic Treaty Organization (NATO), and key European middle powers such as France, Germany, and the United Kingdom have become more central to the political and security components of the South Korean grand strategy. The same applies to Australia. Arguably, it has become integrated into East Asia from an economic point of view, along with New Zealand. But from a political and security point of view, it remains secondary to the region. From a South Korean perspective, it is part of the Greater Eurasia and Indian Ocean region. For South Korea, Australia matters due to its presence in the Indian Ocean, or the "Indo" part of the Indo-Pacific—a geographical and geopolitical concept that became popular from the late 2010s. South Korea pursues all its goals bar inter-Korean reconciliation and reunification in relation to Europe, the Indian Ocean, and Australia. Seoul uses all the means at its disposal to deal with them, except for cybertools.

Central Asia, the Greater Middle East, and South Asia are also part of South Korea's grand strategy toward the Greater Eurasia and Indian Ocean region. Certainly, different countries in these three regions matter most. India, Kazakhstan, Saudi Arabia, and Uzbekistan, for different reasons, are particularly relevant for South Korean grand strategists. But in general these regions as a whole are relevant for economic reasons primarily—with the interest being mutual. Increasingly, certain security developments in these regions also inform South Korean grand strategy as well. Thus, South Korean grand strategy toward Central Asia, the Greater Middle East and South Asia is linked to the goals of deeper integration in the world economy and recognition as an influential middle power above all. In terms of

TABLE 6.1

South Korea's grand strategy toward Greater Eurasia and the Indian Ocean

Key factors	Key ends	Key means
ROK–U.S. alliance, rise of China, economic development, middle power identity, regional integration and globalization	Autonomy, protection from external military threats, deeper integration in the world economy, recognition as an influential middle power	Growing military capabilities; cyber tools; U.S. alliance; diplomatic corps; trade, investment, and aid; public diplomacy; soft power

the means that South Korea uses in these regions, they include diplomatic corps, trade, investment, and aid, and soft power primarily.

Roh Tae-woo (1988–1993)

Roh Tae-woo's signature policy was *Nordpolitik*. This policy elevated the importance of the Soviet Union and then Russia, after the disintegration of the former, as part of South Korea's grand strategy. Putting behind the enmity of the Cold War era, *Nordpolitik* put autonomy, deeper integration in the world economy, and recognition as an influential middle power as the key ends for South Korea to achieve from its relationship with Russia. Other goals including protection from external military threats and inter-Korean reconciliation and reunification also mattered, but only to a lesser extent. In terms of means to implement its strategy toward the Soviet Union/Russia, the Roh government prioritized South Korea's diplomatic corps and trade, investment, and aid. Subsequent governments would go on to do the same.

The Soviet Union participated in the Seoul 1988 Olympic Games, shunning North Korea's calls for boycott. Then, the Korea Trade-Investment Promotion Agency, back then still known as Korea Trade Promotion Corporation, opened an office in Moscow in 1989 after Russia opened a Chamber of Commerce and Industry branch in Seoul.[1] South Korea then normalized diplomatic relations with the Soviet Union in September 1990. Shortly after, Roh paid an official visit to the Soviet Union to meet with President Mikhail Gorbachev and became the first South Korean president to ever set foot in the country.[2] Following the collapse of the Soviet Union, South Korea and Russia quickly established diplomatic relations. In 1992, South Korea was the first Asian country that new Russian President Boris Yeltsin visited, and Roh and Yeltsin signed the Treaty on Basic Relations Between the Republic of Korea and Russia.[3] Meanwhile, Seoul had provided Moscow a $3 billion loan in 1990. Payment was partially made in natural gas and oil. And by 1991, discussions between the two countries were focusing on the construction of an oil pipeline to export Russian oil. The plan was that this pipeline would go through North Korea, thus also helping to support inter-Korean links.[4] The pipeline would also boost South Korea's transit security, as a country heavily reliant on overseas oil and gas and with a need to diversify its energy import routes. This line of thought has not fully disappeared in 2023, in spite of the vagaries of inter-Korean relations. In a relatively short period of time South Korea and the Soviet Union/Russia went from being part of the opposite camps during the Cold War to having a burgeoning diplomatic and economic relationship.

Arguably, however, an even bigger shift in South Korea-Russia relations took place in the security field. The Roh government wanted to boost Seoul's autonomous ability to protect itself against potential attacks by boosting its military capabilities. Russia had highly developed military technology as well as a need for economic support. Already in 1991, Moscow offered MiG jets to Seoul. In 1992, the Roh government announced that it wanted to partner with Russian firms to acquire and commercialize their military equipment.[5] Shortly afterward, Seoul and Moscow signed a memorandum of understanding on military exchanges.[6] This way, Roh laid the groundwork for deeper security ties between the two countries.

In terms of relations with Europe, the Roh government focused on diplomatic relations as a means to strengthen its autonomy by diversifying partners, as well as trade and investment to deepen its integration in the world economy. Most notably, South Korea exchanged ambassadorial-level permanent missions with Hungary in 1989 and exchanged trade offices with Hungary and Yugoslavia that same year.[7] One year later, Roh completed a multicountry tour of Europe also including Central and Eastern Europe.[8] In subsequent years, as communist regimes fell while Yugoslavia disintegrated, Seoul normalized diplomatic relations with the newly independent states.[9] South Korean *chaebol*, for their part, started to open offices and invest in these countries.[10] As for Western Europe, In Seoul opened its permanent mission to the European Community (EC) in 1989—the predecessor of the European Union. One year later, the EC reciprocated by opening its representation to South Korea.[11] Trade and investment relations increased during the Roh years, but Europe remained a relatively small partner compared to other countries and regions.[12]

South Korea grand strategy toward Greater Eurasia and the Indian Ocean also involved a focus on economic links with the Greater Middle East and diplomatic relations with Central Asia. The former was the largest source of oil for South Korea. Saudi Arabia, above all, and Iran, the United Arab Emirates, and Oman were the largest sources. Around 80 percent of South Korean oil imports came from the region, a percentage that has remained relatively constant all the way until 2023.[13] South Korea focused on maintaining strong diplomatic relations with these countries to maintain access to their oil. This helped, among others, for the Korea National Oil Corporation (KNOC) to sign a contract with the Libyan government to participate in an oil production project.[14] This also informed a growing interest in transit security from the region that remains as of 2023, including the development and deployment of blue water naval capabilities. As for Central Asia, South Korea established diplomatic relations with the newly independent countries in the region in 1992.[15] In other words, Seoul sought to normalize relations within months of their independence. They were potential energy suppliers, but Uzbekistan and Kazakhstan were also home to some of the biggest Korean diasporas around the world and might serve as an entry point for stronger economic and diplomatic links.[16]

South Korea also participated in the Gulf War of 1990–1991 involving a U.S.-led coalition fighting against Iraq.[17] The Roh government dispatched more than three hundred military medics and transport support specialists. The coalition was set up under UN Security Council Resolution 678 in the first war mission approved by that body since the Korean War.[18] It was the first time since the Vietnam War that the ROK Army was being deployed to fight a war. From Seoul's perspective, participation in the war helped to show South Korean autonomy within a multilateral coalition, helped to boost the security of South Korea, and showed its position as a middle power.[19] Certainly participation in the Gulf War also helped South Korea to show its support to its close ally, the United States.

Kim Young-sam (1993–1998)

The Kim Young-sam government picked up where the Roh government left off with regard to relations with Russia. In 1993, Seoul and Moscow signed an agreement on mutual cooperation in the military industry.[20] This paved the way for deeper military links. One year later, South Korea launched the "Brown Bear Project."[21] The objective was for Seoul to acquire technology and know-how that would accelerate development of the capabilities of the ROK Armed Forces and thus boost the country's security. That same, year, Russian engineers were dispatched to South Korea and Moscow agreed to provide missiles, jet fighters, and other weaponry as part payment for the loan provided by the Roh government previously.[22] Arms and military technology transfers and sales continued to increase, reaching their peak in 1997. In the meantime, South Korean defense firms established partnerships with Russian counterparts to develop high-tech products such as submarines.[23]

South Korea also sought to enhance its economy by strengthening links with Russia. The two countries continued to explore the possibility of building a pipeline crossing North Korea.[24] This seemed unrealistic considering the internal turmoil there, but a small amount of Russian oil was making its way toward South Korea.[25] Meanwhile, South Korean firms increased exports to Russia while seeking potential joint ventures in the country as its economy opened up.[26] The Kim government also saw soft power as a way to boost links with Russia, also considering the Korean diaspora in the country.[27] In 1995, the Korean Cultural Center opened a branch in Moscow.[28]

The Kim government deepened the focus of South Korea's grand strategy toward trade and investment in Europe. In 1996, South Korea and the European Union signed a Trade and Cooperation Agreement.[29] The two parties wanted to reduce barriers to bilateral trade and investment as well as to start promoting political cooperation. From a South Korean perspective, the agreement with the European Union was a way to both deepen its economic integration with the region and boost its autonomy by forging stronger links with the second biggest economy in the world, which was only poised to grow as new members were joining and Central and Eastern European countries were lining up to be granted membership.[30] In addition, the Ministry of Culture and Sports opened its second Korean

Cultural Center in Europe in Berlin in 1994.[31] Seoul now had cultural centers to seek to use its soft power to boost links with Europe in both France and Germany.

At the same time, South Korea also wanted to boost its economic and diplomatic links with the European Union via East Asian regionalism. In 1996, Seoul was one of the founding members of the Asia–Europe Meeting (ASEM). South Korea, the European Union, ASEAN, China, and Japan launched this meeting, including political and economic pillars.[32] ASEM served to counterbalance their respective relationships with the United States. From a South Korean perspective, ASEM could serve to boost its autonomy as well, by strengthening diplomatic links with a new partner, the European Union , which promised to become a stronger voice in international politics.

In the case of the Greater Middle East, the region continued to provide the bulk of oil imported by South Korea.[33] Seoul maintained its resource diplomacy toward the region. That is, the Kim government continued to use South Korean diplomats as the means to preserve good economic relations. In addition, South Korea deployed peacekeepers to the UN mission in Western Sahara in 1994.[34] This way, Seoul also started to make use of its military capabilities in support of its grand strategy toward the region. Meanwhile, Australia started to export liquefied natural gas (LNG) to South Korea in 1993.[35] This was part of South Korea's resource diplomacy and strategy to deepen integration with different parts of the world. Differently, relations with Central Asia did not take off to the extent that normalization in 1992 may have promised. There were incipient economic exchanges, but they were minimal compared to other parts of the Greater Eurasia and Indian Ocean region. In this respect, Seoul also started to provide aid to South Asian countries.[36] And in 1994, Seoul dispatched peacekeepers to the UN mission on the Indo-Pakistani border.[37] South Korea was thereby using aid and its military capabilities to boost its image as a middle power.

The Indian Ocean itself, meanwhile, started to become a bigger focus of South Korean grand strategists. In 1995, Kim agreed for the ROK Navy to start to prepare to develop blue-water capabilities. Discussions about a blue-water navy dated back to the Roh years, but it was Kim who made clear that this was an imperative for South Korea.[38] The Kim government approved a long-term plan for the ROK Navy to build the autonomous capabilities to have a blue-navy fleet.[39] The Indian Ocean was a key focus of this plan because it was the main route for oil and gas imports coming from the Greater Middle East. It also was the main trade route between South Korea and the growing EU market and essential for the purposes of transit security.

Kim Dae-jung (1998–2003)

Kim Dae-jung's grand strategy toward Greater Eurasia and the Indian Ocean continued from his predecessors' policies while deepening relations with some of the countries and subregions in this vast region. Starting with Russia, stronger military links continued to be a feature of the relationship as Seoul sought to upgrade its military to provide for its own security. In fact, the year 1997 had marked a record in terms of arms sales and military technology transfers from Russia to South Korea that would never be matched again, but both sales and transfers continued to be high during the Kim years.[40] Meanwhile, Moscow and Pyongyang signed a new Treaty of Friendship, Good Neighborliness, and Cooperation that did not commit the former to protect the latter in case of war—a key difference with their Soviet-era agreement.[41] In 2001, newly elected Russian president Vladimir Putin visited South Korea in one of his first foreign policy visits and even before meeting with North Korean leader Kim Jong-il.[42] This suggested that the military relationship between Seoul and Moscow was stronger than the relationship between the latter and Pyongyang. A second "Brown Bear Project" followed, with Russia providing tanks, armored vehicles, anti-tank guided missiles, or helicopters to South Korea in 2002–2006.[43] Putin's visit to South Korea shortly after his inauguration likewise indicated that the Kim government was also using diplomacy to boost links with Russia in the quest to gain support for its "Sunshine Policy," giving the Putin administration a role in supporting inter-Korean relations.

In addition, the Kim government saw Russia playing a greater role in South Korea's integration in the world economy by diversifying economic links. In 2000, Seoul and Moscow signed an energy and resources agreement.[44] The agreement granted South Korea preferential access to Russian oil, gas, and minerals. Indeed, Russian oil exports to South Korea increased during the Kim years compared to earlier periods.[45] Yet Russian oil remained a small share of South Korean imports, and LNG transfers continued to represent a small amount of South Korea's overall consumption.

Moving on to the Greater Middle East, energy links continued to dominate the relationship. Oil from countries including Saudi Arabia, Iran, United Arab Emirates, and Oman and LNG from Qatar or Oman were crucial for South Korean quest for economic security.[46] In fact, the Greater Middle East became the main source of LNG for South Korea during the Kim years, a position it maintained all the way to 2023. To this end, South Korea flexed its diplomatic and trade and investment muscles. In 1999, the Korea Gas Corporation (KOGAS)—South Korea's state-owned gas firm—signed an agreement with the Qatari government to procure LNG from the country. A year later, the firm did the same with the government of Oman.[47] This secured reliable access to gas from the two countries. Meanwhile, Seoul also continued to deploy its peacekeepers in Western Sahara.[48]

Other than the Greater Middle East, South Korea also engaged in resource diplomacy in Australia and Central Asia. Australian direct LNG exports helped Seoul to further integrate in the world economy beyond its traditional partners.[49] The Kim government signed an energy and resources agreement with a country located at the intersection between Central Asia and East Asia, Mongolia, in 1999.[50] As for Central Asia proper, links with South Korea were strengthened, especially via diplomacy and soft power, but they did not produce any significant breakthrough. In the case of South Asia, aid flows continued to be the dominant feature of South Korean grand strategy in the region.[51]

In the case of Europe, the Kim government focused on the diversification of South Korea's economic links and support for its "Sunshine Policy" toward North Korea. And diplomacy was also upgraded during Kim's tenure, with South Korea and the European Union holding their first bilateral head-of-government summit in September 2002. Trade and investment grew bigger, thanks partly to the entry into force of the bilateral Trade and Cooperation Agreement in 2001.[52] As for North Korea policy, Seoul supported the European Union's move to establish a bilateral Political Dialogue with Pyongyang.[53] The first session was held in 1998. The Kim government then hosted the ASEM summit in 2000. The summit was held in October, only four months after the first-ever inter-Korean summit. In the chairman's statement prepared by Seoul, ASEM members including the European Union and European countries pledged to support stronger inter-Korean links.[54] During this period, Kim toured several European countries. His main focus was to gather their support for his North Korea policy, most notably with a speech in Berlin.[55] The combination of the

ASEM summit and the trip was successful in helping the European Union and Western European countries including Germany, Spain, and the United Kingdom to establish diplomatic relations with Pyongyang.[56]

The Kim government also continued to prioritize the development of a blue-water navy to project South Korean capabilities into the Indian Ocean, among other ends. This would support South Korea's goals of strengthening its own security and being recognized as a middle power. Kim announced the creation of an "Strategic Mobile Fleet" in 2001.[57] This fleet would be the basis of a blue-water navy capable of operating in waters across the world, a plan dating back to the Kim Young-sam years but launched only under Kim Dae-jung. In 2001–2003, the ROK Navy dispatched amphibious vessels to the Indian Ocean and elsewhere to support the U.S. Global War on Terror.[58] This was considered a stepping stone in South Korea's development of a full-scale blue-water navy.

Roh Moo-hyun (2003–2008)

The Roh Moo-hyun government took office and continued implementation of South Korea's grand strategy, but upgraded relations with Europe, the Greater Middle East, and Central Asia by diversifying the means used in each of these regions. Russia continued to be the main focus of South Korean grand strategy in the Greater Eurasia and Indian Ocean region. The Roh government established a "Bilateral Strategic Partnership" in 2004.[59] Arms sales and military technology transfers continued to be part of the bilateral relationship, but there was a decline in both as South Korea developed its indigenous capabilities and it had already acquired most of the technology that it wanted to get from Russia.[60] Resource diplomacy arguably became more important, and in 2006 Seoul and Moscow signed a new energy and resource agreement.[61] The Roh government believed that the previous deal was inadequate. The agreement resulted in oil exports from Russia to South Korea more than doubling.[62] Also, South Korea saw public diplomacy as a means to strengthen relations with Russia. In 2005, the Korea Foundation opened an office in Moscow.[63]

Arguably, however, it was the goal of improving inter-Korean relations that in which South Korea-Russia relations reached a new level. Russia was one of the founding members of the Six-Party Talks launched in 2003 to solve the second North Korean nuclear crisis. In the beginning, there were doubts about whether to include Russia in the talks.[64] Once Moscow became part of the Six-Party Talks process, however, South Korean diplomats found it easy to work with their Russian counterparts. They felt that Russia was taking a pragmatic approach, and their emphasis on the need for the United States to normalize relations with North Korea fit the Roh government's approach.[65]

In the case of Europe, South Korea pursued autonomy, deeper economic integration, and middle power recognition using a variety of means. Seoul formally asked the European Union to launch bilateral FTA negotiations. With the European Union being one of the two biggest economies in the world along with the United States, South Korea saw the potential benefits of easier market access to its firms.[66] Brussels rejected Seoul's proposal, though. On the other hand, deeper economic ties between South Korea and Europe also created greater frictions. The Kim government brought three cases against the European Union through the WTO's dispute-settlement mechanism in 2003–2004. The cases focused on countervailing measures on dynamic random access memory chips from South Korea, trade in commercial vessels, and aid for commercial vessels.[67] Meanwhile, South Korea focused on launching an FTA with the European Free Trade Association (EFTA), led by Norway. Negotiations proceeded smoothly, and South Korea and EFTA signed a bilateral trade deal in 2005 that entered into force only one year later.[68] At the same time, South Korea introduced the use of public diplomacy in its strategy toward Europe with the opening of a Korea Foundation office in Berlin in 2005.[69] Seoul consolidated the use of its diplomatic corps by holding two more rounds of its bilateral summit with Brussels.[70] In addition and significantly, South Korea's growing military capabilities and diplomatic corps also led to South Korea becoming a dialogue partner with NATO in 2005.[71] The relationship between the two of them would strengthen substantially from then on.

The Roh government built on the grand strategy pursued by previous governments in the Greater Middle East but was also the first to have a well-developed foreign policy toward the region. Oil and gas transfers continued to dominate the relationship, with Greater Middle Eastern countries being the largest suppliers of both to South Korea.[72] In 2005, KNOC was part of a consortium awarded an oil development project by the Yemeni government.[73] But the Roh government also sought to boost broader economic relations, in particular by supporting the presence of South Korean firms in the region to benefit from its middle-class consumers and to push for economic diversification. South Korea launched negotiations with the Gulf Cooperation Council to establish a free trade agreement with the region in 2006 via a country-to-region format. It also supported South Korean firms involved in the building of new infrastructure across countries in the region.[74] South Korea also increased its security ties in the Greater Middle East, making use of its military capabilities. To begin with, South Korea deployed troops to Iraq in 2004 in support of the U.S.-led Coalition of the Willing.[75] In 2006, South Korea and the United Arab Emirates signed their first military memorandum of understanding.[76] This was a first for Seoul with a country in the region. In 2007, South Korean peacekeepers joined the UN mission in Lebanon, and peacekeepers in Western Sahara continued to be deployed until 2006.[77]

Similarly, the Roh government arguably was the first in South Korean history to launch a well-developed Central Asia strategy. In 2005, the Roh government announced a Comprehensive Central Asia Initiative. The pillars of the strategy were the deepening of bilateral economic ties and strengthening South Korea's credentials as a middle power. With regards to the former, KNOC signed an agreement in 2005 to secure access to oil from the country.[78] KOGAS, meanwhile, signed an agreement of its own with Uzbekistan in 2006 to facilitate the extraction and export of gas from the Central Asian republic to South Korea.[79] In 2007, the Korea Foundation launched the Korea-Central Asia Cooperation Forum.[80] This was developed under the Roh presidency with the goal of using public diplomacy to strengthen country-to-region links.

As for Australia and the Indian Ocean, the Roh government also deepened relations based on long-standing South Korean grand strategy. In 2004, Seoul and Canberra signed an energy and resources agreement to facilitate South Korean access to Australian gas and minerals.[81] The agreement, indeed, helped Australian LNG exports to South Korea to more than double.[82] South Korea's development of its blue-water capabilities allowed the ROK Navy to support humanitarian efforts following the 2004 tsunami that hit Indonesia.[83] This implied the use of military capabilities to strengthen South Korean credentials as a middle power. In contrast, relations with South Asia continued to be heavily dominated by aid flows.[84]

Lee Myung-bak (2008–2013)

The Lee Myung-bak government took office and set to create a "Global Korea." In the case of the Greater Eurasia and Indian Ocean region, in practical terms this implied building on the grand strategy pursued by previous South Korean governments yet expanding the number of ends and means included. Russia continued to be at the center of South Korean strategy toward the region, even if the relative importance of the country's neighbor declined as other countries and subregions such as the European Union became more relevant for Seoul. Lee labeled his policy toward Russia a "Bilateral Strategic Partnership," which referred to a push for a comprehensive relationship.[85] South Korea continued to focus on its resource diplomacy. If anything, this only grew in importance as it became a central pillar of Lee's foreign policy. Oil exports from Russia to South Korea continued to grow, albeit still not to the extent that Moscow's relative importance in this area increased significantly.[86]

Russia also remained an actor in South Korea's policy toward North Korea. The Six-Party Talks had stopped, but the Lee government saw Moscow as a potential player in the resumption of diplomacy with Pyongyang.[87] On the other hand, Russia was also considered to be an important player in the application of the sanctions regime to force North Korea to reverse its nuclear and missile program. To this end, South Korea used its diplomatic corps to try to influence Russia to support its policy.

In the case of Europe, bilateral relations between South Korea and the European Union received a significant boost during the Lee government's time in office. In 2010, the two of them signed an FTA that would already provisionally enter into force one year later.[88] For South Korea, this was its first FTA with one of the "big three" major economies. Plus, Seoul was the first Asian country to ink an agreement with Brussels, thus giving it a comparative advantage vis-à-vis other Asian countries. The FTA also served the Lee government to bargain with the United States as Washington demanded a revision of the Korea–United States Free Trade Agreement (KORUS) before the U.S. Congress would approve it.[89] On the other side, this was the European Union's first new-generation FTA covering areas such as services, the environment, or labor issues. It was also its first FTA with an Asian country, and it served as a blueprint for future FTAs with other Asian countries such as Japan, Singapore, and Vietnam, a positive aspect for South Korea since its firms had longer time to adapt to the demands of the EU market. In addition, South Korea also launched FTA negotiations with Turkey in 2010. The two countries signed an agreement in 2012.[90] In short, relations with Europe served South Korea its purpose of deepening integration in the global economy. Besides, South Korea used its growing military capabilities to strengthen relations with Europe. Turkey was the largest market for South Korean arms exporters during this period.[91] Seoul continued to strengthen its relations with NATO as well. Most notably, South Korea's deployment in Afghanistan in 2010–2014 was part of the organization's International Security Assistance Force (ISAF).[92]

Seoul also used diplomacy in its relationship with Europe and in its quest to be recognized as a relevant middle power. In 2010, South Korea and the European Union upgraded their relationship to a strategic partnership.[93] The two partners vowed to cooperate in a wide range of political and security issues and launched or upgraded dozens of dialogues in the coming years covering these two areas. Meanwhile, their bilateral summits continued. Beyond politics and security, the Lee government pledged to make public diplomacy a central pillar of its foreign policy. The Korea Foundation increased the number of its projects in Europe.[94] Korean Cultural centers opened in Hungary, Poland, Spain, Turkey, and the United Kingdom during Lee's tenure.[95] King Sejong institutes started to open across Europe as well.[96] The Lee government also started to systematically use soft power to boost its middle power credentials and support its economic integration. France hosted KBS's Music Bank World Tour in 2012 and Turkey also hosted KBS's festival one year later.[97]

In the meantime, South Korean policy toward the Greater Middle East became more diversified as South Korea saw opportunities to attain different goals in the region. Economic diversification certainly continued to be a top priority. The Greater Middle East continued to be the largest provider of oil and gas to South Korea, with its share in the case of the latter growing even further.[98] State-owned enterprises continued to sign new contracts across the region to secure access to its energy resources. KNOC and KOGAS signed an agreement with Yemen in 2009.[99] That same year, KOGAS was part of a consortium awarded an oil development project, and a year later KOGAS again was a member of a consortium awarded a gas development project.[100] In addition, South Korea joined the multilateral coalition involved in post-conflict reconstruction in Afghanistan and Libya.[101] This boosted Seoul's middle power credentials. And in 2009,

South Korea and the GFC launched FTA negotiations.[102] The objective of the Lee government was not only to support its resource diplomacy, but also to facilitate South Korean exports including goods and cultural products as well as market access for infrastructure firms. Most notably, South Korean firms won a $40 billion contract to develop nuclear power plants in the United Arab Emirates and engaged in negotiations about similar deals in other countries across the region. The Lee government was directly involved in the negotiations.[103]

South Korea also made use of its military capabilities to boost its middle power status and to deepen economic integration. The mission in Afghanistan was the clearest example. In addition, the ROK Armed Forces deployed the Akh unit to the United Arab Emirates at the request of the host country to provide support in training the country's special forces and conducting joint exercises.[104]

Similarly, South Korea launched a multifaceted policy toward Central Asia during this period of time. The Lee government included Central Asia in its New Asia Initiative to link together the different parts of Asia through a mixture of economic, security, and diplomatic links.[105] The most noteworthy developments were two oil access agreements signed between KNOC and the government of Kazakhstan in 2009 and 2011.[106] Oil from the country would eventually start to flow to South Korea, thus further diversifying the energy sources of the country.[107] Also in Kazakhstan, the Ministry of Culture, Sports and Tourism opened a Korean Cultural Center in 2010.[108] This way, soft power reached the region.

Similarly, India and the Indian Ocean became more prominent in South Korean grand strategy. In 2006, Seoul and Delhi had launched FTA negotiations. Finally, an economic partnership agreement was signed in 2009 and entered into force one year later.[109] South Korea and India also signed a strategic partnership in 2010 to boost political and security ties.[110] More broadly, South Asia was included in the New Asia Initiative that the Lee government hoped would boost links among Asian countries. The subregion continued to be a large recipient of South Korean aid.[111] In the case of the Indian Ocean, a crucial development took place in 2009, when the ROK Navy deployed the Cheonghae Unit to the Gulf of Aden in support of the UN-approved multilateral task force mandated with countering piracy in these waters.[112] South Korea's development of blue-water capabilities was thus having a clear role in support of its security and status as a middle power. The unit would remain in place during at least the next three presidencies.

The Lee government pushed to take relations with Australia to a new level. It was included in the aforementioned New Asia Initiative, symbolizing that from Seoul's perspective the boundaries of the continent were broadening. In 2008, South Korea launched FTA negotiations with Australia.[113] At the same time, energy and natural resources continued to flow from Australia to South Korea.[114] In 2009, Seoul and Canberra signed a memorandum of understanding to boost defense and security ties.[115] This was a significant development in that it signaled that Seoul was using its growing military capabilities to strengthen relations with like-minded partners. Finally, the Lee government opened a Korean Cultural Center in Australia in 2011, adding the country to the list of those targeted by South Korean soft power.[116]

Park Geun-hye (2013–2017)

The Park Geun-hye government had a more conflictual relationship with Russia. On the positive side, economic relations continued to improve. Most notably, Russian oil exports to South Korea grew during the time of the Park government in office.[117] Furthermore, Park's Northeast Asia Peace and Cooperation Initiative (NAPCI) included Russia. This gave renewed political impetus to the idea of the development of a pipeline from Russia through North Korea and into South Korea.[118] For also on the positive side, the Park government believed that Russia could play a role in finding a diplomatic solution to the North Korean nuclear issue. Moscow therefore continued to be afforded a role in South Korea's goal of improving inter-Korean relations. On the negative side, South Korea perceived Russia to be more aggressive. In particular, Seoul was wary of growing Sino-Russian ties, and Moscow's annexation of Ukraine's Crimea region in 2014 sent shockwaves in Seoul, which criticized Russian actions due to their disregard for international law.[119] The invasion led to the cancellation of a planned third "Brown Bear Project."[120] South Korea's development of its jet fighter, missile, and other military program plus its growing focus on cybersecurity now also had Russia in mind.[121] Seoul's extension of its Air Defense Identification Zone (ADIZ) in December 2013 also affected

Russia because it overlapped with Moscow's own ADIZ.[122] South Korea's end when it came to Russia started to involve the defense of its own security.

In the other parts of Eurasia, meanwhile, South Korea continued to develop a set of policies that supported a broad set of goals and boosted its autonomy. Starting with Europe, the European Union became the largest investor in South Korea partly thanks to the bilateral FTA signed in 2010.[123] The FTA with Turkey entered into force in 2013, leading to a boost to bilateral trade flows.[124] Furthermore, KOGAS signed an agreement with Cyprus to participate in a consortium to produce gas.[125] Together with oil exports from the United Kingdom, including thanks to a KNOC deal to take a local firm dating back to 2010, this embedded Europe into South Korea's resource diplomacy. In the meantime, cultural diplomacy and soft power continued to be part of the mix of South Korea's grand strategy toward the region as it pushed to boost its middle power credentials. Two new Korean cultural centers opened in Belgium and Italy in 2013 and 2016, respectively.[126] The Korea Foundation continued its operations, while the number of King Sejong institutes across Europe increased. Furthermore, KBS's Music Bank was held in Germany in 2018, and KCON reached France in 2016.[127] And in terms of the use of diplomatic corps, the Park government included Turkey in its MIKTA initiative as a means to boost its middle power credentials.[128]

Security was the area in which South Korea–Europe relations took a qualitative jump. In 2014, South Korea and the European Union signed the Framework Agreement for the Participation of the ROK in EU Crisis Management Operations.[129] This agreement allowed the ROK Armed Forces to be embedded in EU peacekeeping missions. This way, South Korea became the first country in the world to sign the three key agreements covering economics, politics, and security with the European Union. Also in 2014, Seoul joined NATO's Partnership Interoperability Initiative, allowing the ROK Armed Forces to participate in a platform bringing together NATO members and partners from across the world.[130] As Seoul continued to boost its military capabilities, it was deepening its security ties with Europe. At the same time, the Park government embedded the European Union in its policy toward inter-Korean relations. Indeed, the European Union became a NAPCI dialogue partner upon its inception in 2014.[131] For the first time, Seoul involved the European Union in a multilateral process to try to strengthen inter-Korean links.

The diversification of ends and means of previous presidents continued in the Greater Middle East. Oil and gas exports from the region toward South Korea arguably remained the strongest link between both. Greater Middle East oil exports continued to account for around 80 percent of the oil reaching South Korea, and the region also provided more than half of the gas consumed by South Korean firms and households.[132] In the meantime, South Korea also continued to seek ways to boost trade and investment links with the region. In 2016, South Korea launched FTA negotiations with Israel.[133] Park continued to promote South Korean firms across the region. This included arms exports, with South Korea selling arms to Iraq.[134] Plus, South Korea continued to make use of its soft power and public diplomacy to gain a greater foothold in the Greater Middle East in support of its ends. The Korean Cultural Center opened two new venues in Egypt in 2014 and in the United Arab Emirates in 2016.[135] KCON was held in the region for the first time, with Abu Dhabi hosting the K-pop festival in 2016.[136] Meanwhile, South Korean peacekeepers continued to operate in Lebanon, with Seoul making use of its military capabilities.[137]

In the case of Central Asia, the Park government launched the Eurasia Initiative.[138] This initiative built on the grand strategy of previous governments but expanded the range of tools used by Seoul to achieve its goals. To begin with, South Korea used its diplomatic corps, soft power, and public diplomacy to systematically reach out to the Korean diaspora in Central Asia. For the first time, a South Korean government was treating the diaspora as potential agents to support the country's ultimate goals. In 2015, Seoul opened a Korean Cultural Center in Kazakhstan.[139] And the Korea Foundation was tasked with establishing the Korea–Central Asia Cooperation Forum Secretariat, which would finally launch only a few months after Park left office.[140] Furthermore, oil from Kazakhstan continued to flow to South Korea, and KOGAS launched an LNG extraction and export project in Uzbekistan to secure access to gas from the country.[141] Park included Mongolia in NAPCI since she saw the potential for the country to change the behavior of North Korea as a fellow small power surrounded by more powerful and more developed countries.[142]

In the case of Australia, South Korean grand strategy reached new heights and also became more diversified. In 2013, Seoul and Canberra held their inaugural 2+2 meeting involving the ministries of Foreign Affairs and Defense.[143] One year later, the two countries signed a Vision Statement to serve as the basis for political, economic, and security relations.[144] In 2014,

South Korea and Australia signed their FTA, which entered into force later in the year.[145] In 2015, the two countries came up with a Defense and Security Cooperation Blueprint. That same year, KOGAS launched an LNG project granted by the Australian government.[146] Within a year, Australian exports of LNG to South Korea more than doubled.[147] Park also invited Australia to join MIKTA.[148] The Korean Cultural Center continued to operate, while the Korea Foundation also continued to provide grants to Australian institutions.[149] The Park government was using trade and investment, its diplomatic corps, growing military capabilities, soft power, and public diplomacy to boost economic and political links with Australia.

The Cheonghae Unit continued to operate in the Gulf of Aden. The ROK Navy was conducting joint exercises, patrols, and counterpiracy activities together with the navies of other countries.[150] This symbolized South Korea's use of its growing military assets to protect its own security but also to project its image as a middle power. Meanwhile, in the case of India and the rest of South Asia trade links with the former and aid to the former and the latter continued to dominate the relationship.[151]

Moon Jae-in (2017–2022)

The Moon Jae-in government built on the grand strategy of previous governments in its approach to Eurasia. In the particular case of Russia, Seoul pressed to strengthen trade and investment links to boost autonomy and greater integration in the world economy. To this end, oil continued to flow from Russia to South Korea and exports increased in terms of volume even if not share.[152] More notably and strategically, however, South Korea launched FTA negotiations with the Russia-led Eurasian Economic Union in 2017.[153] This was followed by bilateral trade deal negotiations with Russia itself in 2019.[154] The Moon government wanted to lower the costs of importing Russian oil, but also to increase the competitiveness of South Korean exports by lowering entry tariffs.

The Moon government also sought to directly involve Russia in its strategy to improve inter-Korean relations. Moon unveiled his New Northern Policy in Russia shortly after taking office.[155] This policy sought to establish "economic bridges" between South Korea and Russia via North Korea, thus integrating the latter in Northeast Asian economic flows.[156] In addition, the Moon government believed in using South Korean diplomatic corps and military capabilities to manage the potential threat that Seoul felt coming from Moscow. In November 2021, the navies and air forces of the two countries agreed to open military hotlines to avoid accidental clashes.[157] However, this decision was taken after Russian jets entered South Korea's ADIZ and, at least once, even the country's airspace during joint maneuvers with China.[158] The ROK Air Force had to send its own jets whenever this happened, proving the need for a hotline. South Korea also had to contend with growing cyberattacks from Russia by using its cybersecurity capabilities. Most notably, Russian forces launched a cyberattack on South Korea on the day of the inauguration of the PyeongChang Winter Olympic Games.[159] Last, once Russia invaded Ukraine in February 2022 South Korea used its diplomatic corps to coordinate condemnation of Moscow with other partners, as well as trade and investment to hit Russia economically.[160] This showed the deterioration in South Korea–Russia links.

In the case of Europe, South Korea's grand strategy continued to become more comprehensive. With the three key agreements already in effect, the European Union continued to be the largest investor in South Korea, the ROK Navy and its officials continued to cooperate with the EU naval mission in the Gulf of Aden, and Seoul and Brussels discussed ways to boost links in the Indo-Pacific region based on their own strategies.[161] The two sides also continued to hold their regular summits. The Moon government also believed that the European Union could support its inter-Korean policy. The European Union was included in Seoul's Northeast Asia Peace and Cooperation Platform (NAPC) as one of its members.[162] In October 2018, Moon toured Europe and attended the ASEM summit in Brussels to request support for its North Korea policy.[163] Also, South Korea emphasized broader economic links. In 2019, Seoul signed an FTA with the United Kingdom after it left the European Union.[164] The United Kingdom also became a new market for South Korean arms exports.[165] Meanwhile, King Sejong institutes continued to open across Europe.

Arguably, in any case, South Korea–Europe relations strengthened more clearly in the area of security. Seoul saw cooperation with Europe through its military capabilities as a way to boost its autonomy and protection against external military threats. South Korea and NATO renewed their bilateral cooperation agreement in 2019. One year later, South Korea was one of four Asia-Pacific NATO partners along with Australia, Japan, and New Zealand to participate in a meeting of ministers of foreign affairs.[166] In 2021,

South Korea and NATO expanded the scope of their dialogue and practical cooperation in the context of NATO's growing focus on the Asia–Pacific region.[167] In the meantime, the ROK Navy carried out joint drills with the navies of France, Germany, and the United Kingdom as European countries sent their navies to the waters of the Indo-Pacific.[168]

In the Greater Middle East, certainly securing oil and gas exports continued to underpin Seoul's grand strategy. The Greater Middle East remained the main region of origin for South Korean imports of both.[169] But trade and investment to promote deeper economic integration continued to grow in importance. In 2021, South Korea signed an FTA with Israel.[170] In early 2022, state-run Korea Hydro & Nuclear Power Co. (KHNP) joined a consortium to build a nuclear power plant in Egypt.[171] Meanwhile, South Korean firms continued their arms sales to Iraq.[172] Beyond economics, South Korea used its expanding military capabilities and diplomatic corps to increase its recognition as a middle power and also its integration in the world economy. In 2020, the Cheonghae Unit expanded its theater of operation to the Strait of Hormuz, a key oil and gas transport route crucial for exports from the region to the outside world—including South Korea itself.[173] That same year, the ROK Armed Forces carried their first-ever evacuation of foreign nationals when it participated in the rescue of Afghan nationals from their country before the Taliban took power again.[174] One year later, Seoul joined multilateral negotiations with Iran to revive the nuclear agreement that had halted Tehran's nuclear program but that the Trump administration had later disowned.[175] For the first time, South Korea was a player in a high-level diplomatic initiative in the Greater Middle East. And in 2022, South Korea signed its biggest-ever defense contract with the United Arab Emirates to sell a domestically produced missile system.[176] In the meantime, South Korean peacekeepers continued to be deployed in Lebanon.[177]

As for Central Asia, Seoul saw the Eurasian Economic Union as a pathway to boost trade and investment links with its Central Asian members: Kazakhstan and Kyrgyzstan. The former also increased the volume of its energy exports to South Korea.[178] In addition, the Korean Cultural Center in Kazakhstan and the Korea–Central Asia Cooperation Forum Secretariat carried on with their activities. South Korea continued its engagement with the Korean diaspora across the region, using a range of means to pursue its ends of recognition as a middle power and becoming more integrated in the world economy.

Regarding South Asia, the status of India in particular was elevated by the Moon government. The country was included in the New Southern Policy (NSP), Moon's signature foreign policy initiative. Trade and investment between the two countries increased.[179] In the case of South Asia more broadly, aid still flowed to the region.[180] Equally relevant, the ROK Navy and its Indian counterpart conducted joint drills as part of multilateral exercises in the Indo-Pacific on several occasions.[181] Seoul and Delhi also signed a military logistics support agreement in 2019 for their navies, only the fourth such agreement for India and second with an Asian country after a previous one with Singapore.[182] This way, Seoul also started to make use of its military capabilities in its relationship with India as well.

In terms of relations with Australia, they continued to go from strength to strength as South Korea saw the potential of deeper engagement with a like-minded partner as a way to boost its autonomy, economic integration globally, and status as a middle power. To begin with, South Korea and Australia were part of the Regional Comprehensive Economic Partnership (RCEP) when it finally launched in January 2022. South Korea also announced that it would apply to join the Comprehensive and Progressive Agreement for Trans-Pacific Partnership (CPTPP) later that year, an agreement where Australia was a key economy. Earlier, KOGAS had signed an agreement to get access to Australian gas in 2019, and South Korea had signed a deal to secure mineral resources from the country in 2021.[183] Focusing on security, Seoul and Canberra signed a bilateral security partnership in 2021.[184] This was possible, to an extent, thanks to the close relationship that both of them had with the United States but also because of their reservations toward China's military rise. This same reason led the two of them to have quadrilateral naval exercises together with Japan and the United States in 2019 in the Western Pacific, new quadrilateral exercises in 2021 and six-way exercises also including Canada and India in 2022,[185] among others. Soft power was also part of South Korean grand strategy toward Australia, as it had been in the past. KCON was held in the country in 2017, and the Korean Cultural Center and the Korea Foundation continued their activities.[186]

Last, South Korea took relevant steps toward strengthening its presence in the Indian Ocean to protect against external threats and boost its position as a middle power. In 2018, the Ministry of National Defense launched Navy Vision 2045. The strategy called for power projection in the Indian Ocean, among others. Significantly, the Moon government commissioned an aircraft carrier. When completed, the ship would allow South Korea to boost its presence in the South China Sea and elsewhere in the Indian Ocean.[187] Furthermore, the Cheonghae Unit carried on with its mission in the Gulf of Aden. South Korea seemed to be seeking to become a maritime power as well.

Yoon Suk-yeol (2022)

The Yoon Suk-yeol government continued the strategy of previous governments toward Greater Eurasia and the Indian Ocean. In the case of Europe, security was the area in which this was clearest. Yoon became the first South Korean president to attend a NATO summit when he traveled to a meeting held in Madrid in June 2022.[188] A month later South Korea signed one of its biggest arms sales deals ever with Poland, a NATO member and one of the largest contributors to Ukraine's defense against Russia.[189] South Korea became the only Asian country to condemn Russia for the invasion, impose sanctions on Moscow, and transfer arms to Ukraine (albeit via third parties such as Poland). Yoon presented Seoul's support for Ukraine in terms of values and international norms.[190] On the other hand, relations with Russia deteriorated as a result of South Korea's response to Moscow's invasion of Ukraine. Economic links weakened as a result of the sanctions imposed by Seoul, along with its partners, in an instance of South Korea flexing its trade and investment muscles to punish another country.

In the case of the Greater Middle East, the Yoon government continued to emphasize the use of trade and investment to achieve deeper integration in the world economy. In fact, his government launched a Council on Economic Cooperation with Middle East in September 2022. Bringing together the government and the private sector, the council was tasked with boosting economic links with the region—particularly energy imports, in the context of poorer relations with Russia, and technology exports.[191] The latter was particularly central to Yoon's strategy toward the region. As a case in point, in August 2022 South Korea signed a deal with Egypt to build the country's first nuclear power plant. This was the first such deal with a South Korean firm leading the consortium since 2013.[192]

The Yoon government's more focused approach on the Indo-Pacific boosted links with both Australia and India. Yoon indicated his hope to join the Quad, which would deepen ties with Canberra and Delhi. In the case of Australia, South Korea agreed to boost arms industry and military exercises ties in August 2022.[193] Seoul and Canberra had already enhanced security ties during the NATO summit, which the leaders of the two countries attended. India was included in the ABCD Strategy launched by the Yoon government, which also targeted Southeast Asia. Thus, trade and investment were two means prioritized by Seoul to enhance links with Delhi. But South Korea saw security cooperation as the area of greater potential upside in its links with India.[194] The focus would be on arms industry ties and joint exercises.

As a region, Greater Eurasia and the Indian Ocean has become increasingly relevant to South Korean grand strategy. After all, it is an area of great economic importance to South Korea as its economic links have expanded. But the region has also become more prominent for South Korean foreign policymakers on account of its impact on South Korean security as time has gone by. Furthermore, the region has also become more relevant for Seoul as its quest to be recognized as a middle power has become more explicit.

Russia is South Korea's most important focus when it comes to the Greater Eurasia and Indian Ocean region, but its relative importance has decreased as time has gone by. In any case, the ends that South Korea has sought to achieve in its relations with the country have remained relatively stable over time: protection from external military threats, first with the support from Russia but later on from Russia itself, autonomy, support for inter-Korean reconciliation and reunification, and deeper integration in the world economy. In terms of tools, South Korea has prioritized trade and investment dating back to its last transition to democracy and diplomatic normalization with Russia. This has been key in relation to Seoul's security and economic ends, as well as its quest for autonomy. South Korea has also used its growing military capabilities in its relations with Russia, eventually to protect itself against potential Russian aggression. And South Korea has also used its diplomatic corps as a means to achieve its goals related to security and inter-Korean relations.

In contrast to Russia, Europe has become more relevant for South Korean grand strategy as the years have gone by. From a South Korean perspective, stronger relations with the European Union, NATO, and particular European countries primarily serve the goals of autonomy, deeper integration in the world economy, and recognition as a middle power. In recent years, protection from external military threats has also become a goal in which South Korea sees potential European involvement. In terms of means, South Korea has focused on trade and investment particularly since Roh Moo-hyun launched FTA negotiations with the EU. The diplomatic corps and public diplomacy have been tools that South Korea has used dating back to the Roh Tae-woo and Kim Young-sam administrations, respectively. As for soft power, its use is more recent and can be traced back to the 1990s, but especially to the Roh Moo-hyun years.

Central Asia, South Asia, Australia, and the Indian Ocean obviously are quite different. In the case of the first two, South Korea has pursued autonomy as well as recognition as a middle power above all. In the case of the last two, South Korea has focused primarily on autonomy, recognition as a middle power, and, more recently, protection from external military threats. Seoul has used trade, investment, and aid to pursue its goals in Central and South Asia. It has also made use of diplomacy, public diplomacy, and soft power across these three regions and one country.

CHAPTER VII

The Rest of the World and Global Governance

South Korea's grand strategy also covers the rest of the world and global governance structures. This is the final, larger circle surrounding the three first concentric circles that South Korea prioritizes in its foreign policy. As a self-described middle power, Seoul feels the need but arguably also *has* the need to take a global outlook. This means that its grand strategy ought to have a global focus, meaning both countries and regions not included in its first three concentric circles plus multilateral institutions in place—at least in theory—to govern interstate relations at the global level. Historically, South Korea paid limited attention to regions outside of its immediate neighborhood and wanted to but could not be part of the United Nations, excluded as it was from the organization due to inter-Korean competition. But Seoul has developed a more proactive grand strategy toward the rest of the world and global governance.

South Korea's grand strategy toward the rest of the world prioritizes Latin America and sub-Saharan Africa, as well as Canada. Indeed, Latin America and Canada are part of South Korea's approach to transpacific relations and the Pacific half of the Asia-Pacific and, more recently, Indo-Pacific regions. Certainly, specific countries in Latin America and sub-Saharan Africa are more relevant to South Korea. But from a South Korean perspective, its approach toward the different countries and subregions in each of these two regions is anchored by the same ends and means. Canada, Latin America, and sub-Saharan Africa matter for South Korea, primarily,

TABLE 7.1
South Korea's grand strategy toward the rest of the world and global
governance

Key factors	Key ends	Key means
Economic development, democracy, middle power identity, regional integration and globalization	Autonomy, deeper integration in the world economy, recognition as an influential middle power	Diplomatic corps; trade, investment, and aid; public diplomacy; soft power

to promote autonomy and for economic reasons including access to
resources. Over time, however, South Korea's middle power status and, in
specific cases, security considerations have also become drivers of the
country's grand strategy toward these countries and regions.

Global governance institutions are the other key priority of South Korean
grand strategy beyond its first three concentric circles. South Korea's presence in and contributions to global governance structures were handicapped
during the Cold War. South Korea was prevented from joining the United
Nations for geopolitical considerations, along with North Korea. Furthermore, South Korea was a developing country, and the size of its economy
was relatively small. This prevented Seoul from being part of certain institutions reserved for developed countries, and it also created a level of dependency on global financial institutions. As a case in point, South Korea
received World Bank loans until 1994. It then received an IMF bailout and
World Bank funds during the AFC. Yet South Korea joined the United
Nations in 1991 and a host of other organizations from the mid-1990s
onward. This has given Seoul a platform to further develop and implement its grand strategy. The main focus has been autonomy, economics,
and middle power recognition.

Roh Tae-woo (1988–1993)

The Roh Tae-woo government had a clear top priority in mind when it
came to office: UN membership. His key grand strategy-related slogan was

"End of the Cold War" (냉전 종식).[1] From Roh's perspective, Cold War détente and its eventual end created the conditions for South Korea to join the United Nations, a decades-old goal that South Korea had been unable to achieve because North Korea's allies China and especially the Soviet Union held veto power in the UN Security Council. In the context of the final years of the Cold War, Roh used South Korea's diplomatic corps and trade and investment to achieve this goal. Roh's *Nordpolitik* helped to reduce tensions with the Soviet Union and China. It also asked for the United States to improve relations with North Korea. Seoul then established diplomatic relations with the Soviet Union (and later with Russia) and promised investment. This way, South Korea was able to join the United Nations in September 1991, together with North Korea.[2] UN membership would serve support Seoul's ends of autonomy and recognition as an influential middle power over the decades.

Concurrently, the Roh government also prioritized membership of other international organizations to achieve these means. Above all, Seoul pursued OECD membership. Joining this "rich country" club would help cement South Korea's status at the global level and, indirectly, strengthen its economic integration since it would imply (neo)liberal economic reforms. In addition, South Korea became actively involved in the Uruguay Round of trade negotiations to replace the GATT with what would eventually be the WTO, as discussed previously. South Korea also became an Antarctic Treaty Consultative Party in 1989.[3] This signaled Seoul's ambition to broaden the horizon of its grand strategy. In short, the Roh government believed that South Korea was in a position to play a more active role at the global level, commensurate with its economic growth.

Beyond global governance institutions, the Roh government also started to focus on the Americas beyond the United States. Most notably, South Korea was one of the founding members of the APEC group in 1989. This forum to promote trade included East Asian countries and the United States, but Canada and Mexico had also joined by the end of Roh's time in office. Furthermore, South Korea hosted the 1991 APEC summit. For South Korea, stronger links with Canada and Latin America held the promise of deeper integration in the world economy and autonomy. In addition, KOICA grants, EDCF loans, and other aid flowed to countries across Latin America.[4] South Korea was using aid to strengthen its economic links and middle power status. Similarly, Seoul also started to provide aid to sub-Saharan Africa.[5] Both sub-Saharan Africa and Latin America became two of the three largest destinations of South Korean aid, a status that they retained all the way until at least 2022.

Kim Young-sam (1993–1998)

Kim Young-sam deepened South Korea's integration in global governance structures for the purposes of enhancing middle power recognition and autonomy. This fit with Kim's approach to foreign policy, which presented South Korea as a more responsible member of the international community. This was underpinned by Kim's *segyehwa* policy. Most notably, South Korea took an active approach in the United Nations from early on. Above all, South Korea was elected as a nonpermanent member of the UN Security Council. It took this position for the first time ever in 1996–1997.[6] In addition, Seoul made use of its growing military capabilities to dispatch peacekeepers to the UN Assistance Mission in Somalia in 1993, to Western Sahara in 1994, to the India-Pakistan border that same year, and to the UN Angola Verification Mission in 1995.[7]

Beyond the United Nations, South Korea became one of the founding members of the WTO when it was established in 1995.[8] The WTO became the main institution to promote trade liberalization and to settle trade disputes. One year later, South Korea became only the second Asian country to join the OECD.[9] Also in 1996, Seoul became a member of the Bank for International Settlements (BIS).[10] The BIS was a central bank hub to promote international cooperation in pursuit of monetary and financial stability. It was also a bank for central banks.[11] Membership of these institutions was directly linked to South Korea's quest to boost trade link across the world. Furthermore, South Korea graduated from borrower status in the World Bank in 1995.[12] This way, Seoul was able to use its aid in support of other countries. That same year, South Korea hosted the Antarctic Treaty Consultative meeting.[13] This was a sign of Seoul's using its diplomacy to boost its position as a middle power.

Focusing on Latin America, the Kim government broadened the number of means used to pursue its ends. To begin with, Kim went on a five-country tour of Central and South America in 1996.[14] Kim was the first South Korean president to visit the region. He was using diplomacy to boost

South Korea's diplomatic and economic standing in the region. Among others, the Korea National Oil Corporation (KNOC) signed an agreement in Peru to produce hydrocarbons in a basin on the north of the country.[15] South Korea also continued to provide aid to Latin America as well, increasing the net amount delivered.[16] Meanwhile, Chile joined APEC.[17] This further cemented South Korea's use of this institution to boost economic links with Latin America. In the case of sub-Saharan Africa, South Korea increased the amount of aid delivered to the region.[18] It also sent its peacekeepers to Angola and Somalia, thus introducing a new means in its grand strategy toward the region.

Kim Dae-jung (1998–2003)

Kim Dae-jung doubled down on the approach from his predecessors to make South Korea a more active participant in global governance. Seoul continued to be actively involved in the UN. Among others, it contributed peacekeepers to the International Security Assistance Force (ISAF) in Afghanistan. During Kim's tenure, South Korea also signed the United Nations Framework Convention on Climate Change's (UNFCC) Kyoto Protocol in 1998, which it then ratified in 2002.[19] The agreement sought to combat climate change by limiting greenhouse gas emissions. In 2000, the Kim government signed the International Criminal Court (ICC) statute as well, ratifying it in 2002.[20] Tracing its origins to the 1940s when the UN General Assembly recommended the establishment of an international court, the ICC was launched to prosecute individuals accused of certain egregious crimes. South Korea was one of a handful of Asian countries that signed and ratified membership of the ICC. The ROK Armed Forces were also dispatched to East Timor in 1999 as part of the peacekeeping mission there.[21]

In the case of economic institutions, South Korea became actively involved in the WTO and the OECD. Furthermore, South Korea became one of the founding members of the G20 in 1999.[22] Launched in the aftermath of the AFC and comprising twenty member countries, as reflected in its name, the G20 was tasked with ensuring financial stability. In the area of economics but beyond global governance, the Kim government also laid the groundwork for South Korea to become more active in the use of trade and investment as a tool to deepen economic integration. In 1998, the Ministry of Foreign Affairs (MOFA) became the Ministry of Foreign Affairs and Trade (MOFAT) as trade was incorporated into its tasks. That same year, Seoul launched a set of guidelines for the negotiation of trade agreements as the basis for the FTA network that it would create in future decades.

Latin America was the first region in which Seoul's new, more strategic approach to trade was tested. In 1999, South Korea launched bilateral FTA negotiations with Chile. The agreement was signed only a few days before Kim left office, becoming South Korea's first-ever FTA. When it comes to APEC, Peru also joined.[23] This further boosted ties between South Korea and this country. In the meantime, South Korea continued to provide aid to Latin America even after taking the economic hit of the AFC. Likewise, sub-Saharan Africa also continued to be a recipient of South Korean aid.[24] This showed the importance of aid, trade, and investment for South Korea to boost economic links with Latin America and sub-Saharan Africa, as well as Seoul's position as a middle power.

Roh Moo-hyun (2003–2008)

Roh Moo-hyun started his mandate following the 9/11 terrorist attacks on the United States. He implemented a "Post-9/11 World Order" approach. At the UN level, the Roh government campaigned for Ban Ki-moon to become the organization's secretary general.[25] South Korea was successful, and Ban was inaugurated as the UN's eight secretary general in 2007. This was a clear use of diplomacy to boost the country's middle power credentials. South Korea also continued to be an active participant in the institution's activities. As a case in point, Seoul was one of the original members of the newly launched UN Human Rights Council (UNHRC) in 2006–2008.[26] In addition, South Korea sent peacekeepers to the United Nations mission in Liberia established in 2003 while continuing to participate in the Afghanistan mission. It also joined the UN's mission in Lebanon in 2007.[27] Outside of the United Nations, South Korea continued with its participation in economic institutions such as the BIS, G20, OECD, and WTO. And after FTA negotiations with Chile had proved much more difficult than expected, the Roh government launched an FTA Roadmap in August 2003.[28] The roadmap led South Korea to significantly deepen its interest in FTA negotiations and became the basis of Seoul's policy in this area in the following decades.

In the case of the Americas, the Roh government launched FTA negotiations with Canada in 2005,[29] and with Mexico one year later.[30] Coupled with the launch of trade negotiations with the United States, South Korea was prioritizing trade agreements with the three North American Free Trade Agreement (NAFTA) members. Meanwhile, South Korea continued to use APEC as a forum to strengthen economic links with the Americas and hosted the 2005 meeting. In addition, South Korea continued to increase its aid to Latin America now that it was leaving behind the worst effects of the AFC. Furthermore, South Korea took a significant step in its economic engagement with Latin America by becoming a member of the Inter-American Development Bank (IDB) in 2005.[31] The largest Americas-specific development bank, South Korea's membership married its economic and diplomatic strength to develop the country's grand strategy toward the region. Besides economic power to improve trade and investment links and its middle power image, South Korea introduced a new element in its relations with Latin America: soft power. In 2006, the Ministry of Culture and Tourism opened its first Korean Cultural Center in Latin America in Argentina.[32] South Korea's *Hallyu* (Korean wave) was becoming popular in Latin America, and the government decided to take advantage of this opportunity to boost its middle power credentials.

As for sub-Saharan Africa, Roh was the first president in South Korean history to really devise a multifaceted strategy toward the region. Stronger links with the region could help South Korea to deepen its integration in the world economy beyond traditional markets, boost the country's credentials as a middle power, and strengthen its autonomy. Thus, Roh launched an Africa strategy in 2006.[33] That same year, Seoul hosted the First Africa Leader Forum with leaders from the continent. This was followed by an interministerial meeting one year later.[34] In 2006, South Korea held the first Korea-Africa Economic Cooperation (KOAFEC) ministerial meeting to boost economic links. KOAFEC became a permanent funding mechanism.[35] Resource diplomacy also made its way into Roh's Africa strategy. In 2006, KNOC signed an oil production agreement with Nigeria, even though it would be rescinded three years later.[36] In 2007, the Korea Gas Corporation (KOGAS) signed an agreement for a gas exploration project in Mozambique.[37] South Korea's aid agencies also increased their transfers to the region.[38] Leaving economics aside, South Korea continued its contribution to peacekeeping efforts in Liberia.

Lee Myung-bak (2008–2013)

Lee Myung-back launched a "Creative Pragmatism" (실용외교) policy upon entering office. His approach to global governance and the rest of the world, in any case, built on that of his predecessors. Ban Ki-moon continued to be the secretary general of the United Nations. But South Korea became more involved in the institution's activities thanks to its participation in new peacekeeping operations in Haiti, the Gulf of Aden, and South Sudan, to add to ongoing participation in the missions in Afghanistan, Lebanon, and Liberia.[39] South Korea also had a second term as a UN Security Council nonpermanent member starting from 2013, shortly before Lee left office.[40] Also, South Korea had a second term as UNHRC member in 2009–2011.[41] But Lee took South Korea's involvement in the United Nations to a higher level when Incheon became the host of the newly created Green Climate Fund (GCF) in 2010, founded to fund the fight against climate change, and United Nations Office for Sustainable Development (UNOSD) in 2011. The office was opened to support member states to achieve the UN's sustainable development goals.[42] One year later, Seoul's Global Green Growth Institute (GGGI)—launched by the Lee government in 2010—became an international organization following the Rio+2020 UN Conference on Sustainable Development.[43] For South Korea, active participation in the UN and its activities continued to constitute a way to use diplomacy and military capabilities to show its middle power credentials. And hosting two UN-linked, development-related organizations gave South Korea a leading role as a middle power thanks to its diplomatic corps and economic strength.

In the case of economic institutions, South Korea was invited to join new and older institutions in the aftermath of the GFC. For the Lee government, this was a way to use South Korea's trade and investment prowess as well as its diplomatic corps for economic and middle power purposes. In 2008, the G20 was upgraded to the head of government level. South Korea continued to be part of it, and in 2010 it became the first Asian country to host its annual summit. In 2008 and 2009, South Korea was invited as a "limited guest" to the G8 to address the economic effects of the GFC.[44] In 2009, South Korea was one of the founding members of the Financial Stability Board (FSB). The G20 launched the FSB as a permanent institution for countries to prevent future financial crises via rule-making, monitoring and early warning.[45] South Korea also joined the Basel Committee on Banking Supervision (BCBS) in 2009.[46] The BCBS aimed at improving surveillance of the banking sector to prevent banking crises. South Korea also continued to actively participate in the BIS, OECD, and WTO. But the Lee government also boosted South Korean participation in global bodies focused on development. In 2009, South Korea became the first former aid recipient to join the OECD's Development Assistance Committee. The committee was the body for donors to discuss and coordinate aid giving. Busan then went on to host the fourth and last in a series of OECD High Level forums on Aid Effectiveness.[47] In 2011, Seoul and the World Bank also launched the Korea Green Growth Trust Fund.[48] This was a funding mechanism for South Korea to provide financing for green growth projects in developing countries.

Looking at South Korea's grand strategy toward the Americas, Lee built on the pillars implemented by his predecessors to continue to promote economic integration, middle powerness, and autonomy. In the case of Canada, Lee prioritized his resource diplomacy. In 2009, KNOC signed a deal to acquire a Canadian firm involved in the oil and gas sectors.[49] In 2010, KOGAS signed an agreement to join the Umiak SDL project. Two years later, it signed another agreement to develop the Horn River Development Project.[50] Elsewhere in the Americas, South Korea launched FTA negotiations with Peru in 2009 and signed an agreement two years later.[51] Also in 2009, the Lee government started to negotiate an FTA with Colombia.[52] Meanwhile, South Korea continued to provide aid to Latin America.[53] This included via the IDB.[54] Furthermore, APEC continued to function as a way for South Korea to have stronger economic links with the region. In addition, Seoul significantly boosted its use of soft power in Latin America. In 2012 and 2013, respectively, South Korea opened Korean cultural centers in Mexico and Brazil.[55] In 2012, Chile became the first Latin American country to host KBS's Music Bank World Tour.[56] Plus, South Korea started to open King Sejong institutes across the Americas.[57] In addition, South Korea deployed peacekeepers to the Americas for the first time in 2009. That year, South Korean peacekeepers participated in the UN stabilization mission in Haiti.[58] Seoul also launched the Korea-Caribbean

Partnership Forum in 2011.[59] The forum served to boost economic and diplomatic links with the countries in the region. And even though not part of the Americas but located in the Pacific and a member of APEC, Seoul launched FTA negotiations with New Zealand.[60]

As for Africa, Lee built on the grand strategy of his predecessors and in particular the extensive set of activities launched by Roh Moo-hyun. The second and third Korea-Africa forums were held in 2009 and 2012, respectively.[61] KOAFEC and other ministerial meetings continued to take place.[62] South Korea also continued to prioritize sub-Saharan Africa as one of the key destinations of its aid.[63] In the other direction, South Korea started to import oil from Nigeria in substantial amounts.[64] However, oil imports from the West African country did not become a significant share for South Korea, even if growing significantly in terms of volume. In Nigeria, too, the Ministry of Culture, Sports and Tourism started to use public diplomacy for the first time. In 2010, it opened a Korean Cultural Center in Abuja.[65] Meanwhile, South Korea continued its peacekeeping missions in the Gulf of Aden and Liberia, while launching a new one in South Sudan.[66]

Park Geun-hye (2013–2017)

Park Geun-hye became South Korean president at a time when South Korea was very active in global governance institutions. Ban Ki-moon remained as secretary general of the United Nations until the end of his second term in 2016. South Korea continued to hold a seat as a nonpermanent member of the UN Security Council until the end of 2014. South Korean peacekeepers continued to operate in Afghanistan, the Gulf of Aden, Haiti, Lebanon, Liberia, the Philippines, and South Sudan. And South Korea was getting used to hosting its first UN institution—UNOSD. In addition, during Park's tenure Seoul was a member of the UNHRC in both 2013–2015 and 2016–2018.[67] On top of that, South Korea signed and promptly ratified in 2016 the Paris Agreement on climate change promoted by the UNFCCC.[68] In other words, South Korea was cementing its position as a middle power through a combination of its diplomatic corps and growing military capabilities.

Meanwhile, South Korea also continued to participate in the trade, finance, and development institutions it was part of: BCBS, BIS, FSB, G20, and WTO. In this case, Seoul was using its trade, investment, and aid as a means to deepen economic integration globally and to be recognized as an influential middle power. In this area as well, the Park government launched the New FTA Roadmap in 2013, ten years after the original road-map from the Roh Moo-hyun government.[69] The updated roadmap, in any case, built on similar open trade principles. Park also removed trade from MOFAT's responsibilities, to better differentiate diplomacy from trade functions. This way, the ministry became MOFA once more.

Park's grand strategy toward the Americas built on that of her predecessors. South Korea and Colombia signed their FTA in 2013 and Seoul followed suit with Canada in 2015. In addition, the Park government launched trade negotiations with Central America in 2015.[70] But Seoul did not confine its use of economic instruments in the region to FTAs. Park increased South Korea's financial commitments to the IDB and branched out into infrastructure building with the launch of the Korea Infrastructure Development Co-Financing Facility, as well as into capacity-building with the Public Capacity Building Korea Fund for Economic Development.[71] In 2013, South Korea was granted observer status by the Pacific Alliance.[72] This was a trade bloc launched by Chile, Colombia, Mexico, and Peru to boost links among themselves as well as with countries on the other side of the Pacific. In the Pacific as well, South Korea signed its FTA with New Zealand in 2015.[73] Meanwhile, South Korea continued to participate in APEC. Plus, it also carried on providing aid to Latin American countries. Besides economics, the Park government continued to use soft power to boost links with the region. A Korean Cultural Center opened in Canada in 2016.[74] Brazil and Mexico hosted KBS's Music Bank World Tour in 2014.[75] And KCON reached Mexico in 2017, only one week after Park left office.[76] In the case of Mexico, South Korea included the country in its MIKTA middle power initiative.[77] Therefore, Seoul was using its diplomatic corps to present itself as a middle power in a grouping also including the Latin America country. Seoul also continued its participation in the Haiti peacekeeping mission until it folded in 2014.

Regarding sub-Saharan Africa, the Park government convened the fourth Korea-Africa Forum in 2016.[78] It also carried on convening the ministerial meetings first launched with Roh Moo-hyun. Aid continued to flow to the region, and South Korea continued to import oil from Nigeria, yet this remained a small share of the total.[79] Besides, South Korea continued its peacekeeping missions in the Gulf of Aden, Liberia, and South Sudan. Its military capabilities had become a permanent feature of its grand strategy toward the sub-Saharan Africa region. Furthermore, South Korea started to open King Sejong institutes across the region.[80] Therefore, Seoul began to use soft power as a means to boost its middle power credentials.

Moon Jae-in (2017–2022)

Moon Jae-in entered office with South Korea in a strong position as an influential middle power within the UN system. Moon's grand strategy built on this strength. Seoul continued to participate in peacekeeping missions in the Gulf of Aden, Lebanon, Liberia, and South Sudan.[81] For Seoul, the use of its military capabilities to contribute to UN peacekeeping missions and therefore show its position as a middle power was well entrenched. What is more, South Korea hosted the 2021 UN Peacekeeping Ministerial.[82] This was an annual gathering of world leaders and ministers to agree on how to improve peacekeeping. Seoul was using its diplomatic corps to show its commitment to peacekeeping. In addition, South Korea continued to be a member of the UNHRC until 2018 and had a new term in 2020–2022.[83] Also at the UN level, UNCTAD promoted South Korea to "developed economy" status in 2021. Even though the upgrade came decades after South Korea had actually attained this status, the country was only the first one in UNCTAD's history dating back to 1964 to be promoted.[84] This served to cement South Korea's middle power status.

South Korea was also invited to attend the G7 summit in 2020, before its cancellation due to the COVID-19 pandemic, and in 2021, with the latter meeting being hosted by the United Kingdom. This time South Korea was a full "guest" rather than a "limited guest," marking Seoul's first proper and full-fledged participation in the summit. South Korea was thus benefiting from its diplomatic corps and economic strength to demonstrate its role as a middle power. In addition, South Korea was among a small number of middle powers and developing countries to launch Partnership for Green Growth and the Global Goals 2030 (P4G) in 2018. Seoul also hosted P4G's 2021 summit.[85] This was a partnership to finance and provide other support for sustainable growth. South Korea was using its diplomatic corps and aid to take a leading role on a global issue. In addition, South Korea showed its commitment to the WTO when it joined a select group of countries launching an alternative dispute-settlement mechanism in 2020 after U.S.–China competition threatened the original body.[86] Seoul also continued to participate in the BCBS, BIS, G20, or OECD.

South Korea–Canada relations broadened during Moon's tenure. Most notably, South Korea and Canada were part of joint naval drills together with the United States and Australia in 2019 as well as with the two of them plus India, and Japan in the Western Pacific in January 2022.[87] Thus, South Korea's military capabilities were serving to strengthen its own security in cooperation with Canada and other partners. As for Latin America, there was a proposal in 2018 for an FTA between South Korea and the Pacific Alliance. This could be a first step toward signing an FTA.[88] Arguably even more relevant, in April 2022 South Korea announced that it would apply to join the Comprehensive and Progressive Agreement for Trans-Pacific Partnership (CPTPP).[89] Canada, Chile, Mexico, and Peru, as well as New Zealand, were among the signatories, so membership of this FTA covering a wide range of areas would significantly boost trade links. Seoul also signed an FTA with Central America in 2018, and launched negotiations with Mercosur that same year.[90] Furthermore, Moon substantially increased Seoul's commitment to the IDB to the extent that South Korea became the third largest contributor, trailing only China and Spain.[91] APEC also continued to function, and Latin America continued to be a preferred destination for South Korean aid.[92] The Moon government also continued to use soft power to boost its middle power credentials in the region. KBS's Music Bank World Tour held a concert in Chile in 2018, and the Ministry of Culture, Sports and Tourism opened more King Sejong institutes across the Americas.[93] In the specific case of Mexico, MIKTA continued to serve as a diplomatic vehicle for relations. As for New Zealand, the entry into force of the Regional Comprehensive Economic Partnership (RCEP) in 2022 created a new platform to deepen trade and investment relations.

With regard to sub-Saharan Africa, the Moon government continued to build on the strategy pursued by previous governments. The fifth Korea–Africa Forum had to be first postponed and finally canceled due to the COVID-19 pandemic, but Seoul intended to convene it when possible. It finally took place in March 2022.[94] And other ministerial meetings were held as well.[95] In 2018, meanwhile, South Korea launched an energy investment facility for Africa during the KOAFEC meeting.[96] This way, Seoul was seeking to use its investment to deepen economic relations. In addition, KNOC joined an oil development project in Senegal in 2020.[97] South Korea also continued to import oil from Nigeria.[98] In the other direction, aid carried on flowing to the region.[99] The Ministry of Culture, Tourism and Sports also opened a Korean Cultural Center in South Africa in 2021, along with King Sejong institutes across different countries.[100] This demonstrated the importance that Seoul attached to soft power means to boost its middle powerness end.

Yoon Suk-yeol (2022)

Yoon Suk-yeol continued South Korea's commitment to the United Nations as part of the country's grand strategic goal to be seen as a middle power. In this respect, South Korea continued to participate in peacekeeping missions and also its participation in the UNHRC. South Korea launched FTA negotiations with the Pacific Alliance in June 2022.[101] The Yoon government also indicated its willingness to restart FTA negotiations with Mexico.[102] And CPTPP, which the Yoon government remained committed to join, involved countries in the region, as mentioned above. One of those countries was Canada. The Yoon government prioritized improving relations with Ottawa, mainly as a way to boost the import of Canadian natural resources in the context of deteriorating relations with Russia but also as a valuable diplomatic partner. The Yoon government also appointed a special envoy to the Pacific Island Nations and planned to host South Korea's first-ever summit with the countries in the region in 2023.[103] Thus, diplomatic corps and trade and investment, as well as military capabilities, continued to be the main tools for South Korea to pursue its ends of middle power recognition and economic integration at the global level.

On top of all this, South Korea's growing links with NATO also reinforced relations with two countries in the rest of the world: Canada and New Zealand. Security links with both of them were strengthened, and Canada entered discussions with South Korea to purchase military equipment to transfer to Ukraine.[104] In the case of New Zealand, broader links were also reinforced via ongoing negotiations for South Korea to join CPTPP and the Digital Economy Partnership Agreement (DEPA). This would increase trade and investment links on top of the boost resultant from RCEP.

Together, the rest of the world outside of the first three concentric circles and global governance are the final area of operation of South Korea's grand strategy. As the number of Seoul's ends expanded and the range of means grew, successive South Korean governments paid more attention to and became more active in regions outside South Korea's traditional areas of interest. Likewise, Seoul became more active in global governance institutions upon being able to join the United Nations in 1991.

Starting with global governance institutions, South Korea has become very active in both UN system-related institutions and activities as well as economic institutions in the space of barely three decades. Starting with the Roh Tae-woo government, Seoul focused on being an active player in global governance. For Seoul, its key ends from its grand strategy toward global governance were threefold: autonomy, recognition as a middle power, and deeper integration in the world economy. With regard to means, successive South Korean governments prioritized the use of diplomatic corps, trade, investment, and aid, and military capabilities. Diplomatic corps were used to boost autonomy and, especially, middle power recognition. Trade, investment, and aid were also employed to attain these two goals, together with economic integration. Military capabilities served South Korea to improve its image as a middle power.

In the case of the Americas, South Korea also pursued autonomy, deeper economic integration, and middle power recognition. In the case of the first end, South Korea made use of its economic tools to achieve it. This was even clearer in the case of deeper economic integration with Seoul employing trade, investment, and aid to attain this goal. In particular, the Kim Dae-jung government laid the foundations for trade to became Seoul's means of choice to boost economic links with the region. As for middle power recognition, South Korea made use of aid and soft power to achieve this end. In the case of soft power, South Korea focused on its use from the Roh Moo-hyun government onward.

Finally, South Korea focused on deeper economic integration and middle power recognition as the two key goals of its grand strategy toward sub-Saharan Africa. This was particularly the case after Roh Moo-hyun took office To meet the first of these goals, Seoul used aid primarily—together with investment in the energy sectors. As for the second of the goals, governments dating back to the Lee Myung-bak government have seen soft power as a way for South Korea to have stronger relations with sub-Saharan Africa.

Conclusion

The Past, Present, and Future of South Korea's Grand Strategy

South Korea has a well-defined grand strategy. Dating back to the start of the Sixth Republic in 1988 and at least until the first six months of the Yoon Suk-yeol government in 2022, South Korea has pursued a clear set of ends and used a number of specific means to achieve them. This is logical when considering that South Korean elites have a single, overarching ultimate end: autonomy. They want South Korea to make its own destiny, to be able to independently make decisions on the most appropriate policies that serve the interests of their country, by achieving the goals that they set for themselves. This overarching goal is unsurprising. Arguably, it is the ultimate goal of all countries. But it is particularly important for middle and weak powers, on the assumption that they face structural constraints limiting their independence of action. As a middle power with a history of being colonized (as unified Korea) and then protected yet also constrained by the security umbrella extended by the United States after the Korean War, South Korea indeed craves autonomy.

South Korean elites include four key ends within the overarching aim of autonomy. First of all, they want security, meaning South Korea being able to protect itself from external military threats. This is common for all countries, but arguably more so for South Korea in that it faces the direct threat of North Korea—a country with which it remains technically at war, and which lays claim to the whole of the Korean Peninsula. Furthermore, South Korean elites want security and status by achieving inter-Korean reconciliation and reunification. Only reunification—or at least reconciliation—can elimi-nate the security threat coming from North Korea, and only reunifica-tion can create a single, more powerful Korea. In addition, Seoul seeks prosperity in the form of deeper integration in the world economy. South Korea is not one of the "big three" economies that arguably could enjoy prosperity focusing on their internal market primarily; it was the tenth biggest economy in the world as of 2022, but one that needs economic links with the rest of the world to prosper. Finally, South Korea wants status through recognition as an influential middle power. The country is indeed a middle power, but it wants to yield influence—in other words, to con-tribute to shape international relations.

Middle powers have a range of means to achieve their ends. South Korea is no different. Thus, South Korean policymakers use different tools to achieve their aims. In order of importance in attendance to South Korea's goals, they include military means including autonomous growing military capabilities, cybertools, and the ROK–U.S. alliance; diplomatic means, which amount to the country's diplomatic corps; economic means including trade, investment, and aid; informational means in the form of public diplo-macy; and soft means, namely soft power. (South Korea, however, has only recently began to use cyber means to fulfill its ends.) These means have been part of South Korea's toolkit throughout the Sixth Republic.

Considering all this, a key question is whether South Korea's grand strat-egy has served the country to fulfill these goals. Even though the main aim of this book is primarily to describe and analyze the process whereby South Korea defines and implements its grand strategy, ascertaining the country's success in fulfilling said grand strategy should be briefly explored. This way it is possible to understand whether South Korean grand strategy is serving the country's interests or not.

The Goals of South Korea's Grand Strategy

The Overarching End: Autonomy

Postdemocratization South Korea has developed a global strategy that spans the whole world. In this context, the overarching goal of autonomy is pur-sued on a global scale. This includes the triangular core of South Korean grand strategy, East Asia, Greater Eurasia and the Indian Ocean—as well as the rest of the world and global governance. For South Korea, autonomy is a goal that it can only achieve by being active across the three core layers of its grand strategy, as well as globally. In terms of temporal scope, it is decades-long in that South Korea has been pursuing this goal and will continue to do so in the future. In other words, South Korea sees autonomy as its overarching long-term goal.

Arguably, all the factors explaining South Korean grand strategy in general explain the end of autonomy in particular. That is, no factors are more salient than others in any significant way. Take the case of the ROK–U.S. alliance, economic development, democracy, or middle power identity. They serve as enablers of South Korea's quest for autonomy by giving South Korea some of the means to search for it, as well as by informing its self-perception calling for greater autonomy. Or take the case of the rise of China or the Asian financial crisis, which enable autonomy insofar they are perceived as threats against which autonomy can serve. In the case of China's rise, together with regional integration and globalization they act as enablers as well by giving South Korea other potential partners an options. The division of Korea drives the search for autonomy in that it helps South Korea to develop some of the means that it can divert toward this goal as a result of inter-Korean competition and enmity.

In terms of the means that South Korea uses to try to seek autonomy, they include all the available types—with the partial exception of cyber. Starting with military means, South Korea's own capabilities are used to both protect the country and to support security elsewhere. In addition, the U.S. alliance helps South Korea to protect itself as well, but also to project power beyond the Korean Peninsula. As for diplomatic means, South Korean diplomatic corps help implement South Korean grand strategy through their engagement with other countries and in global governance. Seoul's economic means include trade, investment, and aid, instruments that one of the biggest economies in the world and an increasingly important donor can use to pursue its goals. As for informational means, South Korean public diplomacy instruments help to present the country in a particular way advantageous to it. Soft means, meanwhile, have become more prevalent in South Korean grand strategy as its soft power has become global. Regarding cyber means, South Korea has only started to really utilize them in recent years. They are yet to be as well integrated within its grand strategy as the other means.

As of 2023, South Korea has partially achieved the goal of autonomy. South Korea is more autonomous in its grand strategy than at any point since the foundation of the country. Seoul has set up goals for itself that it is seeking to achieve, regardless of the views and positions of great powers—including its ally, the United States, and its neighbor, China. South Korean policymakers also have a wide range of means at their disposal compared to 1988, when South Korea became a democracy. And they use these means with a high degree of autonomy. Having said that, South Korea is not fully autonomous in that there remain constraints to its actions. Arguably, all countries including great powers are constrained as long as they are part of the international system. But there are actions such as invading third countries, imposing crippling sanctions on third parties, or leading the creation of new multilateral institutions that South Korea cannot pursue autonomously. Hence it can be argued that South Korea autonomy is partial even if it grew dramatically in the 1988–2022 period.

Security: Protection from External Military Threats

The most basic goal of any state is survival. To this end, all countries seek protection from external military threats. Indeed, a military strike or even invasion from a foreign power remains a real possibility in the third decade of the twenty-first century. In the case of South Korea, there is a clear danger from North Korea. In recent years, however, Seoul has been on the receiving end of incursions and cyberattacks from China and Russia, and South Korean policymakers perceive China as a threat in the South China Sea as well. There is also the lingering threat that Japan poses to Dokdo, even if very unlikely. Therefore, the geographical scale of South Korea's grand strategy to protect itself against military threats encompasses the first three layers. As for the temporal scope, it is long-term insofar as threats to South Korean existence have existed for decades and will continue into the future.

Four main factors drive South Korea's focus on protection from external military threats. To begin with and more obviously, the division of Korea continues to pose a threat to South Korea. North Korea not only claims the whole of the Korean Peninsula as its territory, but it also has formidable military power including nuclear weapons. This is the ultimate threat to South Korea. The rise of China is another factor explaining South Korea's focus on this end. China is a treaty security ally of North Korea, which it helped during the Korean War and which it helps to prop up today. Plus, it has become more assertive as the years have gone by—therefore becoming a (perceived) threat for South Korea in its own right. The Asian financial crisis (AFC) is yet another crucial factor explaining South Korea's focus on protection from external military threats. The AFC created a sense of vulnerability among South Korean elites that is yet to fully disappear. Finally, the ROK–U.S. alliance also explains Seoul's end. The alliance helps protect South Korea, and maintaining it helps as a reminder of the threat that Seoul feels from Pyongyang.

South Korea uses three main means to seek to protect itself from third-party military threats. The key two are South Korean own military capabilities and the U.S. alliance. These are the military means that South Korea uses to deter North Korea as well as any other potential threat. Over time, Seoul has both boosted its independent military assets while also deepening the alliance with the United States. In addition, South Korea also uses its diplomatic corps. Diplomats help Seoul to maintain the alliance with the United States and cooperation with other partners. They also serve to address potential threats from China, Russia, and, sometimes, North Korea to reduce military risks. In recent years, South Korea has also started to use cyber means to prevent and protect against cyberattacks from China, North Korea, and Russia.

South Korea has partially achieved the goal of protection from military threats as of 2023. Above all, a nuclear North Korea continues to exist and therefore remains a direct threat to South Korea. The situation has not changed since 1988 and arguably has only gotten worse following North Korea's successful development of a nuclear weapons program. In addition, China and Russia are a threat to South Korea. Arguably, they are a bigger threat in 2023 than they were in 1988 due to their use of cyberattacks. Full-blown war with any of the two countries is very unlikely, but the threat cannot be completely disregarded considering Russia's willingness to invade other countries and China's growing military assertiveness across East Asia. The two of them have been launching cyberattacks on South Korea for years—which North Korea also does. South Korea is arguably safer in 2023 compared to previous years, but this goal is not fully fulfilled.

Security and Status: Inter-Korean Reconciliation and Reunification

If there is one end specific to South Korea, it is inter-Korean reconciliation and reunification. Korea remains a divided country, and the South

Korean constitution states that South Korea's territory encompasses what today is North Korea as well. The geographical scale of this end is mainly reduced to South Korea's triangular core of North Korea, the United States, and China. Along with South Korea itself, these three countries—especially the first two—are the ones that really matter if Seoul is to achieve reconciliation and reunification. South Korea certainly engages with countries in other layers to support this end, but these are secondary to those in the core. The temporal scope of this end is certainly long-term: dating back to the de facto division between south and north and the de jure division between South and North, and only to be achieved if and when reunification takes place.

Four key factors explain this end. The first and most obvious one is the division of Korea into two. As long as the division remains, South Korea will continue to seek reconciliation and reunification. The second important factor is the ROK–U.S. alliance. The alliance has helped protect South Korea since the days after the outbreak of the Korean War, including since it was formally codified in 1953 via a bilateral treaty. The alliance helps Seoul to approach relations with North Korea from a position of strength, including potential unification. China's rise also underpins South Korea's focus on this end. Seoul has to deal with a more powerful China that both is an ally of North Korea and sees the country as a buffer state against the United States. Meanwhile, South Korean middle power identity is another factor underpinning this goal. South Korea is a middle power, but many policymakers believe that only reunification can make Korea whole and more powerful in global affairs.

South Korean elites agree that four main means can help achieve reconciliation and reunification. The country's diplomatic corps and trade, investment, and aid are used for engagement purposes. Every single South Korean president since democratization has sought to engage North Korea. Diplomatic corps support this engagement, hence their role in attaining this goal. Meanwhile, South Korea became richer than the North in the 1970s, and the gap has only continued to grow in the decades since. Any reconciliation and reunification process will involve economic transfers from South Korea to the North, as has been attempted several times. At the same time, South Korean policymakers see the country's own military capabilities and the alliance with the United States as part of the tools to attain reconciliation and reunification. To this they add cybertools, also part of Seoul's military capabilities. These means guarantee that North

Korea cannot defeat South Korea in a war, thus underpinning diplomatic and economic engagement with Pyongyang.

South Korea has not achieved this end as of 2023, obviously. Korea continues to be divided, and even inter-Korean reconciliation remains elusive. Certainly relations between the two Koreas are better in 2023 than they were when Roh Tae-woo launched his *Nordpolitik*—the blueprint for successive South Korean presidents to lay the groundwork for reunification. But even true reconciliation seems years away at best. North Korea's behavior certainly has not helped, with the development of its nuclear weapons program, threats to South Korea and cyberattacks, and more general oppression of its population and behavior denting reconciliation efforts. Arguably, the actions of great powers have not helped either. Neither China nor the United States has consistently supported reconciliation over the decades. This is a case of South Korea being unable to overcome structural barriers to achieve a key end.

Prosperity: Deeper Integration in the World Economy

All countries want to be prosperous. Development is the end goal of any leader who wants to retain power and/or provide for their country's population. Throughout history, successive South Korean presidents implemented policies for the country to escape poverty. Once it did from the 1980–1990s onward, South Korean elites have strived to maintain and increase the country's prosperity. And they see deeper integration in the world economy as the key to achieve this end. This is due to South Korea's trade-oriented economy and (relatively) small market. This serves to explain why the geographical scope of this end is global. South Korean policymakers believe that their country has to deepen economic integration with as many countries as possible in order to maintain its prosperity. And the scope for this goal is long-term in that South Korea sought to become more deeply integrated in the global economy before it became prosperous, and it has retained this end after becoming developed.

Five main factors explain South Korea's quest for greater economic integration globally. To begin with, the country's own economic development. It was achieved thanks to this integration, and South Korean policymakers remain fixated on it. A second factor is China's economic rise. Seoul sees this as an opportunity but also as a risk in that a developed China exporting the goods, especially, and services that South Korea is known for would mean a hit to the South Korean economy. In addition, democracy is another factor informing this end. A more open political system and more open society are usually associated with a more open economy, and vice versa. This is not always the case, but for South Korea it has been since democratization. The AFC also pushed South Korea toward this goal. South Korean policymakers believe that diversification can prevent a new crisis, and this can be best achieved through integration. Finally, the ongoing processes of globalization since at least the 1970s and deeper regional integration since at least the 1990s also inform this goal. South Korean elites believe that Seoul has to tie its prosperity to these two goals, even if some indicators of globalization have gone in reversal since the global financial crisis (GFC) and also the Sino-American trade and technology war.

Trade, investment, and aid is the main mean that South Korea uses to try to achieve this end. South Korea is one of the largest trading countries in the world, ranked as the seventh largest exporter and ninth largest importer of goods worldwide in 2021.[1] Its firms drive this phenomenon. They are also behind South Korea's position as the tenth largest source of foreign direct investment (FDI) in 2020.[2] South Korea has become an increasingly important aid donor. All these economic flows ensure stronger economic links with both developed and developing countries. But South Korea also uses its diplomatic corps as a means to achieve this end. This includes, especially, participation in economic governance institutions and negotiation of free trade agreements (FTAs).

South Korea has achieved the goal of deeper integration in the world economy. In terms of trade-to-GDP ratio, it is ranked second among the fifteen biggest economies in the world as of 2020.[3] The South Korea of 2023 is fully developed, the tenth biggest economy in the world the year earlier, and regularly ranked as one of the most innovative countries worldwide. In other words, it is a prosperous country, thanks in part to FTAs with the "big three," with its main trading partners, and at the regional level.

Status: Recognition as an Influential Middle Power

Recognition as an influential middle power is a key end for South Korea. Arguably, most if not all countries want international recognition, including middle powers. But South Korea is a country that did not even exist eight decades ago, and which before then was part of a colonized Korea. Plus, South Korea used to be a very poor country until at least the 1960s if not the 1970s. Recognition as an influential middle power is thus a powerful end for South Korea. This goal is global in scope, since South Korea has sought and continues to seek said recognition across the different parts of the world and also in global institutions. And it is a long-term aspiration, which Roh Tae-woo set on upon becoming South Korean president in 1988.

Three are the main factors sustaining South Korean elite aspirations for the country to be recognized as an influential middle power. The first one is development. South Korean policymakers believe that Seoul should act and be seen as a middle power commensurate to the size of the South Korean economy and its status as a developed county. The second factor is democracy. South Korea is an example of a country that successfully transitioned to and then consolidated a strong democracy. South Korean elites believe that this is an example to other would-be democracies, and South Korea should be seen as such. The third and final factor is middle power identity. South Korean presidents and policymakers see their country as a middle power themselves, but this would necessitate external recognition as such.

South Korea uses almost all of its means to pursue the end of recognition as an influential middle power. To begin with, South Korea uses its military capabilities to protect other countries and also to transfer arms. This way, it can be seen as a capable military power. Seoul also makes use of its diplomatic corps, in this case to be part of politics at the regional and global levels. South Korean policymakers also see trade, investment, and aid as tools to project economic power, which other countries can see as an expression of the country's middle powerness. South Korea also uses public diplomacy and soft power to present itself to the rest of the world in a particular way that links to its self-perception as a middle power.

Recognition as an influential middle power is an end that South Korea has achieved as of 2023. The country is part of exclusive clubs such as the G20, OECD, BCBS, BIS, or FSB. It has been invited to attend G7 and NATO summits, is home to UN bodies, and hosts prestigious international meetings regularly. It is ranked twelfth in the world in terms of soft power. And it has become an indispensable economic, political, and security partner for countries ranging from its traditional ally, the United States, to more recent newcomers to the Indo-Pacific such as the European Union. More broadly, South Korea has become one of the key Asian voices in a global politics that are becoming more multipolar and less Western-centric in the twenty-first century. In short, South Korea has been able to "expand its horizon."[4]

Middle Power Grand Strategy

In chapter 1, I presented a middle power grand strategy model laying out the geographical scale, temporal scope, types of ends, and types of power (i.e., means) that should inform our analysis of any middle power's grand strategy. The case of South Korea's grand strategy during the Sixth Republic underscores the validity of this model. If middle powers want to implement a successful grand strategy, it needs to have a global geographic scale when possible but at least regional always; a long-term temporal scope measured in decades; clear, highest-order political ends along with autonomy; and implementation of a variety of means to pursue those ends.

Starting with the global scope of a middle power's grand strategy, the case of South Korea shows the advantages of this approach. South Korea pursues autonomy, deeper integration in the world economy, and recognition as an influential middle power at a global level because it serves its interests. A middle power may be able to achieve autonomy by only focusing on its region, but taking a global outlook serves to find more potential partners, contribute to a greater number of issues, deploy a wider range of tools, and, more generally, to be perceived as a more active member of the international community. As for deeper integration in the world economy, this helps to reduce dependency on a smaller number of economic counterparts compared to taking a regional approach. The type of economic links will also vary per region or partner, thus giving middle powers the opportunity to deploy tools that can be then used elsewhere. Regarding recognition as an influential middle power, middle powers have long strived to influence events beyond their region. Some middle powers may only seek influence within their neighborhood, but that would imply that recognition is not global. A country's claim to middle powerness will be weaker if only focusing on the region where it is located.

Yet there are times when a middle power will pursue regional goals. In the case of South Korea, these goals include protection from external military threats and inter-Korean reconciliation and reunification. Starting with the former, it is certainly true that Seoul increasingly sees its security tied to global developments or even developments in another region. But the definition of "region" has expanded over the years. In fact, middle powers often see their security tied to the behavior of great powers in other parts of the world. This is due to the global nature of some of middle powers' ends. As for inter-Korean reconciliation and reunification, this is an end which no other middle power shares. Likewise, middle powers with territorial issues, political problems with particular countries, or economic disputes with third parties, among others, will have goals that are regional in scale. In this case, South Korea has sought to limit the number of actors central to the attainment of this goal to make its grand strategy less complex. The same could apply to other middle powers with certain goals that cannot be solved, for example, via global governance institutions or through the intervention of a large number of actors.

Focusing now on the temporal scope of a middle power's ends, it has to be long-term for a proper grand strategy to be in place. Indeed, this is the basis of any grand strategy and great powers also have a long-term temporal scope in theirs. This is the case for South Korea in every of its five key ends. Indeed, if South Korean policymakers were constantly shifting their ultimate goals, the result would be an erratic foreign policy rather than a coherent grand strategy. Similarly, different means may be used at different times to attain a particular end. This is especially the case when new means become available or others become obsolete. But constantly changing the means to attain a particular end would also prevent a middle power from having a coherent grand strategy. Thus why it is not only ends but also means that should be long-term in nature. Certainly, sometimes critical junctures may affect the ends by making some of them redundant, introducing newer ones, or affecting the means used to achieve them. In the case of South Korea, for example, the AFC did not bring any new ends but helped accelerate the push for deeper integration in the world economy by making use of more means than previously. But most elements of a grand strategy should be able to survive a critical juncture to make it successful.

Middle powers cannot afford to pursue as many ends as great powers. After all, the power capabilities of middle powers are more constrained than those of great powers. Middle powers do not have the same pressures to get involved in as many global issues and regions as great powers are. This is a blessing in disguise, for it allows middle powers to focus on their core interests only. In the case of South Korea, its key ends "only" include autonomy—which is or should be common to all middle powers—plus four others linked to high politics. And even in the case of autonomy, this end should be understood as partial in nature insofar no middle power can credibly claim to have full autonomy from the actions of great powers in an interconnected global community. Arguably, therefore, the goals of middle powers should include partial autonomy—or as much agency as possible within existing structural constraints—plus a small number of others.

In the case of these other ends, they should be understood as interlinked. This is logical, for security, prosperity, and status reinforce—or undermine—each other. But they should be defined in ways that are well understood, broadly agreed upon, and distinguishable from other ends. In the case of South Korea, protection from external military threats mainly refers to the territorial integrity of the country. This is a common goal for all middle powers. As for inter-Korean reconciliation and reunification, there is a consensus that they mean an end to enmity between the two Koreas and being one country again, respectively. In fact, the origins of this goal and its meaning go back to the partition of Korea into two itself. The meaning of deeper integration in the world economy, meanwhile, is clear to South Korean elites as well and traces its origins to South Korea's time as a poor country. It means South Korea being an important part of regional and global trade and investment flows. Recognition as an influential middle power may be less clear than the meaning of other ends, for "influence" is difficult to measure. But South Korean policymakers agree that they want their country to help shape developments elsewhere and to be seen as doing so. The case of South Korea thus shows that a broadly shared understanding of the ends that a middle power wants to pursue is key to a coherent grand strategy.

When it comes to the means to achieve ends, middle powers ought to have a menu to choose from. Each goal will demand a different set of tools to achieve them, and the mix of tools being used will evolve over time according to availability and external circumstances. South Korea, for example, is adept at using traditional military, diplomatic, and economic means, but it is also a keen user of informational and soft means. In contrast, it has only in recent years started to use other means. But in general, South Korea uses a range of means to pursue its ends rather than relying on one or two means only. Other middle powers with, for example, weaker military capabilities may prioritize diplomacy or aid. Or middle powers that have stronger cyber capabilities may make less use of public diplomacy and soft power compared to Seoul. But it is necessary for middle powers not to rely on one or perhaps two means only. They should develop and utilize as many of them as possible, for this makes it more likely that they will achieve their goals.

The Future of South Korea's Grand Strategy

South Korea has a clear grand strategy that is set to remain fairly recognizable for years to come. South Korean elites of (nominally) different political movements may sometimes bicker among themselves regarding the course of South Korean foreign policy. Yet they agree on the ends that they want to achieve and the means to pursue those ends. Furthermore, their grand strategy choices are informed by a series of factors that have remained relatively unchanged over the years. Open political bickering is normal in any vibrant democracy, which explains why South Korea is not immune to it. But behind the facade of disagreement lays a consensus about the ends and means that serve South Korean interests best. The current president at the time of writing, the conservative Yoon Suk-yeol, shares these views.

What would take for South Korea to overturn a grand strategy that can be traced back to 1988? Perhaps an intensification of great power competition between China and the United States to the point that the world is divided into two blocs fully confronting each other once more. Or perhaps North Korea doing the unthinkable, such as a missile or nuclear strike on South Korea. These, however, would be developments completely overturning decades of Sino-American relations and of inter-Korean dynamics, respectively. They may occur, but they are very unlikely. South Korean policymaking elites, therefore, can assume that the international environment in which they have developed their grand strategy for over three decades will remain relatively stable for the time being.

South Korea will thus continue to pursue autonomy as an overarching end well into the future. It is an essential element of South Korea's grand strategy insofar without autonomy South Korea would see itself as a "shrimp among whales," as Korea—and South Korea—itself saw itself in the past. South Korea may not become a "big whale" such as the United States or China. But it does not want to be a shrimp like Korea was in the past. Yet, autonomy need not be understood as South Korea going it alone. South Korea is a democracy, a developed (market) economy, and a strong ally of the United States. Thus, South Korean elites see their autonomy anchored in closer relations with Western countries, and especially the United States. They see cooperation and shared values with the United States, Europe, Australia, Canada, or Japan as enablers of South Korean autonomy. Thus, we can expect Seoul to continue to pursue autonomy, but anchored in its relationship with key partners.

The country should also be less exposed to external military threats than in the past. Certainly, threats are not going to disappear—especially the existential threat of North Korea, but also the growing threat of a rising China under its current assertive foreign policy. But the South Korea of the future will be less vulnerable than in the past. Thanks to its more advanced military capabilities, its alliance with the United States, which also enables stronger security relations with other partners, its adept use of diplomacy, and its status as a developed economy, South Korea will be less vulnerable than it was before. New threats will emerge, for sure, including in the cyber domain. But South Korea has more means at its disposal to address these threats.

Arguably, the question of whether there will be inter-Korean reconciliation—never mind reunification—is the most fundamental for South Korea. Simply put, predicting reconciliation or reunification in the reasonably near future is a futile exercise. Yet, the trajectory of inter-Korean relations over the past few decades suggests that (partial) reconciliation may be possible. Certainly, inter-Korean relations are better today than they were during the Cold War. Thus, at the time of writing one can argue that partial reconciliation but no reunification for the time being is a plausible scenario. This, of course, is ultimately contingent on the domestic politics of North Korea.

South Korea should also become more central to the world economy in years to come. Successive South Korean presidents have created the conditions for this to happen through a growing network of bilateral and regional FTAs, and multiple South Korean firms have become fundamental to the working of the global economy. South Korean firms have been increasing their investment overseas, while the government has been boosting aid to developing countries. Ultimately, South Korea has a well-rounded set of economic tools and a desire to diversify its trade and investment flows across the globe. Even as globalization has slowed down as a result of the GFC and the Sino-American trade and technology war suggests growing protectionism, South Korea is well placed to boost its economic standing.

Undoubtedly, more countries and actors recognize South Korea as a middle power today than at any point in the country's history. It is an active military actor well beyond the Korean Peninsula, involved in a growing number of diplomatic forums, an economic powerhouse, and a country with strong public diplomacy and soft power tools. It is thus very likely that South Korea will maintain its position as an influential middle power into the future, particularly as the relative decline of the West and the "rise of the rest" but especially Asia will draw more attention toward countries such as South Korea. Some analysts and policymakers may consider a multipolar, less Western-centric world as more unstable. But it will clearly give greater say in global affairs to countries from other parts of the world. And an Asian middle power such as South Korea will be among the middle powers to benefit from this shift.

In short, a bright future awaits South Korea and its grand strategy. As I have shown, South Korea's global and long-term grand strategy with clear ends and means is positive for the country and increases its influence. South Korea is more proactive, more capable, more willing to express its views than ever before. As of 2023, South Korea is more able to make its own destiny than at any point in its history.

Notes

Introduction

1. Nina Silove, "Beyond the Buzzword: The Three Meanings of "Grand Strategy," *Security Studies* 27, no. 1 (2018): 31–32.
2. Hal Brands, *What Good Is Grand Strategy? Power and Purpose in American Statecraft from Harry S. Truman to George W. Bush* (Ithaca, NY: Cornell University Press, 2004), 3.
3. International Monetary Fund, *World Economic Outlook Database*, 2021, https://www.imf.org/en/Publications/WEO/weo-database/2021/October; Military Factory, *2022 Military Strength Ranking*, 2022, https://www.globalfirepower.com/countries-listing.php; Brand Finance, *Global Soft Power Index 2022* (London: Brand Finance, 2022).
4. Thierry Balzacq, Peter Dombrowski, and Simon Reich, eds., *Comparative Grand Strategy: A Framework and Cases* (Oxford: Oxford University Press, 2019).
5. There is, however, a growing policy literature on South Korean grand strategy. Recent examples include Seong Whun Cheon, *Managing a Nuclear-Armed North Korea: A Grand Strategy for a Denuclearized and Peacefully Unified Korea* (Seoul: Asan Institute for Policy Studies, 2017); Stephan Haggard, *Grand Strategies on the Korean Peninsula* (La Jolla, CA: UC San Diego Study of Innovation and Technology in China); Han Sung-Joo, *Grand Strategy for South Korea? An Overview*, August 13, 2015, http://www.theasanforum.org/grand-strategy-for-south-korea-an-overview/; Chung Min Lee, *South Korea's Grand Strategy in Transition: Coping with Existential Threats and New Political*

Forces, November 1, 2017, https://carnegieendowment.org/2017/11/01/south
-korea-s-grand-strategy-in-transition-coping-with-existential-threats-and
-new-political-forces-pub-77007.

6. David C. Kang, *American Grand Strategy and East Asian Security in the Twenty-First Century* (Cambridge: Cambridge University Press, 2017).

7. Uk Heo and Terence Roehrig, *South Korea's Rise: Economic Development, Power, and Foreign Relations* (Cambridge: Cambridge University Press, 2014).

8. Jeffrey Robertson, *Diplomacy Style and Foreign Policy: A Case Study of South Korea* (London: Routledge, 2019).

9. Wonjae Hwang, *South Korea's Changing Foreign Policy: The Impact of Democratization and Globalization* (Lanham, MD: Rowman & Littlefield, 2017).

10. Patrick Flamm, *South Korean Identity and Global Foreign Policy: Dream of Autonomy* (London: Routledge, 2019).

11. Sung-Wook Nam, Sang-Woo Rhee, Myongsob Kim, Young-Ho Kim, Yong-Sub Han, Young-Soon Chung, and Sung-Ok Yoo, *South Korea's 70-Year Endeavor for Foreign Policy, National Defense, and Unification* (London: Palgrave Macmillan, 2019).

12. Gabriel Jonsson, *South Korea in the United Nations: Global Governance, Inter-Korean Relations and Peace Building* (Singapore: World Scientific, 2017).

13. Scott A. Snyder, *South Korea at the Crossroads: Autonomy and Alliance in the Era of Rival Powers* (New York: Columbia University Press, 2018).

14. Uk Heo and Terence Roehrig, *The Evolution of the South Korea–United States Alliance* (Cambridge: Cambridge University Press, 2018).

15. Terence Roehrig, *Japan, South Korea, and the United States Nuclear Umbrella: Deterrence After the Cold War* (New York: Columbia University Press, 2017).

16. Min Ye, *China-South Korea Relations in the New Era: Challenges and Opportunities* (Lanham, MD: Rowman & Littlefield, 2017).

17. Brad Glosserman and Scott A. Snyder, *The Japan-South Korea Identity Clash: East Asian Security and the United States* (New York: Columbia University Press, 2015).

18. The names of some of these ministries have changed over time. These were their names as of February 2023.

19. Giovanni Capoccia, "Critical Junctures," in *The Oxford Handbook of Historical Institutionalism*, ed. Orfeo Fioretos, Tulia G. Falleti, and Adam Sheingate (Oxford: Oxford University Press, 2016), 89.

20. The importance of critical junctures for grand strategy is implicit in the existing literature. Some authors explicitly discuss how critical junctures result in a new grand strategy—or how the absence of a critical juncture allows for a grand strategy to continue. See, for example, Melvyn P. Leffler, "9/11 and American Foreign Policy," *Diplomatic History* 29, no. 3 (2005):

395–413; Carlos R. S. Milani and Tiago Nery, "Brazil," in Balzacq, Dombrowski, and Reich, *Comparative Grand Strategy*, 149–70; Brad Williams, *Japanese Foreign Intelligence and Grand Strategy* (Washington, DC: Georgetown University Press, 2021).

1. The Grand Strategy of Middle Powers

1. Carl von Clausewitz, *On War*, ed. and trans. Michael Howard and Peter Paret (Princeton, NJ: Princeton University Press, 1976), 87, 605.
2. Nina Silove, "Beyond the Buzzword: The Three Meanings of "Grand Strategy," *Security Studies* 27, no. 1 (2018): 31–32.
3. Basil Henry Liddell Hart, *Strategy: The Indirect Approach*, 2nd rev. ed. (New York: Praeger, 1974), 357.
4. Liddell Hart, *Strategy*, 321–22.
5. William C. Martel, *Grand Strategy in Theory and Practice: The Need for an Effective America Foreign Policy* (Cambridge: Cambridge University Press, 2015), 24–25.
6. Thierry Balzacq, Peter Dombrowski, and Simon Reich, "Introduction: Comparing Grand Strategies in the Modern World," in *Comparative Grand Strategy: A Framework and Cases*, ed. Thierry Balzacq, Peter Dombrowski, and Simon Reich (Oxford: Oxford University Press, 2019), 6–7.
7. Paul Kennedy, *The Rise and Fall of the Great Powers: Economic Change and Military Conflict from 1500 to 2000* (New York: Random House, 1987).
8. Paul Kennedy, "Grand Strategy in War and Peace: Toward a Broader Definition," in *Grand Strategies in War and Peace*, ed. Paul Kennedy (New Haven, CT: Yale University Press, 1991), 4.
9. Kennedy, "Grand Strategy in War and Peace," 7–8.
10. See, for example, Hans J. Morgenthau, *Politics Among Nations: The Struggle for Power and Peace* (New York: Knopf, 1948); Kenneth Waltz, *Theory of International Politics* (New York: McGraw-Hill, 1979).
11. See, most notably, Alexander Wendt, *Social Theory of International Politics* (Cambridge: Cambridge University Press, 1999).
12. Alexander Wendt, "Anarchy Is What States Make of It: The Social Construction of Power Politics," *International Organization* 46, no. 2 (1992): 391.
13. Wendt, *Social Theory of International Politics*.
14. Liddell Hart, *Strategy*, 321–22.
15. Liddell Hart, *Strategy*, 321–22.
16. Kennedy, "Grand Strategy in War and Peace," 4.
17. Kennedy, "Grand Strategy in War and Peace," 4.

18. Barry Posen, *The Sources of Military Doctrine: France, Britain, and Germany Between the World Wars* (Ithaca, NY: Cornell University Press, 1984), 13.

19. Hal Brands, *What Good Is Grand Strategy? Power and Purpose in American Statecraft from Harry S. Truman to George W. Bush* (Ithaca, NY: Cornell University Press, 2004), 3.

20. Brands, *What Good Is Grand Strategy?*, 3–4.

21. Martel, *Grand Strategy in Theory and Practice*, 32–33.

22. Colin Dueck, *Reluctant Crusaders: Power, Culture, and Change in American Grand Strategy* (Princeton, NJ: Princeton University Press, 2006), 9–10; Silove, "Beyond the Buzzword," 28.

23. Silove, "Beyond the Buzzword," 34–45.

24. Silove, "Beyond the Buzzword," 31–32.

25. Arthur F. Lykke Jr., "Defining Military Strategy = E + W + M," *Military Review* 69, no. 5 (1989): 3.

26. Lykke, "Defining Military Strategy," 3.

27. Jeffrey W. Meiser, "Ends + Ways + Means = (Bad) Strategy," *Parameters*, 46, no. 4 (2016–2017): 82–83.

28. Richard E. Berkebile, "Military Strategy Revisited: A Critique of the Lykke Formulation," *Military Review Online Exclusive* (2018): 1.

29. Berkebile, "Military Strategy Revisited," 3.

30. Lawrence Freedman, *Strategy: A History* (Oxford: Oxford University Press, 2013), 4.

31. Freedman, *Strategy*, 4.

32. Meiser, "Ends + Ways + Means," 81.

33. Silove, "Beyond the Buzzword," 45.

34. Silove, "Beyond the Buzzword," 45.

35. Brands, *What Good Is Grand Strategy?*; Kennedy, "Grand Strategy in War and Peace"; Liddell Hart, *Strategy*; Martel, *Grand Strategy in Theory and Practice*; Posen, *The Sources of Military Doctrine*.

36. Martel, *Grand Strategy in Theory and Practice*, 30

37. Balzacq, Dombrowski, and Reich, "Introduction," 1.

38. Balzacq, Dombrowski, and Reich, "Introduction," 2.

39. Silove, "Beyond the Buzzword," 51.

40. Williamson Murray, "Thoughts on Grand Strategy," in *The Shaping of Grand Strategy: Policy, Diplomacy, and War*, ed. Williamson Murray, Richard Hart Sinnreich, and James Lacey (Cambridge: Cambridge University Press, 2011), 1.

41. Kennedy, *Grand Strategies in War and Peace*.

42. Athanasios G. Platias and Konstantinos Koliopoulos, *Thucydides on Strategy: Grand Strategies in the Peloponnesian War and Their Relevance Today* (New York: Columbia University Press, 2010).

43. Edward N. Luttwak, *The Grand Strategy of the Roman Empire: From the First Century A.D. to the Third* (Baltimore, MD: Johns Hopkins University Press, 1976).

44. Edward N. Luttwak, *The Grand Strategy of the Byzantine Empire* (Cambridge, MA: Harvard University Press, 2009).

45. Steven E. Lobell, *The Challenge of Hegemony: Grand Strategy, Trade, and Domestic Politics* (Ann Arbor: University of Michigan Press, 2003).

46. Mark R. Brawley, *Political Economy and Grand Strategy: A Neoclassical Realist View* (London: Routledge, 2010).

47. Richard Rosecrance and Arthur A. Stein, eds., *The Domestic Bases of Grand Strategy* (Ithaca, NY: Cornell University Press, 1993).

48. Posen, *The Sources of Military Doctrine.*

49. Jeffrey W. Taliaferro, Norrin M. Ripsman, and Steven E. Lobell, eds., *The Challenge of Grand Strategy: The Great Powers and the Broken Balance Between the World Wars* (Cambridge: Cambridge University Press, 2012).

50. Brands, *What Good Is Grand Strategy?*

51. Dueck, *Reluctant Crusaders.*

52. Christopher Hemmer, *American Pendulum: Recurring Debates in U.S. Grand Strategy* (Ithaca, NY: Cornell University Press, 2015).

53. Martel, *Grand Strategy in Theory and Practice.*

54. Robert J. Art, *A Grand Strategy for America* (Ithaca, NY: Cornell University Press, 2003).

55. Hal Brands, *American Grand Strategy in the Age of Trump* (Washington, DC: Brookings Institution Press, 2018).

56. A. Trevor Thrall and Benjamin H. Friedman, eds., *US Grand Strategy in the 21st Century: The Case for Restraint* (London: Routledge, 2018).

57. Lukas K. Danner, *China's Grand Strategy: Contradictory Foreign Policy?* (London: Palgrave Macmillan, 2018).

58. Avery Goldstein, *Rising to the Challenge: China's Grand Strategy and International Security* (Stanford, CA: Stanford University Press, 2005).

59. Sulmaan Wasif Khan, *Haunted by Chaos: China's Grand Strategy from Mao Zedong to Xi Jinping* (Cambridge, MA: Harvard University Press, 2018).

60. Hongua Men, *China's Grand Strategy: A Framework of Analysis* (Singapore: Springer, 2020).

61. Ye Zhicheng, *Inside China's Grand Strategy: The Perspective from the People's Republic*, ed. and trans. Steven I. Levine and Guoli Liu (Lexington: University Press of Kentucky, 2011).

62. Rush Doshi, *The Long Game: China's Grand Strategy to Displace American Order* (Oxford: Oxford University Press, 2021).

63. Andrew F. Cooper, Richard A. Higgott, and Kim R. Nossal, *Relocating Middle Powers: Australia and Canada in a Changing World Order* (Vancouver: University of British Columbia Press, 1993).

64. Andrew Carr, "Is Australia a Middle Power? A Systemic Impact Approach," *Australian Journal of International Affairs* 68, no. 1 (2014): 73–76.
65. Eduard Jordaan, "The Concept of a Middle Power in International Relations: Distinguishing between Emerging and Traditional Middle Powers," *Politikon* 30, no. 1 (2003): 165.
66. Balzacq, Dombrowski, and Reich, "Introduction," 11.
67. Silove, "Beyond the Buzzword," 51.
68. Richard J. Samuels, *Securing Japan: Tokyo's Grand Strategy and the Future of East Asia* (Ithaca, NY: Cornell University Press, 2007).
69. Brad Williams, *Japanese Foreign Intelligence and Grand Strategy* (Washington, DC: Georgetown University Press, 2021).
70. Michael Green, *Line of Advantage: Japan's Grand Strategy in the Era of Abe Shinzo* (New York: Columbia University Press, 2022).
71. Etel Solingen, *Regional Orders at Century's Dawn: Global and Domestic Influences on Grand Strategy* (Princeton, NJ: Princeton University Press, 1998).
72. Michael Wesley, "Australia's Grand Strategy and the 2016 Defence White Paper," *Security Challenges* 12, no. 1 (2016): 19–30.
73. William I. Hitchcock, Melvyn P. Leffler, and Jeffrey W. Legro, *Shaper Nations: Strategies for a Changing World* (Cambridge, MA: Harvard University Press, 2016).
74. Cooper, Higgott, and Nossal, *Relocating Middle Powers*, 20.
75. Charalampos Efstathopoulos, "Middle Powers and the Behavioural Model," *Global Society* 31, no. 1 (2018): 57; Jordaan, "The Concept of a Middle Power," 167–69.
76. Gareth J. Evans and Bruce Grant, *Australia's Foreign Relations in the World of the 1990s* (Melbourne: Melbourne University Press, 1995), 397; Cooper, Higgott, and Nossal, *Relocating Middle Powers*, 20.
77. See, for example, Brands, *What Good Is Grand Strategy?*
78. See, for example, Ian Manners, "Normative Power Europe: A Contradiction in Terms?" *Journal of Common Market Studies* 40, no. 2 (2002): 235–58.
79. Efstathopoulos, "Middle Powers and the Behavioural Model," 56; Jordaan, "The Concept of a Middle Power," 177.
80. Efstathopoulos, "Middle Powers and the Behavioural Model," 56–57.
81. F. H. Soward, "On Becoming a Middle Power: The Canadian Experience," *Pacific Historical Review* 32, no. 2 (1963): 134.
82. Jordaan, "The Concept of a Middle Power," 172.
83. Richard A. Higgott and Andrew Fenton Cooper, "Middle Power Leadership and Coalition Building: Australia, the Cairns Group, and the Uruguay Round of Trade Negotiations," *International Organization* 44, no. 4 (1990): 592; Rory Miller and Sarah Cardaun, "Multinational Security Coalitions

and the Limits of Middle Power Activism in the Middle East," *International Affairs* 96, no. 6 (2020): 1510.

84. Cooper, Higgott, and Nosall, *Relocating Middle Powers*, 24–25.

85. Andrew F. Cooper, "Niche Diplomacy: A Conceptual Overview," in *Niche Diplomacy: Middle Powers after the Cold War*, ed. Andrew F. Cooper (London: Macmillan Press, 1997), 4; Alan K. Henrikson, "Niche Diplomacy in the World Public Arena," in *The New Public Diplomacy: Soft Power in International Relations*, ed. Jan Melissen (London: Palgrave Macmillan, 2005), 71.

86. Heather Smith, "Unwilling Internationalism or Strategic Internationalism: Canadian Climate Policy Under the Conservative Government," in *Readings in Canadian Foreign Policy: Classic Debates and New Ideas*, ed. Duanne Bratt and Christopher J. Kurucha (Oxford: Oxford University Press, 2007), 59.

87. Manners, "Normative Power Europe."

88. Anu Bradford, *Brussels Effect: How the European Union Rules the World* (Oxford: Oxford University Press, 2020).

89. Efstathopoulos, "Middle Powers and the Behavioural Model," 68; Jordaan, "The Concept of a Middle Power," 172.

90. Ralf Emmers and Sarah Teo, "Regional Security Strategies of Middle Powers in the Asia-Pacific," *International Relations of the Asia-Pacific* 15, no. 2 (2015): 192; Jordaan, "The Concept of a Middle Power," 177.

91. Efstathopoulos, "Middle Powers and the Behavioural Model," 53.

92. Ziya Onis and Mustafa Kutlay, "The Dynamics of Emerging Middle-power Influence in Regional and Global Governance," *Australian Journal of International Relations* 71, no. 2 (2017): 165.

93. Kennedy, "Grand Strategy in War and Peace"; Kennedy, *The Rise and Fall of Great Powers*.

94. Jordaan, "The Concept of a Middle Power," 168.

95. Dongmin Shin, "The Concept of Middle Power and the Case of the ROK: A Review," in *Korea 2012: Politics, Economy and Society*, ed. Rudiger Frank, Jim Hoare, Patrick Kollner, and Susan Pares (Leiden: Brill, 2012), 148.

96. Soon-ok Shin, "South Korea's Elusive Middlepowermanship: Regional or Global Player?" *Pacific Review* 29, no. 2 (2016): 188.

97. Jordaan, "The Concept of a Middle Power," 171; Hakan Edstrom and Jacob Westberg, "The Defense Strategies of Middle Powers: Competing for Security, Influence and Status in an Era of Unipolar Demise," *Comparative Strategy* 39, no. 2 (2020): 171.

98. Edstrom and Westberg, "The Defense Strategies of Middle Powers," 172, 182.

99. Martel, *Grand Strategy in Theory and Practice*, 30.

100. Martel, *Grand Strategy in Theory and Practice*, 30.

101. Brands, *What Good Is Grand Strategy?*; Hemmer, *American Pendulum*.

102. Brawley, *Political Economy and Grand Strategy*, ch. 7.

103. Doshi, *The Long Game*; Men, *China's Grand Strategy*.

104. Meunier, Sophie, *Trading Voices: The European Union in International Commercial Negotiations* (Princeton, NJ: Princeton University Press, 2007).

105. Martel, *Grand Strategy in Theory and Practice*, 30, 34.

106. Martel, *Grand Strategy in Theory and Practice*, 30, 33.

107. Brands, *What Good Is Grand Strategy?*; Hemmer, *American Pendulum*.

108. Martel, *Grand Strategy in Theory and Practice*, 30, 50.

109. Martel, *Grand Strategy in Theory and Practice*, 50.

2. Historical Background, 1948–1987

1. UN General Assembly, Resolution 112 (II), "The Problem of the Independence of Korea," 14 November 1947, https://documents-dds-ny.un.org/doc/RESOLUTION/GEN/NR0/038/19/PDF/NR003819.pdf?OpenElement.

2. Charles Kraus, "Kim Gu on Reunification and War, 1948," *NKIDP e-Dossier* 19, June 2015, https://www.wilsoncenter.org/publication/kim-gu-reunification-and-war-1948.

3. Young Ick Lew, *The Making of the First Korean President: Syngman Rhee's Quest for Independence, 1875–1948* (Honolulu: University of Hawai'i Press, 2014), 278.

4. Ministry of National Defense of the Republic of Korea, *2000 Defense White Paper* (Seoul: Ministry of the National Defense of the Republic of Korea, 2000), 372.

5. Ministry of National Defense, *2000 Defense White Paper*, 372.

6. Ministry of National Defense, *2000 Defense White Paper*, 372.

7. Office of the Historian of the Department of State of the United States of America, "Report of the National Security Council to the President," *Foreign Relations of the United States, 1949, the Far East and Australasia*, vol. 7, pt. 2, https://history.state.gov/historicaldocuments/frus1949v07p2/d209.

8. William Stueck, *The Korean War: An International History* (Princeton, NJ: Princeton University Press, 1995), 18–19.

9. Department of State of the United States of America, "Review of the Position as of 1950: Address by the Secretary of State, January 12, 1950," *American Foreign Policy 1950–1955: Basic Documents* (Washington, DC: U.S. Government Printing Office, 1957), 2:2310–28.

10. Clayton Knowles, "2 Votes Block Korea Aid Bill; House Test a Blow to Truman," *New York Times*, 20 January 1950.

11. UN Security Council, Resolution 82 (1950), 25 June 1950, https://digitallibrary
.un.org/record/112025?ln=en.

12. UN Security Council, Resolution 83 (1950), 27 June 1950, https://digitallibrary
.un.org/record/112026?ln=en.

13. United Nations Command, Under One Flag, 2022, https://www.unc.mil
/About/About-Us/.

14. Stueck, *The Korean War*, 65.

15. Stueck, *The Korean War*, 168–69.

16. United Nations Command, Armistice Negotiations, 2022, https://www
.unc.mil/History/1951-1953-Armistice-Negotiations/.

17. Edward C. Keefer, ed., "The President of the Republic of Korea (Rhee) to
President Eisenhower," *American Foreign Policy 1952–1954, Korea* (Washington, DC: US Government Printing Office: 1984), 15:1224–26.

18. United Nations Command, *Armistice Negotiations*.

19. Syngman Rhee, "Memorandum, President Syngman Rhee to All Diplomatic
Officials," 14 August 1953, https://digitalarchive.wilsoncenter.org/document
/119394.

20. UN General Assembly, Resolution 195 (III), "The Problem of the Independence of Korea," 12 December 1948, https://digitallibrary.un.org/record
/210026?ln=en.

21. Chi Young Pak, *Korea and the United Nations* (The Hague: Kluwer Law
International, 2000), 66–67.

22. Ministry of Foreign Affairs of the Republic of Korea, "외교관계수립현황"
(Status of Establishment of Diplomatic Relations), December 2021, https://
www.mofa.go.kr/www/wpge/m_4181/contents.do.

23. As of 2022, the UN Digital Library holds more than 1,100 records on the
"Korean question" covering the period 1947–2017, with periods of special
intensity throughout the decades including 1950–1954, 1961–1963, 1971–1976,
1979–1981, 1986–1992, or 1995–2000. See https://digitallibrary.un.org/search
?ln=en&as=0&p=subjectheading:[KOREAN+QUESTION].

24. Ministry of Foreign Affairs of the Republic of Korea. "Presidential Proclamation of Sovereignty over Adjacent Seas," trans. T. T. Yynn, 28
September 1953.

25. Ministry of Foreign Affairs, "외교관계수립현황."

26. Mutual Defense Treaty Between the Republic of Korea and the United
States of America, 1 October 1953.

27. Office of the Historian of the Department of State of the United States of
America, "Memorandum by the Executive Officer of the Operations Coordinating Boards (Staats) to the Executive Secretary of the National Security
Council (Lay)," *Foreign Relations of the United States, 1952–1954, Korea*, https://
history.state.gov/historicaldocuments/frus1952-54v15p2/d980.

28. Ramon Pacheco Pardo, *Shrimp to Whale: South Korea from the Forgotten War to K-Pop* (London: Hurst, 2022), 41.

29. Victor Cha, "Powerplay: Origins of the U.S. Alliance System in Asia," *International Security* 34, no. 3 (2009–2010): 158–59.

30. Office of the Historian of the Department of State of the United States of America, "The Truman Doctrine, 1947," *Milestones in the History of U.S. Foreign Relations*, https://history.state.gov/milestones/1945-1952/truman-doctrine.

31. Office of the Historian of the Department of State of the United States of America, "Southeast Asia Treaty Organization (SEATO), 1954," *Milestones in the History of U.S. Foreign Relations*, https://history.state.gov/milestones/1945-1952/truman-doctrine.

32. Hans M. Kristensen and Robert S. Norris, "A History of US Nuclear Weapons in South Korea," *Bulletin of the Atomic Scientists* 73, no. 6 (2017): 349–50.

33. Ministry of Foreign Affairs of the Republic of Korea, "변영태 외무장관의 한국 통일 방안 제시" (Foreign Minister's Byeon Yeong Tae Proposal for Korean Unification), 22 May 1954, 대한민국 외교부 60년 (60 Years of the Ministry of Foreign Affairs of the Republic of Korea) (Seoul: Ministry of Foreign Affairs of the Rebuplic of Korea, 2009).

34. Pacheco Pardo, *Shrimp to Whale*, 39.

35. Pacheco Pardo, *Shrimp to Whale*, 31.

36. Ministry of Foreign Affairs of the Republic of Korea, "외교관계수립현황."

37. See https://digitallibrary.un.org/search?ln=en&as=0&p=subjectheading:[KOREAN+QUESTION].

38. Pacheco Pardo, *Shrimp to Whale*, 57.

39. Peter Banseok Kwon, "Building Bombs, Building a Nation: The State, *Chaebol*, and the Militarized Industrialization of South Korea, 1973–1979," *Journal of Asian Studies* 79, no. 1 (2020): 52–54.

40. SIPRI, "Military Expenditure by Country, in Constant (2019) US$m. 1949–2020," 2021, https://sipri.org/sites/default/files/SIPRI-Milex-data-1949-2020_0.xlsx.

41. Hannah Fischer, *North Korea Provocative Actions, 1950–2007* (Washington, DC: Congressional Research Service, 2007), 4–5.

42. Tim Kane, *Global U.S. Troop Deployment, 1950–2005* (Washington, DC: The Heritage Foundation, 2006), 9.

43. Kristensen and Norris, "A History of US Nuclear Weapons in South Korea," 349.

44. Ministry of National Defense of the Republic of Korea, *2000 Defense White Paper*, 375.

45. Korea Herald, "98 Peace Corps Volunteers Arrive Here for Assignments," *Korea Herald*, 17 September 1966.

46. Min Yong Lee, "The Vietnam War: South Korea's Search for National Security," in *The Park Chung Hee Era: The Transformation of South Korea*, ed. Byung-Kook Kim and Ezra F. Vogel (Cambridge, MA: Harvard University Press, 2011), 403–29.

47. Craig R. Whitney, "Korean Troops End Vietnam Combat Role," *New York Times*, 9 November 1972.

48. Ministry of Unification of the Republic of Korea, *White Paper on Korean Unification 1996* (Seoul: Ministry of Unification of the Republic of Korea, 1996), 42–44.

49. World Bank, "Population, Total—Korea, Dem. People's Rep.," 2022, https://data.worldbank.org/indicator/SP.POP.TOTL?locations=KP; World Bank, "Population, total—Korea, Rep.," 2022, https://data.worldbank.org/indicator/SP.POP.TOTL?locations=KR.

50. Treaty of Friendship, Co-operation and Mutual Assistance Between the Union of Soviet Socialist Republics and the Democratic People's Republic of Korea, 6 July 1961; Treaty of Friendship, Co-operation and Mutual Assistance Between the People's Republic of China and the Democratic People's Republic of Korea, 11 July 1961.

51. Ministry of National Defense, *2000 Defense White Paper*, 375.

52. B. C. Koh, "Dilemmas of Korean Unification," *Asian Survey* 11, no. 5 (1971): 485.

53. Park Chung-hee, "평화통일 구상 선언" (Peaceful Unification Initiative Declaration), 15 August 1970.

54. Treaty on Basic Relations Between the Republic of Korea and Japan, 22 June 1965.

55. Pacheco Pardo, *Shrimp to Whale*, 53–54.

56. Chae-Jin Lee, "South Korea: Political Competition and Government Adaptation," *Asian Survey* 12, no. 1 (1972): 45; Sungjoo Han, "South Korea: The Political Economy of Dependency," *Asian Survey* 14, no. 1 (1974): 46; John K. C. Oh, "South Korea 1975: A Permanent Emergency," *Asian Survey* 16, no. 1 (1976): 79; Cong-Sik Lee, "South Korea 1979: Confrontation, Assassination, and Transition," *Asian Survey* 20, no. 1 (1980): 74.

57. Richard Nixon, "Address to the Nation on the War in Vietnam," 3 November 1969.

58. Kane, *Global U.S. Troop Deployment*, 9.

59. USAID, "U.S. Foreign Assistance Trends," 2022, https://foreignassistance.gov/aid-trends.

60. Seung-Young Kim, "Security, Nationalism, and the Pursuit of Nuclear Weapons and Missiles: The South Korean Case, 1970–82," *Diplomacy and Statecraft* 12, no. 4 (2001): 53–80.

61. Joint Communiqué of the United States of America and the People's Republic of China, 27 February 1972.

62. Sungjoo Han, "South Korea in 1974: The "Korean Democracy" on Trial," *Asian Survey* 15, no. 1 (1975): 40.

63. Ministry of National Defense, *2000 Defense White Paper*, 376.

64. Bae Young-kyung, "北의지따라 반복된 연락채널 차단·복원 . . . 국면전환 '신호탄'" (Blocking and Restoring Contact Channels Repeatedly at North Korea's Will: Change of Phase 'A Signal'"), *Yonhap News*, 27 July 2021.

65. The July 4 South-North Joint Communiqué, 4 July 1972.

66. Park Chung-hee, "평화통일 외교정책에 관한 특별성명" (Special Statement on Foreign Policy for Peaceful Unification), 23 June 1973.

67. Letter to the Congress of the United States of America from the Supreme People's Assembly of the Democratic People's Republic of Korea, 6 April 1973.

68. Letter to the Congress of the United States of the United States of America from the Supreme People's Assembly of the Democratic People's Republic of Korea, 13 May 1974.

69. Ministry of National Defense, *2000 Defense White Paper*, 376.

70. Bae, "北의지따라 반복된 연락채널 차단·복원 . . . 국면전환 '신호탄.'"

71. Jutta Bolt, Robert Inklaar, Herman de Jong, and Jan Luiten van Zanden, "Maddison Project Database 2020," 7 December 2021, https://www.rug.nl/ggdc/historicaldevelopment/maddison/releases/maddison-project-database-2020.

72. Tae Dong Chung, "Korea's Nordpolitik: Achievements & Prospects," *Asian Perspective* 15, no. 2 (1991): 151–52.

73. Ministry of National Defense, *2000 Defense White Paper*, 377.

74. UN General Assembly, Resolution 3390, "Question of Korea," 18 November 1975, https://digitallibrary.un.org/record/639969.

75. Select Committee on Ethics of the United States Senate, *Korean Influence Enquiry* (Washington, DC: U.S. Government Printing Office, 1978); Lewis M. Simons, "SEATO's Flags Are Coming Down for the Last Time," *Washington Post*, 29 June 1977; J. Bruce Jacobs, "Taiwan 1979: The "'Normalcy' after 'Normalization,'" *Asian Survey* 20, no. 1 (1980): 86.

76. Chong-Sik Lee, "South Korea 1979: Confrontation, Assassination, and Transition," *Asian Survey* 20, no. 1 (1980): 76.

77. Ministry of National Defense, *2000 Defense White Paper*, 377.

78. Brian Kim, "US Lifts Restrictions on South Korea, Ending Range and Warhead Limits" *Defense News*, 25 May 2021.

79. Kristensen and Norris, "A History of Nuclear Weapons in South Korea," 353.

80. Ministry of Foreign Affairs of the Republic of Korea, "외교관계수립현황."

81. Glenn D. Paige, "1966: Korea Creates the Future," *Asian Survey* 7, no. 1 (1967): 27.

82. Soon Sung Cho, "North Korea and South Korea: Stepped-Up Aggression and the Search for New Security," *Asian Survey* 9, no. 1 (1969): 31–32.

83. Joungwon Alexander Kim, "Divided Korea 1969: Consolidating for Transition," *Asian Survey* 10, no. 1 (1970): 33.

84. Park Chung-hee, "평화통일 외교정책에 관한 특별성명."

85. See https://digitallibrary.un.org/search?ln=en&as=0&p=subjectheading:[KOREAN+QUESTION].

86. KOICA, *Annual Report 1993* (Seoul: KOICA, 1993), 9–10.

87. KOCIS, "History," 2022, https://www.kocis.go.kr/eng/openHistory.do.

88. Pacheco Pardo, *Shrimp to Whale*, 89–90.

89. Joint Statement Following Meetings with President Chun Doo Hwan of the Republic of Korea, 14 November 1983.

90. Kim, "Security, Nationalism, and the Pursuit of Nuclear Weapons and Missiles."

91. Kane, *Global U.S. Troop* Deployment, 9.

92. Kristensen and Norris, "A History of Nuclear Weapons in South Korea," 359.

93. Pacheco Pardo, *Shrimp to Whale*, 87.

94. Pacheco Pardo, *Shrimp to Whale*, 106.

95. Dae-Sook Suh, "South Korea in 1982: The First Year of the Fifth Republic," *Asian Survey* 22, no. 1 (1982): 111.

96. Chun Doo-hwan, "민족화합 민주평화통일 제의" (Formula for National Reconciliation, Democratic Peace and Unification), 22 January 1982.

97. William Chapman, "North Korean Leader's Son Blamed for Rangoon Bombing," *Washington Post*, 3 December 1983.

98. Clyde Haberman, "Korean Families Visit After Border Is Opened," *New York Times*, 21 September 1985.

99. Clyde Haberman, "5 Dead, 36 Hurt in an Explosion at Seoul Airport," *New York Times*, 15 September 1986.

100. Associated Press, "Woman Says She Put Bomb on a Korean Jet, Killing 115," *New York Times*, 15 January 1988.

101. Chae-Jin Lee, "South Korea in 1984: Seeking Peace and Prosperity," *Asian Survey* 25, no. 1 (1985): 86–87.

102. Chae-Jin Lee, "South Korea in 1983: Crisis Management and Political Legitimacy," *Asian Survey* 24, no. 1 (1984): 113–14.

103. Chae, "South Korea in 1984," 85.

104. Chung, "Korea's Nordpolitik," 151.

105. Chae, "South Korea in 1984," 85.

106. Han Sung-Joo, "South Korea in 1987: The Politics of Democratization," *Asian Survey* 28, no. 1 (1988): 59–60.

107. Han Sung-Joo, "South Korea in 1987."

108. KOICA, "Annual Report 1993," 9–10.

109. Pacheco Pardo, *Shrimp to Whale*, 99.

110. Victor Cha, *Beyond the Final Score: The Politics of Sport in Asia* (New York: Columbia University Press, 2009), 56.

111. Alon Levkowitz, "Korea and the Middle East Turmoil: A Reassessment of South Korea–Middle East Relations," *The Korean Journal of Defense Analyses* 24, no. 2 (2012): 228–29.

112. See https://digitallibrary.un.org/search?ln=en&as=0&p=subjectheading: [KOREAN+QUESTION].

3. South Korea's Grand Strategy

1. Thierry Balzacq, Peter Dombrowski, and Simon Reich, eds., *Comparative Grand Strategy: A Framework and Cases* (Oxford: Oxford University Press, 2019), 8.

2. Roh Tae-woo, "남북이 함께 번영하는 민족공동체: 민족자존과 통일번영을 위한 특별 선언" (A National Community Where the Two Koreas Prosper Together: Special Declaration for National Self-Esteem, Unification, and Prosperity), 7 July 1988.

3. Constitution of the Republic of Korea, 29 October 1987.

4. Socialist Constitution of the Democratic People's Republic of Korea, 29 August 2019.

5. South Korea's Ministry of National Defense (MND) has published twenty-four defense white papers between the first one of 1988 and the last one at the time of writing, issued in 2022. All of them discuss North Korea in these terms.

6. Interview with ROK Ministry of Foreign Affairs (MOFA) official, phone, September 29, 2020; interview with ROK MOFA official, Seoul, 6 August 2021; interview with ROK government advisor, Seoul, 11 August 2021.

7. Interview with MOFA official, phone, 20 July 2020; interview with ROK Army official, phone, 5 August 2020; interview with ROK MOFA official 1, online, 17 November 2020.

8. South Korea was placed under the U.S. nuclear umbrella after the two countries signed their mutual defense treaty in 1953, and this policy continues to be in place as of 2022.

9. International Institute for Strategic Studies, *The Military Balance 2022* (London: Routledge, 2022), 9.

10. Interview with ROK Army official 2, phone, 5 August 2020; interview with ROK MOFA official, online, 16 September 2020; interview with ROK MOFA official, Seoul, 11 August 2021.

11. See, for example, the Joint Statement Between the United States and the Republic of Korea, 20 October 2003 (under Roh Moo-hyun); Joint Vision for the Alliance of the United States of America and the Republic of Korea, 16 June 2009 (under Lee Myung-bak); Joint Statement by President Barack Obama of the United States and President Park Geun-hye of South Korea, 7 May 2013 (under Park Geun-hye); U.S.-ROK Leaders' Joint Statement, 21 May 2021 (under Moon-Jae-in); and United States-Republic of Korea Leaders' Joint Statement, 21 May 2022 (under Yoon Suk-yeol).

12. See, for example, the white papers issued by the ROK MOFA between 1990 and 2021.

13. Interview with ROK government advisor, online, 1 November 2020; interview with ROK MND official, Seoul, 13 August 2021; interview with ROK MOFA official, Seoul, 16 August 2021.

14. Interview with U.S. Department of State official, phone, 20 July 2020; interview with U.S. Department of State official, phone, 22 July 2020.

15. See, for example, the white papers issued by the ROK MOFA between 1990 and 2021.

16. Interview with ROK Army official 1, phone, 5 August 2020; with ROK MOFA official, Seoul, 24 July 2021; interview with ROK government advisor, Seoul, 21 August 2021.

17. Treaty of Friendship, Co-operation and Mutual Assistance between the People's Republic of China and the Democratic People's Republic of Korea.

18. Interview with ROK government advisor, phone, 18 August 2020; interview with ROK MOFA official, online, 16 September 2020; interview with ROK MOFA official, Seoul, 16 August 2021.

19. International Institute for Strategic Studies, *The Military Balance 2022*, 9.

20. Jessica Chen Weiss, "What China's Assertiveness in the South China Sea Means—and What Comes Next," *Washington Post*, 30 May 2019.

21. Joe Biden, "Remarks by President Biden on America's Place in the World," 4 February 2021.

22. World Bank, "GDP per Capita (Current US$)—Korea, Rep," 2022, https://data.worldbank.org/indicator/NY.GDP.PCAP.CD?locations=KR.

23. Interview with ROK MOFA official, phone, 29 September 2020; interview with ROK MOFA official, Seoul, 15 August 2021.

24. OECD, "List of OECD Members," 2022, https://www.oecd.org/about/document/ratification-oecd-convention.htm.

25. Bank of Korea, "Overview," 2022, https://www.bok.or.kr/eng/main/contents.do?menuNo=400198.

26. G20, "About the G20," 2022, https://g20.org/about-the-g20/; OECD, "Development Assistance Committee (DAC)," 2022, https://www.oecd.org/dac/development-assistance-committee/; G7 UK 2021, "Members &

Guests," 2021, https://www.g7uk.org/members-guests/; IMF, "World Economic Outlook Database: October 2021 Edition," 2022, https://www.imf.org/en/Publications/WEO/weo-database/2021/October.

27. Kiseon Chung and Hyun Choe, "South Korean National Pride: Determinants, Changes, and Suggestions," *Asian Perspective* 32, no. 1 (2008): 99–127; Hanwool Jeong, "South Korean National Pride Beyond 'Patriotism Highs' and 'Hell Chosun,'" *East Asia Institute Issue Briefing* (2020).

28. Interview with ROK MOFA official, Seoul, 24 August 2021; interview with ROK MOFA official, Seoul, 26 April 2022.

29. Samuel Huntington, *The Third Wave: Democratization in the Late Twentieth Century* (Norman: University of Oklahoma Press, 1991).

30. See, for example, the V-Dem Dataset available at https://www.v-dem.net/vdemds.html.

31. Chung and Choe, "South Korean National Pride"; Jeong, "South Korean National Pride."

32. Chung and Choe, "South Korean National Pride"; Jeong, "South Korean National Pride."

33. Interview with ROK government advisor, Seoul, 12 August 2021; interview with ROK MOFA official, Seoul, 15 August 2021; interview with ROK MOFA official, Seoul, 27 April 2022.

34. The most recent example at the time of writing would be South Korea siding with the United States, Europe, and other fellow democracies including in Asia to call out Russia's invasion of Ukraine and impose sanctions on Moscow.

35. G7 UK 2021, "Members & Guests."

36. Department of State of the United States of America, "Official Interventions," 2021, https://www.state.gov/official-interventions-the-summit-for-democracy/.

37. Alexander Wendt, *Social Theory of International Politics* (Cambridge: Cambridge University Press, 1999).

38. This is a common reference to South Korea as a foreign policy actor in official government documents, policy speeches, and interviews with policymakers.

39. Interview with ROK MOFA official, online, 21 December 2020; with ROK MOFA official, Seoul, 24 July 2021; interview with ROK MOFA official, Seoul, 15 August 2021.

40. Kim Young-sam, "세계화 구상에 대한 대통령 말씀(옛껍질을 깨고 새로 태어납시다)" (President's Message on the Globalization Initiative [Let's Break the Old Shell and Be Reborn]), 26 January 1995.

41. APEC, "History," March 2022, https://www.apec.org/about-us/about-apec/history.

42. World Bank, "Trade (% of GDP)," 2022, https://data.worldbank.org/indicator/NE.TRD.GNFS.ZS?most_recent_value_desc=true.

43. Interview with ROK MOFA official, Seoul, 30 July 2021; interview with ROK government advisor, Seoul, 12 August 2021; interview with ROK MOFA official, Seoul, 26 August 2021.

44. Interview with ROK MOFA official, phone, 20 July 2020; interview with ROK MOFA official, Seoul, 26 August 2021; interview with ROK government advisor, Seoul, 9 August 2021.

45. Interview with ROK MOFA official, phone, 20 July 2020; interview with ROK MOFA official, Seoul, 26 August 2021; interview with ROK government advisor, Seoul, 11 August 2021.

46. See, for example, Carmen M. Reinhart and Kenneth S. Rogoff, *This Time Is Different: Eight Centuries of Financial Folly* (Princeton, NJ: Princeton University Press, 2011).

47. World Bank, "GDP Growth (Annual %)—Korea, Rep," 2022, https://data.worldbank.org/indicator/NY.GDP.MKTP.KD.ZG?locations=KR.

48. International Monetary Fund, "Republic of Korea—IMF Stand-By Arrangement—Summary of the Economic Program," 5 December 1997.

49. South Korean interviewees asked about this point agreed that this is a driving force behind South Korean grand strategy ever since the AFC.

50. ASEAN Plus Three, "History," 2022, https://aseanplusthree.asean.org/about-apt/history/.

51. G20, "About the G20."

52. Bank of Korea, "Basel Committee on Banking Supervision (BCBS)," 2022, https://www.bok.or.kr/eng/main/contents.do?menuNo=400103.

53. Paul Kennedy, *The Rise and Fall of the Great Powers: Economic Change and Military Conflict from 1500 to 2000* (New York: Random House, 1987).

54. David C. Kang, "Hierarchy and Legitimacy in International Systems: The Tribute System in Early Modern East Asia," *Security Studies* 19, no. 4 (2010): 591–622.

55. John Sudworth, "How South Korean Ship Was Sunk," *BBC*, May 20, 2010; BBC "North Korean Artillery Hits South Korean Island," *BBC*, November 23, 2010.

56. This is a recurrent theme in all South Korean defense white papers after 2010, regardless of the government in power and the state of inter-Korean relations.

57. Oh Seok-min, "Russian Aircraft Violates S. Korea's Airspace Above East Sea Twice," *Yonhap News*, 23 July 2019.

58. Yonhap, "S. Korea To Resume Seizure of Illegal Chinese Fishing Boats," *Yonhap News*, 23 October 2020.

59. Russia renounced the 1961 Soviet Union-North Korea treaty in 1995, allowing it to expire in 1996. https://www.tandfonline.com/doi/abs/10.1080/014959301753428018. Moscow and Pyongyang signed a Treaty of Friendship, Good Neighborliness, and Cooperation, but this agreement does not commit Russia to protect North Korea in case of war. https://www.tandfonline.com/doi/abs/10.1080/014959301753428018 (original text).

60. See, for example, the white papers issued by the ROK MND between 1988 and 2022.

61. Ministry of National Defense of the Republic of Korea, *2018 Defense White Paper* (Seoul: Ministry of National Defense of the Republic of Korea, 2018), 15, 22.

62. Interview with ROK MOFA official, phone, 29 September 2020; interview with ROK MOU official, Seoul, 9 August 2021; interview with ROK government advisor, Seoul, 11 August 2021.

63. Interview with ROK MOFA official, phone, 20 July 2020; interview with ROK MOFA official, phone, 29 September 2020; interview with ROK government advisor, Seoul, 11 August 2021.

64. Interview with ROK government advisor, phone, 18 August 2020; ROK MOFA official, phone, 29 September 2020; interview with ROK MOU official, Seoul, 9 August 2021.

65. Elizabeth Thurbon, *Developmental Mindset: The Revival of Financial Activism in South Korea* (Ithaca, NY: Cornell University Press, 2016).

66. See, for example, the white papers issued by MOEF and MOTIE from the 1990s onwards.

67. Interview with ROK MOFA official, phone, 20 July 2020; interview with ROK Army official 2, phone, 5 August 2020; interview with ROK MOFA official, Seoul, 11 August 2021.

68. Interview with ROK government advisor, phone, 8 January 2021; interview with ROK MOFA official, Seoul, 11 August 2021; interview with ROK MOFA official, Seoul, 15 August 2021.

69. Interview with ROK MOFA official, phone, 20 July 2020; interview with ROK MOFA official, online, 16 September 2020; interview with ROK government advisor, 8 January 2021.

70. Interview with ROK government advisor, phone, 18 August 2020; interview with ROK MOFA official, Seoul, 16 August 2021; interview with ROK MOFA official, Seoul, 24 August 2021.

71. SIPRI, "Military Expenditure by Country as Percentage of Gross Domestic Product 1949–2020," 2021, https://sipri.org/sites/default/files/SIPRI-Milex-data-1949-2020_0.xlsx.

72. Military Factory, "2022 Military Strength Ranking."

73. SIPRI, "Military Expenditure by Country, in Constant (2019) US$m. 1949–2020," 2021, https://sipri.org/sites/default/files/SIPRI-Milex-data-1949-2020_0.xlsx.

74. SIPRI, "Military Expenditure by Country as Percentage of Gross Domestic Product."

75. International Institute for Strategic Studies, *The Military Balance 2022*, ch. 6.

76. Kim, "US Lifts Restrictions on South Korea."

77. South Korea did not have a proper cybersecurity strategy until April 2019, when the National Security Office launched the National Cybersecurity Strategy. The strategy is available here: https://www.itu.int/en/ITU-D/Cybersecurity/Documents/National_Strategies_Repository/National%20Cybersecurity%20Strategy_South%20Korea.pdf

78. SIPRI, "SIPRI Arms Transfers Database," 2022, https://www.sipri.org/databases/armstransfers.

79. Pieter D. Wezeman, Alexandra Kuimova and Siemon T. Wezeman, "Trends in International Arms Transfers, 2021," *SIPRI Fact Sheet* (2022): 2.

80. SIPRI, "SIPRI Arms Transfers Database."

81. Lowy Institute, "Global Diplomacy Index: 2019 Country Ranking," 2022, available at https://globaldiplomacyindex.lowyinstitute.org/country_rank.html.

82. Ministry of Foreign Affairs of the Republic of Korea, *2022년도 외교부 예산 개요* (Outline of the 2022 Ministry of Foreign Affairs Budget) (Seoul: Ministry of Foreign Affairs of the Republic of Korea, 2022), 42, 44.

83. United Nations, "Former Secretaries-General," 2022, https://www.un.org/sg/en/content/former-secretaries-general.

84. Ramon Pacheco Pardo, Tongfi Kim, Linde Desmaele, Maximilian Ernst, Paula Cantero Dieguez, and Riccardo Villa, *Moon Jae-in's Policy Towards Multilateral Institutions: Continuity and Change in South Korea's Global Strategy* (Brussels: KF-VUB Korea Chair, 2019).

85. Eun Mee Kim and Nancy Y. Kim, "The South Korean Development Model," in JeongHun Han, Ramon Pacheco Pardo, and Youngho Cho, eds., *The Oxford Handbook of South Korean Politics* (Oxford: Oxford University Press, 2023), ch. 35.

86. Sohyun Zoe Lee, "Foreign Economic Policy," in Han, Pacheco Pardo, and Cho, *Oxford Handbook of South Korean Politics*, ch. 34.

87. Institute for International Trade, *"한국 FTA 추진 10년의 발자취"* (Ten Years of Korea FTA Promotion), *Trade Focus* 13, no. 18 (2014): 1–7.

88. Lee, "Foreign Economic Policy."

89. Kim and Kim, "The South Korean Development Model."

90. KOICA, *Annual Report 1993* (Seoul: KOICA, 1993), 10.

91. OECD, "Total Net ODA Disbursements from All Donors to Developing Countries," 2022, https://www.oecd.org/dac/financing-sustainable
-development/development-finance-data/idsonline.htm

92. OECD, "Development Co-operation Profiles—Korea," 2022, https://
www.oecd-ilibrary.org/sites/d919ff1a-en/index.html?itemId=/content
/component/d919ff1a-en.

93. OECD, *China's Belt and Road Initiative in the Global Trade, Investment and Finance
Landscape* (Paris: OECD, 2018), 3–4; OECD, "Development Co-operation
Profiles—Japan," 2022, https://www.oecd-ilibrary.org/sites/b8cf3944-en
/index.html?itemId=/content/component/d919ff1a-en&_csp_=5da8b1c38c60
2446d658c9ebe2b44c25&itemIGO=oecd&itemContentType=chapter.

94. Carnes Lord, "The Past and Future of Public Diplomacy," *Orbis* 42, no.1
(1998): 51–54.

95. The Academy of Korean Studies, 'Timeline,' 2021, http://intl.aks.ac.kr/english
/usr/wap/detail.do?app=21&seq=10328&lang=eng.

96. Yonhap News Agency, "History," 2022, https://en.yna.co.kr/aboutus/history.

97. Korea Foundation, "Who We Are," 2022 https://www.kf.or.kr/kfEng/cm
/cntnts/cntntsView2.do?mi=2126.

98. Arirang, "About Arirang," 13 November 2018, https://www.arirang.com
/prroom/About_ArirangN1.asp.

99. Ministry of Foreign Affairs of the Republic of Korea, "Introduction of Public
Diplomacy," 2013, https://www.mofa.go.kr/eng/wpge/m_22841/contents.do.

100. Terry Flew, *Understanding Global Media*, 2nd ed. (London: Palgrave Macmillan, 2018), 110–16; Times Higher Education, "World University Rankings
2022," 2022, https://www.timeshighereducation.com/world-university
-rankings/2022/world-ranking#!/page/0/length/25/sort_by/rank/sort
_order/asc/cols/stats.

101. Joseph Nye, "Soft Power: The Origins and Political Progress of a Concept,"
Palgrave Communications 3 (2017): 2.

102. Ramon Pacheco Pardo, *Shrimp to Whale: South Korea from the Forgotten War to
K-Pop* (London: Hurst, 2022), 162–63.

103. Framework on the Promotion of Cultural Industries, 8 February 1999.

104. Ministry of Culture, Sports and Tourism, "History," 2022, http://www.mcst
.go.kr/english/about/history.jsp.

105. King Sejong Institute, "Communicating with the World Through the King
Sejong Institute," 2022, https://www.ksif.or.kr/ste/ksf/hkd/lochkd.do
?menuNo=31101100.

106. KOCIS, "History," 2022, https://www.kocis.go.kr/eng/openHistory.do.

107. Interview with ROK MND official, Seoul, 13 August 2021; interview with
ROK MOFA official, Seoul, 24 August 2021; interview with ROK MOFA
official, Seoul, 26 August 2021.

108. Interview with ROK Army official 1, phone, 5 August 2020; interview with ROK government advisor, phone, 28 August 2020; interview with ROK MOFA official, Seoul, 4 August 2021.

109. Interview with ROK Army official 1, phone, 5 August 2020; with ROK MOFA official, Seoul, 24 July 2021; interview with ROK government advisor, Seoul, 11 August 2021.

110. Interview with ROK MOU official, Seoul, 9 August 2021; interview with ROK MOFA official, 15 August 2021; interview with ROK MOFA official, 24 August 2021.

111. World Bank, World Integrated Trade Solution Database, 2022, https://wits.worldbank.org/Default.aspx?lang=en.

112. IMF, Direction of Trade Statistics, 25 March 2022, https://data.imf.org/?sk=9d6028d4-f14a-464c-a2f2-59b2cd424b85.

113. ADB, *Asian Economic Integration Report 2021: Making Digital Platforms Work for Asia and the Pacific* (Manila: ADB, 2021), 17.

114. Interview with ROK MOFA official, online, 17 November 2020; interview with ROK MOFA official, Seou, 30 July 2021; interview with ROK government advisor, Seoul, 11 August 2021.

115. Kaewkamol Pitakdumrongkit, *Negotiating Financial Agreement in East Asia: Surviving the Turbulence* (London: Routledge, 2015), ch. 5.

116. See both the ROK MND's Defense white papers and the ROK MOFA's Diplomatic white papers from 1988 and 1990 onward, respectively.

117. Interview with Japan MOFA official, online, 16 September 2008; interview with Japan MOFA official, London, 10 January 2014.

118. Interview with ROK MOFA official, Seoul, 6 August 2021; interview with ROK MOU official, Seoul, 9 August 2021; interview with ROK government advisor, Seoul, 12 August 2021.

119. Ministry of Foreign Affairs of the Republic of Korea, "외교관계수립현황" (Status of Establishment of Diplomatic Relations), December 2021, https://www.mofa.go.kr/www/wpge/m_4181/contents.do.

120. U.S. Energy Information Administration, "South Korea," 6 November 2020, https://www.eia.gov/international/analysis/country/KOR.

121. Presidential Committee on New Southern Policy, *New Southern Policy Plus* (Seoul: Government of the Republic of Korea, 2021), 8.

122. Interview with Russia government advisor, Washington, DC, 25 March 2008; interview with U.S. Department of State official, Washington, DC, 25 March 2008; interview with ROK MOFA official, phone, 29 September 2020.

123. Presidential Committee on Northern Economic Cooperation, *9-BRIDGE Strategy*, 2017, https://www.bukbang.go.kr/bukbang_en/vision_policy/9-bridge/.

124. Australian Government Department of Foreign Affairs and Trade, *2017 Foreign Policy White Paper* (Canberra: Australian Government Department of Foreign Affairs and Trade, 2017), ch. 3.

125. Ministry of Foreign Affairs of the Republic of Korea, "재외동포 정의 및 현황" (Total Number of Overseas Koreans), 2022, https://www.mofa.go.kr/www/wpge/m_21509/contents.do.

126. Interview with EU official, Seoul, 5 August 2021; interview with ROK MOFA official, Seoul, 21 August 2021; interview with ROK MOFA official, Seoul, 24 August 2021.

127. ADB, "Republic of Korea-Chile Free Trade Agreement," 2015, https://aric.adb.org/fta/korea-chile-free-trade-agreement.

128. Carolina Urrego-Sandoval and Ramon Pacheco Pardo, eds., *Exploring Trade Cooperation Between the Pacific Alliance and South Korea* (Bogota: Universidad de los Andes, 2021).

129. Interview with ROK Ministry of Economy and Finance official, phone, 14 June 2017; interview with ROK government advisor, phone, 18 August 2020; interview with ROK MOFA official, Seoul, 15 August 2021.

130. Interview with ROK MOFA official, phone, 20 July 2020; interview with ROK government advisor, phone, 18 August 2020; interview with ROK MOFA official, Seoul, 16 August 2021.

131. Urrego-Sandoval and Pacheco Pardo, *Exploring Trade Cooperation*.

4. Triangular Core

1. Roh Tae-woo, "남북이 함께 번영하는 민족공동체: 민족자존과 통일번영을 위한 특별 선언" (A National Community Where the Two Koreas Prosper Together: Special Declaration for National Self-Esteem, Unification, and Prosperity), 7 July 1988.

2. Interview with ROK Ministry of Foreign Affairs (MOFA) official, phone, 29 September 2020; interview with ROK MOFA official, Seoul, 28 July 2021.

3. Roh, "남북이 함께 번영하는 민족공동체."

4. Ministry of Unification of the Republic of Korea, 남북대화 50년 (50 Years of Inter-Korean Dialogue) (Seoul: Ministry of Unification of the Republic of Korea, 2021), 44–45.

5. Roh, "남북이 함께 번영하는 민족공동체."

6. United Nations, "Member States," 2022, https://www.un.org/en/about-us/member-states.

7. Agreement on Reconciliation, Non-aggression and Exchanges and Cooperation Between the South and the North, 13 December 1991.

8. Hans M. Kristensen and Robert S. Norris, "A History of US Nuclear Weapons in South Korea," *Bulletin of the Atomic Scientists* 73, no. 6 (2017): 349–50.

9. Joint Declaration on the Denuclearization of the Korean Peninsula, 20 January 1992.

10. International Atomic Energy Agency, Agreement of 30 January 1992 between the Government of the Democratic People's Republic of Korea and the International Atomic Energy Agency for the Application of Safeguards in Connection with the Treaty on the Non-Proliferation of Nuclear Weapons, 30 January 1992.

11. IAEA, "Fact Sheet on DPRK Nuclear Safeguards," 2022, https://www.iaea .org/newscenter/focus/dprk/fact-sheet-on-dprk-nuclear-safeguards.

12. CSIS, "Missiles of South Korea," 10 August 2021, https://missilethreat.csis .org/country/south-korea/.

13. Korea Aerospace Research Institute, "History," 2022, https://www.kari.re .kr/eng/sub01_04.do.

14. Alexander A. Sergounin and Sergey V. Subbotin, *Russian Arms Transfers to East Asia in the 1990s* (Oxford: Oxford University Press, 1999), 112.

15. Ministry of National Defense of the Republic of Korea, *1988 국방백서1988* (1988 Defense White Paper) (Seoul: Ministry of National Defense of the Republic of Korea, 1988), ch. 2.

16. Roh Tae-woo, "새로운 세계질서(世界秩序)와 한(韓)·미(美) 동반관계" (A New World Order and Korea–U.S. Partnership), 23 September 1992.

17. Kristensen and Norris, "History of Nuclear Weapons in South Korea."

18. Introduced in August 1988, the 818 Plan to modernize the ROK military was laid out in more detail in Ministry of National Defense of the Republic of Korea, *1989 국방백서* (1989 Defense White Paper) (Seoul: Ministry of National Defense of the Republic of Korea, 1989).

19. Andrea Matles Savada and William Shaw, eds., *South Korea: A Country Study* (Washington, DC: Federal Research Division, Library of Congress, 1992), 295–96.

20. Savada and Shaw, *South Korea*, 295–96.

21. Ministry of National Defense of the Republic of Korea, *1992–1993국방백서* (1992–1993 Defense White Paper) (Seoul: Ministry of National Defense of the Republic of Korea, 1993), 191–4.

22. Ministry of National Defense of the Republic of Korea, *1988 국방백서*.

23. Kang Young-jin, "사우디가 공습의 6% 수행/다국적군 참가국 역할분담(걸프전)" (Saudi Arabia Conducted 6% of Strikes/Role Sharing among the Participating Countries in the Multinational Forces [Gulf War]), *JoongAng Ilbo*, 6 February 1991.

24. "S. Korea To Join U.S.-Led Maritime Drills Next Month: Officials," *Yonhap News*, 17 May 2022.

25. See the GATT documents available via the World Trade Organization, https://www.wto.org/english/docs_e/gattdocs_e.htm.

26. Roh, "남북이 함께 번영하는 민족공동체."

27. Interview with ROK MOFA official, phone, September 29, 2020.

28. KBS, "중국, 서울올림픽 참가 공식통보" (China Officially Announces Its Participation in the Seoul Olympics), *KBS News*, 14 January 1988.

29. KBS, "개막식" (Opening Ceremony), *KBS News*, 22 September 1990.

30. Interview with ROK MOFA official, phone, 29 September 2020.

31. ADB, "Integration Indicators," 2022, https://aric.adb.org/database/integration.

32. ADB, "Integration Indicators."

33. ADB, "Integration Indicators."

34. China's Statistic Yearbook, published by the National Bureau of Statistics of China, started recording data on South Korean FDI into China from 1992.

35. "대상: '중국은행서울사무소'" (Target: People's Bank of China Seoul Office), *Hankyung News*, 2 April 2006.

36. Interview with ROK MOFA official, phone, 29 September 2020.

37. Qian Qichen, *Ten Episodes in China's Diplomacy* (New York: HarperCollins, 2005), 114–16.

38. Qichen, *Ten Episodes*, ch. 5.

39. 한중수교 공동성명 (Joint Statement on the Establishment of Republic of Korea–China Diplomatic Relations), 24 August 1992.

40. KBS, "중국 방문 노태우 대통령 북경공항 환영식" (President Roh Tae-woo's Visit to China Welcome Ceremony at Beijing Airport," *KBS News*, 27 September 1992.

41. Kim Young-sam, "제49주년 광복절 경축사 (위대한 한민족의 시대를위한 매진)" (49th Liberation Day Congratulatory Speech: Striving for a Great Korean Era), 15 August 1994.

42. Interview with ROK MOU official, Seoul, 26 August 2008; with ROK MOFA official, Seoul, 19 September 2008.

43. Interview with ROK MOU official, Seoul, 26 August 2008; with ROK MOFA official, Seoul, 19 September 2008.

44. Kim, "제49주년 광복절 경축사."

45. IAEA, "Fact Sheet on DPRK Nuclear Safeguards."

46. IAEA, "Fact Sheet on DPRK Nuclear Safeguards."

47. Interview with ROK MOFA official, Seoul, 18 September 2008.

48. Marion Creekmore, *A Moment of Crisis: Jimmy Carter, the Power of a Peacemaker, and North Korea* (New York, NY: PublicAffairs, 2006).

49. Interview with ROK MOFA official, Seoul, 18 September 2008.

50. Agreed Framework between the United States of America and the Democratic People's Republic of Korea, 21 October 1994.

51. KEDO, "About Us: Our History," 1999–2022, http://www.kedo.org/au _history.asp.

52. Department of State of the United States of America, "Readout on August 1997 Four-Party Talks re. Korean Peninsula," 8 August 1997.

53. Ministry of Unification of the Republic of Korea, 통일백서 *1994* (White Paper on Korean Unification 1994) (Seoul: Ministry of Unification of the Republic of Korea, 1994), 24, 26.

54. James Kim, "N. Korea's Kim Il-sung, 82, Dies," *UPI*, 9 July 1994.

55. Minn Chung, "Seoul Will Become a Sea of Fire . . .," *Bulletin of Concerned Asian Scholars* 26, no. 1–2 (1994): 132.

56. Bae, "北의지따라 반복된 연락채널 차단·복원 . . . 국면전환 '신호탄.'"

57. Kim, "US Lifts Restrictions on South Korea."

58. Oh Dongryong, "金泳三 대통령, 1994년 한국형 핵추진 잠수함 제작 지시" (President Kim Young-sam Gave Orders to Build a Korean Nuclear-Powered Submarine in 1994), *Monthly Chosun*, July 2009.

59. Kim Jihoon, "러시아에 빌려준 돈, 탱크로 대신 받았다 . . .'불곰 사업'이란" (Money Lent to Russia, Received in Exchange for Tanks . . . What Is the 'Brown Bear Project'), *Moneytoday*, 17 November 2021.

60. Joint Ministries, 제3차 우주개발 진흥 기본계획—*2021*년도 우주개발 진흥 시행 계획 (The Third Space Development Promotion Basic Plan [2018–2040]—2021 Space Development Promotion Implementation Plan) (Sejong City: Ministry of Science and ICT, 2021).

61. Korea Aerospace Research Institute, "History."

62. Kim Young-sam, "한·미 정상 공동기자회견 서두말씀(미래지향적 동맹관계로 향한 발걸음)" (Introductory Remarks at the Joint Press Conference between the ROK and the United States [Toward a Future-Oriented Alliance]), 27 July 1995.

63. Interview with ROK MOFA official, Seoul, 18 September 2008; interview with U.S. Department of State official, phone, 20 July 2020.

64. Kim Young-sam, "한·미 정상 공동기자회견 서두말씀(미래지향적 동맹관계로 향한 발걸음)."

65. Interview with ROK MOFA official, Seoul, 18 September 2008; interview with U.S. Department of State official, phone, 20 July 2020.

66. Interview with ROK MOFA official, Seoul, 18 September 2008.

67. Kristensen and Norris, "A History of Nuclear Weapons in South Korea," 353–54.

68. Interview with ROK MOFA official, Seoul, 18 September 2008.

69. See ROK MND Defense white papers from 1988 to 2020.

70. SIPRI, "SIPRI Arms Transfers Database," 2022, https://www.sipri.org /databases/armstransfers.

71. Interview with ROK MOU official, Seoul, 26 August 2008.

72. See the GATT documents available via the World Trade Organization, https://www.wto.org/english/docs_e/gattdocs_e.htm.

73. UNFCC, *Parties—Republic of Korea*, 7 August 2018, https://unfccc.int/node/61147.

74. 2021 Seoul UN Peacekeeping Ministerial Preparatory Secretariat, "ROK Contribution to UN Peacekeeping," 2021, https://www.unpko2021.kr/EN/PKO/korea.

75. KOCIS, "History," 2022, https://www.kocis.go.kr/eng/openHistory.do.

76. ADB, "Integration Indicators."

77. National Bureau of Statistics of China, "Statistical Database," 2012, http://www.stats.gov.cn/english/Statisticaldata/AnnualData/ (see annual "Actually Used Foreign Direct and Other Investment by Country or Territory" data).

78. KBS, "김영삼 대통령, 일본.중국 순방 6박7일" (President Kim Young-sam Tours Japan and China for 7 Days and 6 Nights," *KBS News*, 30 March 1994.

79. Teresa Watanabe, "China's President Begins Milestone Visit to South Korea," *Los Angeles Times*, 14 November 1995.

80. KOCIS, "History."

81. Interview with ROK MOU official, Seoul, 26 August 2008.

82. James Risen, "U.S. Warns China on Taiwan, Sends Warship to Area," *Los Angeles Times*, 11 March 1996.

83. Interview with ROK MOFA official, Seoul, 18 September 2008.

84. Interview with ROK MOFA official, Seoul, 18 September 2008.

85. Interview with ROK MOFA official, Seoul, 18 September 2008.

86. Kim Dae-jung, "제15 대 대통령 취임사" (15th President's Inaugural Address), 25 February 1998.

87. Kim Dae-jung, "2001년도 예산안 제출에 즈음한 국회 시정연설(평화와 번영의 한반도 시대를 열기 위하여)" (Speech to the National Assembly on the Occasion of the Submission of the Budget for 2001 to Open an Era of Peace and Prosperity on the Korean Peninsula), 8 November 2000.

88. Kim Dae-jung, *Kim Dae-jung' s "Three-Stage" Approach to Korean Unification. Focusing on the South-North Confederal Stage* (Los Angeles: Center for Multiethnic and Transnational Studies, University of Southern California, 1997), 1–36.

89. Kim Dae-jung, "Korean Reunification: A Rejoinder," *Security Dialogue* 24, no. 4 (1993): 410–11.

90. South-North Joint Declaration, Pyongyang, 15 June 2000.

91. Ministry of Unification of the Republic of Korea, 남북대화 50년, 69.

92. Statistics Korea, "남북 이산가족 상봉 추이" (South–North Korean Family Reunions), 2022, http://www.index.go.kr/potal/main/EachDtlPageDetail.do?idx_cd=1696.

93. Ministry of Unification of the Republic of Korea, "Inter-Korean Dialogue," 2022, https://www.unikorea.go.kr/eng_unikorea/relations/statistics/dialogue/.

94. Interview with Cheong Wa Dae official, Seoul, 30 July 2020; interview with ROK MOU official, Seoul, 26 August 2008.

95. Sheryl WuDunn, "North Korea Fires Missile Over Japanese Territory," *New York Times*, 1 September 1998.

96. Nicholas Macfie, "Factbox: The Battles of the Korean West Sea," *Reuters*, 29 November 2010.

97. Macfie, "Factbox."

98. Kim, "US Lifts Restrictions on South Korea."

99. Kim Dae-jung, "한·미 정상회담 공동기자회견 서두말씀(21세기를 향한 한차원 높은 동반자 관계)" (Preface to the Joint Press Conference of the Korea-U.S. Summit [A Higher-Lever Partnership for the 21st Century]), 9 June 1998.

100. Interview with Cheong Wa Dae official, Seoul, 1 August 2008.

101. Interview with Cheong Wa Dae official, Seoul, 1 August 2008.

102. Kim Dae-Jung, *Conscience in Action: The Autobiography of Kim Dae-jung*, trans. Jeon Seung-hee (London: Palgrave Macmillan, 2019), 501.

103. White House, *A New National Security Strategy for a New Century* (Washington, DC: White House, 1998), 42.

104. Interview with U.S. Department of State official, Washington, DC, 9 April 2008.

105. IAEA, "Fact Sheet on DPRK Nuclear Safeguards."

106. George W. Bush, "State of the Union Address," 29 January 2002.

107. Kim, *Conscience in Action*, 733–37, 772–76.

108. Interview with U.S. White House official, Washington, DC, 9 April 2008; interview with Cheong Wa Dae official, Seoul, 30 July 2008.

109. See Korea Foundation, "Annual Reports," 2022, https://www.kf.or.kr/kfEng/cm/cntnts/cntntsView.do?mi=2129&cntntsId=1630.

110. Interview with ROK MOFA official, London, 30 October 2008.

111. See WTO, "Disputes by Member," 2022, https://www.wto.org/english/tratop_e/dispu_e/dispu_by_country_e.htm.

112. Kim Dae-jung, "중국 베이징 대학교 연설(동북아지역의 평화와 안정을 위한 한·중 협력)" (Speech at Peking University, China [Korea-China Cooperation for Peace and Stability in Northeast Asia]), 12 November 1998.

113. Kim, 중국 베이징 대학교 연설(동북아지역의 평화와 안정을 위한 한·중 협력).

114. Kim, 중국 베이징 대학교 연설(동북아지역의 평화와 안정을 위한 한·중 협력).

115. Interview with Cheong Wa Dae official, Seoul, 30 July 2008.

116. ADB, "Integration Indicators."

117. World Bank, World Integrated Trade Solution Database, 2022, https://wits.worldbank.org/Default.aspx?lang=en.

118. National Bureau of Statistics of China, "Statistical Database."

119. Interview with Cheong Wa Dae official, Seoul, 30 July 2008.

120. Interview with Cheong Wa Dae official, Seoul, 30 July 2008.

121. Ramon Pacheco Pardo, *Shrimp to Whale: South Korea from the Forgotten War to K-Pop* (London: Hurst, 2022), 162–63.

122. Interview with ROK MOFA official, London, 30 October 2008.

123. KBS, "2014 KBS한중가요제 26일 개최. . . 엑소·블락비 등 참가" (14th KBS Korea-China Music Festival Held on the 26th . . . Participation of EXO, Block B, etc), *KBS News*, 20 November 2014.

124. Pacheco Pardo, *Shimp to Whale*, 160.

125. "Chronology of Key Events Since Establishment of S. Korea-China Diplomatic Ties," *Yonhap News*, 18 August 2017.

126. Ministry of National Defense of the Republic of Korea, *2004 Defense White Paper* (Seoul: Ministry of National Defense of the Republic of Korea, 2004).

127. Interview with ROK MOFA official, Seoul, 4 August 2008; interview with ROK Army official 1, phone, 5 August 2020.

128. Ministry of National Defense of the Republic of Korea, *2006 Defense White Paper* (Seoul: Ministry of National Defense of the Republic of Korea, 2006).

129. Interview with ROK MOU official, Seoul, 11 September 2008.

130. IAEA, "Fact Sheet on DPRK Nuclear Safeguards"; Roh Moo-hyun, "제16대 대통령 취임사" (16th President's Inaugural Address), 25 February 2003.

131. Korea Herald, "Koreas Celebrate First Joint Venture Production," *Korea Herald*, 16 December 2014.

132. Ministry of Unification of the Republic of Korea, "Humanitarian Cooperation," 2022, https://www.unikorea.go.kr/eng_unikorea/relations/statistics/humanitarian/.

133. Ministry of Unification of the Republic of Korea, "Inter-Korean Exchanges & Cooperation," 2022, https://www.unikorea.go.kr/eng_unikorea/relations/statistics/exchanges/.

134. Bae, "北의지따라 반복된 연락채널 차단·복원 . . . 국면전환 '신호탄.'"

135. Presidential Committee on Northeast Asian Cooperation, *Toward a Peaceful and Prosperous Northeast Asia* (Seoul: Government of the Republic of Korea, 2004).

136. Joint Statement of the Fourth Round of the Six-Party Talks, Beijing, 19 September 2005.

137. Initial Actions to Implement Six-Party Talks Joint Statement, Beijing, 13 February 2007.

138. The Opening of the 2nd Working Group Meeting on Northeast Asia Peace and Security Mechanism, Moscow, 20 August 2007.

139. UN Security Council, *Security Council Committee Established Pursuant to Resolution 1718 (2006)*, 2022, https://www.un.org/securitycouncil/sanctions/1718.

140. Declaration on the Advancement of South-North Korean Relations, Peace and Prosperity, Pyongyang, 4 October 2007.

141. Oh, "金泳三 대통령, 1994년 한국형 핵추진 잠수함 제작 지시." (President Kim Young-sam Gave Orders to Build a Korean Nuclear-Powered Submarine in 1994)

142. Ministry of National Defense of the Republic of Korea, 국방개혁 2020—이렇게 추진합니다 (Defense Reform Plan 2020—We Wil Proceed as Follows) (Seoul: Ministry of National Defense of the Republic of Korea, 2005).

143. Ministry of National Defense of the Republic of Korea, *2006 Defense White Paper*, 40.

144. Interview with ROK MOFA official, Seoul, 4 August 2008.

145. Ministry of National Defense of the Republic of Korea, 국방개혁 *2020*, 4.

146. Roh Moo-hyun, "한 . 미 동맹의 미래지향적 조정" (Forward-looking Coordination of the Korea–U.S. Alliance), February 2009.

147. Interview with ROK MOFA official, Seoul, 4 August 2008.

148. Mark Bromley, Paul Holton, Pieter D. Wezeman, and Siemon T. Wezeman, "SIPRI Arms Transfers Data, 2008," *SIPRI Fact Sheet* (2009): 2.

149. Reuters Staff, "South Korea Launches $1 bln Advanced Destroyer," *Reuters*, 25 May 2007.

150. Voice of America, "S. Korea, US Fail to Reach Agreement on Troop Withdrawal," *Voice of America*, 20 August 2004.

151. Department of State of the United States of America, "U.S., South Korea to Transfer Wartime Force Command in 2012," 23 February 2007.

152. Interview with U.S. White House official, Washington, DC, 3 April 2008; interview with ROK MOFA official, London, 30 October 2008.

153. Interview with ROK MOU official, 11 September 2008.

154. Interview with ROK MOFA official, 4 August 2008.

155. Interview with ROK MOFA official, 4 August 2008.

156. 2021 Peacekeeping Secretariat, "ROK Contribution to UN Peacekeeping."

157. Roh Moo-hyun, "[미국 방문]귀국보고" ([Visit to the United States] Report on Return), 17 May 2003; Roh Moo-hyun, "2004년 신년기자회견 모두연설" (2004 New Year's Press Conference Full Transcript), 14 January 2004.

158. Reuters Staff, "All South Korea Troops to Leave Iraq by End of '08," *Reuters*, 19 September 2008.

159. ADB, "Republic of Korea-United States Free Trade Agreement," 2015, https://aric.adb.org/fta/korea-united-states-free-trade-agreement.

160. Interview with U.S. White House official, Washington, DC, 9 April 2008; interview with ROK MOFA official, online, 12 November 2020.

161. ADB, "Republic of Korea-United States Free Trade Agreement."

162. ADB, "Integration Indicators."

163. KNOC, "Operations—USA," 21 January 2022, https://www.knoc.co.kr /ENG/sub03/sub03_1_2_3.jsp.

164. WTO, "Disputes by Member."

165. Korea Foundation, "Who We Are," 2022 https://www.kf.or.kr/kfEng/cm /cntnts/cntntsView2.do?mi=2126; King Sejong Institute, "Communicating with the World Through the King Sejong Institute," 2022, https://www .ksif.or.kr/ste/ksf/hkd/lochkd.do?menuNo=31101100.

166. The Korea Times Music Festival, "About," 2022, http://ktmf.koreatimes.com /?page_id=36.

167. Roh Moo-hyun, "[중국 국빈방문]청화대학 초청 연설" ([China Visit] Speech at Tsinghua University), 9 July 2003.

168. World Bank, World Integrated Trade Solution Database.

169. ADB, "Integration Indicators."

170. ADB, "People's Republic of China-Republic of Korea Free Trade Agreement," 2015, https://aric.adb.org/fta/peoples-republic-of-china-korea-free -trade-agreement.

171. Interview with U.S. White House official, Washington, DC, 3 April 2008; interview with Japan MOFA official, London, 14 May 2009; interview with ROK MOFA official, London, 30 October 2008.

172. Interview with ROK MOFA official, London, 30 October 2008.

173. "Chronology of Key Events."

174. KOCIS, "History."

175. King Sejong Institute, "Communicating with the World."

176. KBS, "2014 KBS한중가요제 26일 개최. . . 엑소·블락비 등 참가" (14th KBS Korea-China Music Festival Held on the 26th . . . Participation of EXO, Block B, etc).

177. Korea Foundation, "Who We Are."

178. Ministry of Foreign Affairs of the Republic of Korea, "Goguryeo," 2013, https://www.mofa.go.kr/eng/wpge/m_5436/contents.do.

179. Ministry of National Defense of the Republic of Korea, 국방개혁 2020.

180. Interview with ROK MOFA official, online, 15 July 2020.

181. Kim Eun-jung, "Lee Aide Says Two Koreas Discussed Schedule, Venue of Possible Summit in 2009," Yonhap News, 29 June 2012.

182. Interviews with ROK MOU official, phone, 24 July 2020.

183. Ministry of National Defense of the Republic of Korea, 2008 Defense White Paper (Seoul: Ministry of National Defense of the Republic of Korea, 2008).

184. Ministry of Unification of the Republic of Korea, 남북대화 50년, 69.

185. Bae, "北의지따라 반복된 연락채널 차단·복원 . . . 국면전환 '신호탄.'"

186. "Chronology of N. Korea's Nuclear Tests Before Inter-Korean Summit Agreement on Nuke Program," Yonhap News, 27 April 2018.

187. CSIS, "Missiles of North Korea," 24 March 2022, https://missilethreat.csis.org/country/dprk/.

188. Ramon Pacheco Pardo, Tongfi Kim, Maximilian Ernst, Sung Kyoo Ahn, and Riccardo Villa, *Beyond Traditional Security: South Korea's Positioning Towards the Cyber, Energy, Maritime and Trade Security Domains* (Brussels: KF-VUB Korea Chair, 2020), 9.

189. Macfie, "Factbox: The Battles of the Korean West Sea."

190. Macfie, "Factbox."

191. Lee Myung-bak, "대국민 담화문" (Public Statement), 24 May 2010.

192. Bae, "北의지따라 반복된 연락채널 차단·복원 . . . 국면전환 '신호탄.'"

193. Macfie, "Factbox."

194. Mark MacDonald, "Crisis Status in South Korea After North Shells Island," *New York Times*, 23 November 2010.

195. Ministry of National Defense of the Republic of Korea, *2010 Defense White Paper* (Seoul: Ministry of National Defense of the Republic of Korea, 2010), 25–27.

196. Pacheco Pardo et al., *Beyond Traditional Security*, 10.

197. Interview with ROK MOFA official, phone, 20 July 2020.

198. Ministry of Unification of the Republic of Korea, "Humanitarian Aid."

199. Bae, "北의지따라 반복된 연락채널 차단·복원 . . . 국면전환 '신호탄.'"

200. Interview with ROK MOFA official, 20 July 2020.

201. Ministry of National Defense of the Republic of Korea, 국방개혁 *307*계획 (Defense Reform Plan 307) (Seoul: Ministry of National Defense of the Republic of Korea, 2011).

202. Ministry of National Defense of the Republic of Korea, *2014 Defense White Paper* (Seoul: Ministry of National Defense of the Republic of Korea), 60–61.

203. Ministry of National Defense, *2014 Defense White Paper*, 60–62.

204. Kim, "US Lifts Restrictions on South Korea."

205. Kim Min-seok and Ser Myo-ja, "South Korean Navy Dominating," *Korea JoongAng Daily*, 12 May 2008.

206. Digital News Team, "이명박 정부, '한국형 핵추진 잠수함' 건조 추진" (Lee Myung-bak Pushes Ahead to Build "Korean Nuclear-Powered Submarine"), *Kyunghyang Shinmun*, 23 September 2010.

207. Korea Aerospace Research Institute, "History."

208. Ministry of National Defense of the Republic of Korea, 국방개혁 *307*계획.

209. Lee Myung-bak, "제17 대 대통령 취임사" (17th President's Inaugural Address), 25 February 2008.

210. Joint Vision for the Alliance of the United States of America and the Republic of Korea, Washington, DC, 16 June 2009.

211. Joint Vision, 16 June 2009.

212. Ministry of National Defense of the Republic of Korea, *2010 Defense White Paper* (Seoul: Ministry of National Defense of the Republic of Korea, 2010), 79.

213. BBC, "Submarine Focus for US–South Korea Military Drill," *BBC*, 26 July 2010.

214. John D. Banusiewicz, "Clinton, Gates Reaffirm U.S. Commitment to South Korea," American Forces Press Service, 22 July 2010.

215. Trilateral Statement Japan, Republic of Korea, and the United States, Washington, DC, 6 December 2010.

216. Remarks by President Obama and President Lee Myung-bak of the Republic of Korea After Bilateral Meeting, 26 June 2010.

217. Interview with Cheong Wa Dae official, phone, 23 July 2020.

218. Lee Myung-bak, *The Uncharted Path: An Autobiography* (Naperville: Sourcebooks, 2011).

219. ADB, "Republic of Korea–United States Free Trade Agreement."

220. Bank of Korea, *2008 Annual Report* (Seoul: Bank of Korea, 2009), 25.

221. ADB, "Integration Indicators."

222. KNOC, "Operations—USA."

223. WTO, "Disputes by Member."

224. Pacheco Pardo, *Shrimp to Whale*, 174.

225. The G20 Seoul Summit Leaders' Declaration, Seoul, 12 November 2010.

226. Seoul Nuclear Security Summit Communiqué, Seoul, 27 March 2012.

227. Ministry of National Defense of the Republic of Korea, "소말리아 해역 청해부대('09. 3. ~ 현재)" (Cheonghae Unit in the Waters of Somalia (March 2009–Present)), 2022, https://www.mnd.go.kr/user/boardList.action?command=view&page=1&boardId=O_46599&boardSeq=O_50274&titleId=mnd_010700000000&id=mnd_010702000000.

228. Combined Maritime Forces, "CTF 151: Counter-Piracy," 2022, https://combinedmaritimeforces.com/ctf-151-counter-piracy/.

229. 2021 Peacekeeping Secretariat, "ROK Contribution to UN Peacekeeping."

230. Embassy of the Republic of Korea in Afghanistan, "Ambassador's Greetings," 2022, https://overseas.mofa.go.kr/af-en/wpge/m_2593/contents.do.

231. 2021 Peacekeeping Secretariat, "ROK Contribution to UN Peacekeeping."

232. KOCIS, "History."

233. Korea Foundation, "Who We Are."

234. KCON USA, "About Us," 2021, https://www.kconusa.com/about-us/.

235. James Minor, "K-Pop Night Out's 5-Year Anniversary at SXSW," 23 January 2017, https://www.sxsw.com/music/2017/k-pop-night-5-year-anniversary/.

236. Ministry of National Defense of the Republic of Korea, *2010 Defense White Paper*, 93.

237. ADB, "People's Republic of China-Republic of Korea Free Trade Agreement."

238. Interview with ROK MOFA official, online, 16 September 2020.

239. Interview with ROK MOFA official, 16 September 2020.

240. Bank of Korea, *2008 Annual Report*, 25.

241. ADB, "Integration Indicators."

242. Interview with ROK MOFA official, online, 16 September 2020.

243. "Chronology of Key Events."

244. Interview with ROK MOFA official, phone, 20 July 2020.

245. Joint Statement for Tripartite Partnership, Fukuoka, 13 December 2008.

246. Trilateral Cooperation Secretariat, "What Is TCS," 2022, https://www.tcs -asia.org/en/about/overview.php.

247. Sarah Kim, "Korea, China to Establish a New Defense Phone Line," *Korea JoongAng Daily*, 24 July 2014.

248. Interview with ROK MOFA official, online, 16 September 2020.

249. KBS, "2014 KBS한중가요제 26일 개최. . . 엑소·블락비 등 참가" (14th KBS Korea-China Music Festival Held on the 26th . . . Participation of EXO, Block B, etc).

250. Interview ROK MOFA official, Seoul, 26 August 2021; interview with U.S. Department of State official, phone, 22 July 2020.

251. "Wen Calls for Defusing Tensions over ROK Warship Sinking," *Xinhua*, May 30, 2010; Lee Myung-bak, "대국민 담화문."

252. Interview with China MFA official, London, 26 July 2011.

253. Interview with ROK MOFA official, phone, 4 September 2020.

254. Ministry of Unification of the Republic of Korea, *Trust-Building Process on the Korean Peninsula*, September 2013.

255. See ROK MND Defense white papers of 2014 and 2016.

256. BBC, "Koreas Restart Operations in Kaesong Industrial Zone," *BBC*, 16 September 2013.

257. Ministry of Unification of the Republic of Korea, "Humanitarian Cooperation."

258. Chang Jae-soon, "Park Willing to Meet N. Korean Leader Anytime," *Yonhap News*, 3 November 2013.

259. Ministry of Foreign Affairs of the Republic of Korea, *2016 Diplomatic White Paper* (Seoul: Ministry of Foreign Affairs of the Republic of Korea, 2016), 50–51.

260. Ministry of Foreign Affairs of the Republic of Korea, "Northeast Asia Peace and Cooperation Initiative: Moving beyond the Asian Paradox Towards Peace and Cooperation in Northeast Asia," 2013.

261. "Chronology of N. Korea's Nuclear Tests."

262. Pacheco Pardo et al., *Beyond Traditional Security*, 9.

263. CSIS, "Missiles of North Korea."

264. "Chronology of N. Korea's Nuclear Tests."

265. Pacheco Pardo et al., *Beyond Traditional Security*, 10.

266. Trilateral Information Sharing Arrangement Concerning the Nuclear and Missile Threats Posed by North Korea Among the Ministry of National Defense of the Republic of Korea, the Ministry of Defense of Japan and the Department of State of the United States of America, December 2014.

267. BBC, "South Korea Halts Joint Venture after North's Test," *BBC*, 10 February 2016.

268. Bae, "北의지따라 반복된 연락채널 차단·복원 . . . 국면전환 '신호탄.'"

269. North Korea Human Rights Act, 3 March 2016.

270. Ministry of National Defense of the Republic of Korea, *2016 Defense White Paper* (Seoul: Ministry of National Defense of the Republic of Korea, 2016), 52, 107.

271. Ministry of National Defense of the Republic of Korea, *2016 Defense White Paper*, 72–73.

272. Ministry of National Defense, *2016 Defense White Paper*, 71–72.

273. Agreement Between the Government of Japan and the Government of the Republic of Korea on the Protection of Classified Military Information, Seoul, 23 November 2016.

274. Interview with ROK MOFA official, Seoul, 16 August 2021.

275. Joint Declaration in Commemoration of the 60th Anniversary of the Alliance between the Republic of Korea and the United States of America, 7 May 2013.

276. Joint Statement Following the U.S.-Japan-ROK Trilateral Meeting in New York, 18 September 2016.

277. UN Security Council, *Security Council Committee Established Pursuant to Resolution 1718* (2006).

278. North Korean Human Rights Act of 2004, 18 October 2004.

279. The 46th ROK–U.S. Security Consultative Meeting Joint Communiqué, Washington, DC, 23 October 2014.

280. Ministry of National Defense, *2014 Defense White Paper*.

281. Embassy of the Republic of Korea in Afghanistan, "Ambassador's Greetings."

282. 2021 Peacekeeping Secretariat, "ROK Contribution to UN Peacekeeping."

283. ADB, "Integration Indicators."

284. ADB, "Integration Indicators."

285. Interview with ROK MOFA official, online, 16 September 2020.

286. WTO, "Disputes by Member."

287. Park Geun-hye, "칭화대학교 연설" (Tsinghua University Speech), 28 June 2013.

288. Ministry of Foreign Affairs of the People's Republic of China, "State Councilor Dai Bingguo Meets with ROK President-Elect's Special Envoy Kim Moon-sung," 22 January 2013, https://www.fmprc.gov.cn/mfa_eng/wjb _663304/zzjg_663340/yzs_663350/gjlb_663354/2767_663538/2769_663542 /201301/t20130125_522191.html.
289. "Chronology of Key Events."
290. Park Geun-hye, "한중 비즈니스포럼 연설" (Speech at the Korea-China Business Forum), 27 June 2013.
291. Yonhap, "Chronology of Key Events."
292. Interview with ROK MOFA official, Seoul, 16 August 2021.
293. Kim, "Korea, China To Establish a New Defense Phone Line."
294. Guo Yuandan, "China Notifies South Korea of Its Flight Information in KADIZ, Reflecting Friendly Relationship," *China Military Online*, 30 October 2019.
295. Kim Kwang-tae, "Park Attends Military Parade in China," *Yonhap News*, 3 September 2015.
296. Joint Declaration for Peace and Cooperation in Northeast Asia, Seoul, 1 November 2015.
297. ADB, "People's Republic of China-Republic of Korea Free Trade Agreement."
298. ADB, "Japan-Republic of Korea-People's Republic of China Free Trade Agreement," 2015, https://aric.adb.org/fta/peoples-republic-of-china-japan -korea-free-trade-agreement.
299. AIIB, "Members and Prospective Members of the Bank," 2022, https:// www.aiib.org/en/about-aiib/governance/members-of-bank/index.html.
300. ADB, "Integration Indicators."
301. KBS, "2014 KBS한중가요제 26일 개최. . . 엑소·블락비 등 참가" (14th KBS Korea-China Music Festival Held on the 26th . . . Participation of EXO, Block B, etc).
302. Choe Sang-Hun, "South Korea Announces Expansion of Its Air Defense Zone," *New York Times*, 8 December 2013.
303. Interview with China MFA official, London, 22 October 2014.
304. Pacheco Pardo et al., *Beyond Traditional Security*, 10.
305. Chang Jae-soon, "China FM: THAAD Could Jeopardize, Threaten China's Security Interests," *Yonhap News*, 26 February 2016.
306. Ethan Meick and Nargina Salidjanova, *China's Response to U.S.-South Korean Missile Defense System Deployment and Its Implications* (Washington, DC: U.S.-China Economic and Security Review Commission, 2017).
307. Guo, "China Notifies South Korea of Its Flight Information."
308. Pacheco Pardo et al., *Beyond Traditional Security*, 10.

309. 2018 Inter-Korean Summit Preparation Committee, *2018 Inter-Korean Summit*, 27 April 2018.
310. 2018 Inter-Korean Summit Preparation Committee, *2018 Inter-Korean Summit*.
311. Ministry of National Defense of the Republic of Korea, *2018 Defense White Paper* (Seoul: Ministry of National Defense of the Republic of Korea, 2018), 12.
312. "Chronology of N. Korea's Nuclear Tests"; CSIS, "Missiles of North Korea."
313. Pacheco Pardo et al., *Beyond Traditional Security*, 9.
314. Mira Rapp-Hooper, "Saving America's Alliances: The United States Still Needs the System That Put It on Top," *Foreign Affairs* 99:2 (2020): 127–40.
315. Ministry of National Defense, *2018 Defense White Paper*, 48–51.
316. Ministry of National Defense, *2018 Defense White Paper*, 366.
317. Kim, "US Lifts Restrictions on South Korea."
318. Pacheco Pardo et al., *Beyond Traditional Security*, 10–2.
319. Ministry of National Defense, *2018 Defense White Paper*, 42.
320. Moon Jae-in, "Speech at the Korber Foundation," 7 July 2017.
321. Ramon Pacheco Pardo, *North Korea–US Relations from Kim Jong Il to Kim Jong Un* (London: Routledge, 2019), 158–80.
322. Bae, "北의지따라 반복된 연락채널 차단·복원 . . . 국면전환 '신호탄.'"
323. Moon Jae-in, "Speech at the Korber Foundation."
324. Ministry of National Defense of the Republic of Korea, *2020 Defense White Paper*.
325. "S. Korea Renames 'Three Axis' Defense System Amid Peace Efforts," *Yonhap News*, 10 January 2019.
326. Ministry of Unification of the Republic of Korea, "Humanitarian Cooperation."
327. Ministry of Unification of the Republic of Korea, "Inter-Korean Dialogue."
328. Ministry of Foreign Affairs of the Republic of Korea, *Northeast Asia Peace and Cooperation Platform* (Seoul: Ministry of Foreign Affairs of the Republic of Korea, 2018).
329. Ministry of Foreign Affairs, *Northeast Asia Peace and Cooperation Platform*.
330. Ministry of Foreign Affairs, *Northeast Asia Peace and Cooperation Platform*.
331. Interview with ROK MND official, Seoul, 13 August 2021.
332. Kim Min-san, "문재인 "핵잠수함 우리에게도 필요한 시대... 미국과 원자력 협정 개정하겠다" (Moon Jae-in: "We Need Nuclear Submarines . . . Will Revise Our Nuclear Agreement with the United States"), *JoongAng Ilbo*, 27 April 2017.
333. Ankit Panda, "'Five Eyes' Countries Eye Expanded Cooperation Amid North Korea Challenges," *The Diplomat*, 28 January 2020.
334. Moon Jae-in, "Address by President Moon Jae-in on 73rd Armed Forces Day," 1 October 2021.

335. Moon Jae-in, "Address by President Moon Jae-in at 76th Session of United Nations General Assembly," 21 September 2021.

336. Bae, "北의지따라 반복된 연락채널 차단·복원 . . . 국면전환 '신호탄.' "

337. DAPA, "산학연 중심의 미래첨단기술 개발 추진" (Promotion of Future Advanced Technology Development Centered on Industry-University Research), 22 March 2021, https://www.dapa.go.kr/dapa/na/ntt/selectNttInfo .do?bbsId=326&nttSn=36392&menuId=678.

338. Moon Jae-in, "Remarks by President Moon Jae-in at Meeting with Ruling and Opposition Party Leaders to Discuss Recent ROK-U.S. Summit," 26 May 2021.

339. Moon Jae-in, "Remarks by President Moon Jae-in at Rollout Ceremony for KF-X Prototype," 9 April 2021; "S. Korea to Develop Indigenous Marine Corps Chopper by 2031," *Yonhap News*, 26 April 2021; Daehan Lee, "South Korea Conducts Submarine-launched Ballistic Missile Test," *Naval News*, 4 July 2021; "Navy Receives First 3,000-Ton-Class SLBM Submarine," *Yonhap News*, 13 August 2021; Choi Soo-hyang, "S. Korea Develops Supersonic Cruise Missile Amid Tensions with N. Korea," *Yonhap News*, 15 September 2021.

340. Korea Aerospace Research Institute, "History."

341. Song Sang-ho and Kang Yoon-seung, "Seoul, Washington React Sternly to Provocative North Korean ICBM Firing," *Yonhap News*, 24 March 2022.

342. Moon Jae-in, "Korea–US Business Summit," 28 June 2017.

343. Interview with Cheong Wa Dae official, Seoul, 26 April 2022.

344. Interview with Cheong Wa Dae official, 26 April 2022.

345. White House, "Remarks by Republic of Korea National Security Advisor Chung Eui-Yong," 8 March 2018.

346. U.S. Department of State, "U.S.-ROK Working Group," 20 November 2018.

347. Interview with ROK MOFA official, phone, 4 September 2020.

348. Interview with Cheong Wa Dae official, Seoul, 28 July 2021.

349. Song Sang-ho, "Allies' Push to Update War Plans Likely to Boost Deterrence against N.K. Threats," *Yonhap News*, 2 December 2021.

350. Yeo Jun-suk, "Will OPCON Transfer Take Place Earlier Than Expected?" *The Korea Herald*, 3 July 2017.

351. Michael Lee, "Assessment for OPCON Transfer to Be Held in the Summer," *Korea JoongAng Daily*, 14 December 2021.

352. Kim Seung-yeon, "391 Afghan Evacuees to Be Airlifted to S. Korea Thursday: Foreign Ministry," *Yonhap News*, 25 August 2021.

353. National Security Council of the United States of America, *U.S. Strategic Framework for the Indo-Pacific*, February 2018.

354. U.S.–ROK Leaders' Joint Statement.

355. U.S. Indo-Pacific Command, "U.S., Allied Forces Conduct Exercise Pacific Vanguard 2021 off Coast of Australia," 9 July 2021, https://www

.pacom.mil/Media/News/News-Article-View/Article/2689702/us-allied
-forces-conduct-exercise-pacific-vanguard-2021-off-coast-of-australia/.

356. Park Si-soo, "US, South Korea Agree to Enhance Security Cooperation in Outer Space," *SpaceNews*, 30 August 2021.

357. The draft letter is available in Bood Woodward, *Fear: Trump in the White House* (New York: Simon & Schuster, 2019).

358. ADB, "Republic of Korea-United States Free Trade Agreement."

359. WTO, "Disputes by Member."

360. Bank of Korea, *2020 Annual Report* (Seoul: Bank of Korea, 2021), 62.

361. ADB, "Integration Indicators."

362. White House, "Chair's Statements on Principles Supply Chain Resilience," 31 October 2021.

363. Samsung, "Samsung Electronics Announces New Advanced Semiconductor Fab Site in Taylor, Texas," 24 November 2021.

364. Ministry of Culture, Sports and Tourism, "History."

365. Hayden Bagot, "KOCCA Return to SWSW for 7th Annual Showcase," 28 January 2019, https://www.sxsw.com/music/2019/kocca-return-to-sxsw -for-7th-annual-showcase/.

366. Jane Perlez, Mark Landler and Choe Sang-Hun, "China Blinks on South Korea, Making Nice after a Year of Hostilities," *New York Times*, 1 November 2017.

367. Cheong Wa Dae, "Results of State Visit to China by the President," 17 December 2017, https://english1.president.go.kr/BriefingSpeeches/Briefings/155.

368. Joint Declaration of the Seventh Japan-China-ROK Trilateral Summit, Tokyo, 9 May 2018.

369. Interview with Cheong Wa Dae official, Seoul, 28 July 2021.

370. Interview with Cheong Wa Dae official, Seoul, 26 April 2022.

371. Interview with Cheong Wa Dae official, 26 April 2022.

372. Interview with ROK MOFA official, Seoul, 24 July 2021.

373. Cheong Wa Dae, "Results of State Visit to China by the President."

374. Ministry of Foreign Affairs of the People's Republic of China, "Xi Jinping Arrives in Pyongyang for a State Visit to the Democratic People's Republic of Korea (DPRK)," 20 June 2019, https://www.fmprc.gov.cn/mfa_eng/wjb _663304/zzjg_663340/yzs_663350/gjlb_663354/2701_663406/2703_663410 /201906/t20190624_511673.html.

375. China Daily, "DPRK Détente Will Not Last if US Insists in All Take, No Give," *China Daily*, 29 August 2018.

376. Guo, "China Notifies South Korea of Its Flight Information in KADIZ, Reflecting Friendly Relationship."

377. ADB, "People's Republic of China-Republic of Korea Free Trade Agreement."

378. RCEP, "RCEP Agreement Enters into Force," 1 January 2022, https://rcepsec.org/2022/01/14/rcep-agreement-enters-into-force/.

379. Kim Soo-yeon, "S. Korea Launches Process to Join CPTPP: Finance Minister," *Yonhap News*, 13 December 2021.

380. ADB, "Integration Indicators."

381. Interview with ROK *chaebol* manager, Seoul, 13 August 2022.

382. KOCIS, "History."

383. Lee Sang-hyeop, "2021년 한중가요제 성료 . . . 한중문화교류의 장을 열다" (2021 Korea-China Music Festival Held . . . Opening the Door for Cultural Exchanges between China and Korea), *WCE News*, 9 December 2021.

384. Yoon Suk-yeol, "Address by President Yoon Suk Yeol on Korea's 77th Liberation Day," 15 August 2022.

385. "Yoon Says Any Meetings with N.K. Leader Should Be for 'Tangible' Results," *Yonhap News*, 7 May 2022.

386. Interview with ROK Presidential Office official, Seoul, 5 August 2022.

387. Interview with ROK MOFA official, Seoul, 20 August 2022.

388. U.S. Department of State, "United States of America-Republic of Korea Extended Deterrence Strategy and Consultation Group (EDSCG)," 8 September 2022.

389. Ji Da-gyum, "US Aircraft Carrier, South Korea Navy Conduct Drills Off Peninsula to Deter N.Korea," *Korea Herald*, 26 September 2022.

390. Kim Soo-yeon and Chae Yun-hwan, "N. Korea's Missile Flies across NLL for 1st Time; S. Korea Sends Missiles Northward in Its Show of Force," *Yonhap News*, 2 November 2022.

391. "S. Korea Successfully Launches Homegrown Space Rocket in Second Attempt," *Yonhap News*, 21 June 2022.

392. Shin Ji-hye, "Yoon Says 'Preemptive Strike' Is 'to Protect Peace,'" *Korea Herald*, 3 February 2022.

393. Yi Wonju, "S. Korea Co-sponsors U.N. Draft Resolution on N.K. Human Rights: Ministry," *Yonhap News*, 1 November 2022.

394. United States-Republic of Korea Leaders' Joint Statement, 21 May 2022.

395. Ramon Pacheco Pardo, *South Korea: A Pivotal State Under Construction* (Brussels: KF-VUB Korea Chair, 2022).

396. "Yoon Says Will 'Positively Review Joining' Quad if Invited: Report," *Yonhap News*, 26 April 2022; White House, "Fact Sheet: In Asia, President Biden and Dozen Indo-Pacific Partners Launch the Indo-Pacific Economic Framework for Prosperity," 23 May 2022; Pacheco Pardo, *South Korea*.

397. Jung Da-min, "What's Behind Deployment of Largest-ever Navy Fleet to RIMPAC?" *Korea Times*, 8 July 2022.

398. SK, "SK Announces $22 Billion in New Investments in the U.S. in Semiconductors, Clean Energy, and Bioscience," 29 July 2022.

399. Interview with ROK MOFA official, Seoul, 20 August 2022.

400. United States Forces Korea, "CFC, USFK and UNC Begin Ulchi Freedom Shield," 23 August 2022.

401. Interview with ROK MOFA official, Seoul, 2 August 2022.

402. "Amid Tensions Over Taiwan, S. Korea Expresses Objection to Changing Status Quo by Force," *Yonhap News*, 6 August 2022.

403. Hyonhee Shin, "South Korea, China Clash over U.S. Missile Shield, Complicating Conciliation," *Reuters*, 11 August 2022.

404. UN Human Rights Council, "Human Rights Council Adopts 21 Texts and Rejects One Draft Decision, Extends Mandates on Older Persons, Right to Development, Arbitrary Detention, Mercenaries, Slavery, Indigenous Peoples, Safe Drinking Water and Sanitation," 6 October 2022, https://www.ohchr.org/en/news/2022/10/human-rights-council-adopts-21-texts-and-rejects-one-draft-decision-extends-mandates.

405. "Yoon Invites Chinese Leader Xi to Visit S. Korea," *Yonhap News*, 16 September 2022.

406. Interview with ROK MOFA official, Seoul, August 2, 2022; interview with ROK *chaebol* manager, Seoul, August 13, 2022.

407. Ji Da-gyum, "S.Korea, China Commit to Revitalizing Military Exchanges, Cooperation on N. Korean Issues," *Korea Herald*, 10 June 2022.

408. Interview with ROK MOFA official, Seoul, 2 August 2022.

5. East Asia

1. Roh Tae-woo, "참된 역사인식으로 마음의 벽 허물어야—미야자와 일본 총리를 위한 만찬만찬사" (Breaking Down the Walls in Our Hearts with True Historical Awareness—Dinner Remarks for Prime Minister Miyazawa of Japan), 16 January 1992.

2. Fred Hiatt, "Japan Offers Apology for Colonizing Korea," *Washington Post*, 25 May 1990.

3. Hong Yung Lee, "South Korea in 1991: Unprecedented Opportunity, Increasing Challenge," *Asian Survey* 32, no. 1 (1992): 73.

4. Hong Yung Lee, "South Korea in 1992: A Turning Point in Democratization," *Asian Survey* 33, no. 1 (1993): 49.

5. Ministry of National Defense of the Republic of Korea, *1988*년 국방백서 (1988 Defense White Paper) (Seoul: Ministry of National Defense of the Republic of Korea, 1988).

6. CSIS, "Missiles of South Korea," 10 August 2021, https://missilethreat.csis .org/country/south-korea/.

7. Interview with ROK Ministry of Foreign Affairs (MOFA) official, phone, 29 September 2020; interview with ROK government advisor, Seoul, 11 August 2021.

8. Song Sang-ho, "S. Korea Conducted Dokdo Defence Drills Last Week: Source," *Yonhap News*, 29 December 2021.

9. KOCIS, "History," 2022, https://www.kocis.go.kr/eng/openHistory.do.

10. See Korea Foundation, "Annual Reports," 2022, https://www.kf.or.kr /kfEng/cm/cntnts/cntntsView.do?mi=2129&cntntsId=1630.

11. Interview with ROK MOFA official, Seoul, 30 July 2021.

12. ASEAN-Korea Cooperation Fund, "ASEAN-Republic of Korea Cooperation Fund (AKCF)," 9 December 2019, https://www.aseanrokfund.com/lib /upload/files/resources/AKCF_Leaflet.pdf.

13. KOICA, "Total Flows by Region," 2022, https://stat.koica.go.kr/ipm/os /acms/smrizeAreaList.do?lang=en.

14. UNCTAD, "The ASEAN-Republic of Korea Investment Agreement," https:// investmentpolicy.unctad.org/international-investment-agreements/treaties /treaties-with-investment-provisions/3257/asean-korea-investment-agreement.

15. Korea Energy Statistical Information System, "Annual LNG Imports by Country of Origin," 2022, http://www.kesis.net/sub/subChartEng.jsp.

16. KNOC, "Operations—Vietnam," 31 December 2021, https://www.knoc.co .kr/ENG/sub03/sub03_1_1_6.jsp.

17. Ministry of Foreign Affairs of the Republic of Korea, "외교관계수립현황."

18. ADB, "Integration Indicators," 2022, https://aric.adb.org/database/integration.

19. APEC, "History," March 2022, https://www.apec.org/about-us/about-apec /history.

20. CSCAP, "About Us," 2008, http://www.cscap.org.

21. Interview with ROK MOFA official, Seoul, 18 September 2008.

22. Paul Shin, "Hosokawa Apologizes for Korean Suffering," Associated Press, 8 November 1993.

23. Interview with ROK MOFA official, phone, 3 September 2020.

24. Bank of Japan, "Bridging Loan Facility for the Bank of Korea," 19 December 1997, https://www.boj.or.jp/en/announcements/release_1997/un9712a .htm/.

25. See the annual editions of KOTRA's 북한의 대외무역동향 (North Korea's Foreign Trade Trends) for data on North Korea's trade relations.

26. Interview with ROK MOFA official, Seoul, 18 September 2008.

27. Interview with ROK Army official 2, phone, 5 August 2020.

28. Maeil Business Newspaper, "한국군함 첫 일본 입항" (First Korean Warship to Enter Japan), *Maeil Business Newspaper*, 20 December 1994.

29. Jere Longman, "South Korea and Japan Will Share World Cup," *New York Times*, 1 June 1996.
30. ADB, "Integration Indicators."
31. Korea Energy Statistical Information System, "Annual LNG Imports by Country of Origin," 2022, http://www.kesis.net/sub/subChartEng.jsp.
32. Memorandum of Understanding between the Government of the Republic of Korea and the Government of Malaysia on Energy and Mineral Resources Cooperation, Seoul, 1 December 1995.
33. KOICA, "Geographical Flows by Region," 2022, https://stat.koica.go.kr /ipm/os/acms/smrizeAreaList.do?lang=en.
34. UNCTAD, "The ASEAN-Republic of Korea Investment Agreement."
35. Ministry of Foreign Affairs of the Republic of Korea, "외교관계수립현황" (Status of Establishment of Diplomatic Relations), December 2021, https:// www.mofa.go.kr/www/wpge/m_4181/contents.do.
36. KBS, "김영삼대통령 베트남 방문" (President Kim Young-sam Visits Vietnam), *KBS News*, 20 November 1996.
37. Ministry of Foreign Affairs, "외교관계수립현황."
38. Korea Foundation, "Annual Reports."
39. CSCAP, "About Us."
40. ASEAN, "ASEAN Regional Forum," 2022, https://aseanregionalforum .asean.org/about-arf/.
41. Desmond Ball, "CSCAP Foundation and Achievements," in *Assessing Track-2 Diplomacy in the Asia-Pacific Region: A CSCAP Reader*, ed. Desmond Ball and Kwa Chong Guan (Singapore: S. Rajaratnam School of International Studies, 2010), 26.
42. ASEAN, "2nd Informal Summit, Kuala Lumpur, 14–16 December 1997," 2020, https://asean.org/speechandstatement/2nd-informal-summit-kuala -lumpur-14-16-december-1997/.
43. Kim Dae-Jung, *Conscience in Action: The Autobiography of Kim Dae-jung*, trans. Jeon Seung-hee (London: Palgrave Macmillan, 2019), 190–91.
44. Republic of Korea–Japan Joint Declaration: A New Republic of Korea–Japan Partnership Toward the 21st Century, Tokyo, 8 October 1998.
45. Washington Post, "Japan Apologizes to Korea for Occupation," *Washington Post*, 8 October 1998.
46. Republic of Korea-Japan Joint Declaration.
47. Ministry of Foreign Affairs of Japan, "The First Japan–ROK High-Level Economic Consultations," 5 March 1999, https://www.mofa.go.jp/announce /announce/1999/3/305-3.html.
48. Republic of Korea–Japan Joint Declaration.
49. Kim, *Conscience in Action*, 795–96.

50. Interview with ROK Army official 2, phone, 5 August 2020.

51. KOCIS, "History."

52. Interview with ROK National Security Council official, Seoul, 1 August 2008.

53. Howard W. French, "Japan's Refusal to Revise Textbooks Angers Its Neighbors," *New York Times*, 10 July 2001.

54. Stephanie Strom, "Japan's Premier Visits War Shrine, Pleasing Few," *New York Times*, 14 August 2001.

55. Ministry of National Defense of the Republic of Korea, *2000 Defense White Paper*, 375.

56. Yonhap, "S. Korea to Participate in Japan's Fleet Review Next Month," *Yonhap News*, 27 October 2022.

57. ADB, "Integration Indicators."

58. Korea Energy Statistical Information System, "Annual LNG Imports by Country of Origin."

59. KNOC, "Operations—Vietnam."

60. KOICA, "Total Flows by Region."

61. 2021 Seoul UN Peacekeeping Ministerial Preparatory Secretariat, "ROK Contribution to UN Peacekeeping."

62. Kim, *Conscience in Action*, 549.

63. The Joint Statement of the 2nd ASEAN+3 Finance Ministers' Meeting, Chiang Mai, 6 May 2000.

64. Kim, *Conscience in Action*, 546–47.

65. East Asia Vision Group, "Towards an East Asian Community: Region of Peace, Prosperity and Progress," *East Asia Vision Group Report* (2001).

66. ADB, "Chiang Mai Initiative (Multilateralisation)," 2015, https://aric.adb .org/initiative/chiang-mai-initiative.

67. ADB, "ASEAN+3 Asian Bond Markets Initiative (ABMI)," 2015, https:// aric.adb.org/initiative/asean3-asian-bond-markets-initiative.

68. Interview with ROK National Security Council official, Seoul, 30 July 2007.

69. Interview with ROK National Security Council official, Seoul, 1 August 2008.

70. Interview with ROK MOFA official, Seoul, 4 August 2008.

71. ADB, "Japan–Republic of Korea Free Trade Agreement," 2015, https://aric .adb.org/fta/japan-republic-of-korea-free-trade-agreement.

72. Interview with ROK National Security Council official, Seoul, 12 August 2008.

73. Bank of Korea, *2005 Annual Report* (Seoul: Bank of Korea, 2006), 18.

74. See WTO, "Disputes by Member," 2022, https://www.wto.org/english/tratop _e/dispu_e/dispu_by_country_e.htm.

75. Interview with ROK MOFA official, London, 30 October 2008; interview with Japan MOFA official, London, 10 January 2014.

76. Interview with ROK National Security Council official, Seoul, 12 August 2008; interview with Japan MOFA official, London, 10 January 2014.

77. See ROK MND defense white papers.

78. Korea Herald, "Remembering 'Winter Sonata,' the Start of Hallyu," *Korea Herald*, 30 December 2011.

79. Korea Foundation, "Who We Are," 2022 https://www.kf.or.kr/kfEng /cm/cntnts/cntntsView2.do?mi=2126.

80. King Sejong Institute, "Communicating with the World Through the King Sejong Institute," 2022, https://www.ksif.or.kr/ste/ksf/hkd/lochkd.do ?menuNo=31101100.

81. Song Sang-ho, "S. Korea Conducted Dokdo Defence Drills."

82. Ministry of Defense of Japan, *Defense of Japan 2005* (Tokyo: Ministry of Defense of Japan, 2005), 42.

83. Ministry of Defense of Japan, *Defense of Japan 2021* (Tokyo: Ministry of Defense of Japan, 2021), 40.

84. Kyodo, "Government Representative Attends Annual Takeshima Day Event for 10th Year in a Row," *Japan Times*, 22 February 2022.

85. See ROK MND defense white papers.

86. Interview with ROK National Security Council official, Seoul, 12 August 2008.

87. ASEAN–Korea Cooperation Fund, "ASEAN-Republic of Korea Cooperation Fund (AKCF)."

88. ADB, "ASEAN–Republic of Korea Comprehensive Economic Cooperation Agreement," 2015, https://aric.adb.org/fta/asean-korea-comprehensive -economic-cooperation-agreement.

89. ADB, "Republic of Korea–Singapore Free Trade Agreement," 2015, https:// aric.adb.org/fta/korea-singapore-free-trade-agreement.

90. ADB, "Integration Indicators."

91. OECD, "Total Flows by Region."

92. Interview with ROK Ministry of Economy and Finance official, phone, 14 June 2017.

93. Korea Foundation, "Who We Are."

94. KOCIS, "History."

95. APEC, "History."

96. Interview with ROK Ministry of Economy and Finance official, phone, 14 June 2017.

97. Lee Myung-bak, "[일본 방문]일본 경제단체 주최 오찬사" ([Visit to Japan] Luncheon Hosted by Japanese Economic Groups), 21 April 2008.

98. Chisa Fujioka, "S. Korea, Japan Look to Future, Plan to Talk Trade," *Reuters*, 21 April 2008.

99. KBS, "12th Defense Trilateral Talks to be Held Wed.," *KBS World*, 12 May 2020.

100. Yonhap, "S. Korea to Participate in Japan's Fleet Review Next Month."

101. U.S. Department of Defense, "Trilateral Meeting," 2009, https://www.defense.gov/Multimedia/Photos/igphoto/2001997296/.

102. See ROK MND defense white papers.

103. Interview with ROK MOFA official, phone, 21 July 2020.

104. Ser Myo-ja, "Lee Myung-bak Makes Historic Visit to Dokdo," *Korea JoongAng Daily*, 10 August 2002.

105. RCEP, "RCEP Agreement Enters Into Force."

106. KBS, "Music Bank Live from Tokyo," *KBS World*, 20 May 2011.

107. ASEAN–Korea Cooperation Fund, "ASEAN–Republic of Korea Cooperation Fund (AKCF)."

108. SIPRI, "SIPRI Arms Transfers Database," 2022, https://www.sipri.org/databases/armstransfers.

109. ADB, "Indonesia–Republic of Korea Free Trade Agreement," 2015, https://aric.adb.org/fta/korea-indonesia-free-trade-agreement; ADB, "Republic of Korea-Viet Nam Free Trade Agreement," 2015, https://aric.adb.org/fta/korea-viet-nam-free-trade-agreement.

110. ADB, Integration Indicators; KOICA, "Total Flows by Region."

111. KOGAS, "Exploration Projects," 2017, https://www.kogas.or.kr:9450/eng/contents.do?key=1555.

112. KOCIS, "History."

113. KBS, *KBS 2013 Annual Report* (Seoul: KBS, 2013), 8.

114. King Sejong Institute, "Communicating with the World."

115. Ministry of Foreign Affairs of the Republic of Korea, *2009 Diplomatic White Paper* (Seoul: Ministry of Foreign Affairs of the Republic of Korea, 2009), 68–79.

116. AMRO, "Overview of the Chiang Mai Initiative Multilateralization," 2017, https://www.amro-asia.org/wp-content/uploads/2017/02/For-website-updating-Overview-of-CMIM.pdf.

117. ASEAN, "About the ASEAN Defence Ministers," 6 February 2017, https://admm.asean.org/index.php/about-admm/about-admm-plus.html.

118. AMRO "Overview," 2018, https://www.amro-asia.org/about-amro/who-we-are/#overview.

119. The Joint Statement of the 15th ASEAN+3 Finance Ministers and Central Bank Governors' Meeting, Manila, 3 May 2012.

120. Park Geun-hye, "제69주년 광복절 경축사" (69th Liberation Day Congratulatory Address), 15 August 2014.

121. "S. Korea to Participate in Japan's Fleet Review Next Month."

122. Trilateral Information Sharing Arrangement Concerning the Nuclear and Missile Threats Posed by North Korea among the Ministry of National

Defense of the Republic of Korea, the Ministry of Defense of Japan, and the Department of Defense of the United States of America, 29 December 2014.

123. Interview with ROK MOFA official, Seoul, 16 August 2021.

124. U.S. Indo-Pacific Command, "Trilateral Pacific Dragon Ballistic Missile Defense Exercise Concludes," 28 June 2016, https://www.pacom.mil/Media /News/News-Article-View/Article/816829/trilateral-pacific-dragon-ballistic -missile-defense-exercise-concludes/.

125. Interview with ROK MOFA official, Seoul, 16 August 2021.

126. See ROK MND defense white papers.

127. Sarah Kim, "Korea Expands ADIZ," *Korea JoongAng Daily*, 8 December 2013.

128. Choi Soo-hyang, "S. Korea Unveils Prototype of First Homegrown Fighter Aircraft KF-21," *Yonhap News*, 9 April 2021.

129. ADB, "Japan–Republic of Korea-People's Republic of China Free Trade Agreement."

130. Interview with ROK MOFA official, online, 17 November 2020.

131. Hyonhee Shin and Tetsushi Kajimoto, "South Korea Says Currency Swap Accord with Japan Desirable," *Reuters*, 27 March 2020.

132. BBC, "South Korea Warns Japan Over Comfort Women Review," *BBC*, 1 March 2014.

133. BBC, "Comfort Women: Japan and South Korea Hail Agreement," *BBC*, 28 December 2015.

134. MWave, "KCON," 2022, https://www.mwave.me/en/kcon.

135. ADB, "Republic of Korea–Viet Nam Free Trade Agreement."

136. World Bank, World Integrated Trade Solution Database, 2022, https://wits .worldbank.org/Default.aspx?lang=en.

137. ADB, "Integration Indicators."

138. KOICA, "Total Flows by Region."

139. Ministry of Foreign Affairs of the Republic of Korea, "Northeast Asia Peace and Cooperation Initiative: Moving beyond the Asian Paradox Towards Peace and Cooperation in Northeast Asia," 2013.

140. MIKTA, "History," 2022, http://mikta.org/about/our-history/.

141. SIPRI, "SIPRI Arms Transfers Database."

142. KOCIS, "History."

143. KBS, *KBS 2015 Annual Report* (Seoul: KBS, 2015).

144. Interview with ROK MOFA official, Seoul, 9 August 2021.

145. Interview with ROK National Security Council official, Seoul, 26 April 2022.

146. U.S. Indo-Pacific Command, "U.S., Allied Forces Launch Inaugural Pacific Vanguard Exercise," 23 May 2019, https://www.pacom.mil/Media /News/News-Article-View/Article/1856643/us-allied-forces-launch -inaugural-pacific-vanguard-exercise/.

147. U.S. Indo-Pacific Command, "U.S., Allied Forces Conduct Exercise Pacific Vanguard 2021 off Coast of Australia," 9 July 2021, https://www.pacom.mil/Media/News/News-Article-View/Article/2689702/us-allied-forces-conduct-exercise-pacific-vanguard-2021-off-coast-of-australia/.
148. U.S. Indo-Pacific Command, "Six Indo-Pacific Nations Begin Exercise Sea Dragon," 6 January 2022, https://www.pacom.mil/Media/News/News-Article-View/Article/2890954/six-indo-pacific-nations-begin-exercise-sea-dragon/.
149. Ministry of Defense of Japan, "Bilateral Anti-Piracy Training with EU Maritime Force and Republic of Korea Navy," October 2018, https://www.mod.go.jp/en/jdf/no128/column.html.
150. Interview with U.S. National Security Council official, phone, 6 December 2018.
151. Interview with ROK National Security Council official, Seoul, 26 April 2022.
152. Yonhap News, "S. Korea Decides to Join CPTPP Trade Agreement," *Yonhap News*, 15 April 2022.
153. Reuters Staff, "South Korea Removes Japan from Fast-track Trade 'White List,'" *Reuters*, 17 September 2019.
154. WTO, "Disputes by Member."
155. MND, *2020 Defense White Paper*, 216.
156. Presidential Committee on New Southern Policy, *New Southern Policy Plus* (Seoul: Presidential Committee on New Southern Policy, 2020).
157. Lee Chi-dong, "Moon Revs Up ASEAN Diplomacy, Breaks Ice with Abe," *Yonhap News*, 5 November 2019.
158. ADB, "Indonesia–Republic of Korea Free Trade Agreement."
159. ADB, "Republic of Korea–Malaysia Free Trade Agreement," 2015, https://aric.adb.org/fta/malaysia-korea-free-trade-agreement; ADB, "Cambodia-[Republic of] Korea Free Trade Agreement," 2015, https://aric.adb.org/fta/cambodia-republic-of-korea-fta.
160. World Bank, World Integrated Trade Solution Database.
161. ADB, "Integration Indicators."
162. KOICA, "Total Flows by Region."
163. Korea Foundation, "Who We Are."
164. KBS, *KBS 2017 Annual Report* (Seoul: KBS, 2017), 29.
165. MWave, "KCON."
166. Korea Foundation, "Who We Are."
167. Presidential Committee on New Southern Policy, *New Southern Policy Plus*.
168. Moon Jae-in, "Remarks by President Moon Jae-in at ASEAN–Republic of Korea Commemorative Summit," 27 November 2019.

169. Ministry of Foreign Affairs of the Republic of Korea, *Northeast Asia Peace and Cooperation Platform*.

170. Yonhap, "S. Korea Holds Talks on Joining DEPA Pact," *Yonhap News*, 27 January 2022.

171. Yonhap, "Yoon Calls for Joint Efforts with Japan for Future-oriented Relationship," *Yonhap News*, 4 July 2022.

172. Yoon, "Address by President Yoon Suk Yeol on Korea's 77th Liberation Day."

173. David Brunnstrom and Hyonhee Shin, "S.Korea, Japan Hold First Bilateral Talks since 2019, Seek Stronger Ties," *Reuters*, 22 September 2022.

174. Yonhap, "S. Korea, U.S., Japan Agree on Strong Response in Case of N. Korea's Nuke Test," *Yonhap News*, 2 September 2022.

175. U.S. Department of Defense, "U.S., Republic of Korea, and Japan Participate in Missile Defense Exercise in Hawaii," 15 August 2022; Song Sang-ho, "S. Korea, U.S., Japan to Hold Trilateral Anti-sub Drills in East Sea," *Yonhap News*, 29 September 2022.

176. Park Hyun-ju and Esther Chung, "Korea, Japan Inching Back to Intelligence-sharing Pact," *Korea JoongAng Daily*, 16 June 2022.

177. "S. Korea to Participate in Japan's Fleet Review Next Month," *Korea JoongAng Daily*, 16 June 2022.

178. Ina Choi, "ASEAN-ROK Partnership: What's Next After the New Southern Policy?," August 11, 2022, https://www.kiep.go.kr/galleryDownload.es?bid=0008&list_no=10269&seq=1.

179. SIPRI, "SIPRI Arms Transfers Database."

180. Priam Nepomuceno, "Japan, SoKor Troops to Act as Observers in 'KAMANDAG' Drills," *Philippine News Agency*, 3 October 2022.

181. Ministry of Trade, Industry and Energy of the Republic of Korea, "Outcomes of ASEAN Ministers' Meetings," 19 September 2022.

182. Interview with ROK Presidential Office official, Seoul, 12 August 2022.

6. Greater Eurasia and the Indian Ocean

1. Jane Gross, "Gorbachev, Ending U.S. Trip, Meets South Korean Leader, Who Sees a Renewal of Ties," *New York Times*, 5 June 1990.

2. KBS, "노태우 대통령 1990년 12월 소련 방문 확정" (President Roh Tae-woo Confirms His Visit to Russia in December 1990), *KBS News*, 17 November 1990.

3. Sam Jameson, "Yeltsin Ends S. Korea Visit with Treaties," *Los Angeles Times*, 21 November 1992; Treaty on Basic Relations Between the Republic of Korea and Russia, 20 November 1992.

4. Interview with ROK MOFA official, phone, 29 September 2020.
5. Alexander A. Sergounin and Sergey V. Subbotin, *Russian Arms Transfers to East Asia in the 1990s* (Oxford: Oxford University Press, 1999), 111.
6. Jameson, "Yeltsin Ends S. Korea Visit with Treaties."
7. Ministry of Foreign Affairs of the Republic of Korea, "외교관계수립현황" (Status of Establishment of Diplomatic Relations), December 2021, https://www.mofa.go.kr/www/wpge/m_4181/contents.do.
8. KBS, "노태우 대통령 유럽순방, 각국 보도" (President Roh Tae-woo's European Tour, Reports from Around the World," *KBS News*, 6 November 1989.
9. Ministry of Foreign Affairs of the Republic of Korea, "외교관계수립현황."
10. Samsung, *Samsung Electronics Co., Ltd. 2019 Business Report* (Seoul: Samsung, 2020).
11. KF-VUB Korea Chair, "Europe–South Korea Relations," June 2020, https://www.korea-chair.eu/timeline/.
12. ADB, "Integration Indicators," 2022, https://aric.adb.org/database/integration.
13. Korea Energy Statistical Information System, "Annual Imports of Crude Oil by Country," 2022, http://www.kesis.net/sub/subChartEng.jsp.
14. KNOC, "Operations—Libya," 31 December 2021, https://www.knoc.co.kr/ENG/sub03/sub03_1_3_1.jsp.
15. Ministry of Foreign Affairs of the Republic of Korea, "외교관계수립현황."
16. Ministry of Foreign Affairs of the Republic of Korea, "재외동포 정의 및 현황" (Total Number of Overseas Koreans), 2022, https://www.mofa.go.kr/www/wpge/m_21509/contents.do.
17. Ministry of Foreign Affairs of the Republic of Korea, *1991 외교백서* (1991 Diplomatic White Paper) (Seoul: Ministry of Foreign Affairs of the Republic of Korea, 1991).
18. UN Security Council, *Resolution 678* (1990), 29 November 1950, https://www.securitycouncilreport.org/atf/cf/%7B65BFCF9B-6D27-4E9C-8CD3-CF6E4FF96FF9%7D/Chap%20VII%20SRES%20678.pdf.
19. Interview with ROK MOFA official, Seoul, 15 August 2021.
20. Interview with ROK MOFA official, Seoul, 18 September 2008.
21. Kim Jihoon, "러시아에 빌려준 돈, 탱크로 대신 받았다 . . .'불곰 사업'이란" (Money Lent to Russia, Received in Exchange for Tanks . . . What Is the 'Brown Bear Project'), *Moneytoday*, 17 November 2021.
22. Chong-sik Lee and Hyuk-Sang Shon, "South Korea in 1994: A Year of Trial," *Asian Survey* 35, no. 1 (1994): 35.
23. Sergounin and Subbotin, *Russian Arms Transfers to East Asia in the 1990s*, 111–15.
24. Interview with ROK MOFA official, phone, 29 September 2020.
25. Korea Energy Statistical Information System, "Annual Imports of Crude Oil by Country."

26. Samsung, *Samsung Electronics Co., Ltd. 2019 Business Report.*
27. Ministry of Foreign Affairs, "재외동포 정의 및 현황."
28. KOCIS, "History," 2022, https://www.kocis.go.kr/eng/openHistory.do.
29. KF-VUB Korea Chair, "Europe–South Korea Relations."
30. Interview with ROK MOFA official, Seoul, 11 August 2021.
31. KOCIS, "History."
32. ASEM InfoBoard, "Overview," 2022, https://www.aseminfoboard.org/about/overview.
33. Korea Energy Statistical Information System, "Annual Imports of Crude Oil."
34. 2021 Seoul UN Peacekeeping Ministerial Preparatory Secretariat, "ROK Contribution to UN Peacekeeping," 2021, https://www.unpko2021.kr/EN/PKO/korea.
35. Korea Energy Statistical Information System, "Annual LNG Imports by Country of Origin," 2022, http://www.kesis.net/sub/subChartEng.jsp.
36. KOICA, "Geographical Flows by Country."
37. 2021 Peacekeeping Secretariat, "ROK Contribution to UN Peacekeeping."
38. Kim Young-sam, "해군사관학교 제49기 졸업 및 임관식 연설(세계평화에 기여하는 대양해군)" (Speech at the 49th Naval Academy Graduation and Commissioning Ceremony: Blue-Water Navy Contribution to World Peace)," 24 March 1995.
39. Ministry of National Defense of the Republic of Korea, *1995–1996 국방백서* (1995–1996 Defense White Paper) (Seoul: Ministry of National Defense of the Republic of Korea, 1996).
40. SIPRI, "SIPRI Arms Transfers Database," 2022, https://www.sipri.org/databases/armstransfers.
41. Treaty of Friendship, Good Neighborliness, and Cooperation between the Russian Federation and the Democratic People's Republic of Korea, Pyongyang, 9 February 2000.
42. Patrick E. Tyler, "South Korea's New Best Friend?," *New York Times*, 1 March 2001.
43. Kim, "러시아에 빌려준 돈, 탱크로 대신 받았다 . . .'불곰 사업'이란."
44. Agreement Between the Government of the Russian Federation and the Republic of Korea on Cooperation in the Fuel and Energy Sector, Moscow, 10 October 2000.
45. Korea Energy Statistical Information System, "Annual Imports of Crude Oil."
46. Korea Energy Statistical Information System, "Annual Imports of Crude Oil"; Korea Energy Statistical Information System, "Annual LNG Imports by Country of Origin."
47. KOGAS, "LNG Projects."

48. 2021 Peacekeeping Secretariat, "ROK Contribution to UN Peacekeeping."

49. Korea Energy Statistical Information System, "Annual LNG Imports by Country of Origin."

50. Agreement Between the Government of the Republic of Korea and the Government of Mongolia on Cooperation in the Fields of Energy and Natural Resources, Seoul, 8 November 1999.

51. KOICA, "Geographical Flows by Country."

52. KF-VUB Korea Chair, "Europe–South Korea Relations."

53. KF-VUB Korea Chair, "Europe–North Korea Relations," June 2020, https://www.korea-chair.eu/timeline/.

54. Chairman's Statement of the Third Asia–Europe Meeting, Seoul, 21 October 2000.

55. Kim Dae-jung, "Address by President Kim Dae-jung of the Republic of Korea at Free University of Berlin," 9 March 2000.

56. KF-VUB Korea Chair, "Europe–North Korea Relations."

57. Kim Dae-jung, "Speech Before Graduating Midshipmen, Korea Naval Academy, Chinhae," 20 March 2001.

58. Republic of Korea Air Force, "Counterterrorism," 2013, http://go.airforce .mil.kr:8081/user/indexSub.action?codyMenuSeq=56576&siteId=airfo rce-eng&menuUIType=sub.

59. Roh Moo-hyun, "[러시아 방문]푸틴 러시아 대통령내외 주최 만찬 답사" ([Visit to Russia] Participation in Dinner Hosted by Russian President Putin), 21 September 2004.

60. Interview with ROK MOFA official, phone, 29 September 2020.

61. Agreement Between the Government of the Russian Federation and the Government of the Republic of Korea on Cooperation in the Gas Sector, Seoul, 17 October 2006.

62. Korea Energy Statistical Information System, "Annual Imports of Crude Oil by Country."

63. Korea Foundation, "Who We Are," 2022 https://www.kf.or.kr/kfEng/cm /cntnts/cntntsView2.do?mi=2126.

64. Interview with US National Security Council official, Washington, DC, 9 April 2008.

65. Interview with ROK National Security Council official, Seoul, 12 August 2008.

66. Interview with ROK MOFA official, Seoul, 11 August 2021.

67. See WTO, "Disputes by Member," 2022, https://www.wto.org/english /tratop_e/dispu_e/dispu_by_country_e.htm.

68. ADB, "Republic of Korea–European Free Trade Association Free Trade Agreement," 2006, https://aric.adb.org/fta/korea-european-free-trade-association -free-trade-agreement.

69. Korea Foundation, "Who We Are."

70. KF-VUB Korea Chair, "Europe–South Korea Relations."

71. NATO, "Relations with the Republic of Korea," 2 September 2021, https://www.nato.int/cps/en/natohq/topics_50098.htm.

72. Korea Energy Statistical Information System, "Annual Imports of Crude Oil by Country"; Korea Energy Statistical Information System, "Annual LNG Imports by Country of Origin."

73. KNOC, "Operations—Yemen," 31 December 2021, https://www.knoc.co.kr/ENG/sub03/sub03_1_5_2.jsp.

74. Interview with ROK MOFA official, 6 August 2021.

75. Esther Schrader and Barbara Demick, "Troops in S. Korea to Go to Iraq," *Los Angeles Times*, 18 May 2004.

76. Emirates News Agency-WAM, "UAE, South Korea Sign Military Cooperation Agreement," *WAM*, 16 November 2006.

77. 2021 Peacekeeping Secretariat, "ROK Contribution to UN Peacekeeping."

78. KNOC, "Operations—Kazakhstan," 31 December 2021, https://www.knoc.co.kr/ENG/sub03/sub03_1_1_2.jsp.

79. KOGAS, "Production Projects," 2017, https://www.kogas.or.kr:9450/eng/contents.do?key=1556.

80. Korea Foundation, "Who We Are."

81. Agreement Between the Government of Australia and the Government of the Republic of Korea on Cooperation in the Fields of Energy and Mineral Resources, Canberra, 30 August 2004.

82. Korea Energy Statistical Information System, "Annual LNG Imports by Country of Origin."

83. Yonhap, "쓰나미 피해지원 해군제중부대 귀항" (Jejung Unit Supporting Tsunami Damage Relief Returns to Port), *Yonhap News*, 9 March 2005.

84. KOICA, "Geographical Flows by Region."

85. Cheong Wa Dae, *Global Korea: The National Security Strategy of the Republic of Korea* (Seoul: Office of the President, 2009), 25.

86. Korea Energy Statistical Information System, "Annual Imports of Crude Oil by Country."

87. Interview with ROK National Security Council official, online, 13 October 2020.

88. ADB, "Republic of Korea–European Union Free Trade Agreement," 2011, https://aric.adb.org/fta/korea-european-union-free-trade-agreement.

89. Interview with ROK MOFA official, Seoul, 4 August 2021.

90. ADB, "Republic of Korea–Turkey Free Trade Agreement," 2015, https://aric.adb.org/fta/korea-turkey-free-trade-agreement.

91. SIPRI, "SIPRI Arms Transfers Database."

92. NATO, "Relations with the Republic of Korea."

93. KF-VUB Korea Chair, "Europe–South Korea Relations."

94. See Korea Foundation, "Annual Reports," 2022, https://www.kf.or.kr/kfEng /cm/cntnts/cntntsView.do?mi=2129&cntntsId=1630.

95. KOCIS, "History."

96. King Sejong Institute, "Communicating with the World Through the King Sejong Institute," 2022, https://www.ksif.or.kr/ste/ksf/hkd/lochkd.do?menu No=31101100.

97. KBS, *KBS 2012 Annual Report* (Seoul: KBS, 2012); KBS, *KBS 2013 Annual Report* (Seoul: KBS, 2013), 8.

98. Korea Energy Statistical Information System, "Annual Imports of Crude Oil by Country"; Korea Energy Statistical Information System, "Annual LNG Imports by Country of Origin."

99. KNOC, "Operations—Yemen"; KOGAS, "LNG Projects."

100. KOGAS, "Exploration Projects," 2017, https://www.kogas.or.kr:9450/eng /contents.do?key=1555.

101. Embassy of the Republic of Korea in Afghanistan, "Ambassador's Greet- ings"; Embassy of the Republic of Korea in Libya, "공관장 인사" (Ambassa- dor's Greetings), 2022, https://overseas.mofa.go.kr/ly-ko/wpge/m_10851 /contents.do.

102. ADB, "Republic of Korea-Gulf Cooperation Council Free Trade Agree- ment," 2015, https://aric.adb.org/fta/korea-gulf-cooperation-council-free-trade -agreement.

103. Interview with ROK MOFA official, Seoul, 6 August 2021.

104. Yonhap, "S. Korean Troops Arrive in UAE," *Yonhap News*, 11 January 2011.

105. Ministry of Foreign Affairs of the Republic of Korea, *2009 Diplomatic White Paper*, 68–79.

106. KNOC, "Operations—Kazakhstan."

107. Korea Energy Statistical Information System, "Annual Imports of Crude Oil by Country."

108. KOCIS, "History."

109. ADB, "India–Republic of Korea Comprehensive Economic Partnership Agreement," 2015, https://aric.adb.org/fta/india-korea-comprehensive-econo mic-partnership-agreement.

110. India–Republic of Korea Joint Statement: Towards a Strategic Partnership, New Delhi, 25 January 2010.

111. Ministry of Foreign Affairs of the Republic of Korea, *2009 Diplomatic White Paper*, 68–79.

112. Ministry of National Defense of the Republic of Korea, "소말리아 해역 청해 부대('09. 3. ~ 현재)" (Cheonghae Unit in the Waters of Somalia (March 2009– Present)), 2022, https://www.mnd.go.kr/user/boardList.action?command=view &page=1&boardId=O_46599&boardSeq=O_50274&titleId=mnd_01070000 0000&id=mnd_010702000000.

113. ADB, "Australia–Republic of Korea Free Trade Agreement," 2015, https://aric.adb.org/fta/australia-korea-free-trade-agreement; ADB, "Republic of Korea-New Zealand Closer Economic Partnership," 2015, https://aric.adb.org/fta/new-zealand-korea-closer-economic-partnership.

114. Korea Energy Statistical Information System, "Annual LNG Imports by Country of Origin."

115. Joint Statement on Enhanced Global and Security Cooperation Between Australia and the Republic of Korea, Canberra, 5 March 2009.

116. KOCIS, "History."

117. Korea Energy Statistical Information System, "Annual Imports of Crude Oil by Country."

118. Ministry of Foreign Affairs of the Republic of Korea, *Northeast Asia Peace and Cooperation Initiative: Moving beyond the Asian Paradox Towards Peace and Cooperation in Northeast Asia*, 2013.

119. Interview with ROK MOFA official, Seoul, 16 August 2021.

120. Kim, "러시아에 빌려준 돈, 탱크로 대신 받았다 . . .'불곰 사업'이란."

121. Interview with ROK MOFA official, Seoul, 16 August 2021.

122. Sarah Kim, "Korea Expands ADIZ."

123. KF-VUB Korea Chair, East-West Center, Asan Institute for Policy Studies and KIEP, *Korea Matters for Europe/Europe Matters for Korea* (Washington, DC: East-West Center, 2020), 14.

124. ADB, "Republic of Korea–Turkey Free Trade Agreement."

125. KOGAS, "Exploration Projects."

126. KOCIS, "History."

127. KBS, *KBS 2018 Annual Report* (Seoul: KBS, 2018), 27; MWave, "KCON," 2022, https://www.mwave.me/en/kcon.

128. MIKTA, "History," 2022, http://mikta.org/about/our-history/.

129. KF-VUB Korea Chair, "Europe–South Korea Relations."

130. NATO, "Relations with the Republic of Korea."

131. Ministry of Foreign Affairs of the Republic of Korea, *Northeast Asia Peace and Cooperation Initiative*.

132. Korea Energy Statistical Information System, "Annual Imports of Crude Oil by Country"; Korea Energy Statistical Information System, "Annual LNG Imports by Country of Origin."

133. ADB, "Republic of Korea-Israel Free Trade Agreement," 2015, https://aric.adb.org/fta/korea-israel-free-trade-agreement.

134. SIPRI, "SIPRI Arms Transfers Database."

135. KOCIS, "History."

136. MWave, "KCON."

137. 2021 Peacekeeping Secretariat, "ROK Contribution to UN Peacekeeping."

138. Ministry of Foreign Affairs of the Republic of Korea, *Diplomatic White Paper 2014* (Seoul: Ministry of Foreign Affairs of the Republic of Korea, 2014), 117–22.

139. KOCIS, "History."

140. Korea Foundation, "Who We Are."

141. Korea Energy Statistical Information System, "Annual Imports of Crude Oil by Country"; Korea Energy Statistical Information System, "Annual LNG Imports by Country of Origin."

142. Ministry of Foreign Affairs of the Republic of Korea, *Northeast Asia Peace and Cooperation Initiative.*

143. Department of Foreign Affairs and Trade of the Government of Australia, "Republic of Korea (South Korea)," 2022, https://www.dfat.gov.au/geo /republic-of-korea.

144. Vision Statement for a Secure, Peaceful and Prosperous Future between the Republic of Korea and Australia, 8 April 2014.

145. ADB, "Australia-Republic of Korea Free Trade Agreement."

146. KOGAS, "LNG Projects," 2017, https://www.kogas.or.kr:9450/eng/contents .do?key=1557.

147. Korea Energy Statistical Information System, "Annual LNG Imports by Country of Origin."

148. MIKTA, "History."

149. Korea Foundation, "Annual Reports."

150. Ministry of National Defense of the Republic of Korea, "소말리아 해역 청해부대 ('09. 3.~현재)" (Cheonghae Unit in the Waters of Somalia (March 2009–Present)).

151. KOICA, "Total Flows by Region," 2022, https://stat.koica.go.kr/ipm/os /acms/smrizeAreaList.do?lang=en; World Bank, World Integrated Trade Solution Database, 2022, https://wits.worldbank.org/Default.aspx?lang=en.

152. Korea Energy Statistical Information System, "Annual Imports of Crude Oil by Country"; World Bank, World Integrated Trade Solution Database.

153. ADB, "[Republic of] Korea–Eurasian Economic Union Free Trade Agreement," 2015, https://aric.adb.org/fta/[republic-of]korea-eurasian-economic-union-free-trade-agreement.

154. ADB, "Republic of Korea-Russia Bilateral Economic Partnership Agreement," 2015, https://aric.adb.org/fta/korea-russia-bilateral-economic-partnership -agreement.

155. Moon Jae-in, "제3차 동방경제포럼(EEF) 전체회의" (The Third Eastern Economic Forum Plenary Meeting), 7 September 2017.

156. The Presidential Committee on Northern Economic Cooperation, "Vision-Strategy," 2017, http://www.bukbang.go.kr/bukbang_en/vision_policy /history/.

157. Yonhap, "S. Korea, Russia to Set Up Military Hotlines: Defense Ministry," *Yonhap News*, 11 November 2021.

158. Oh Seok-min, "Russian Aircraft Violates S. Korea's Airspace Above East Sea Twice," *Yonhap News*, 23 July 2019.

159. Yonhap, "Russia Found Behind Cyber Attacks on PyeongChang Olympics," *Yonhap News*, 20 October 2020.

160. United States Mission to the United Nations, "Joint Statement Following a Vote on a UN Security Council Resolution on Russia's Aggression Towards Ukraine," 25 February 2022, https://usun.usmission.gov/joint-statement -following-a-vote-on-a-un-security-council-resolution-on-russias -aggression-toward-ukraine/; Ministry of Foreign Affairs of the Republic of Korea, "MOFA's Spokesperson Statement on Situation Regarding Ukraine," 25 February 2022, https://www.mofa.go.kr/eng/brd/m_5676/view.do?seq =322002&page=1.

161. KF-VUB Korea Chair, *Korea Matters for Europe/Europe Matters for Korea*, 14; interview with ROK MOFA official, Seoul, 16 August 2021.

162. Ministry of Foreign Affairs of the Republic of Korea, *Northeast Asia Peace and Cooperation Platform*.

163. Yonhap, "Moon Pitches Vision of Regional Railway Bloc at Asia–Europe Summit," *Yonhap News*, 19 October 2018.

164. ADB, "[Republic of] Korea–United Kingdom Free Trade Agreement," 2015, https://aric.adb.org/fta/republic-of-korea-united-kingdom-fta.

165. SIPRI, "SIPRI Arms Transfers Database."

166. Up until 2022, NATO referred to the four countries as "Asia–Pacific partners" or AP4.

167. NATO, "Relations with the Republic of Korea."

168. Yonhap, "S. Korea to Take Part in India-led Joint Naval Exercises: Sources," *Yonhap News*, 22 February 2022.

169. Korea Energy Statistical Information System, "Annual Imports of Crude Oil by Country"; Korea Energy Statistical Information System, "Annual LNG Imports by Country of Origin."

170. ADB, "Republic of Korea–Israel Free Trade Agreement."

171. Lee Ho-Jeong, "Korea Selected to Participate in Egypt's Nuclear Power Project," *Korea JoongAng Daily*, 2 January 2022.

172. SIPRI, "SIPRI Arms Transfers Database."

173. Ministry of National Defense of the Republic of Korea, "소말리아 해역 청해 부대('09. 3. ~ 현재)" (Cheonghae Unit in the Waters of Somalia (March 2009–Present)).

174. Kim Seung-yon, "378 Afghan Co-workers, Family Members on Way to S. Korea on Aerial Tanker," *Yonhap News*, 26 August 2021.

175. Kim Eun-jung, "Seoul Diplomat Meets Negotiators of Iran Nuclear Talks in Vienna," *Yonhap News*, 6 January 2022.
176. Kim Deok-hyun, "S. Korea Signs Deal to Sell M-SAM Missiles to UAE," *Yonhap News*, 17 January 2022.
177. 2021 Peacekeeping Secretariat, "ROK Contribution to UN Peacekeeping."
178. Korea Energy Statistical Information System, "Annual Imports of Crude Oil by Country."
179. World Bank, World Integrated Trade Solution Database.
180. KOICA, "Total Flows by Region."
181. "S. Korea to Take Part in India-led Joint Naval Exercises: Sources."
182. Roby Thomas, "Military Logistics Agreements: Wind in the Sails for Indian Navy," *IDSA Comment*, 26 November 2019.
183. KOGAS, "LNG Projects"; Department of Industry, Science, Energy and Resources of the Government of Australia, "Australia, Republic of Korea to Work Closer on Critical Minerals," 13 December 2021, https://www.minister.industry.gov.au/ministers/pitt/media-releases/australia-republic-korea-work-closer-critical-minerals.
184. Australia–ROK Comprehensive Strategic Partnership, 13 December 2021.
185. U.S. Indo-Pacific Command, "U.S., Allied Forces Conduct Exercise Pacific Vanguard 2021 off Coast of Australia," 9 July 2021, https://www.pacom.mil/Media/News/News-Article-View/Article/2689702/us-allied-forces-conduct-exercise-pacific-vanguard-2021-off-coast-of-australia/; U.S. Indo-Pacific Command, "Six Indo-Pacific Nations Begin Exercise Sea Dragon," 6 January 2022, https://www.pacom.mil/Media/News/News-Article-View/Article/2890954/six-indo-pacific-nations-begin-exercise-sea-dragon/.
186. MWave, "KCON."
187. Interview with ROK MND official, Seoul, 13 August 2021.
188. NATO, "Bilateral Meeting with the Republic of Korea," 30 June 2022.
189. Ramon Pacheco Pardo, *South Korea: A Pivotal State Under Construction* (Brussels: KF-VUB Korea Chair, 2022).
190. Yonhap, "Yoon Offers to Carry Out Aid Projects as Long as N.K Shows Denuclearization Commitment," *Yonhap News*, 17 August 2022.
191. Yonhap, "S. Korea Launches Council on Economic Cooperation with Middle East," *Yonhap News*, 2 September 2022.
192. Reuters, "S.Korea Wins S2.25 bln Order to Build Nuclear Power Plants in Egypt," *Reuters*, 25 August 2022.
193. Australia Department of Defence, "Deputy Prime Minister Meeting with ROK Minister for National Defense," 4 August 2022.
194. Interview with ROK Presidential Office official, Seoul, 12 August 2022.

7. The Rest of the World and Global Governance

1. Roh Tae-woo, "미국 Washington Post 지 회견" (Interview with the *Washington Post*), 4 June 1991.

2. United Nations, "Member States," 2022, https://www.un.org/en/about
-us/member-states.

3. Ministry of Foreign Affairs of the Republic of Korea (MOFA), "The Antarctic Treaty System," 2022, https://www.mofa.go.kr/eng/wpge/m_5433
/contents.do.

4. KOICA, "Total Flows by Region," 2022, https://stat.koica.go.kr/ipm/os/acms
/smrizeAreaList.do?lang=en.

5. KOICA, "Total Flows by Region."

6. UN Security Council, "Republic of Korea," 2022, https://www.un.org
/securitycouncil/content/republic-korea.

7. 2021 Seoul UN Peacekeeping Ministerial Preparatory Secretariat, "ROK
Contribution to UN Peacekeeping," 2021, https://www.unpko2021.kr/EN
/PKO/korea.

8. WTO, "Members and Observers," 2022, https://www.wto.org/english/thewto
_e/whatis_e/tif_e/org6_e.htm.

9. OECD, "List of OECD Member Countries—Ratification of the Convention
of the OECD," 2022, https://www.oecd.org/about/document/ratification
-oecd-convention.htm.

10. BIS, "BIS Invites Nine New Members to Join It," 9 September 1996, https://
www.bis.org/press/p960909b.htm.

11. BIS, "About BIS—Overview," 2022, https://www.bis.org/about/index.htm.

12. World Bank Group, *World Bank and Republic of Korea: 60 Years of Partnership*
(Incheon: World Bank Group Korea Office, 2015), 9.

13. Ministry of Foreign Affairs, "The Antarctic Treaty System."

14. Interview with ROK MOFA official, Seoul, 18 September 2008.

15. KNOC, "Operations—Peru," 31 December 2021, https://www.knoc.co
.kr/ENG/sub03/sub03_1_2_2.jsp.

16. KOICA, "Total Flows by Region."

17. APEC, "History," March 2022, https://www.apec.org/about-us/about-apec
/history.

18. KOICA, "Total Flows by Region."

19. UNFCC, *Parties—Republic of Korea*, 7 August 2018, https://unfccc.int/node
/61147.

20. International Criminal Court, "Republic of Korea," 11 March 2003, https://
asp.icc-cpi.int/states-parties/asian-states/republic-of-korea.

21. 2021 Peacekeeping Secretariat, "ROK Contribution to UN Peacekeeping."

22. G20, "About the G20," 2022, https://g20.org/about-the-g20/;

23. ADB, "Republic of Korea-Chile Free Trade Agreement"; APEC, "History."

24. KOICA, "Total Flows by Region."

25. Interview with ROK Presidential Committee official, phone, 12 September 2020.

26. UN Human Rights Council, "Membership of the Human Rights Council 19 June 2006–18 June 2007 by Regional Groups," 2022, https://www.ohchr.org/en/hr-bodies/hrc/group20062007.

27. 2021 Seoul UN Peacekeeping Ministerial Preparatory Secretariat, "ROK Contribution to UN Peacekeeping," 2021, https://www.unpko2021.kr/EN/PKO/korea.

28. Institute for International Trade, *"한국 FTA 추진 10년의 발자취"* (Ten Years of Korea FTA Promotion), *Trade Focus* 13, no. 18 (2014): 1–7.

29. ADB, "Republic of Korea––Canada Free Trade Agreement," 2015, https://aric.adb.org/fta/korea-canada-free-trade-agreement.

30. ADB, "Republic of Korea–Mexico Strategic Economic Complementation Agreement," 2015, https://aric.adb.org/fta/korea-mexico-strategic-economic-complementation-agreement.

31. IDB, "The IDB and Korea," 14 February 2005, https://www.iadb.org/en/news/background-papers/2005-02-14/the-idb-and-korea%2C2791.html.

32. KOCIS, "History," 2022, https://www.kocis.go.kr/eng/openHistory.do.

33. Ministry of Foreign Affairs of the Republic of Korea, *2006 Diplomatic White Paper* (Seoul: Ministry of Foreign Affairs of the Republic of Korea, 2006), 138–39.

34. Ministry of Foreign Affairs of the Republic of Korea, "2007 Inter-sessional Meeting of the Korea-Africa Forum to Be Held," 14 November 2007, https://www.mofa.go.kr/eng/brd/m_5676/view.do.

35. African Development Bank Group, "Korea," 2022, https://www.afdb.org/en/countries/non-regional-member-countries/coree.

36. BBC, "Nigeria Scraps S Korea Oil Deal," *BBC*, 29 January 2009.

37. KOGAS, "Exploration Projects," 2017, https://www.kogas.or.kr:9450/eng/contents.do?key=1555.

38. KOICA, "Total Flows by Region."

39. 2021 Peacekeeping Secretariat, "ROK Contribution to UN Peacekeeping."

40. UN Security Council, "Republic of Korea."

41. UN Human Rights Council, "Membership of the Human Rights Council 19 June 2009–18 June 2010 by Regional Groups," 2022, https://www.ohchr.org/en/HRBodies/HRC/Pages/Group20092010.aspx.

42. GCF, "About GCF," 2022, https://www.greenclimate.fund/about; UNOSD, "About UNOSD," 2022, https://unosd.un.org/content/about.

43. GGGI, "About GGGI," 2022, https://gggi.org/about/.

44. G8 Summit 2009, "Other Countries," 2022, https://web.archive.org/web /20090710005133/http://www.g8italia2009.it/G8/Home/Summit /Partecipanti/G8-G8_Layout_locale-1199882116809_AltriPaesi.htm.
45. FSB, "About the FSB," 16 November 2020, https://www.fsb.org/about/.
46. Bank of Korea, "Basel Committee on Banking Supervision (BCBS)," 2022, https://www.bok.or.kr/eng/main/contents.do?menuNo=400103.
47. OECD, "Fourth High Level Forum on Aid Effectiveness," 2022, https:// www.oecd.org/dac/effectiveness/fourthhighlevelforumonaideffectiveness .htm.
48. World Bank Group, *World Bank and Republic of Korea*, 11.
49. KNOC, "Operations—Canada," 31 December 2021, https://www.knoc.co .kr/ENG/sub03/sub03_1_2_1.jsp.
50. KOGAS, "Production Projects," 2017, https://www.kogas.or.kr:9450/eng /contents.do?key=1556.
51. ADB, "Republic of Korea-Peru Free Trade Agreement," 2015, https://aric .adb.org/fta/korea-peru-fta.
52. ADB, "Republic of Korea-Colombia Free Trade Agreement," 2015, https:// aric.adb.org/fta/korea-colombia-free-trade-agreement.
53. KOICA, "Total Flows by Region."
54. IDB, "Trust Funds," 2022, https://www.iadb.org/en/about-us/trust-funds.
55. KOCIS, "History."
56. KBS, "Music Bank World Tour Begins 2018 Run in Chile," *KBS News*, 12 January 2018.
57. King Sejong Institute, "Communicating with the World Through the King Sejong Institute," 2022, https://www.ksif.or.kr/ste/ksf/hkd/lochkd.do?menu No=31101100.
58. 2021 Peacekeeping Secretariat, "ROK Contribution to UN Peacekeeping."
59. Ministry of Foreign Affairs of the Republic of Korea, "Korea–Caribbean Forum—Overview," 2022, https://www.mofa.go.kr/eng/wpge/m_20061 /contents.do.
60. ADB, "Republic of Korea–New Zealand Closer Economic Partnership."
61. Ministry of Foreign Affairs of the Republic of Korea, "Sub-Saharan Africa— Information on Countries and Other Areas," 2022, https://www.mofa.go.kr /eng/wpge/m_4910/contents.do.
62. African Development Bank Group, "Korea."
63. KOICA, "Total Flows by Region."
64. Korea Energy Statistical Information System, "Annual Imports of Crude Oil by Country," 2022, http://www.kesis.net/sub/subChartEng.jsp.
65. KOCIS, "History."
66. 2021 Peacekeeping Secretariat, "ROK Contribution to UN Peacekeeping."

67. UN Human Rights Council, "Membership of the Human Rights Council 1 January 2013–31 December 2013 by Regional Groups," 2022, https://www .ohchr.org/en/hr-bodies/hrc/group2013; UN Human Rights Council, "Membership of the Human Rights Council 1 January 2016–31 December 2016 by Regional Groups," 2022, https://www.ohchr.org/en/hr-bodies/hrc/group2016.

68. UNFCC, *Parties—Republic of Korea.*

69. Institute for International Trade, *"한국 FTA 추진 10년의 발자취,"* 1–7.

70. ADB, "Republic of Korea-Central America Free Trade Agreement," 2015, https://aric.adb.org/fta/korea-central-america-fta.

71. IDB, "Trust Funds."

72. Ministry of Foreign Affairs of the Republic of Korea "ROK Wins an Observer Status at the Pacific Alliance, a Dynamic and Open Economic Cooperation Bloc in Latin America," 17 July 2013, https://www.mofa.go .kr/eng/brd/m_5676/view.do.

73. ADB, "Republic of Korea-New Zealand Closer Economic Partnership."

74. KOCIS, "History."

75. KBS, *KBS 2014 Annual Report* (Seoul: KBS, 2014).

76. MWave, "KCON," 2022, https://www.mwave.me/en/kcon.

77. MIKTA, "History," 2022, http://mikta.org/about/our-history/.

78. Ministry of Foreign Affairs of the Republic of Korea, "Sub-Saharan Africa—Information on Countries and Other Areas."

79. Korea Energy Statistical Information System, "Annual Imports of Crude Oil by Country."

80. King Sejong Institute, "Communicating with the World Through the King Sejong Institute."

81. 2021 Peacekeeping Secretariat, "ROK Contribution to UN Peacekeeping."

82. 2021 Seoul UN Peacekeeping Ministerial Preparatory Secretariat, "2021 Seoul UN Peacekeeping Ministerial," 2021, https://www.unpko2021.kr /EN.

83. UN Human Rights Council, "Membership of the Human Rights Council 1 January 2016–31 December 2016 by Regional Groups"; UN Human Rights Council, "Membership of the Human Rights Council 1 January 2020–31 December 2020 by Regional Groups," 2022, https://www .ohchr.org/en/hr-bodies/hrc/group2020.

84. Kim Jee-hee, "Korea Promoted to Developed Nation by Unctad," *Korea JoongAng Daily,* 4 July 2021.

85. P4G, "Republic of Korea," 2022, https://p4gpartnerships.org/global-ecosystems /country-partners/republic-korea.

86. European Commission, "EU and 15 World Trade Organization Members Establish Contingency Appeal Arrangement for Trade Disputes," 27

March 2020, https://ec.europa.eu/commission/presscorner/detail/en/IP
_20_538.

87. U.S. Indo-Pacific Command, "U.S., Allied Forces Conduct Exercise Pacific Vanguard 2021 off Coast of Australia," 9 July 2021, https://www.pacom.mil /Media/News/News-Article-View/Article/2689702/us-allied-forces -conduct-exercise-pacific-vanguard-2021-off-coast-of-australia/; U.S. Indo-Pacific Command, "Six Indo-Pacific Nations Begin Exercise Sea Dragon," 6 January 2022, https://www.pacom.mil/Media/News/News-Article-View /Article/2890954/six-indo-pacific-nations-begin-exercise-sea-dragon/.

88. ADB, "Republic of Korea--Pacific Alliance Free Trade Agreement," 2015, https://aric.adb.org/fta/republic-of-korea-pacific-alliance-free-trade -agreement.

89. Yonhap, "S. Korea Decides to Join CPTPP Trade Agreement," *Yonhap News*, 15 April 2022.

90. ADB, "Republic of Korea–Central America Free Trade Agreement"; ADB, "Republic of Korea–MERCOSUS Free Trade Agreement," 2015, https:// aric.adb.org/fta/korea-mercosur-preferential-trading-agreement.

91. IDB, "Trust Funds."

92. KOICA, "Total Flows by Region."

93. KBS, *KBS 2018 Annual Report* (Seoul: KBS, 2018), 27.

94. Ministry of Foreign Affairs of the Republic of Korea, "Outcome of the 5th Korea–Africa Forum," 10 March 2022, https://www.mofa.go.kr/eng /brd/m_5676/view.do?seq=322014.

95. African Development Bank Group, "Korea."

96. African Development Bank Group, "African Development Bank and Korea Launch the Korea–Africa Energy Investment Facility," 23 May 2018, https://www.afdb.org/fr/press-releases/african-development-bank-and -korea-launch-korea-africa-energy-investment-facility.

97. KNOC, "Operations—Senegal," 31 December 2021, https://www.knoc.co .kr/ENG/sub03/sub03_1_3_2.jsp.

98. Korea Energy Statistical Information System, "Annual Imports of Crude Oil by Country."

99. KOICA, "Total Flows by Region."

100. KOCIS, "History."

101. ADB, "Republic of Korea–Pacific Alliance Trade Agreement," 2022, https://aric.adb.org/fta/republic-of-korea-pacific-alliance-free-trade -agreement.

102. Government of Mexico, "The Foreign Ministers of Mexico and South Korea Agree to Promote a Bilateral FTA," 4 July 2022.

103. Interview with ROK Presidential Office official, Seoul, 12 August 2022.

104. Joe Saballa, "Canada Asks South Korea to Supply More Artillery Rounds," *The Defense Post*, 2 June 2022.

Conclusion

1. WTO, *World Trade Statistical Review 2021* (Geneva: World Trade Organization, 2021), 58.
2. United Nations Conference on Trade and Development (UNCTAD), *World Investment Review 2021: Investing in Sustainable Recovery* (New York: United Nations, 2021), 7.
3. World Bank, "Trade (% of GDP)," 2022, https://data.worldbank.org/indicator/NE.TRD.GNFS.ZS?most_recent_value_desc=true.
4. Park Jin, "Dinner Speech at the 17th Jeju Forum," 15 September 2022.

Index

arms exports/sales, 118; ROK, 175, 179–80, 195, 199, 201–2, 204, 230; Russian, 189, 191

ASEAN. *See* Association of Southeast Asian Nations

ASEAN Regional Forum (ARF), 160, 162, 165, 171, 175

ASEM. *See* Asia–Europe Meeting

Asia–Europe Meeting (ASEM), 188, 190–91, 201

Asian and Pacific Council (ASPAC), 47

Asian Development Bank (ADB), 62

Asian financial crisis (AFC), 1, 10, 55, 56, *157*, 163, 208, 211–12; autonomy and, 224; diplomacy around, 160–61; external military threats and, 226; globalization and, 65–66, 229; Kim Dae-jun during, 108, 165, 181

Asian Games (1986), 50–52, 99

Asian Infrastructure Investment Bank (AIIB), 139

Asia-Pacific Economic Cooperation (APEC), 159–60, 162–63, 168–69, 211, 219; Cold War and, 64; under Lee Myung-bak, 215–17; North Korea in, 166; under Roh Tae-woo, 209

ASPAC. *See* Asian and Pacific Council

assassinations, 41, 48

Association of Southeast Asian Nations (ASEAN), 86, 156, 158–59, 161, 174, 177–78; ASEAN+3, 64, 66, 162, 165–66, 169, 171–72, 175, 179; ASEAN+6, 170–71, 173

Australia, 2, 11, 87–89, 188, 190, 193, 203, 213; FTAs with, 197, 199–200; as middle power, 4, 22–23, 26, 62; Yoon Suk-yeol on, 204–5

authoritarianism, 41, 48

autonomy, 7, 10, *28*; strategic, 67–68, 84, 91, 97, 99, 118

autonomy (in ROK grand strategy), 31, 55, 91, *94, 157, 184, 208*, 222–25; Kim Young-sam on, 102–5; military capacities and, 205–6; Moon Jae-in on, 144; postdemocratization, 67–68; predemocratization, 54; Roh Moo-hyun on, 118–19; Roh Tae-woo on, 95–97; ROK–U.S. alliance and, 58, 93

Ballistic Missile Guidelines (1979), U.S.–ROK, 47, 49, 58, 103

Ballistic Missile Guidelines (2001), U.S.–ROK, 110, 112, 126, 131, 141, 143, 145, 147–48

Bank for International Settlements (BIS), 61, 210, 215

Ban Ki-moon, 77, 212, 214, 216

Bank of Japan, 160–61, 167, 173

Bank of Korea (BOK), 146, 167, 173; AFC and, 66, 160–161; GFC and, 128; People's Bank of China and, 100, 106, 130

Basel Committee on Banking Supervision (BCBS), 215

Battle of Yeonpyeong (2002), 110

BCBS. *See* Basel Committee on Banking Supervision

behavioral middle powers, 21–22

Biden, Joe, 144–45, 151–52, 176

big conglomerates. *See* chaebol

"big three" economies, 72, 130, 183, 223

bilateralism, ROK, 77–78, 93, 146, 169, 200, 203; with China, 106, 113–14, 121–22, 130, 139; with Europe, 194, 201–2; with Japan, 44, 158, 160–61, 172, 175–77, 179; with Southeast Asia, 159, 165–66; with Soviet Union, 51–52; trade and, 177, 187, 192. *See also* free trade agreements

BIS. *See* Bank for International
   Settlements
blue water navy, ROK, 118, 186,
   188–89, 191, 193, 196–97
BOK. *See* Bank of Korea
bombs/bombings, 39, 50–51, 97
Brazil, 22–23, 40, 215, 217
Britain, 19–20
"Brown Bear Project," 103, 187, 189, 197
Brunei, 162, 165
Brussels Effect, 26
budgets, ROK, 3–4, 41, 74–75, 78, 141
Burma/Myanmar, 50
Bush, George H. W., 96–97
Bush, George W., 20, 111–12, 119–20
Byeon Yeong-tae, 39

Cambodia, 162, 178
Canada, 176, 207–8, 215, 219–20; FTA
   with, 213, 217; as a middle power, 22,
   26, 62
capitalism, 38, 41
Carter, Jimmy, 46–47, 49
Central Asia, 2, 11, 88, 183, 186, 190,
   197, 199, 202
CFC. *See* Combined Forces Command,
   ROK/US
chaebol (big conglomerates), 41, 52, 72,
   79, 88, 100, 106, 140, 151, 186
Cheonan, ROK, 68, 124–25, 127, 131–32,
   169–170
Cheonghae Unit, ROK Navy, 129, 136,
   145, 196, 200, 202, 204
Chiang Mai Initiative (CMI), 165, 171
Chile, 89, 178–79, 211–13, 215, 219
China, 7–8, 33, 44, 51, 79, 85, 149, 197;
   Civil War, 35, 39; grand strategy, 12,
   29; as a great power, 5, 20–21, 24, 73;
   inter-Korean relations and, 60, 95,
   109; Kim Dae-jung on, 113–15; Kim
   Young-sam on, 106–8; Korean

Cultural Centers in, 107, 122, 139; in
   Korean War armistice, 36–37; Lee
   Myung-bak on, 130–32; Moon Jae-in
   on, 147–49; North Korea and, 32–33,
   59–60, 69, 83–84, 99–100, 106–7,
   225–28; Park Geun-hye on, 137–40;
   PLA, 39, 138, 148; relationship/
   rivalry with U.S., 7, 45, 61, 119,
   146–47, 176, 234–35; rise of, 55, 56,
   59–61, 84, 93–94, *94*, 107, *157*, *184*,
   224; Roh Moo-hyun on, 121–23;
   Roh Tae-woo on, 99–101; ROK
   bilateralism with, 106, 113–14,
   121–22, 130, 139; ROK normalized
   diplomatic relations with, 1, 8, 10,
   100–01, 138, 152; ROK trade with,
   51, 60, 100, 114–15, 130, 138–39;
   sanctions and, 6, 140, 149; in UN
   Security Council, 209; Yoon
   Suk-yeol on, 152–54. *See also* South
   Korea–China relations
Chun Doo-hwan, 48–53, 78, 94
"classicist approach" to grand strategy,
   14, 17–18
Clausewitz, Carl von, 13, 15
climate change, 90, 211, 214
climate diplomacy, 6
Clinton, Bill, 11, 102–3, 105, 164
CMI. *See* Chiang Mai Initiative
Cold War, 1, 10, 20, 27–29, 67–69, 77,
   79–81, 84–84; globalization
   following, 64; great powers and,
   14–15; Roh Tae-woo on, 208–9;
   ROK democratization and, 8, 63
Colombia, 215, 217
colonization of Korea, Japanese, 33, 40,
   67, 84–86, 163, 176–77, 222, 229–30;
   reparations for, 43–44; sex slaves
   during, 157, 160, 174
Combined Forces Command (CFC),
   ROK–U.S., 46, 49, 76, 98

communication, inter-Korean, 45, 103, 116, 125, 133–34, 137, 142–43

communism, 29, 35–40, 61, 84, 87, 94–96, 99

Comprehensive and Progressive Agreement for Trans-Pacific Partnership (CPTPP), 64, 148, 176, 178, 180, 203, 219–20

Comprehensive Countermeasures for National Cyber Security Crisis (2009), ROK, 125

Congress, U.S., 35, 46, 120, 128, 136, 194

conservative presidents/administrations, ROK, 1, 3, 123, 132, 149–50, 234

consolidation, democratic, 4, 62, 76, 230

constitution, ROK, 57–58, 92, 226–27

cooperation, 6, 66, 90; multilateral, 24–25, 142, 175–76; pan–East Asian, 165–66, 168–69; security, 113, 116, 180, 205

cooperation, regional, 26–27, 55, 63–66, 94, 157, 184, 208, 226–29; China and, 56, 224; under Lee Myung-bak, 171–72

Core Technology Plan, ROK, 147–48

Council for Security Cooperation in the Asia Pacific (CSCAP), 64, 160, 162

coups, military, 41, 48

COVID-19 pandemic, 62, 146, 149, 177–78, 218–19

CPTPP. *See* Comprehensive and Progressive Agreement for Trans-Pacific Partnership

critical junctures, 10, 55, 232, 238*n*10

CSCAP. *See* Council for Security Cooperation in the Asia Pacific

cyberattacks/cyber warfare, 69, 75, 124, 126, 133, 139–41, 201, 225

cybersecurity/cyber means, ROK, 2, 30, 94, 153, 184, 224, 255*n*77; under Lee

Myung-bak, 125; as military capabilities, 227–28; Russia and, 197, 201

DAPA. *See* Defense Acquisition Program Administration, ROK

deaths, 46, 50–52, 68, 103, 110, 124–25, 133; by assassination, 41, 48

Defense Acquisition Program Administration (DAPA), ROK, 143

Defense Reform Plan (2020), ROK, 117–18, 123

Defense Trilateral Talks (DTT), 161, 164, 173, 176

demilitarized zone (DMZ), 36–37, 41–42, 46, 50

democracy/democratization (1988), ROK transition to, 1, 3–4, 55, 63, 74, 94, 99, 157, 225; economic development and, 5–6, 61–62; normalization of diplomatic relations with Soviet Union and, 10; South Korea–U.S alliance following, 7–8. *See also* postdemocratization, ROK; predemocratization (1948–1987)

Deng Xiaoping, 51, 59–60, 100

denuclearization, 96, 104, 119, 123, 134–35

DEPA. *See* Digital Economy Partnership Agreement

deterrence policies, ROK, 39, 103–5, 108, 117, 125–26, 148, 150, 226; domestic weapon production as, 96, 110–11, 158; Park Geun-hye on, 132–34; ROK–U.S. alliance in, 58–59, 76, 93, 119

developed country, ROK as, 1, 10

developing country/developmental state, ROK as, 41, 71, 78, 159–60, 208

diaspora, Korean, 88, 186, 199

dictatorial rule, ROK, 10, 41, 82, 85, 89, 158

Digital Economy Partnership Agreement (DEPA), 178, 220

diplomacy, international (ROK), 24, 37, 40, 65, 87, 100–1, 116, 171–72; around AFC, 160–61; with Europe, 185; in the Middle East, 202; under Moon Jae-in, 200–1; with the Soviet Union, 209. *See also* public diplomacy, ROK

diplomatic corps/diplomatic means, ROK, 2, *55*, 74, *94*, *157*, *184*, *208*, 227; China and, 100–1, 122; Japan and, 158, 179; middle power identity and, 77–78; under Park Geun-hye, 198; under Roh Tae-woo, 158–59

dispute-settlement mechanism, WTO, 112–13, 120–21, 137, 146, 167, 177, 192, 218

division of Korea, 32–33, *55*, 56–58, 67, *94*, 225

DMZ. *See* demilitarized zone

Dokdo Islands, 37, 158, 161, 164, 167–68, 170, 173, 177, 180, 225

domestic weapons production, ROK, 41, 76, 97–98, 103; Ballistic Missile Guidelines impacting, 47, 49; as deterrence, 96, 110–11, 158; of missiles, 47, 75, 96, 104, 143, 147–48, 202; nuclear weapons in, 44–45, 74, 96

Douglas, McDonnell, 98

DTT. *See* Defense Trilateral Talks

East Asia, 2, *83*, 137; Kim Dae-jung, 163–66; Kim Young-sam on, 160–62; Lee Myung-bak on, 169–72; Moon Jae-in on, 175–79; Northeast Asia in, 11, 64, 82, 155; Park Geun-hye on, 172–75; regionalism in, 155, 175,

180–81, 188; Roh Moo-hyun, 166–69; Roh Tae-woo on, 157–60; in ROK grand strategy, *55*, *83*, 85–87, 155–56, *157*; security in, 182–83; Yoon Suk-yeol on, 179–81. *See also* Southeast Asia

East Asian Vision Group (EAVG), 165–66

East China Sea, 86, 148

Eastern bloc, 67, 72

EAVG. *See* East Asian Vision Group

economic: governance, 62, 66, 86, 88, 229; power, 14, 33, 62, 213; security, 29, 88, 190, 196

economic development, ROK, 4–6, *55*, 61–62, *94*, *157*, *184*, *208*, 228; under Chun, 48–49, 52; under Park Chung-hee, 41–42; postdemocratization, 56; under Rhee Syngman, 39

Economic Development Cooperation Fund (EDCF), ROK, 52, 78–79, 159, 209–10

economic means, 18, 30, *55*, 74, 128, 158–59, 223–24, 233; China and, 130, 139; in foreign policy, 78; FTAs in, 120–21; under Moon Jae-in, 140; under Park Geun-hye, 133, 136; under Yoon Suk-yeol, 179

EFTA. *See* European Free Trade Association

Egypt, 199, 202

818 Plan, ROK, 97–98

Eisenhower, Dwight D., 39–40

ends (ROK grand strategy), 11, 33, *55*, 67–74, *94*, 153–54, *157*, *184*, *208*, 221

Eurasia Initiative, ROK, 199

Eurasian Economic Union, 200, 202

Europe, 2, 11, 14, 39, 87–88, 183, 190, 201–2, 205–6

independence of action, ROK, 1, 65–67, 222

India, 22, 24, 74, 88, 176, 183, 196, 203–5

Indian Ocean, 2, 11, 55, *83*, 87–89, 182–83, *184*; Kim Dae-jung on, 189–91; Kim Young-sam on, 187–89; Lee Myung-bak on, 194–97; Moon Jae-in on, 200–4; Park Geun-hye on, 197–200; Roh Moo-hyun on, 191–93; Roh Tae-woo on, 184–89; Yoon Suk-yeol on, 204–6

Indonesia, 22, 159, 162, 171, 175, 177–78, 193

Indo-Pacific Economic Framework (IPEF), U.S., 151

industrialization, 41

informational means, 30, 55, 223–24

infrastructure, 52, 79, 159, 179, 193, 217

Inter-American Development Bank (IDB), 213, 217, 219

inter-Korean relations, 7, 10, 69–71, 124, 141, 178; China and, 60, 95, 109; communication in, 45, 103, 116, 125, 133–34, 137, 142–43; family reunions in, 50, 109; Japan in, 88, 161, 163–64, 167; Kim Young-sam on, 101–2, 103; *Nordpolitik* and, 50, 57, 94–95, 99, 158–59, 184, 209, 228; under Park Chung-hee, 42–43, 45–46; Russia in, 88, 200–1, 205. *See also* reconciliation and reunification with North Korea

inter-Korean summits, 70, 103, 109, 115, 116, 117, 140–41, 190

International Atomic Energy Agency (IAEA), 96–97, 101

International Criminal Court (ICC), 211

International Monetary Fund (IMF), 20, 66, 78, 165

international relations (IR), 4, 14–15, 22

International Security Assistance Force (ISAF), 195

interstate conflicts, 14, 68

interwar period, 16, 19

investment, 2, 55, 78–79, *94*, 120, 137, *157*, *184*, *208*; in China, 85, 106, 130, 138–39; in Europe, 187; FDI as, 71, 229; in Japan, 176; in the Middle East, 202; in ROK, 198; in Southeast Asia, 171, 177–78

IPEF. *See* Indo-Pacific Economic Framework, U.S.

Iran, 22, 111, 186, 190, 202

Iraq, 59, 98, 111, 119–20, 136, 186, 193, 199

ISAF. *See* International Security Assistance Force

Israel, 22, 199, 202

Japan, 8, 19–20, 23, 38–40, 51, 79, 81; external military threats and, 156, 158, 167–68, 180, 225; FTAs with, 166–67, 176; in inter-Korean relations, 88, 161, 163–64, 167; Kim Dae-jung on, 163–64; Kim Young-sam on, 160–61; Korean Cultural Centers in, 158, 164, 170, 173; Lee Myung-bak on, 169–70; as a middle power, 22, 67, 72, 156; Moon Jae-in on, 175–77; Park Geun-hye on, 172–74; Roh Moo-hyun on, 166–68; Roh Tae-woo on, 157–58; ROK bilateralism with, 44, 158, 160–61, 172, 175–77, 179; ROK military capabilities and, 164, 169–70, 172–73, 180; ROK normalized diplomatic relations with, 43–44, 85; ROK trade with, 6, 160–61, 164, 166–67, 176–77; South Korea–Japan relations, 155–57, 160, 163–64, 168–70, 172–73; South Korea relations with, 155–57, 160, 163–64, 168–70, 172–73; World

War II and, 32, 37, 106. *See also*
colonization of Korea, Japanese
Jiang Zemin, 106–7
Joint Declaration on the
Denuclearization of the Korean
Peninsula, 96
joint military exercises, 38, 42, 151–52,
179–80
joint naval drills, 145–46, 164–65,
169–70, 176, 200–3, 218

Kaesong Industrial Complex, 116,
124–25, 133–34, 142
Kaifu Toshiki, 157
KAMD. *See* Korea Air and Missile
Defense system, ROK
KARI. *See* Korea Aerospace Institute
Kazakhstan, 88, 183, 186, 196, 199, 202
KCON (music festival), 137, 146, 174,
177–78, 198–99, 203, 217
KEDO. *See* Korean Peninsula Energy
Development Organization
Kill Chain strategy, ROK, 125–26, 133–34
Kim Dae-jung, 66, 81, 108–15, 119, 127,
153, 181, 221; on East Asia, 163–66;
on global governance, 211–12; on
Greater Eurasia and the Indian
Ocean, 189–91
Kim Il-sung, 34–35, 46, 50, 57, 103
Kim Jong-il, 57, 108–9, 115, 123–24, 164,
189
Kim Jong-un, 133–35, 141, 148
Kim Young-sam, 64, 81, 89, 101–8, 127,
206 181; on East Asia, 160–62; on
global governance, 210–11; on
Greater Eurasia and the Indian
Ocean, 187–89
King Sejong institutes, 81, 121, 170–71,
198, 215, 217–20; in China, 131, 139;
in Europe, 195; in Japan, 167, 175; in
U.S., 129

Kishida Fumio, 179
KMPR. *See* Korean Massive
Punishment and Retaliation, ROK
KNOC. *See* Korea National Oil
Corporation
KOAFEC. *See* Korea-Africa Economic
Cooperation
KOCCA. *See* Korea Creative Content
Agency
KOCIS. *See* Korea Overseas Culture
Information Service
KOGAS. *See* Korea Gas Corporation
KOICA. *See* Korea International
Cooperation Agency
Koizumi Junichiro, 164
Korea Aerospace Institute (KARI), 96,
103–4, 150
Korea-Africa Economic Cooperation
(KOAFEC), 213, 219
Korea Air and Missile Defense (KAMD)
system, ROK, 125–26, 133–34
Korea-Caribbean Partnership Forum,
215–16
Korea Creative Content Agency
(KOCCA), 129–30, 137, 146
Korea Gas Corporation (KOGAS), 171,
190, 193, 198–200, 203, 213–15
Korea International Cooperation
Agency (KOICA), 79, 159, 209–210
Korea National Oil Corporation
(KNOC), 120, 186, 192–93, 196, 198,
211, 213, 215, 219; contract with
Vietnam, 159, 165
Korean Cultural Centers, 48, 149,
187–88, 195, 197–200, 202–3, 217,
219–20; in China, 107, 122, 139; in
Japan, 158, 164, 170, 173; in Latin
America, 213, 215; in Southeast Asia,
168, 171, 175; in U.S., 106, 112, 121,
129, 137, 146–47
Korean language (*Hangeul*), 81, 121

Korean Massive Punishment and Retaliation (KMPR), ROK, 134

Korean Peninsula, 5, 35, 59–61, 84, 87, 107, 182

Korean Peninsula Energy Development Organization (KEDO), 102, 111, 115–16

Korean People's Army (KPA, North Korea), 35, 49

"Korean question," UN, 37, 40, 48

Korean studies, 4–9, 12

Korean War, 1, 33–35, 49, 57–59, 67, 186, 225, 227; armistice, 36–37, 58, 60, 74, 84–85, 107; democratization and, 71; military capabilities and, 74; ROK–U.S. alliance and, 38, 42

Korean wave. See Hallyu

Korea Overseas Culture Information Service (KOCIS), 48, 81

Korea Trade-Investment Promotion Agency (KOTRA), 174, 184

Korea-United States Free Trade Agreement (KORUS), 120, 128, 137, 146, 194

KOTRA. See Korea Trade-Investment Promotion Agency

KPA. See Korean People's Army

K-pop music, 81, 137, 167, 170–71, 177, 199; in China, 121–22, 140, 149; in U.S., 136–37

K-Pop Night Out, 129–30, 137

Kyoto Protocol, UNFCC, 105, 211

Lao, 162

Latin America, 77, 207–11; FTAs with, 89, 212–13, 215, 219

Lebanon, 202, 212

Lee Byung-tae, 161

Lee Myung-bak, 80, 122 135, 123–32, 153, 180; East Asia under, 169–72; on global governance, 214–16; Greater

Eurasia and the Indian Ocean under, 194–97

Lee Sang-ock, 100

Lee Teng-hui, 107

legitimacy, 25–26, 42, 59, 70, 99

Liberal International Order, 26–29, 61, 67, 72

liberal presidents/administrations, ROK, 1, 3, 108, 110–11, 115, 126–27, 140, 175

Liberia, 119, 136, 145, 212

Libya, 186, 195

liquefied natural gas (LNG), 188, 190, 193, 199–200; from Southeast Asia, 159, 162, 165, 171

long-term temporal scope of (ROK grand strategy), 1–5, 31

MacArthur, Douglas, 36

Malaysia, 40, 159, 162, 165, 178

Mao Zedong, 21, 45

Maritime Self-Defense Force, Japanese, 163, 164–65, 170, 176

Marshall Plan, U.S., 38–39

Masterplan for National Cybersecurity (2011), ROK, 125

means (ROK grand strategy), 1–2, 11, 55–56, 75–82, 90–91, 94, 154, 157, 208, 221; informational, 30, 55, 223–24; military, 15, 30, 55, 73–74, 223–24, 226. See also cybersecurity/cyber means, ROK; diplomatic corps/diplomatic means, ROK; economic means

methodology, research, 9–10

Mexico, 213, 219–20

Middle East, Greater, 2, 11, 52, 87, 186, 192, 213; oil/natural gas imported from, 188–90, 195, 199, 204

middle power, ROK: recognition as an influential, 1, 55, 68, 72–73, 94, 157,

National Defense Force, ROK, 34–35
NATO. *See* North Atlantic Treaty
Organization
natural gas, 87–88, 159, 185, 188–89, 192,
195, 198–99, 202–3. *See also* liquefied
natural gas
Navy, ROK, 98, 126, 161, 173, 179; blue
water, 118, 186, 188–89, 191, 193,
196–97; *Cheonan*, 68, 124–25, 127,
131–32, 169–70; Cheonghae Unit,
129, 136, 145, 196, 200, 202, 204; in
joint naval drills, 145–46, 164–65,
169–70, 176, 200–3, 218
Navy, U.S., 8, 170
NEASED. *See* Northeast Asia Security
Dialogue
neoliberalism, 71
Netherlands, 26
network diplomacy, 25, 63–64, 77
New Asia Initiative, 171, 196–97
New Southern Policy (NSP/NSP+),
ROK, 145, 177–78, 203
New Zealand, 178–79, 213, 217, 219–20
Nigeria, 22, 213, 218–19
9/11 terrorist attacks, 20, 65, 212
Nixon, Richard, 20, 44–45
NLL. *See* Northern Limit Line
Nordpolitik (Roh foreign policy), 50,
57, 94–95, 99, 158–59, 184,
209, 228
normalized diplomatic relations, ROK,
47, 77, 162, 185–86; with China, 1, 8,
10, 100–1, 138, 152; with Japan,
43–44, 85; with Russia, 205; with
Soviet Union, 1, 10, 100, 184–85;
with Vietnam, 159
normative middle powers, 21–22
norm entrepreneurs, middle powers as,
25–26, 63–64
North American Free Trade Agreement
(NAFTA), 213

North Atlantic Treaty Organization
(NATO), 195, 198, 201–2, 204, 213,
230, 292*n*166; military capabilities
and, 192; under Truman, 38–39;
under Yoon Suk-yeol, 220
Northeast Asia, 11, 64, 82, 155
Northeast Asian Cooperation Initiative
for Peace and Prosperity, ROK,
116
Northeast Asia Peace and Cooperation
Initiative (NAPCI), 132–33, 174–75,
197–99
Northeast Asia Peace and Cooperation
Platform (NAPC), 142, 178, 201
Northeast Asia Security Dialogue
(NEASED), 101–2, 109–10, 116, 133,
142
Northern Limit Line (NLL), 110,
124–25
North Korea, 5, 34, 110–111, 156; armed
forces, 35–36, 45, 70, 74; bombings
by, 50–51; China and, 32–33, 59–60,
69, 83–84, 99–100, 106–7, 225–28;
DMZ provocation by, 41–42; as
external military threat, 57, 68–70,
84, 92–93, 101–3, 161, 176, 222–23,
235; Japan and, 86, 156, 161; Kim
Dae-jung on, 108–10, 166; Kim
Young-sam on, 101–4; in Korean
War armistice, 36–37; Lee Myung-
bak on, 123–26; Moon Jae-in on,
140–44; nuclear crises, 1, 96–97,
101–2, 115–16, 191–92; nuclear
weapons, 68–69, 101–2, 113, 116–18,
122–23, 133–36, 141–43, 226; Park
Geun-hye on, 132–35; pipeline
crossing, 187, 197; Rhee policy on,
36–40; Roh Moo-hyun on, 115–17;
Roh Tae-woo on, 94–96; ROK aid
to, 116, 125, 142; Soviet Union and,
32–33, 35–36; Yoon Suk-yeol on,

212–14; on Greater Eurasia and the Indian Ocean, 191–93

Roh Tae-woo, 4, 63, 70, 72, 94–101, 181, 206, 221; on East Asia, 157–60; on global governance, 208–10; on Greater Eurasia and the Indian Ocean, 184–87; *Nordpolitik* under, 50, 57, 94–95, 99, 158–59, 184, 209, 228

ROK. *See* Republic of Korea

Roosevelt, Theodore, 20

Russia, 2, 11, 22, 24, 88, 182–85, 205, 254n59; arms exports/sales, 189, 191; Kim Dae-jung on, 189; Kim Young-sam, 187; Lee Myung-bak on, 194; Moon Jae-in on, 200–1; Park Geun-hye on, 197; Roh Moo-hyu on, 191–92; Ukraine invaded by, 201, 204, 252n34. *See also* Soviet Union

sanctions, 117, 136, 144, 204; China and, 6, 140, 149

Saudi Arabia, 22, 183, 186, 190

SBLM. *See* submarine-launched ballistic missile

SEATO. *See* Southeast Asia Treaty Organization

security, ROK, 1, 5, 15–16, 29, 55, 184–85, 193, 213, 222–23, 225–28; bilateral, 169, 203; cooperation, 113, 116, 180, 205; economic, 29, 88, 190, 196; European and, 201–2, 204–6; Greater Middle East in, 193; Japan in, 180; multilateral, 175–76; status and, 70–71. *See also* external military threats

Security Council, UN, 26, 37, 40–41, 45, 88, 99, 136, 186, 209–11, 214

segyehwa (globalization) policy, 64, 89

sex slaves under Japanese colonialism, 157, 160, 174

Singapore, 142, 168, 178–79, 194–95, 203

Sino-U.S. relationship/rivalry, 7, 45, 61, 119, 146–47, 176, 234–35

Six-Party Talks, 88, 122–23, 137–38, 167, 191–92, 194; Lee Myung-bak and, 125, 131–32; Roh Moo-hyun and, 116; U.S. in, 119

Sixth Republic era, ROK, 3, 11, 30–31, 222

slavery under Japanese colonialism, 157, 160, 174, 176–77

"small states," 22–23

SOFA. *See* Status of Forces Agreement, U.S.-ROK

soft power, ROK, 2–3, 55, 80–82, *94*, *121–23*, *157*, *184*, *208*, 217–18; bilateralism and, 158; in Japan, 173–74; under Kim Young-sam, 106; under Lee Myung-bak, 195; under Moon Jae-in, 203; under Roh Moo-hyu, 206, 221; in Southeast Asia, 166–68

Somalia, 106, 129, 210–11

South Africa, 22, 219–220

South Asia, 2, 11, 203, 213

South China Sea, 86, 145, 148, 204, 225

Southeast Asia, 64, 82, 85–87, 155, 158–59, 161–62, 165–66, 168–72, 174–75; Moon Jae-in on, 177–79; ROK aid for, 159, 162, 165, 171, 177–78; Yoon Suk-yeol on, 179–81

Southeast Asia Treaty Organization (SEATO), 39, 46–47

Southern Chosun National Defense Security Military Academy, 34

South Korea–Japan relations, 155–57, 160, 163–64, 168–70, 172–73

South Korea-Russia relations, 185,
191–92, 201, 204–5
South Korea–U.S. alliance, 7–8, 55, 56,
58–59, 73–76, 83–84, 94, 153–54, 157,
184, 227; bilateralism of, 93; under
Chun Doo-hwan, 49; dependency
in, 2, 33, 41, 97, 99, 106; under Kim
Dae-jung, 110–13; under Kim
Young-sam, 104–6; under Lee
Myung-bak, 126–30; under Moon
Jae-in, 144–47; under Park Chung-
hee, 41–42, 44, 46–47; under Park
Geun-hye, 135–37; post Korean War,
38–40; under Roh Moo-hyun,
117–21; under Roh Tae-woo,
96–100; under Yoon Suk-yeol,
151–52
sovereignty, 37, 89–90, 105, 143
Soviet Union, 19–20, 51–52, 57, 67, 87;
Cold War and, 14, 29; collapse of, 14,
64; normalized diplomatic relations
with, 1, 10, 100, 184–85; North
Korea and, 32–33, 35–36; in UN
Security Council, 37, 40–41, 209
space program/rockets, ROK, 103–4,
126, 143
Spain, 19, 37
statecraft, 3, 61
status, 1, 6, 11, 31, 55, 72–73, 222–23,
226–28, 229–31; middle powers
seeking, 29–30; security and,
70–71
Status of Forces Agreement (SOFA),
U.S.-ROK, 42
"strategic ambiguity," 119, 121,
147–48
strategic autonomy, 67–68, 84, 91, 97,
99, 118
submarine-launched ballistic missile
(SBLM), 73, 133, 143, 148

sub-Saharan Africa, 77, 213, 219; ROK
aid for, 207–8, 210, 212, 217–18
"Sunshine Policy/North Korea
Reconciliation and Cooperation
Policy," ROK, 108–10, 115, 190
superpowers, 24, 26, 85. See also great
powers
supply chains, 146, 151–53, 165
Sweden, 22, 26

Taiwan, 37–40, 43, 45–47, 51, 62, 100,
107, 152
Taiwan Strait Crisis (1995–1996), 107
tariffs, 71, 98–99, 113–14, 200, 209
TCOG. See Trilateral Coordination and
Oversight Group
technology, 105, 151, 157–58, 177, 189,
204, 235; military, 47, 75–76, 96–98,
103, 118, 185, 187, 191; nuclear
weapons, 44–45
temporal scope (grand strategies), 28,
28–29, 54–55, 68, 90–91, 224,
227–28
Terminal High Altitude Area Defense
(THAAD) antimissile defense
system, 60, 69, 134–35, 140–41,
143–44, 147, 149, 152
territorial waters, 37, 43, 69, 124
THAAD antimissile defense system. See
Terminal High Altitude Area
Defense (THAAD) antimissile
defense system
Thailand, 165, 178
Three Basic Principles for Peaceful
Unification (1972), ROK, 70,
108–9
Tiananmen Square crackdown (1989),
100
TISA. See Trilateral Information
Security Agreement

tourism, 109, 124, 136, 142

TPP. *See* Trans-Pacific Partnership

trade, ROK, 2, *55*, 78–79, *94*, 112, 128, 137, *157*, *208*, 221, 228–29; with China, 51, 60, 85, 100, 114–15, 130, 138–39; globalization and, 65; with Japan, 6, 160–61, 164, 166–67, 176–77; under Kim Young-sam, 187; with North Korea, 133; under Roh Tae-woo, 95; and Southeast Asia, 161–62, 165, 171, 174, 177–78

Trade and Cooperation Agreement (2001), 190

Trade and Cooperation Agreement, EU–ROK, 187

Trans-Pacific Partnership (TPP), 137, 173

Treaty of Friendship, Co-operation and Mutual Assistance, North Korea–China, 43

Treaty of Friendship, Co-operation and Mutual Assistance, North Korea–Soviet Union, 43

Treaty of Friendship, Good Neighborliness, and Cooperation, North Korea–Russia, 189

Treaty on Basic Relations Between Japan and the Republic of Korea, 43–44, 163

Treaty on Basic Relations Between the Republic of Korea and Russia, 185

Treaty on Non-Proliferation of Nuclear Weapons (NPT), 45, 101, 115

triangular core (ROK foreign policy), 2, 11, *55*, 82–85, *83*, 92–94, *94*, 223–24, 227; under Kim Dae-jung, 108–15; under Kim Young-sam, 101–108;

under Lee Myung-bak, 123–32; under Moon Jae-in, 140–49; under Park Geun-hye, 132–40; under Roh Moo-hyun, 115–23; under Roh Tae-woo, 94–101; under Yoon Suk-yeol, 149–54. *See also* China; North Korea; United States (U.S.)

Trilateral Coordination and Oversight Group (TCOG), 164

Trilateral Information Security Agreement (TISA), 134–35, 172–73, 176

trilateralism, ROK, 161, 163–64, 166, 169, 172–74, 177, 179; under Lee Myung-bak, 127; under Moon Jae-in, 147; under Park Chung-hee, 47

troops, North Korean, 35–36, 45, 70

troops, ROK, 38, 42, 119–20, 193

troops, U.S., 35, 60, 75–76; stationed in ROK, 38–39, 42, 44, 46, 49, 92

Truman, Harry, 20, 35–36, 38–40

Truman doctrine, U.S., 38–39

Trump, Donald, 20, 141–42, 144–46, 148, 176, 202

Turkey, 22, 195, 198

Ukraine, 197, 201, 204, 252*n*34

UNC. *See* United Nations Command

UNFCC. *See* United Nations Framework Convention on Climate Change's

UNHRC. *See* United Nations Human Rights Council

United Arab Emirates, 186, 190, 193, 195, 199, 202

United Kingdom, 4, 37, 39, 62, 67, 71, 198, 201

United Nations (UN): General
Assembly, 33, 37, 40–41, 46, 48;
North Korean observer status in, 46,
52–53; peacekeeping, 6, 106, 188, 193,
198–199, 202, 210–12, 214–18, 220;
ROK membership in, 1, 6–7, 10, 72,
77, 208–11, 221; ROK observer status
in, 37, 52–53; Security Council, 26,
37, 40–41, 45, 88, 99, 136, 186,
209–11, 214

United Nations Command (UNC), 36,
38, 46

United Nations Framework Convention
on Climate Change's (UNFCC),
211

United Nations Human Rights Council
(UNHRC), 152, 212, 214, 218

United Nations Office for Sustainable
Development (UNOSD), 214,
216

United States (U.S.), 32, 71, 83–85, 156;
Cold War and, 14, 20; Congress, 35,
46, 120, 128, 136, 194; decline of, 26,
80–81, 236; grand strategy, 12, 20; as
a great power, 5, 19–20, 28–29, 57,
73; Kim Dae-jung on, 110–13;
Kim Young-sam on, 104–6; in
Korean War armistice, 36–37; Lee
Myung-bak on, 126–30; Liberal
International Order, 26–29;
militarization by, 36, 39; Moon
Jae-in on, 144–47; 9/11 terrorist
attacks, 20, 65, 212; nuclear umbrella,
7, 49, 58, 250n8; nuclear weapons,
38–39, 96, 104; relationship/rivalry
with China, 7, 45, 61, 119, 146–47,
176, 234; Roh Moo-hyun on,
117–21; Roh Tae-woo on, 96–99;
Yoon Suk-yeol on, 151–52. See also
armed forces, U.S.; South Korea–
U.S. alliance

UNOSD. See United Nations Office for
Sustainable Development

Uruguay Round, 98–99, 105, 209

U.S. See United States

U.S. Army Military Government in
Korea (USAMGIK), 35

Uzbekistan, 88, 183, 186, 193, 199, 202

Vietnam, 41, 159, 162, 165, 168, 173–74,
178

Vietnam War, 42, 120, 186

Wang Yi, 140

war, 13–15, 27

War on Terror, Global, 65, 119, 191

Washington, George, 20

weak powers, 19, 22, 64, 222; ROK as,
31, 33, 41, 49, 52, 63, 67, 90–91

weapons of mass destruction (WMD),
70, 111, 142. See also nuclear
weapons, tactical

Western Europe, 38–39, 185–86

Winter Olympic Games (2018), 142,
144, 148

WMD. See weapons of mass destruction

World Bank, 78, 208, 210

World Cup (2002), 161, 164

world economy, integration in the, 1, 55,
71–72, 85–88, 91, 94, 154, 157, 184,
189, 208, 221

World Trade Organization (WTO), 71,
98–99, 105, 114, 122, 163, 209–11;
dispute-settlement mechanism,
112–13, 120–21, 137, 146, 167, 177,
192, 218

World War I, 20

World War II, 13–14, 20, 32, 106, 138,
160, 173–74, 176; Liberal
International Order following,
26–29, 61

WTO. See World Trade Organization

Xi Jinping, 21, 60, 138, 140, 148–49, 152–53

Xinjiang Uyghur Autonomous Region, 152

Yeltsin, Boris, 185

Yemen, 68, 182, 195

Yonhap News Agency, 80

Yoon Suk-yeol, 70, 149–54, 180, 222, 234; on East Asia, 179–81; on global governance, 220–21; on Greater Eurasia and the Indian Ocean, 204–6

Yugoslavia, 185–86

GPSR Authorized Representative: Easy Access System Europe, Mustamäe tee
50, 10621 Tallinn, Estonia, gpsr.requests@easproject.com

www.ingramcontent.com/pod-product-compliance
Lightning Source LLC
Chambersburg PA
CBHW022137020426
42334CB00015B/932